MW00861012

"If you're anything like me, it's hard to keep up w
acceptance and commitment therapy (ACT), as
and changes. So, if you want to get up to speed on t. ...innovative research in ACT,
and discover the exciting new directions ACT is heading in, this book is for you!"

—**Russ Harris**, author of ACT *Made Simple* and *The Happiness Trap*

"This book is an example of 'ACT unchained.' For many reasons, ACT has often been
presented as 'a psychotherapy model among models.' This book, reflecting the basic
science perspective that ACT came from, is pointing toward something much more comprehensive: basic principles of effective psychological treatment."

—**Niklas Törneke, MD**, author of *Learning RFT* and *Metaphor in Practice*

"It takes a very talented group of editors to bring together the widely recognized thought
leaders in an area of applied clinical science, and to harness the power and vision of such
brilliant minds. Levin, Twohig, and Krafft have succeeded in accomplishing this difficult
feat. The reader of *Innovations in Acceptance and Commitment Therapy* will quickly realize
that there is something very special about this book. This book has the best of both
worlds: An extremely broad and interesting array of highly relevant topics that are well
written, comprehensive, and thought provoking. If I were to recommend one book that
would instantly get the reader up to speed on the most recent developments in ACT
specifically, and the burgeoning field of contextual behavioral science (CBS) more
broadly, this would be it! Highly recommended!"

—**Kirk Strosahl, PhD**, cofounder of ACT, and coauthor of *Learning ACT*
*in Psychiatry* and *The Mindfulness and Acceptance Workbook for Depression*

"*Innovations in Acceptance and Commitment Therapy* is essential reading for all professionals who want to use the wisdom of ACT ideas in their work. The book provides
cutting-edge and up-to-date coverage of ACT theoretical concepts and practical innovations for practitioners across all settings, such as individual or group psychotherapy,
counseling, coaching, community or organizational interventions, etc. Comprising an
excellent collection of chapters from leading authors in the field, this is a must-read for
those looking to learn about new ACT innovations."

—**Louise McHugh, PhD**, associate professor at University College Dublin,
coauthor of *A Contextual Behavioral Guide to the Self*, peer-reviewed ACT
trainer, and fellow of the Association for Contextual Behavioral Science

"*Innovations in Acceptance and Commitment Therapy* provides an excellent sampling of ACT interventions across clinical issues, populations, and levels of care; and demonstrates how ACT represents a process-based therapy. It's exciting to see how far we've advanced in CBS! This book integrates contemporary applied behavior theory into clinical applications, providing not only an overview of current research, but also clinical tools for immediate use. Thus, it will be a very useful 'state of the union' for clinicians and researchers alike."

> —**Lisa W. Coyne, PhD**, assistant professor in the department of psychiatry at Harvard Medical School; founder of the New England Center for OCD and Anxiety in Boston, MA; and coauthor of *Acceptance and Commitment Therapy*

"*Innovations in Acceptance and Commitment Therapy* not only provides a compendium of up-to-date advances in the intervention, it contextualizes the evolution of ACT and the importance of refining and studying clinical application with varied populations. The research detailed here in conjunction with real-world strategies to improve clients' lives makes it one of the most important books for clinicians, researchers, and teachers to read. Fully digesting the book means learning how to bring new and interesting ACT applications into your work as a mental health researcher and provider. This book not only catches the reader up on innovations, it inspires readers to continue the work of developing this incredible intervention."

> —**Robyn D. Walser, PhD**, codirector of Bay Area Trauma Recovery Clinic; assistant professor at the University of California, Berkeley; author of *The Heart of ACT*; and coauthor of *Learning ACT* and *The Mindful Couple*

# Innovations in Acceptance & Commitment Therapy

*Clinical Advancements*
*and Applications in ACT*

EDITED BY
MICHAEL E. LEVIN, PhD
MICHAEL P. TWOHIG, PhD
JENNIFER KRAFFT, MS

CONTEXT PRESS
An Imprint of New Harbinger Publications, Inc.

## Publisher's Note

*This publication is designed to provide accurate and authoritative information in regard to the subject matter covered. It is sold with the understanding that the publisher is not engaged in rendering psychological, financial, legal, or other professional services. If expert assistance or counseling is needed, the services of a competent professional should be sought.*

Distributed in Canada by Raincoast Books

Copyright © 2020 by Michael Levin, Michael Twohig, and Jennifer Krafft
        Context Press
        An imprint of New Harbinger Publications, Inc.
        5674 Shattuck Avenue
        Oakland, CA 94609
        www.newharbinger.com

Cover design by Amy Shoup

Acquired by Catharine Meyers

Edited by Rona Bernstein

Indexed by James Minkin

All Rights Reserved

Library of Congress Cataloging-in-Publication Data on file

Printed in the United States of America

22    21    20

10    9    8    7    6    5    4    3    2    1                    First Printing

We dedicate this book to the Association for Contextual Behavioral Science, whose curious, open, and supportive community facilitated these advances.

# Contents

## Section Three: Innovations with Targeted Populations and Problems

## Section Four: Innovations in Implementing ACT

# The Rise of Process-Based Therapy Research: Returning to Our Roots

## Kelly G. Wilson

*Professor, University of Mississippi*
*Founder, OneLife, LLC*

At first glance, this book appears to be an exploration of the application of a specific psychotherapy model. However, there is more here than meets the eye. Understanding the significance of this book requires some historical perspective on how the field has evolved and is evolving, and some of the forces that have shaped that evolution.

During the 1970s, the National Institute of Mental Health (NIMH) came under increasing pressure to produce quantitative scientific evidence regarding the efficacy of psychotherapy. There was legislative pressure to convert the NIMH into a sort of Food and Drug Administration for psychotherapies (Wolfe, personal communication, 1997). In pharmaceutical research, randomized controlled trials (RCTs) are used to examine the efficacy of various drugs in the treatment of diseases. NIMH sought the equivalents of metaphorical drug/disease match in RCTs of psychotherapy approaches.

Prior to the 1970s, psychotherapy research had been predominantly psychodynamic; however, psychodynamic researchers' process model and historical development through narrative case studies did not convert readily into experiments. Psychodynamic researchers simply did not produce grant proposals that suited the new experimental aims of the NIMH (see Rosner's outstanding 2005 article), and with a few exceptions, their research programs languished. Likewise, the first two iterations of psychiatry's *Diagnostic and Statistical Manual* (DSM; American Psychiatric Association [APA], 1952, 1968) suffered from notorious unreliability (e.g., Rosenhan, 1973).

In order to proceed with the psychotherapy equivalent of pharmaceutical RCTs, researchers needed the equivalents of both drug and disease treated. In 1980, the publication of DSM-III (APA, 1980) converged with NIMH's spending priorities in a way that changed the face of research in psychotherapy and psychopathology. The new DSM-III, mostly scoured of psychodynamic theory, provided at least some reasonably reliable identifiable syndromes. Syndromes were seen as the pathway to disease identification. In the mid-1980s, NIMH was decentralized and reorganized around these syndrome clusters. The stage was set for the modern era of RCTs. Highly specified protocols were treated as the equivalent of static pharmaceutical molecules, and DSM syndromes were treated as if they were bona fide diseases.

This convergence of events exerted tremendous selective pressure on which theories would be examined using federal research dollars. Of course, biological theories tied to new pharmaceuticals prospered. Among psychological theories, those which lent themselves to practical application and the gathering of evidence began to consume the vast majority of research dollars (Rosner, 2005). Setting aside pharmacotherapy, two broad and often overlapping theoretical positions dominated the research landscape from the mid 1980s to the present day. Cognitive therapy (CT), behavior therapy (BT), and the many combination cognitive-behavioral therapies (CBTs) generated vastly more evidence than all other theories combined. Beck describes his aims eloquently in *Cognitive Therapy and the Emotional Disorders*:

> Before starting to evaluate the psychotherapies, we should distinguish between a system of psychotherapy and a simple cluster of techniques. A system of psychotherapy provides both a format for understanding the psychological disorders it purports to treat and a clear blueprint of the general principles and specific procedures of treatment. A well-developed system provides (a) a comprehensive theory or model of psychopathology and (b) a detailed description of and guide to therapeutic techniques related to this model (1976, p. 278).

Beck's (1976) process model suggests a number of immediate lines of empirical examination. If inaccurate cognitions were the culprit, measurement studies would be able to gather data on prevalence of such pathogenic thinking and interventions could be crafted to alter those patterns. He suggested studies in experimental psychology as an additional way to test the process model. Beck was not offering a treatment for a specific psychiatric illness; rather, he offered a strategy document centered on a process-oriented approach to understanding, treating, and evaluating psychotherapy.

Behaviorists of all stripes were likewise well positioned to enter a psychotherapy research world that demanded experiments. Most behaviorists either had one foot still in the lab or were trained by faculty who were trained in basic labs. These ties between the basic behavioral lab and the clinic were very longstanding. The first published exposure-based treatment was carried out by Mary Cover Jones in 1924. Jones, a student at the time, reverse engineered John B. Watson's famous Little Albert experiment. Watson had shown that carefully organized stimulus pairings in the lab could create fearful avoidance in the presence of harmless small animals. Jones (1924), the mother of behavior therapy, showed that these same principles could be harnessed to reverse fearful avoidance. Twenty-five years later, the likes of Ogden Lindsley, Murray Sidman, Joseph Wolpe, and Arnold Lazarus, among a host of others, created the beginnings of modern behavioral applied psychology. These behavior theories, born in the lab, were quite well suited to quantitative examination of outcomes and became increasingly effective at securing NIMH research funding. But as NIMH organized around the treatment of psychiatric diagnoses, there was a price to be paid. Both BT and CT researchers were increasingly required to focus treatment development on specific syndromes.

Although this book is not about the diagnosis or classification of human suffering, it is part of a response to the pernicious effects of three decades of the organization of psychological science around syndromal classification. DSM-III in the hands of NIMH hijacked the development of promising process-oriented treatments. Barry Wolfe provides a candid case study of the pressing of psychology into the mold of cures for psychiatric diseases:

> It soon became virtually impossible to get a grant in the area of psychotherapy, particularly outcome, unless it was focused on DSM. We actually had to tell certain grantees who weren't working on specific categories that they were going to have to shift their research… Marsha Linehan originally started her research of a 12-week behavior therapy [for what] she called parasuicidal women. And these were folks who were rather frequently attempting in a mild way or at least making suicidal gestures. She was trained behaviorally, had no interest in diagnostic categories. We went out there, this was again around 1980 or so, and said "Look, these folks look a lot like Borderline and so you'd probably be better off if you start calling them Borderlines" (Barry Wolfe as quoted in Rosner, 2005).

This reorganization around syndromes had an extraordinary, rapid, and widespread impact. By the 1990s, departments of counseling, social work, and psychology routinely offered courses explicitly around DSM diagnostics, and reimbursement for professional services was increasingly tied to these diagnostic categories. Abnormal psychology textbooks, study sections at the National Institutes of Health, specialty professional and research organizations, the names of our journals, the names and aims of our assessment instruments, and the specialization and subspecialization of our best and brightest researchers, including both experimental psychopathologists and clinical trialists, became increasingly organized around DSM syndromes.

In the midst of simulating pharmacology research lie two assumptions. The first is that psychosocial treatments are static things, like the molecules they stand in for in this misbegotten metaphor. The second is that that the diagnoses are discrete disease entities, like cancer or the mumps or measles, or at least markers for latent disease states. Both of these assumptions are deeply problematic, even from the perspective of some designers of the DSM. During the most recent revision, leaders of the DSM task force detailed the decades-long failure of syndromal classification in leading to disease identification:

> In the more than 30 years since the introduction of the Feigner criteria by Robins and Guze, which eventually led to DSM-III, the goal of validating these syndromes and discovering common etiologies has remained elusive… Not one laboratory marker has been found to be specific in identifying any of the DSM-defined syndromes… Epidemiological and clinical studies have shown extremely

high rates of comorbidities among disorders, undermining the hypothesis that the syndromes represent distinct etiologies… With regard to treatment, lack of specificity is the rule rather than the exception… Reification of DSM-IV entities, to the point that they are considered to be equivalent to diseases, is more likely to obscure than to elucidate research findings… All these limitations in the current diagnostic paradigm suggest that research exclusively focused on refining the DSM-defined syndromes may never be successful in uncovering their underlying etiologies. For that to happen, an as yet unknown paradigm shift may need to occur (Kupfer, First, & Regier, 2002, pp. xviii–xix).

However well intentioned, that paradigm shift did not come with the publication of the DSM-5 (APA, 2013). In fact, DSM-5 produced dismal reliability in field trials, with common diagnoses like major depression hovering in the .28 range, and with some field trial sites with reliabilities as low as .13 (Regier et al., 2013). However, such a paradigm shift may well be in the offing. The shift is related to the second of the flawed assumptions of the pharmaceutical RCT metaphor—that psychosocial treatments could be made as stable as the molecules in pharmaceutical testing. Even when protocols have been highly specified, with carefully monitored adherence, troubles lurk, though they are often hidden in the aggregated data of treatment outcome studies. For example, studies routinely show more variance between therapists within a given treatment arm than is found between treatment arms (Miller, Hubble, Chow, & Seidel, 2013). And, even if we can produce very close adherence to a protocol, it is not the least clear empirically that outcomes will improve.

There is an alternative. We can let loose of both ends of the disease model—syndrome as disease and treatment manual as tested molecule. The suggestion of letting loose of DSM sometimes prompts "We have to have *something!*" As it turns out, we do have something. In fact, the something we have has been there all along, though it has not been the focus of many of our most important educational and research institutions. That something is a return to a close examination of change processes. And, a recognition that the therapist is every bit a part of the treatment—not just the static receptacle of a delivered protocol. It was this close examination of change processes, both in the clinic, in the case of Beck, and in the lab, as sprung from the behavioral tradition that launched our best-established treatments.

An additional shift that occurred with the move to protocols/syndrome RCTs was a shift to highly aggregated data as the centerpiece of clinical science. Group designs often obscure important and interesting variability. And, of course, our best-established approaches came from the study of individuals, not groups. They were derived from individual response to intervention, not average group response, which may not map onto the response of any individual in the group. Modern computational power, data gathering, and data analytic techniques offer opportunities that were not available in previous decades (e.g., Kurz, Johnson, Kellum, & Wilson, 2019). We may well be seeing the start of a shift as significant as the shift that occurred in the 1980s. Hofmann and Hayes offer a vision of this paradigm shift in motion:

Clinical science might see a decline of named therapies defined by set technologies, a decline of broad schools, a rise of testable models, a rise of mediation and moderation studies, the emergence of new forms of diagnosis based on functional analysis, a move from nomothetic to idiographic approaches, and a move toward processes that specify modifiable elements. These changes could integrate or bridge different treatment orientations, settings, and even cultures (2018, p. 37).

It is in this light that you should read *Innovations in Acceptance and Commitment Therapy.* It is noteworthy that within this volume, you will find more faithfulness to examining change processes than to the brand name of ACT as a therapy. Indeed, several chapters in this ACT innovations text are not even called ACT. Y. Barnes-Holmes, McEnteggart, and D. Barnes-Holmes's ROE (relating, orienting, evoking) model, closely connected to a lab research group, diverges while maintaining similar roots. Villatte's chapter is presented as an ACT enhancement, but not as ACT per se. Kanter, Corey, Manbeck, and Rosen's chapter mixes ACT and functional analytic psychotherapy sensibilities. All of these chapters fall well within the broader contextual behavioral science umbrella. As a codeveloper of ACT, I am delighted that the ACT developmental trajectory has led some researchers to create treatments that might sensibly be thought of as not ACT. Various ways of thinking about ACT, including the matrix, the DNA-V model, and the hexaflex, along with a more traditional clinical behavior analysis construal of ACT processes, are healthy variations within a network of approaches. I expect that some of these approaches will fall away and some will be more useful than others in different contexts.

Readers should also note the variation in content addressed. Most of the chapters targeting a particular content area are unrelated to any DSM diagnosis, including those on racism and providing treatment sensitive to cultural context. It is too easy to fall into the trap of seeing the world through the dominant culture's lens and mistaking "a way" of seeing things as "the way" of seeing things. Generalizability is always an empirical question. No number of replications can dictate generalizability as a settled matter. Other chapters explore health concerns of great social significance. Even chapters, such as Merwin's on anorexia, that examine an identifiable disorder do not adhere to the typical formal properties of the DSM diagnoses. In fact, Merwin focuses persistently on the application of ACT principles to overcontrol. That focus on overcontrol may well lead to understanding difficulties very different from eating disorders, but with shared variance in process and intervention on overcontrol.

The shift is not about leaving behind anything we have learned. Rather it is an exemplar of broad, process-oriented treatment development. This model represents a welcome return to the roots of our best-supported treatments' focus on change processes rather than diagnoses. In addition, a more process-oriented treatment development effort provides an opportunity to bring together researchers of psychodynamic and common factors models who have suffered under the current dominant disease/protocol RCT model. Process has always been their focus. A reorientation to process brings these often-conflicting factions into the same strategic effort. We could join in a systematic empirical examination to answer Gordon Paul's (1969) clinical question: "What treatment, by whom, is most effective for this individual with that specific problem, under which set of circumstances, and how does it come about?" (p. 44).

The era of fixed protocols matched to misbegotten DSM diagnoses is coming to an end. This is very good news. It is good news for a progressive psychological science, both basic and applied, and ultimately good news for consumers of applied science.

# References

American Psychiatric Association. (1952). *Diagnostic and statistical manual of mental disorders* (1st ed.). Washington, DC: Author.

American Psychiatric Association. (1968). *Diagnostic and statistical manual of mental disorders* (2nd ed.). Washington, DC: Author.

American Psychiatric Association. (1980). *Diagnostic and statistical manual of mental disorders* (3rd ed.). Arlington, VA: Author.

American Psychiatric Association. (2013). *Diagnostic and statistical manual of mental disorders* (5th ed.). Arlington, VA: Author.

Beck, A. T. (1976). *Cognitive therapy and the emotional disorders.* New York, NY: Penguin.

Hofmann, S. G., & Hayes, S. C. (2018). *The future of intervention science: process-based therapy. Clinical Psychological Science, 7,* 37–50.

Jones, M. C. (1924). A laboratory study of fear. The case of Peter. *Pedagogical Seminary, 31,* 308–315.

Kupfer, D. J., First, M. B., & Regier, D. A. (2002). *A research agenda for DSM-V.* Arlington, VA: American Psychiatric Association.

Kurz, A. S., Johnson, Y., Kellum, K. K., & Wilson, K. G. (2019). How can process-based researchers bridge the gap between individuals and groups? Discover the dynamic p-technique. *Journal of Contextual Behavioral Science, 13,* 60–65.

Miller, S. D., Hubble, M. A., Chow, D. L., & Seidel, J. A. (2013). The outcome of psychotherapy: Yesterday, today, and tomorrow. *Psychotherapy, 50,* 88–97.

Paul, G. L. (1969). Behavior modification research: Design and practice. In C. M. Franks (Ed.), *Behavior therapy: Appraisal and status.* New York, NY: McGraw-Hill.

Regier, D. A., Narrow, W. E., Clarke, D. E., Kraemer, H. C., Kuramoto, S. J., Kuhl, E. A., & Kupfer, D. J. (2013). DSM-5 field trials in the United States and Canada, Part II: Test-retest reliability of selected categorical diagnoses. *American Journal of Psychiatry, 170,* 59–70.

Rosenhan, D. L. (1973). On being sane in insane places. *Science, 179,* 250–258.

Rosner, R. I. (2005). Psychotherapy research and the National Institute of Mental Health, 1948-1980. In W. E. Pickren, Jr., & S. F. Schneider (Eds.), *Psychology and the National Institute of Mental Health: A historical analysis of science, practice, and policy* (pp. 113–150). Washington, DC: American Psychological Association.

# CHAPTER 1

# Introduction
## *Refining Acceptance and Commitment Therapy to Meet the Challenges of the Human Condition*

Michael E. Levin

Jennifer Krafft

Michael P. Twohig

*Utah State University*

## Overview

Acceptance and commitment therapy (ACT) has seen exponential growth since the publication of the first book-length description in 1999 (Hayes, Strosahl, & Wilson, 1999). The Association for Contextual Behavioral Science (ACBS) was founded in 2005 as a community of scholars, practitioners, and students involved in ACT and, more broadly, contextual behavioral science (CBS). Since then, it has grown to nearly 8,000 members across 76 countries (ACBS, 2018). Randomized controlled trials (RCTs) of ACT now total over 300, with at least 51 in 2018 alone, spanning a wide range of topics including depression, anxiety disorders, obsessive compulsive and related disorders, addiction, eating disorders, psychosis, chronic pain, weight management, coping with medical conditions, work stress, and stigma (ACBS, 2019). ACT is recognized by leading organizations as an evidence-based treatment for a range of problem areas (e.g., Division 12 of the American Psychological Association, 2019). ACT is being adopted and widely disseminated by organizations including the United States Veterans Health Administration (e.g., Walser, Karlin, Trockel, Mazina, & Barr Taylor, 2013) and the World Health Organization (Tol et al., 2018) and integrated into settings including hospitals (see chapters 14 and 15 of this volume), schools (e.g., Livheim et al., 2015), athletics (e.g., Moore, 2009), workplaces (e.g., Flaxman & Bond, 2010), and criminal justice (e.g., Zarling, Bannon, & Berta, 2019). Furthermore, professions outside of clinical/counseling psychology, including social work, behavior analysis, education, coaching, nursing, and others, are increasingly adopting ACT (ACBS, 2018). This rapid development may be attributed in part to the rich collaboration and open communication between basic researchers, applied researchers, and practitioners of ACT and the underlying CBS approach.

As a sign of a healthy field, the current practice of ACT looks quite different from that of the 1990s. Preliminary work applying ACT to specific problem areas and settings has evolved into sophisticated and refined adaptations. New ways of conceptualizing and applying ACT have progressed out of developments within basic and applied research. Although this rapid, expansive growth is exciting, it raises challenges for professionals in staying up to date on the latest innovations and developments in ACT across settings, cultures, problem areas, and programs of research.

Practitioners and researchers of ACT may not be aware of major innovations in these areas, leading to missed opportunities and potential fragmenting of knowledge. We run the risk of "reinventing the wheel" by adapting ACT for specific challenges and populations without considering previous relevant work that could provide a useful starting point for further development. Insofar as these innovations are important for overcoming challenges and maximizing gains, we may fail to provide the most effective treatment to those we serve. At the risk of hyperbole, over time, this could lead to the ACT community's becoming more and more fragmented, with the mutual interest and collaboration shared by basic researchers, applied researchers, and practitioners in ACBS breaking down. Gaps can form and widen between basic and applied research, and between treatment protocols tested in studies and new clinical strategies used by clinicians.

These are natural challenges that emerge from a rich, thriving therapy and professional community, particularly one such as ACBS that takes a strongly nonhierarchical, open approach to treatment development and dissemination. As the number of researchers and clinicians increases worldwide, it will be more complicated to keep up with developments within ACT. Part of this can be solved with efforts to share ongoing developments in the field in an accessible manner.

## The Purpose of This Book

Our aim for this book is to provide an up-to-date review of some of the largest innovations in ACT that warrant increased dissemination. This could easily fill up several volumes, so we focused in particular on significant new techniques, models, and other adaptations of ACT that are notable additions or changes to how it has traditionally been taught, practiced, and researched. We tried to avoid more "surface-level" adaptations, which, although still meaningful, might be more readily in line with readers' base knowledge.

We also tried to include innovations about which less has been written from an applied perspective to date and for which materials are less available. As a result, the chapters tend to be written more by researchers who have been developing and studying new ACT approaches but may not yet have widely disseminated applied training materials on their innovations. That said, we tried to include a diverse array of authors, including researchers who have developed innovations through basic translational work and treatment development as well as clinicians who have developed novel treatment strategies through their own clinical work. We chose to forego reviews of work in major areas where the innovations have been widely disseminated (e.g., anxiety, depression, chronic pain, substance use, workplace settings, focused ACT in primary care). Those materials are available in recent publications and books.

Each chapter is practically focused, with an emphasis on describing how the innovation could actually be used with clients through specific exercises and/or clinical examples. You will learn cutting-edge treatment strategies to integrate into your practice or research. Although the space afforded in each chapter may not necessarily be enough to fully appreciate the depth and details of the innovation and to competently deliver it to clients, this will provide at least an introduction and basic knowledge you can practically use. We hope this helps raise your awareness of innovations in the field and areas you might want to learn more about through trainings or readings. You may find that areas you work in have developed since you were last trained. You may also find inspiration for your own innovations.

There is a natural tension between adopting new, innovative clinical strategies and using empirically validated therapeutic strategies. Going too far on the innovation side, without direct research, risks drifting enough from tested therapeutic methods that it is no longer clear if these innovations are evidence based. Going too far on the empirical validation side (i.e., only using strategies that have been directly proven effective), without new innovations, risks stagnation that can lead to treatment protocols that are less effective or even ineffective for the contexts they are applied to.

This book aims to help relieve tension between clinical innovation and treatment research by identifying current gaps in the literature where innovations need further study. In addition to a practical "how to" description of using the innovation in practice, chapters also provide a brief summary of supporting research, challenges applying the innovation, and future directions. We hope this serves to identify not only treatment protocols that need empirical validation, but also areas where CBS researchers and practitioners can collaborate in the future to refine these innovations and overcome challenges encountered.

## Brief Overview of ACT

In order to keep a focus on notable innovations, each chapter assumes a base knowledge of ACT, including the underlying theoretical model (i.e., psychological [in]flexibility and its component processes) and basic research (i.e., behavior analysis including relational frame theory [RFT]). We will provide a brief overview of these concepts so that each chapter will not need to do so.

ACT emerged from and builds on traditional behavior analysis, as detailed in chapter 2 by Dixon and Paliliunas. The ACT approach to clinical behavior analysis is distinct because of its underlying philosophy, called *functional contextualism* (Hayes, Hayes, & Reese, 1988), and its basis in RFT, a modern behavior analytic account of cognition (Hayes, Barnes-Holmes, & Roche, 2001).

In functional contextualism, the unit of analysis in research and practice is the "act in context" (Hayes et al., 1988). ACT therapists work to influence the behavior of their clients by observing the impact of context (i.e., antecedents and consequences) and altering the context (private and public) to foster new and more effective behavior. Consistent with this, all events are looked at functionally more so than topographically. Thus, in functional contextualism we look at the effects of all internal and external events, rather than what they are. This can be notable, as someone may have, for example a suicidal thought, which on the surface can be scary, but if that thought is observed mindfully, it may have a small behavioral impact. Functional contextualism also entails a pragmatic understanding of truth: that truth is defined by what works to accomplish a specific goal (Hayes et al., 1988). This is highlighted in ACT, as goals are not assumed and each client is asked what their goals are for therapy. This can conflict at times with a traditional goal within psychology of disorder reduction. ACT therapists do often work on disorder reduction, but it is not assumed to be our goal and it is always tied in to increased functioning for the client.

Many of the strategies used in ACT are guided by RFT (Hayes et al., 2001). At the core of RFT is the idea that verbal behavior entails the ability to respond to stimuli not solely based on their formal properties, but also based on contexts that indicate how they are related to other stimuli. This results in a transfer of information about a stimulus as well as functional effects of how one should respond in the presence of that stimulus. Again, this applies to internal and external stimuli. Put simply, we can relate anything to anything, and how we relate things affects how we see the world and what we do in response to those stimuli. This might lead to a world of suffering, with one's options feeling small and unworkable, or it can lead to a world of meaning and opportunities.

Core ACT processes (e.g., defusion, self-as-context) are derived from RFT principles, and ACT therapists use conversations with clients to alter relational responding. The chapters by Villatte (chapter 3) and Barnes-Holmes, Y., McEnteggart, and Barnes-Holmes D. (chapter 4) describe innovations in using RFT to inform ACT in detail. The primary way that ACT affects relational responding is by altering the functional context in which stimuli (internal and external) are experienced. By and large, we work to help clients experience certain events mindfully or with distance rather than with literal meaning. This allows a moment of choice in how to respond to that stimulus, rather than automatically following the literal functions of stimuli (e.g., acting on the thought *I will fail* literally and thus giving up versus as just a thought and continuing to try). Other elements of ACT are more additive and seek to build or tie relational frames together to support meaningful actions (e.g., linking trying something difficult to personal values).

ACT is a model of treatment organized around a set of key therapeutic processes of change, rather than defined by specific techniques or protocols. The diversity of ACT methods reviewed in this book exemplifies the flexibility and creativity this functional approach to behavior change affords. There are countless ways to do ACT—provided they function to target the therapeutic processes identified in the underlying psychological flexibility model.

Psychological flexibility is defined as the ability to flexibly pursue one's values in a context-sensitive manner, with awareness of and openness to inner experiences as they are. Psychological flexibility theoretically consists of six interrelated processes: acceptance of internal experiences (as opposed to experiential avoidance), defusion (seeing internal experiences as they are, as opposed to their relationally constructed versions), self-as-context (recognizing oneself as an observer of one's experiences, rather than defining oneself with verbal content), flexible attention to the present moment (as opposed to attention being dominated by thoughts of the past or future), values clarity (intentionally choosing personal values), and committed action (as opposed to inaction or impulsivity that interferes with values). In broad terms, ACT is done by instigating, modeling, and reinforcing psychological flexibility in the moment, with the aim of helping clients build more meaningful, effective patterns of activity in their lives. Some innovative treatment models, such as the ACT matrix (Schoendorff & Olaz, chapter 6) and DNA-V (L. Hayes & Ciarrochi, chapter 7), take a unique and novel approach to developing psychological flexibility or integrate other perspectives (see section 2). The flexibility of this model allows for many adaptations to the needs and characteristics of different populations, as described throughout section 3 of this book, and for many types of implementation methods, as seen in section 4.

## CBS Perspective on Treatment Innovation

The rapid growth and innovation in ACT can be attributed to its underlying CBS strategy (Hayes, Barnes-Holmes, & Wilson, 2012). Appreciating this approach can provide context for how the innovations included in this book have developed within ACT and how they maintain their theoretical and scientific coherence.

CBS is best understood in terms of its functional contextual philosophical assumptions (Hayes et al., 1988). As a pragmatic approach to knowledge building, the truth of an analysis is defined in terms of what works to predict *and* influence behavior (i.e., understanding behavior means being able to reliably predict and change it). More specifically, CBS aims to develop theories that allow us to predict and influence behavior with precision, scope, and depth. This orients us to a more specific form of knowledge building in which analyses use a limited set of terms (precision) that cohere across levels of analyses (depth) and account for a wide range of phenomena (scope), ultimately because these qualities help ensure a progressive science of behavior. The CBS emphases on (1) context in understanding behavior and (2) a pragmatic truth criterion defined by prediction and influence with precision, scope, and depth have a number of downstream implications for how CBS approaches research, treatment development, and the more specific topic of this book, ongoing innovations in treatment.

## Engaging in Reticulated, Iterative Development

Developing analyses that have precision, scope, and depth requires a tight integration with basic science (where highly technical, abstracted principles are ideally developed and refined). However, the pragmatic truth criterion of CBS suggests that treatment development and refinement need not be unidirectional (Hayes, 1998). New insights are not only predicated on developments in basic science but rather may come from any level of analysis or practice including basic research, theory refinement, applied research, or practice. Thus, rather than a bottom-up approach, CBS encourages a reticulated, iterative approach in which all levels proceed simultaneously with innovations at any one level informing and being refined by the others. That said, it is critical these levels communicate and value each other for the system to work, as innovations and findings at any one level gain impact through iterating and refining across levels (Hayes, 1998). A well-developed basic account needs to be translated and evaluated in treatment protocols, treatment protocols need to be acceptable to practitioners and coherent with basic principles, and so on. This is critical to CBS in which the success of the whole endeavor is defined in relation to a practical outcome of prediction and influence of behavior, but with the progressive, sophisticated qualities of precision, scope, and depth, which come from careful basic research and theory refinement.

This book highlights examples of how the reticulated CBS approach is progressing with ACT. Chapters written by basic and translational scientists describe how ACT can be interpreted and informed from advances in evolutionary science (S. Hayes et al., chapter 5), RFT (Barnes-Holmes et al., chapter 4; Villatte, chapter 3), and behavior analysis (Dixon & Paliliunas, chapter 2), highlighting novel theoretical conceptualizations and practical treatment strategies to be applied and evaluated (i.e., innovations guided by basic science). Other chapters describe how the ACT theoretical model might be adapted based on unique applications of ACT such as to children and adolescents (L. Hayes & Ciarrochi, chapter 7) or integration with other models such as exposure (Twohig, Ong, Petersen, Barney, & Fruge, chapter 8) and affective science (Luoma & LeJeune, chapter 9). These chapters are examples of innovations guided by theory refinement. Chapters written by treatment developers describe innovative adaptations to ACT based on applied research and practice in specific problem areas such as obesity (Lillis, Dallal, & Forman, chapter 10), cancer (Arch, Fishbein, & Kirk, chapter 12), and eating disorders (Merwin, chapter 13) as well as settings such as partial hospitalization programs (Dalrymple, D'Avanzato, & Morgan, chapter 14), medical settings (Dindo, Weinrib, & Marchman, chapter 15), and lower income countries (Ebert, Bockarie, Stewart, Szabo, & White, chapter 18). This book aims to further support the reticulated

CBS approach, raising awareness of developments in basic research, applied research, and practice to be further evaluated and adopted at other levels of analysis.

## Refining Applied Theoretical Models

Theory provides a common language that organizes the knowledge gained in each level of analysis in CBS. The high precision and scope principles developed in basic science are organized into analytic abstractive theories aiming to predict and influence behavior in more specific, applied domains (e.g., experiential avoidance, cognitive defusion). These applied theoretical constructs, often referred to as "middle-level" terms (Hayes et al., 2012), help contextualize the application of basic principles such that they can be more readily organized into therapeutic processes and procedures for researchers to research and practitioners to practice. When the connections between basic and applied theoretical models are strong and active, this can help ensure treatment protocols are closely linked to more broadly applicable and precise therapeutic processes that are closely linked to even higher scope and precision basic principles, all of which serve a progressive approach to predicting and influencing behavior. That said, these connections need ongoing attention and refinement to ensure the theoretical model remains true to its goals, rather than "hand waving" tight connections between levels of analysis. Furthermore, theory should continue to be refined based on work occurring at each level of analysis, which should translate into better prediction and influence over time (e.g., more effective, efficient interventions).

The chapters in this book illustrate how researchers and practitioners continue to refine ACT through findings in basic research, applied research, and practice. For example, Barnes-Holmes and colleagues (chapter 4) describe novel theoretical constructs (relating, orienting, evoking, or ROE) that are more closely linked to RFT principles that could be used to conceptualize psychopathology and its amelioration. S. Hayes and colleagues (chapter 5) describe how broader evolutionary processes across multiple dimensions and levels might guide innovations in the psychological flexibility model. Schoendorff and Olaz (chapter 6) describe an applied theoretical model for ACT focused on noticing and engaging in behaviors based on appetitive versus aversive control. Luoma and LeJeune (chapter 9) describe how a combination of clinical practice, outcome research, and basic research in affective science has been incorporated into an innovative ACT model for highly shame-prone clients. Other examples abound throughout the book, highlighting how the theoretical model underlying ACT continues to grow and be refined based on careful basic and applied work.

## Emphasizing Function over Form

CBS focuses on what works for changing behavior in a given context, which naturally leads to intervention strategies defined by their function rather than their form (i.e., how they affect behavior, not what they look like). CBS-based protocols are flexible in that they are oriented toward various techniques and strategies that can have an intended effect on a client and can engage a particular therapeutic process. This contrasts with more prescriptive, technique-based protocols, which might focus more on what you *specifically* do with clients. From a CBS perspective, the latter risks ignoring context and failing to have the intended effect on a client. A more flexible approach focused on function may increase challenges initially with developing competence and delivering the treatment with fidelity. However, it also provides an ideal opportunity for innovation as researchers and practitioners vary their behaviors in creative ways to identify what best produces the intended function for clients. New innovations are found based on what works to increase psychological flexibility and meaningful behavior change in given applied contexts.

The contributions in this book highlight a range of creative ways ACT has been adapted and applied to produce its intended functions. Rather than providing prescriptive, formal protocols outlining what to do with clients, these chapters focus more on key therapeutic processes to target and provide example strategies for how to produce these functions. For example, Merwin (chapter 13) provides a number of new ACT exercises that evolved out of work applying ACT for eating disorders. Kanter and colleagues (chapter 11) outline an approach that integrates diversity training methods with a variety of CBS-based methods (including from ACT and functional analytic psychotherapy), which can be flexibly applied to reduce racism and improve effective intergroup contact. This functional approach also allows ACT to be delivered effectively in different treatment modalities such as web-based interventions, as described in Lappalainen and Lappalainen (chapter 16). As you read the chapters in this book, we encourage you to take note of the flexibility and creativity with which ACT can be applied and adapted to those being served.

## Applying Broadly, but Refining to Context

Guided by CBS, researchers have sought to explicitly test the scope of ACT and its underlying psychological flexibility model across various populations and targets. This is in part a theoretical test, determining what the boundary conditions are for psychological (in)flexibility (i.e., testing its scope) and what areas might require additions, refinements, or simply a different approach. This is also in part a practical test, identifying what areas ACT can be effectively applied to and its potential as a more transdiagnostic treatment organized around a key set of therapeutic processes. Preliminary research initially led to a sense that ACT can be applied far and wide to various psychological and behavioral health areas, often with minimal adaptations to protocols being evaluated (Hayes, Luoma, Bond, Masuda, & Lillis, 2006).

Although there are benefits to applying an intervention universally to target a wide range of problems (e.g., treating comorbidity, reducing training burden), CBS also recognizes the importance of idiographic case conceptualizations and adapting treatment to clients' unique contexts. As preliminary work has evolved into robust programs of research and clinical services in these areas, ACT has been adapted to the unique needs, challenges, and opportunities these contexts afford.

The chapters in this book provide a number of examples outlining how ACT has been applied and adapted for specific problems and settings. In some cases, authors describe finding boundary conditions where the existing ACT protocols and its applied model were arguably insufficient, such as in applying ACT to children and adolescents where adaptations had to be made to address the unique needs during development (L. Hayes & Ciarrochi, chapter 7). In other cases, authors describe how integrating other behavior therapy methods was clearly indicated, providing new opportunities to effectively combine ACT with other evidence-based strategies. For example, Twohig and colleagues (chapter 8) describe how to implement exposure methods within ACT for anxiety and related disorders, highlighting ways ACT adds to exposure therapy (e.g., linking values to approaching regularly avoided stimuli, using acceptance and mindfulness to increase contact with previously avoided stimuli). Finally, other authors describe challenges presented in certain populations where adaptations to ACT are needed, such as in addressing the unique needs of cancer patients (Arch et al., chapter 12) and diverse clients (Masuda, chapter 17). For example, Kanter and colleagues (chapter 11) describe how CBS-based methods such as ACT have been adapted to reduce racism, including navigating the challenging interpersonal processes that arise when conducting this work within diverse groups.

Overall, the chapters in this book provide an excellent review of how the treatment strategies and underlying theoretical model for ACT have been adapted as a result of in-depth work in target populations and settings. This work largely supports the broad scope of the psychological flexibility model and ACT for treating a wide range of problems, but also reminds readers of the importance of developing competencies in these target areas and adapting ACT to the unique needs and opportunities afforded.

## Focusing on What Works in Practice

The pragmatic truth criterion in CBS does not stop at the level of basic research, theory, or well-controlled outcome studies. Ultimately, it means developing a science of behavior that reduces human suffering and improves well-being, which is not achieved at the point at which RCTs indicate ACT is efficacious. CBS includes a deep commitment to applied theories and treatment methods reaching those who would benefit. For example, ACT has always maintained a focus on developing theoretical models and treatment strategies that clinicians can and want to adopt in their practice (Hayes, 2002). Early treatment studies included effectiveness research to confirm ACT is effective when provided in routine care by clinicians receiving training (Strosahl, Hayes, Bergan, & Romano, 1998). Subsequent developments have continued to maintain a strong emphasis on implementation and creativity in the ways that ACT might reach those who would benefit.

The chapters in this book outline a variety of innovative ways that ACT researchers and practitioners have sought to implement ACT. These include chapters describing how ACT has been integrated into medical settings as a one-day workshop (Dindo et al., chapter 15), developed as a partial hospital program for psychiatric patients (Dalrymple et al., chapter 14), disseminated through a task-sharing approach in Sierra Leone (Ebert et al., chapter 18), adapted to diverse cultures (Masuda, chapter 17), implemented by behavior analysts (Dixon & Paliliunas, chapter 2), and delivered as an online therapy (Lappalainen & Lappalainen, chapter 16). Although in no way is this comprehensive, these chapters provide rich examples of how ACT can be creatively adapted for practitioners and settings to reach those in need.

## Overview of Book Chapters

This book is organized around major types of innovation that have occurred within ACT based on its CBS approach. The first section will explore innovations in ACT informed from basic research and associated fields including behavior analysis (Dixon & Paliliunas, chapter 2), RFT (Villatte, chapter 3; Barnes-Holmes et al., chapter 4), and evolution science (Hayes et al., chapter 5). These chapters focus more on conceptual developments in ACT and refinements to the theoretical model as a result of basic research. That said, they also provide clinical examples and specific strategies based on these conceptual advancements.

The second section will provide examples of how ACT has been adapted into novel treatment models and integrated with other approaches. Two chapters provide alternative models for case conceptualization and treatment from an ACT perspective: the matrix (Schoendorff & Olaz, chapter 6) and DNA-V (L. Hayes & Ciarrochi, chapter 7). In-depth examples are also provided of how ACT can be informed by and integrated with other models such as exposure therapy for anxiety and related disorders (Twohig et al., chapter 8) and affective science for shame-prone clients (Luoma & LeJeune, chapter 9). These chapters illustrate adaptations that have been made to ACT, including its theoretical model and integrating this model with other approaches.

The third section will cover innovative uses of ACT in targeted populations and problem areas. A key area of advancement in ACT is in adapting and refining treatment protocols for specific problems. Chapters in this section present particularly innovative examples of adapting ACT based on years of careful research and clinical work. Areas include applying ACT for obesity (Lillis et al., chapter 10), racism (Kanter et al., chapter 11), cancer (Arch et al., chapter 12), and eating disorders (Merwin, chapter 13). These cover a range of areas in which ACT has been applied and has grown, including mental health, behavioral medicine, and societal challenges.

The final section will include chapters describing innovative ways ACT has been adapted and implemented in various settings. Significant challenges often arise when implementing a treatment in new settings, particularly those that vary from typical outpatient therapy settings. Chapters in this section represent exemplary programs where ACT has been implemented in novel ways to maximize its uptake, reach, and impact in new settings. These include implementing ACT in partial hospitalization programs (Dalrymple et al., chapter 14), medical settings (Dindo et al., chapter 15), online formats (Lappalainen & Lappalainen, chapter 16), diverse cultures (Masuda, chapter 17), and lower-income countries (Ebert et al., chapter 18).

Three chapters (13, 14, and 15) have online supplements, which you can download at the website for this book, http://www.newharbinger.com/43102. (See the very back of this book for more details.)

## How to Use This Book

One way this book may differ from other scholarly texts is that each chapter stands on its own. While a lot can be gained from reading the whole book, you can read the chapters in any order you choose and are also welcome to skip chapters. The chapters do not build on each other. Each chapter will introduce you to an innovative approach with ACT, providing novel perspectives, case conceptualizations, and treatment strategies that you might consider integrating into your practice or research or exploring further through trainings and writings on the topic. We encourage you to use this book as an opportunity to expand your awareness and knowledge of the various ways ACT has been adapted and refined over the years.

If you want to further develop your foundational knowledge of functional contextualism, RFT, psychological flexibility and its six processes, and ACT in general, you might wish to read all the chapters and focus on some key concepts, using the following strategies to guide you:

1. Pay attention to the way functional contextualism and its main tenets resonate throughout the book. Look for a focus on function of events over their topography, as well as explicated goals of the chapter author(s) and the clients they suggest using these techniques with.

2. Notice ties back to many forms of basic science, most commonly behavior analysis and RFT.

3. You will most often see RFT guiding the writing; note the authors' focus on altering the context of inner experiences and increasing the power of certain actions through expanding relations with values discussions. Pay attention to the discussions in certain chapters of building relational abilities to increase skills; these will often pertain to younger clients.

4. Assessment of psychological inflexibility, and a resulting case conceptualization, is an important aspect of delivering ACT. Notice how chapters discuss the ways psychological inflexibility manifests in target settings and populations,

considering how you might assess for inflexibility and integrate it into case conceptualizations.

5.  The authors demonstrate cultural competence in knowing how to best foster psychological flexibility in a functional manner in the populations they most often work with. Notice the various ways they teach psychological flexibility and implement ACT based on the issues being targeted.

6.  Watch for instances where related therapies are integrated into these treatments. These can be nice illustrations of how many methods can be used to move similar processes of change.

7.  Try something new! As you go through the book, watch for and keep an open mind with novel ways to conceptualize and implement ACT. You might even apply ACT with yourself, noticing your mind saying what "won't work" or is "nothing new" as you continue to open yourself up to learning about the innovations outlined in each chapter.

ACT and the underlying CBS approach offer a world of opportunities for innovation as researchers, practitioners, and other professionals continue to flexibly adapt and refine it to meet the unique needs of their settings and populations. We hope this book helps you to explore recent developments in ACT and ways to continue moving toward a therapy more adequate to addressing the challenges of the human condition.

# References

Association for Contextual Behavioral Science (2018). *ACBS Annual Report.* Retrieved from https://contextualscience.org/files/2018%20Annual%20Report.pdf

Association for Contextual Behavioral Science. (2019). *ACT randomized controlled trials since 1986.* Retrieved from https://contextualscience.org/ACT_Randomized_Controlled_Trials

Division 12 of the American Psychological Association (2019). *Psychological treatments.* Retrieved from https://www.div12.org/treatments/

Flaxman, P. E., & Bond, F. W. (2010). A randomised worksite comparison of acceptance and commitment therapy and stress inoculation training. *Behaviour Research and Therapy, 48,* 816–820.

Hayes, S. C. (1998). Building a useful relationship between "applied" and "basic" science in behavior therapy. *The Behavior Therapist, 21,* 109–112.

Hayes, S. C. (2002). Getting to dissemination. *Clinical Psychology: Science and Practice, 9,* 424–429.

Hayes, S. C., Barnes-Holmes, D., & Roche, B. (Eds.). (2001). *Relational frame theory: A post Skinnerian account of human language and cognition.* New York, NY: Plenum.

Hayes, S. C., Barnes-Holmes, D., & Wilson, K. G. (2012). Contextual behavioral science: Creating a science more adequate to the challenge of the human condition. *Journal of Contextual Behavioral Science, 1,* 1–16.

Hayes, S. C., Hayes, L. J., & Reese, H. W. (1988). Finding the philosophical core: A review of Stephen C. Pepper's *World Hypotheses. Journal of the Experimental Analysis of Behavior, 50,* 97–111.

Hayes, S. C., Luoma, J., Bond, F., Masuda, A., & Lillis, J. (2006). Acceptance and commitment therapy: Model, processes, and outcomes. *Behaviour Research and Therapy, 44,* 1–25.

Hayes, S. C., Strosahl, K., & Wilson, K. G. (1999). *Acceptance and commitment therapy: An experiential approach to behavior change.* New York, NY: Guilford Press

Livheim, F., Hayes, L., Ghaderi, A., Magnusdottir, T., Hogfeldt, A., Rowse, J., . . . Tengstrom, A. (2015). The effectiveness of acceptance and commitment therapy for adolescent mental health: Swedish and Australian pilot outcomes. *Journal of Child and Family Studies, 24,* 1016–1030.

Moore, Z. E. (2009). Theoretical and empirical developments of the Mindfulness-Acceptance-Commitment (MAC) approach to performance enhancement. *Journal of Clinical Sport Psychology, 3,* 291–302.

Strosahl, K. D., Hayes, S. C., Bergan, J., & Romano, P. (1998). Assessing the field effectiveness of Acceptance and Commitment Therapy: An example of the manipulated training research method. *Behavior Therapy, 29,* 35–64.

Tol, W. A., Augustinavicius, J., Carswell, K., Leku, M. R., Adaku, A., Brown, F. L., . . . Bryant, R. (2018). Feasibility of a guided self-help intervention to reduce psychological distress in South Sudanese refugee women in Uganda. *World Psychiatry, 17,* 234–235.

Walser, R. D., Karlin, B. E., Trockel, M., Mazina, B., & Barr Taylor, C. (2013). Training in and implementation of Acceptance and Commitment Therapy for depression in the Veterans Health Administration: Therapist and patient outcomes. *Behaviour Research and Therapy, 51,* 555–563.

Zarling, A., Bannon, S., & Berta, M. (2019). Evaluation of acceptance and commitment therapy for domestic violence offenders. *Psychology of Violence, 9,* 257–266.

# SECTION ONE

# Innovations from Basic Research

# CHAPTER 2

# Clinical Behavior Analysis
## *Integrating ACT and ABA*

Mark R. Dixon
*Southern Illinois University*

Dana Paliliunas
*Missouri State University*

## Overview

This chapter will begin by providing a brief historical review of behavior therapy, applied behavior analysis, and clinical behavior analysis and the interaction of these fields in the treatment of complex behavior problems. Then we will describe acceptance and commitment therapy (ACT) using behavior analytic terminology that may serve to clarify the role of ACT in the work of applied behavior analysts. Finally, we will conclude the chapter with a discussion of incorporating ACT techniques within applied behavior analytic interventions, as well as areas for continued advancement in terms of research and practice.

### A Historical Perspective

Behavior therapy is the systematic application of the principles of learning to treat psychological problems (Skinner, Solomon, & Lindsley, 1954). Researchers and practitioners of behavior therapy, as it developed in the mid-1900s, sought to utilize a scientific approach to address human behavior problems (Barlow, 1980). The hallmark of early behavior therapy approaches was an emphasis on "first-order" change or direct symptom reduction, in juxtaposition with the psychoanalytic techniques prominent at that time. The behavioral approach varied in the conditions and behaviors addressed but was consistent in the scientific approach and emphasis on direct environmental contingencies that characterized the interventions.

While behavioral therapeutic techniques were unified under the umbrella of behaviorism, two distinct philosophical perspectives developed. The differences between methodological and radical behaviorism are critical in understanding the evolution of behavioral therapy. *Methodological behaviorists* emphasize stimulus-response relationships with a mechanistic interpretation of behavior, which need not include internal processes or private events for a complete analysis. Conversely, *radical behaviorists* emphasize an operant analysis with a contextual interpretation of behavior, treating both overt and private events as behaviors under environmental control, which are requisite for a complete account. Behavioral therapy approaches were soon divided along this philosophical line; radical behaviorists, driven largely by the work of B. F. Skinner, developed applied behavior analysis (ABA), whereas methodological behaviorists, such as Joseph Wolpe, retained the term "behavior therapy" (Dougher & Hayes, 2004).

Over time, ABA and behavior therapy became increasingly distinct, the former working heavily within the context of developmental disabilities, particularly autism spectrum disorder (ASD), and the latter exhibiting a focus on outpatient clinical populations, despite the considerable conceptual and procedural overlap between the two. The rapid expansion of ABA and its professionalization has been due, in part, to the reported increase in the prevalence of ASD over several decades (Baio et al., 2018), although ABA has also had an increasing role in other areas such as staff and parent training and substance abuse treatment. Similarly, behavior therapy has evolved from initial techniques largely based in stimulus-response learning (e.g., systematic desensitization) to incorporating cognitive theory, resulting in cognitive behavioral therapy. A review of the *Journal of Applied Behavior Analysis,* the flagship journal for ABA, confirmed the increasing predominance of research regarding developmental disabilities and a lack of "interest in studying newer behavioral conceptualizations" (O'Donohue & Fryling, 2007, p. 52). Radical and methodological behaviorist approaches, both strictly behavioral interventions, initially included clinically focused interventions, but the focus of ABA has become more narrowed today.

## Present Conditions

In the past several decades, there has been an influx of conceptual and empirical growth regarding human language and cognition from a radical behaviorist perspective, creating another shift in behavior analysis toward the treatment of psychological and behavior problems. Skinner (1957) crafted a behavior analytic interpretation of human language, presenting a theory that posited verbal behavior is under operant control and can be analyzed in terms of function. Since that time, work regarding stimulus equivalence (Sidman, 1971) and relational frame theory (RFT; Hayes, Barnes-Holmes, & Roche, 2001) has advanced the radical behavior account of human language and cognition with a robust empirical foundation (O'Connor, Farrell, Munnelly, & McHugh, 2017). Accounts of derived relational responding and the transformation of stimulus function have provided a means for a behavior analytic examination of psychological problems in which the effect of mediating verbal behavior on maladaptive behavior is central (e.g., Törneke, Luciano, & Valdivia Salas, 2008). Empirical studies that have demonstrated the effect of rule-governed behavior on contingency sensitivity is another critical component in these interpretations of complex behavior (Catania, Shimoff, & Matthews, 1989). Within the field of ABA, these "post-Skinnerian" accounts of verbal behavior have been increasingly adopted and accepted as part of language acquisition training programs for individuals with ASD or other language delays (e.g., Dixon, 2016). As empirical and technological advances have occurred within the scope of ABA, the interest and ability of behavior analysts to return to treating the breadth of populations observed in the early formation of the discipline have increased.

## Clinical Behavior Analysis

A number of applied behavior analysts have expressed concern for the narrowing of the field as well as the need for expanding the scope of treatment in a manner that is consistent with behavior analytic practice (e.g., O'Donohue & Fryling, 2007). Such has been the interest in developing a robust account of the role of private events from a radical behaviorist account that a unique field of study has emerged in the past several decades: clinical behavior analysis.

Clinical behavior analysis (CBA) has been defined as "the application of the assumptions, principles and methods of modern functional contextual behavior analysis to 'traditional clinical issues,'" meaning those commonly treated by clinical psychologists (Dougher & Hayes, 2004, p. 11). Of significant interest in CBA treatment is the function of verbal behavior, not only in the context of possible mediating effects on behavior in the natural environment, but in the context of the therapy setting (Kohlenberg, Tsai, & Dougher, 1993). Radical behaviorists interested in the treatment of individuals who not only can engage in complex verbal behavior but whose presenting problems are related to verbal behavior have kept a careful eye on how language abilities may in fact alter the antecedent-behavior-consequence relationship, leading to less positive psychological well-being.

ACT is one such CBA approach. ACT research includes a breadth of populations, for example individuals with diagnoses or needs such as obsessive-compulsive disorder, depression, generalized anxiety, chronic pain, weight management, and work stress (Hayes, Levin, Plumb-Vilardaga, Villatte, & Pistorello, 2013). Much of the ACT literature has been published by researchers within the field of clinical psychology, or by behavior analysts who have published outside of the predominant ABA journals. Despite the quantity and scope of the ACT literature, research on this topic found within the applied journals of the Association for Behavior Analysis International (ABAI) is sparse, with a recent search producing only two empirical articles specifically evaluating ACT interventions. Nonetheless, technologies continue to increase the complexity of verbal skills taught by behavior analysts, and the swell of researchers and practitioners seeking to provide more effective treatments for the behavior problems of verbal individuals continues to grow. ACT makes intervention for these types of behavior problems more accessible in a manner that is conceptually consistent with a radical behavior approach.

# Description of ACT from a Behavioral Perspective

Before outlining the utility of ACT within applied behavior analytic intervention, we will provide a description of this approach utilizing behavioral terminology that makes clear the conceptual consistency of ACT within the framework of ABA. This interpretation of ACT elucidates the way in which these techniques fit into behavioral intervention. The ACT perspective holds that "human suffering predominantly emerges from normal psychological processes, particularly those involving human language" (Hayes, Strosahl, & Wilson, 2011, p. 11). Cognitive fusion, or responding to the content of private events as literal, and experiential avoidance, or attempting to regulate or control private events, are two processes central to the ACT conceptualization of psychological distress. These verbal events can mediate overt behavior, resulting in excessive rule governance that reduces sensitivity to environmental contingencies. ACT is designed to decrease the dominance of such verbally mediated behavior when it results in distress and restricts access to reinforcement.

The theoretical foundations for ACT are behavior analytic; however, in practice, and often within ACT literature, much of the strict behavioral language commonly used throughout ABA literature is not utilized. Instead, the terminology used in the application of ACT, often referred to as "middle-level terms," is clinical in nature (Barnes-Holmes, Y., Hussey, McEnteggart, Barnes-Holmes, D., & Foody, 2016). The use of terminology such as "mindfulness" or "values" (for example) does not diminish the behavior analytic nature of such treatments, rather it makes them accessible to the client. The behavior analyst implementing ACT, however, would design and evaluate the treatment using behavior analytic terms. For example, the collection of techniques and processes commonly referred to as mindfulness exercises seeks to train discrimination between stimuli occurring privately and those occurring within the current external environment as well as attending to the current external environment when private verbal behavior is not adaptive. As well, the therapist seeks to determine the function of covert and overt verbal behavior and reduce excessive or ineffective rule following when it is maladaptive. Similarly, the collection of techniques and processes included within the "values" work seeks to train identification of personal reinforcers, abstract these to general verbal descriptions, discriminate between behaviors that access said reinforcers and those that do not, and utilize self-management techniques to increase values-consistent behaviors. The therapist seeks to increase the clients' frequency of optimal choice making, creating larger patterns of behavior that are related to personal reinforcers, often utilizing techniques related to perspective taking in order to do so. These descriptions, while incomplete and representative of only a fraction of the techniques embedded within ACT treatment, exemplify the consistency between a CBA and an ABA approach to intervention.

## The ACT Context

From an ABA perspective, such descriptions allow for a division of the behavioral components of ACT techniques into two distinct "groups": mindfulness and reinforcer seeking. Mindfulness techniques are implemented to determine the function of and increase attending to stimuli, including covert and overt verbal stimuli. An individual learns to discriminate between and among stimuli and their psychological functions, and intervention focuses on reducing the effect of maladaptive verbal behavior by weakening the functions of certain stimuli and strengthening alternative relations among stimuli. Reinforcer-seeking techniques are implemented to increase the frequency of behavior aligned with verbally defined values in order to maximize contact with reinforcers. Given that many reinforcers are delayed in time, and moving them closer temporally is impossible, a creative alternative is to provide verbal descriptions of those reinforcers instead. Here the therapist may reiterate the behavior-consequence relationships and how each alternative behavior will eventually yield a specific consequence. When those consequences are in fact reinforcing, it is very likely that verbal descriptions of them will contain some of the reinforcing functions of the events/items themselves. In contrast, the therapist can also use this technique to emphasize the client's negative long-term outcomes of engaging in maladaptive behavior to immediate reinforcers, for example, avoiding painful thoughts. Intervention then emphasizes increasing optimal choice making, utilizing self-control training techniques to increase the individual's preference for larger delayed reinforcers (Dixon & Tibbetts, 2009). Finally, the therapist implements mindfulness and reinforcer-seeking processes in order to increase psychological flexibility, which, in behavioral terms, can be defined as the ability to engage in adaptive behavior depending on the present environment in order to more successfully obtain reinforcers.

ACT is designed to alter the context in which behavior occurs and the interaction with verbal behavior as well as to reinforce a set of flexible, adaptive behaviors that produce preferred outcomes. In order to respond optimally in terms of the current environmental contingencies and possible competing reinforcers, the individual learns to discriminate when private events are impeding access to reinforcement. They must adjust responding in order to contact the existing environmental contingencies, regardless of private or public verbal descriptions of the events. Therapeutic exercises and behavior change procedures provide a means by which to train mindful behaviors and increase reinforcer seeking.

Perhaps what makes ACT so user-friendly to the behavioral community is its set of methods that can be used to contribute toward obtaining a higher degree of psychological flexibility. Although this term, "psychological flexibility," may initially seem vague, it is a useful metric by which to validate changes in private events that may be beyond the measurements typically used. Constructs such as depression or anxiety are difficult if not impossible to measure. This leaves the behavior analyst to either dismiss the importance of these states or attempt to measure them indirectly, perhaps as a biproduct of some observable behavior. The ACT processes could be thus considered the independent variable manipulations that in isolation or combination have a potential to influence the dependent variable of psychological flexibility. Following this logic, psychological flexibility serves as an indirect metric of a variety of private events that may function as antecedents or consequences of an observable behavior. Therefore, to eventually change behavior under the control of such verbal stimuli, one must work on altering psychological flexibility.

## Present-Moment Awareness

Present-moment awareness can be summarized as one's ability to provide ongoing observation of the current environment without subjective evaluations of the events occurring within that environment. From a behavior analytic perspective, present-moment awareness refers to responding to the present literal environment, interacting with stimulus objects directly rather than the psychological functions of those stimuli. In other words, if one is engaging in a behavior of self-talk whereby they count from one to ten as they breathe in, and from ten to one while they breathe out, it would be somewhat difficult to psychologically interact with other covert verbal behaviors. This is because the self-counting and motor movements necessary to breathe this deliberately would compete with co-occurring supplemental behavior stimulation.

## Acceptance

The process of acceptance involves engaging in psychological and physical approaches to stimuli that could be either reinforcing or punishing. Rather than attempting to escape or avoid aversive events, stimuli, or thoughts, when one engages in an acceptance response it is as if such stimuli are weakened or absent in their ability to affect typical response strength. From a behavior analytic perspective, acceptance can be understood as a continuance of prior response strength, rate, or allocation among alternatives in the presence of newly introduced stimuli. It is naïve to simplify human behavior down to a single schedule of reinforcement and evaluate adaptive or maladaptive behavior as the outcome of persistence on this simple schedule. Instead, the real world is composed of multiple concurrent choice options and their respective reinforcement schedules. When a person engages in the process of acceptance, it tends to be a response allocation to an option that contains both positive and aversive stimuli in the immediacy yet has the potential to yield larger, more preferred reinforcers long term. As a result, the person must opt to experience fewer ideal consequences now for an optimal consequence that is delayed. Unwillingness to accept might be seen as the opposite, whereby the person escapes or avoids aversive events by selecting a less advantageous sooner consequence.

Take, for example, a parent who is scared to fly on a plane but whose children live across an ocean. Neither of the two primary choices, both of which contain some aversive events, is ideal. They could choose to accept the aversiveness of the experience of flying on a plane to obtain the larger reinforcer of a closer relationship with their child, or they could choose to never fly, avoid the aversive experience, but also eliminate acquiring the reinforcers the parent-child relationship might provide. Too often, the person seeks desperately for a third, but illusory, option of not being afraid and seeing their child. Verbally constructed rules may guide the person to seek this third choice, and when not actually found within the environment, may cause unpleasant emotional responses or other maladaptive escape behaviors.

## Defusion

The core process of defusion is one in which the person changes the functions of stimuli by altering the context or creating contexts in which unhelpful functions are diminished. Once a verbally sophisticated human (around age three for a neurotypical child) interacts psychologically with a physical stimulus object, that object of the world takes on supplemental "functions." These functions are not bound by utility, but rather by any variety of reactions, triggers, or conditions that transcend the object itself. For example, if an English speaker encountered the word ZAL on a piece of paper, initially they would interact with it in isolation as a series of three letters, which does not represent an actual word in the English language. However, if shortly after that the same person were to hear another person say, "A ZAL is worse than a killer clown," all of a sudden, the word ZAL would have an infinite number of additional functions that would immediately become attached to it. Whether it be silliness, horror, fear, panic, memories of the circus or of Halloween, ZAL would never be the same again. The process of defusion seeks to work backward on the dominance that verbally derived functions have over actual stimulus objects and weaken such functions to the point that the person may tend to once again interact with the stimulus as just an object—devoid of any evocative responses.

From a behavior analytic perspective, defusion involves the responding to supplemental and oftentimes contradictory functions of a given aversive stimulus. Through the application of additional functions, many of which would be nonaversive, the person tends to demonstrate weakened response strength to the stimulus object. Such an object may even take the form of a thought, or in other words a self-generated rule that produces avoidance or maladaptive behavior. For example, upon seeing oneself in the mirror, that stimulus may occasion the thought *Nobody thinks I am attractive*. This would then set the occasion for maladaptive behavior (e.g., drinking; sleeping with multiple strangers) to escape or avoid such a thought and attempt to provide a competing self-rule response to terminate this thought (*If someone has sex with me, they must think I am attractive*). To defuse from such a thought, one would attempt to alter the function of the stimulus (me in the mirror) to include modified phrases such as *I am having the thought that nobody thinks I am attractive* or by saying the original phrase repeatedly to weaken the consequential emotional response that habituation of the utterance could produce.

## Self-as-Context

The core process termed self-as-context is an attempt to develop awareness of one's own experiences without subjective evaluations of them—in other words, to experience various contingencies of reinforcement without the added consequence of producing a self-rule or commentary that is made to judge the events. When a person engages in a behavior, contacts the consequences of such, and then critiques the experience in any number of ways, we might consider this a maladaptive drift from the present moment. Such drifts tend to result in the person's identifying themselves as a collection of experiences, some good and some bad, rather than as someone who transcends such experiences as a separate entity. This entanglement of oneself within the contingency-behavior-consequence interaction often produces maladaptive behavior patterns and a loss of a sense of self. For example, one spouse may begin to define the endless number of interactions they have with their partner as "good" or "bad," and even if most are deemed "good," over time this could produce unexpected consequences. Further evaluations could include self-rules such as "My spouse is wonderful, and she loves me," "This is the love of my life," or "He is the one that makes me whole." Yet upon the untimely death of this spouse, the individual is unable to see themselves as anything more than someone who generates and believes phrases such as "I have lost everything" or "There is no reason to live anymore."

From a behavior analytic perspective, self-as-context may be best understood as an effective perspective-taking repertoire that allows relation to stimuli in a multitude of ways, such that one perspective is not dominating the behavioral repertoire. Here one may come to see the perspective of others just as readily as their own. Using the previous example, if the mourning spouse were to take the perspective of someone else who had lost their spouse and went on to eventually find new love or develop a closer relationship with their church, this would allow them to "step back" for a moment and psychologically interact with an alternative perspective. If this same event happened to this individual and this other person, and this other person eventually found happiness, then it may be possible for this individual to do so as well. Furthermore, these rule-generating processes weaken the dominance of the existing programmed contingencies. Although this individual is now sleeping alone in an empty house and not contacting the reinforcers of their spouse, it is possible that their behavioral repertoire will include fewer maladaptive responses (e.g., not going to work, failing to engage in self-care, substance use) if they can generate and subsequently follow self-rules that describe alternative potential contingency arrangements.

## Values

The core process of values involves an identification of and engaging in behavior that has purpose to the individual. Values are defined as life paths or directions, rather than goals or items a person can eventually achieve. For a verbally sophisticated individual, values are intangible, verbal descriptions of meaningful life outcomes. However, for young children or individuals with more limited verbal repertoires, values may initially need to be defined in more literal terms and abstracted over time. Maladaptive behaviors may occur if individuals seek out immediate sources of reinforcement that might actually be in opposition to broader values-driven life directions. If one values personal health and vitality yet consumes a container of ice cream every evening, although the immediate reinforcer of the dessert is obtained, it impedes the life value from being substantiated. Increasing the likelihood of engaging in values-consistent behavior is an important component of ACT treatment.

From a behavior analytic perspective, values might be best understood as a response pattern of repeated choices of larger delayed reinforcers that are selected at the expense of smaller more immediate reinforcers. Values are demonstrated not by which choice is made on a single concurrent schedule at a single point in time, but rather by the cumulation of many response patterns over considerable amounts of time. Once these reinforcers are contacted, the process of values requires the person to abstract these actual experiences to verbal descriptions of these experiences—or for others within the verbal community to do so. For example, upon helping a puppy out of a busy street to avoid death, a child may find himself being licked by the puppy and find this reinforcing. Subsequently, his mother may inform him that "you were a good boy" or "saving lives is a wonderful thing to do," which adds a narrative to the event itself. As multiple other responses also yield similar utterances from his mother, the child may develop a value that "helping others" is something that is important to allocate responding toward. In other words, the response class broadens to allow a multitude of topographies not only to contact the response-specific reinforcer, but also to demonstrate congruence with the rule and its implied social reinforcers.

## Committed Action

The core process of committed action involves the development of larger and larger patterns of behavior that will produce an overall increase in reinforcement obtained by the individual. It is all too common for one to articulate what is important, valuable, or reinforcing but never to engage in behavior to alter the actual attainment of such preferred outcomes. Committed action means demonstrating behavior that is consistent with one's values. This will often involve tolerance of aversive stimuli (acceptance) in order to pursue attaining such delayed, optimal reinforcers. To help an individual stay committed, the typical antecedent may need to be enhanced through a verbal description of how responding may produce consistency with previously described values, or how failing to respond may serve non-value-driven ends. For example, when provided a worksheet in math class, a child may have a tendency to tear the paper and put their head down on the desk. Doing so allows for avoidance of the task and a break from the aversiveness of work completion. However, if the usual "do your worksheet" antecedent was supplemented with "all good kids work hard," and wanting to be a "good kid" was a value of the child, there may be an increased probability of tolerating the work task, even though it contains some aversive properties and functions.

From a behavior analytic perspective, committed action is simply response strength. When the strength is high toward response options that lead to optimal reinforcers, we may deem such as commitment. Yet when such strength is low and responding is instead biased toward other consequences that are inconsistent with or opposed to said values, we may conclude a lack of committed action. The goal with this core process is to produce behavior that occurs now and persists across increasing periods of time. Using the previous example, the concurrent choice involves tearing up work and getting the immediate escape reinforcer and failing to obtain the social value-driven pattern of "being a good kid," versus completing work and experiencing the aversive stimulation no break provides, only to eventually be deemed worthy of the value of "being a good kid." As one might expect, the more delayed and abstract a value is, the lower the probability response strength will remain at sufficient levels.

## Incorporating ACT into ABA Interventions

In ABA, the primary objective is to utilize the principles of behavioral learning to solve problems of social importance. The majority of the work within this field of intervention has comprised treatments for persons with intellectual disabilities. Although this is not considered the primary demographic for which clinical interventions such as ACT are utilized, there are indeed many instances in which the traditional behavioral interventions might be improved upon by introducing ACT elements into the treatment package.

Perhaps the decision as to whether a behavioral intervention could be enhanced by incorporating ACT involves first determining if the client is verbally sophisticated enough to understand the language used within ACT. One way to determine the depth of the verbal repertoire is to evaluate whether the client's behavior and/or descriptions of such are limited to the present set of programmed contingencies under which they are exposed. If there is little to no talk about past or future events, most likely such relations between the actual world and their verbal descriptions are absent. For example, during a behavioral interview, if responses to questions regarding the target behavior, antecedent/consequent events, and so on relate only to the present environment (which may not be relevant to the problem behavior), do not refer to specific past events or concerns for possible similar events in the future, describe time or cause/effect in an incoherent manner, or do not include statements suggesting rule governance, such a client will most likely not benefit from adding ACT techniques into the intervention. Instead, the emphasis should rest on identification of controlling variables and behavior functions that are present in the current environment. However, if the client in question does in fact speak of time and places that are not the present in a coherent manner or in a way that suggests possible rule governance, such a client's behavior problems will most likely contain elements of maladaptive rules, choices, and discounting of the relative consequences. It is this type of client—one who is more verbally sophisticated—who has a possibility of benefiting from a behavioral intervention that incorporates ACT techniques. To further evaluate the need for ACT techniques for verbally sophisticated clients, consideration of psychological flexibility is needed. For example, if the individual does adapt or persist in behavior consistent with the current context but demonstrates a deficit in a specific skill needed to produce desired behavior change, then skill training is likely more appropriate than ACT alone. While ACT is not a "one-size-fits-all" approach to intervention for verbal clients, for those who have a sophisticated verbal repertoire, addressing verbally mediated behavior with ACT techniques may supplement, rather than replace, other environmental manipulations.

As a behavior analyst, one must keep in mind that ACT should not be approached as a type of psychotherapy, and the clinician should not practice outside of their competency regarding specific populations, target behaviors, or settings for which they have been trained. Rather, behavioral analysts should approach ACT as a *verbal instruction intervention* that allows for the client to become more aware of the programmed contingencies, the consequences of each choice that is present, and how verbal descriptions of reinforcers (values) might be capable of altering behavior to a meaningful degree. In other words, ACT is designed to enhance the reinforcing elements of certain consequences that can be obtained by engaging in certain behaviors. ACT works as a set of verbal motivating operations that are designed to bias the antecedent-behavior-consequence relationships. The ultimate goal when using ACT within a behavioral intervention is to increase the likelihood of an individual's responding to environmental contingencies that reinforce appropriate behavior by (1) altering the context in which behavior occurs, (2) changing the individual's interaction with verbal behavior about events (ACT), and (3) reinforcing adaptive, flexible behaviors that relate to preferred outcomes. When this is done, the benefits can be substantial.

As with other techniques derived from behavioral principles, ACT intervention is not limited to specific populations or behavior problems, as evidenced by empirical support for ACT in a breadth of areas from children to adults, nonclinical to clinical populations, and brief to intensive intervention. Behavior analysts can utilize these techniques in application with, in theory, any verbal population with whom they work, including individuals with disabilities or behavioral addictions, parents, employees, and so on. From the perspective of the behavior analyst, ACT is not a distinct form of therapy used to treat a distinct set of clients; instead, when private events mediate client behavior, ACT offers techniques to address these variables.

Data collection and the dependent variable targeted for change should be the same as they would be in the absence of ACT techniques. Specifically, the behavior analyst should continue to evaluate success or failure of intervention by measuring objective units of behavior, and not rest treatment efficacy solely on client self-report measures related to hypothesized internal states. Although self-report measures are not sufficient to evaluate treatment effects, psychometrically validated measures of psychological flexibility and ACT processes can be supplements to assess progress and inform treatment decisions. For example, such measures might suggest ACT core processes for emphasis when selecting therapeutic exercises or indicate the client's reported change in psychological flexibility over time.

Data collected on overt behavior can also be utilized in both evaluative and informative ways. Consistent with behavioral intervention in general, change in behavior over time is the primary indicator of the efficacy of treatment. In addition, such data can be used to inform clinical decisions made by the behavior analyst. As suggested previously, if contingency modifications alone are insufficient to produce behavior change, this may be considered an indicator that techniques to address the role of private events may be beneficial. Likewise, if ACT-specific techniques are predominant in an intervention that fails to produce a change in behavior, this may be an indicator that additional environmental manipulations may be needed. A common misconception of the ACT approach in ABA seems to be that performance on ACT exercises or protocols should be treated as a dependent measure in and of itself, which results in the attempt to measure client mastery of ACT targets as a primary indicator of treatment success. However, if ACT is treated as a verbal instruction intervention that seeks to address the function of private events and their effect on the overt behavior of the client, it is clear that the dependent measure of interest remains a change in socially significant behavior.

## Future Directions

Although there have been a number of documented studies showing how ACT can impact behavioral interventions (e.g., Pingo, Dixon, & Paliliunas, 2019; see also Pingo, Dixon, & Paliliunas, in press), and even more showing that ACT may in fact be the primary intervention process, there is a need for considerably more research. First, a more objective analysis needs to be conducted that shows the absolute threshold as to when ACT would be effective for a client with disabilities. Although we provided general guidelines in the previous section, these are currently the best we have. Until there is an empirical definition, a behavior analyst may be wasting time attempting ACT for persons who will not benefit from it, or worse, missing an opportunity to enhance an intervention because it was deduced that the client was too verbally unsophisticated for ACT to have any utility.

Other research that involves treatment integrity of ACT administration would benefit the community, as poor implementation or varied implementation across caregivers will weaken the overall utility of ACT as a set of procedures. For if ACT remains only as a therapy approach, that nebulous repertoire will be difficult for a behavior analyst to capture and implement. We have no doubt that ACT serves the psychological community well; however, in order for it to have an important role on the front line in ABA, it will need to be reconfigured as something less than therapy. That "something less" is in dire need of investigation.

In conclusion, acceptance and commitment therapy has had a rich history within and beyond the domain of clinical psychology. As a therapy approach that rose up from basic behavior analytic principles, ACT has quickly become a dominant force in producing important client outcomes. Many behavior analysts who work in applied settings are beginning to discover that contingency-exclusive interventions are insufficient to produce successful treatments for their more highly verbally sophisticated clientele; thus, ACT is now seeing a resurgence of interest by the very behavioral community that has tried for the past few decades to do without it. Perhaps ACT suffered from its reliance on middle-level terms instead of a technical vocabulary that would have been comfortable to a behavior analyst. However, as this chapter illustrates, ACT processes can be explained in such technical language, have been shown to have value in many areas in which behavior analysts may work, and hold great promise for evolving the types of interventions that have been attempted with clients who stand to benefit from their inclusion. As both the research and practice community explore the potential ACT has for improving the human condition, we believe that all involved stand to substantially benefit by coming in contact with more value-driven lives.

# References

Baio, J., Wiggins, L., Christensen, D. L., Maenner, M. J., Daniels, J., Warren, Z., . . . Dowling, N. F. (2018). Prevalence of autism spectrum disorder among children aged 8 years: Autism and Developmental Disabilities Monitoring Network, 11 sites, United States, 2014. *Centers for Disease Control and Prevention, MMWR Surveillance Summaries, 67*(6), 1–23.

Barlow, D. H. (1980). Behavior therapy: The next decade. *Behavior Therapy, 11,* 315–328.

Barnes-Holmes, Y., Hussey, I., McEnteggart, C., Barnes-Holmes, D., & Foody, M. (2016). Scientific ambition: The relationship between relational frame theory and middle-level terms in acceptance and commitment therapy. In R. D. Zettle, S. C. Hayes, D. Barnes-Holmes, & A. Biglan (Eds.), *The Wiley handbook of contextual behavioral science* (pp. 365–382). Chichester, UK: Wiley/Blackwell.

Catania A. C., Shimoff E., & Matthews B. A. (1989). An experimental analysis of rule-governed behavior. In S. C. Hayes (Ed.), *Rule-governed behavior* (pp. 119–150). Boston, MA: Springer.

Dixon, M. R. (2016). *PEAK relational training system: Transformation.* Carbondale, IL: Shawnee Scientific Press.

Dixon, M. R., & Tibbetts, P. A. (2009). The effects of choice on self-control. *Journal of Applied Behavior Analysis, 42*(2), 243–252. doi: 10.1901/jaba.2009.42-243

Dougher, M. J., & Hayes, S. C. (2004). Clinical behavior analysis. In M. J. Dougher (Ed.), *Clinical behavior analysis* (pp. 11–26). Oakland, CA: Context Press.

Hayes, S. C., Barnes-Holmes, D., & Roche, B. (2001). *Relational frame theory: A post-Skinnerian account of human language and cognition.* New York, NY: Kluwer Academic/Plenum Publishers.

Hayes, S. C., Levin, M. E., Plumb-Vilardaga, J., Villatte, J. L., & Pistorello, J. (2013). Acceptance and commitment therapy and contextual behavioral science: Examining the progress of a distinctive model of behavioral and cognitive therapy. *Behavior Therapy, 44*(2), 180–198. doi: 10.1016/j.beth.2009.08.002

Hayes, S. C., Strosahl, K. D., & Wilson, K. G. (2011). *Acceptance and commitment therapy: The process and practice of mindful change.* New York, NY: The Guilford Press.

Kohlenberg, R. J., Tsai, M., & Dougher, M. J. (1993). The dimensions of clinical behavior analysis. *The Behavior Analyst, 16(2)*, 271–282.

O'Connor, M., Farrell, L., Munnelly, A., & McHugh, L. (2017). Citation analysis of relational frame theory: 2009–2016. *Journal of Contextual Behavioral Science, 6(2)* 152–158. doi: 10.1016/j.jcbs.2017.04.009

O'Donohue, W., & Fryling, M. (2007). How has applied behavior analysis and behavior therapy changed?: An historical analysis of journals. *The Behavior Analyst Today, 8(1)*, 52–62. doi: 10.1037/h0100106

Pingo, J., Dixon, M. R., & Paliliunas, D. (2019). Intervention-enhancing effects of acceptance and commitment training on behavior-analytic treatment for direct service professionals' work performance, stress, and job satisfaction. *Behavior Analysis in Practice.*

Pingo, J., Dixon, M. R., & Paliliunas, D. (in press). An examination of the intervention-enhancing effect of acceptance and commitment therapy-based training on direct service professionals' performance in the workplace. *Behavior Analysis in Practice.*

Sidman, M. (1971). Reading and auditory-visual equivalences. *Journal of Speech, Language, and Hearing Research, 14*, 5–13. doi: 10.1044/jshr.1401.05

Skinner, B. F. (1957). *Verbal behavior.* New York, NY: Appleton-Century-Crofts.

Skinner B. F., Solomon H. C., & Lindsley O. R. (1954). A new method for the experimental analysis of behavior of psychotic patients. *The Journal of Nervous and Mental Disease, 120*, 403–406.

Törneke, N., Luciano, C., & Valdivia Salas, S. (2008). Rule-governed behavior and psychological problems. *International Journal of Psychology and Psychological Therapy, 8(2)*, 141–156.

# CHAPTER 3

# Using Clinical RFT to Enhance ACT Interventions
## *The Example of Values Work*

Matthieu Villatte

*Bastyr University*

## Overview

Even though the vast majority of psychotherapy models rely on language to activate therapeutic processes, only a few of them offer specific guidelines to conduct effective clinical conversations. Among these few exceptions, even fewer use an approach to language based on empirical research. Relational frame theory (RFT; Hayes, Barnes-Holmes, & Roche, 2001) is a functional contextual approach to language based on hundreds of empirical and conceptual publications, demonstrating principles directly applicable to clinical work. These principles are naturally particularly suitable to ACT practice, given that RFT and ACT are both grounded in contextual behavioral science and functional contextualism. This chapter presents a general framework for using RFT in clinical practice (based on Villatte, Villatte, & Hayes, 2016) and an example of enhancing ACT interventions in values work.

## A Framework for Using RFT in Clinical Practice

The clinical RFT approach presented in this section is an attempt to organize RFT technical concepts into a framework that is directly useful to clinicians. While RFT concepts have often been linked to ACT in books and trainings, their direct relevance to clinical interventions has not always been clear. For example, the concept of symbolic generalization of thought suppression (i.e., a target of thought suppression can generalize to stimuli that don't share any formal properties; Hooper, Saunders, & McHugh, 2010) can be linked to the ineffectiveness of experiential avoidance, which can justify the use of acceptance and mindfulness in ACT. However, ACT therapists generally don't use RFT principles to select and craft acceptance and mindfulness interventions. They know why using acceptance and mindfulness makes sense from an RFT perspective, but not how to use RFT to conduct acceptance and mindfulness interventions.

More recent efforts by several RFT researchers and clinicians have begun to change the relationship between RFT and clinical work in general, and between RFT and ACT in particular (Barnes-Holmes, Oliver, McEnteggart, & Thomson, 2018; Dahl, Plumb, Stewart, & Lundgren, 2009; Gil-Luciano, Ruiz, Valdivia-Salas, & Suárez, 2016; Luciano et al., 2011; McHugh, Stewart, & Almada, 2019; Törneke, 2010, 2017). The approach presented in this section constitutes one of the possible ways of using RFT principles to directly guide assessment and intervention in ACT and other models that are sufficiently consistent with contextual behavioral science (see Hayes, Villatte, Levin, & Hildebrandt, 2011). Our framework allows therapists to flexibly navigate among models and techniques in a coherent fashion because the concepts of clinical RFT are situated at a different level than in traditional models. More specifically, our framework is organized around two overarching goals (flexible context sensitivity and functional coherence) and one main strategy (altering the context to shape behaviors) served by a set of tools directly derived from RFT principles.

## THE GOAL OF DEVELOPING FLEXIBLE CONTEXT SENSITIVITY

The first overarching goal of our framework is to develop clients' *flexible context sensitivity*, which can be defined as the ability to notice a variety of elements of the context and to respond to what is most relevant. For example, a person who is arguing with her partner (a behavior) can potentially be influenced by a variety of contextual variables. The place where the argument takes place (e.g., a confined or an open space) may make it more or less likely for her to be angry; the topic of conversation (e.g., receiving or giving feedback) might evoke openness or close-mindedness; the feelings she has for her partner, in general and in this particular moment, might modulate her ability to empathize; the way her partner responds to her (e.g., interruptions or active listening) might reinforce or weaken her expressions of vulnerability; and so on. If this person shows good flexible context sensitivity, she will be able to notice these different contextual sources of influence (awareness) and to respond to the variables that are most helpful to reach her goal (flexibility). For example, she might notice that she is becoming close-minded because of the feedback she is receiving and also notice her feelings of love toward her partner, which could lead her to change her response (e.g., listening more, sharing her feelings).

## THE GOAL OF DEVELOPING FUNCTIONAL COHERENCE

The second overarching goal consists of developing the client's *functional coherence*, that is, a pragmatic and integrative conceptualization of the world (very much in line with the pragmatic truth criterion of functional contextualism; Monestès & Villatte, 2015). In this perspective, what makes sense is what works to reach a given goal, without needing to eliminate any experience. Using our previous example, the person arguing with her partner might choose to be open when hearing feedback because it is the response that will help her reach her goal of improving communication in her relationship (pragmatism). She wouldn't need to eliminate feelings of irritation that show up when hearing feedback because such feelings are parts of the diverse experiences that can be included in a contextual sense of self (integration).

## THE STRATEGY OF ALTERING THE CONTEXT TO SHAPE BEHAVIORS

The main strategy adopted in clinical RFT is similar to what behavior therapists have been doing for decades: altering the context to shape behaviors. However, clinical RFT as we conceptualize it includes *language*, both in the clinically relevant behaviors targeted by assessment and interventions, and in the context allowing transformations to occur. In other words, thinking and talking are ways of influencing the client's behavior, and they are also relevant behaviors we are trying to shape in the client's repertoire. For example, a therapist working with the person from our previous example might ask her what kind of person she wants to be in her relationship, which might help her notice her feelings of love (improved context sensitivity) and clarify her goals and values (improved functional coherence).

## Relational Framing as a Clinical Tool

When language is included in the tools and targets of clinical interventions, the practical relevance of RFT becomes obvious. Indeed, with RFT comes a higher level of precision because language can be analyzed through smaller functional units—or relational frames. Consider for example this client's quote: "I am so anxious. I need to think of something else to feel better." In this phrase, the client is using a frame of coordination between I and anxious (I and anxious come together). He is also using a conditional frame between thinking of something else and feeling better (thinking of something else is the condition to feel better). And finally, he is using a frame of comparison between his current feeling and what he hopes to feel if he thinks of something else (i.e., feeling *better*).

Therapists informed by RFT can interpret their clients' verbal behavior and choose their own verbal responses based on these different types of frames and their specific effects. Take, for example, a client who talks about herself as an empty box. The therapist could interpret this as showing some degree of functional coherence because the metaphor she uses is a container (as in self-as-context; see McHugh & Stewart, 2012) but as indicating a lack of awareness of experiences and/or of hierarchical/inclusive connection between these experiences and her self. The therapist might then use deictic framing (perspective-taking) strategies to help this client become more aware of her experiences and hierarchical/inclusion framing strategies to help her relate to these experiences in a more integrative way. While ACT therapists can use self-as-context techniques without knowledge of RFT principles (e.g., rephrasing the client's thought as "you are having the thought that" as a way of developing a content/context relationship between the self and the thought), using language with the precision offered by RFT allows them to use a variety of techniques activating deictic and hierarchical framing (not just ACT techniques described in manuals). Identifying and intentionally using these relational frames on the fly in natural conversations brings fluidity and flexibility to the therapeutic process. In the next section I will provide several examples of the use of relational framing to assess and shape client behavior related to values work in natural conversations.

# Description of Using RFT in Values Work

From a contextual behavioral—and more specifically RFT—perspective, values can be defined as sources of overarching, intrinsic, and positive reinforcement (Villatte et al., 2016). *Overarching* means that reinforcement is provided by a potentially infinite number of possible actions that can help connect to a given value. For example, a person who values education can read books, attend classes, or have a conversation with an expert. As a result of this overarching characteristic, there are no space and time limits in how people can connect with their values. Even a simple action such as contemplating the sky can be in the service of education as long as the person doing the action builds a symbolic relationship between contemplating the sky and education. It is thus always possible to do something in the service of any given value, anytime, and anywhere, regardless of physical constraints. More specifically, RFT suggests that hierarchical framing is the key type of framing allowing reinforcement to become overarching. Education needs to be situated at the top of a hierarchical network including an infinite variety of actions and goals.

*Intrinsic reinforcement* means that reinforcement doesn't depend on the outcomes of actions but is instead inside the action. Doing the action per se is reinforcing because it is symbolically related to a value. For example, a person who values autonomy can find satisfaction from cooking alone even if he is not a good cook and the meal is not tasty. What matters is that he is doing an action in connection with the value of "autonomy." Independence from outcomes helps people engaged in valued actions not to rely on feelings, social approval, or performance in order to find meaning and purpose in their lives. Regardless of what doing an action feels like, how the social community regards it, or how well it is executed, it is satisfying and reinforcing. As for its overarching quality, the intrinsically reinforcing quality of values is provided by the use of hierarchical framing. A valued action is reinforcing because it is part of a value, not because it can lead to an outcome (action and outcome are in a conditional relationship, or *conditional framing,* IF-THEN). The valued action is satisfying because it is, in and of itself, a way of being and doing that is reinforcing. Feeling good or bad as a result of doing the action is not relevant to its meaningful quality. How other people judge this action, and what it produces as a consequence, is not relevant either in the context of valued living. Of course, people generally desire and find satisfaction from pleasant feelings, social approval, and positive outcomes; but values provide a layer of reinforcement that is more stable, less sensitive to contextual variations, and thus more liberating.

Finally, *positive reinforcement* means that values are approached, rather than avoided. That is, a person might reject arrogance and avoid behaving arrogantly, but a more valued way of guiding her actions would be to behave *with* humility. It is worth noting that not doing an action can still operate as approaching a value as long as not doing this action is symbolically related to the value in a positive way (i.e., through coordination framing rather than distinction or opposition framing). For example, a person who is in a position of power at a meeting with colleagues who have less power might choose not to speak up as a way of connecting with his value of "equity." Formulating values through positive rather than negative reinforcement has the advantage of providing the person engaging in a valued action with satisfying and enriching experiences rather than relief or feelings of guilt. Naturally, relief and guilt can be powerful sources of motivation and have some advantages too. Values don't require negative reinforcement to be eliminated altogether but instead provide an additional layer of reinforcement, which gives meaning and purpose in a more vital way.

Having presented the RFT approach to values, I will now explore ways in which RFT can be used to help clients clarify and build these sources of meaningful reinforcement. In the next section I will demonstrate strategies that specifically target overarching, intrinsic, and positive reinforcement.

## Building Overarching Reinforcement

Overarching reinforcement is provided by hierarchical framing between actions and values. It means that clients need to be able to identify a source of reinforcement that is abstract enough to include an infinite number of actions and goals. Often, they are only able to identify actions and goals as sources of motivation, such as wanting to build a family or spending more time with a partner. In order to extract a value, you can directly target hierarchical framing with questions and reflections that help move the source of motivation to the highest level in the hierarchical network. For example, you might ask, "What is essential about building a family?" "What is meaningful about doing that?" "What bigger purpose does spending more time with your partner serve?" or simply, "Why is it important?" The client might not immediately identify a value, but might identify a goal (e.g., "Because I want to improve my relationship" or "Because I want children"). However, further exploration targeting the extraction of the higher level of abstract reinforcement will eventually lead to a concept that is broad enough to include an infinite number of actions. For example, you might follow up with asking, "And why is it important for you to improve your relationship?"

You can also use conditional framing to climb levels in the hierarchical network step by step, that is, exploring the goal of an action, then the goal of this goal, and so on. For example, you might ask, "And if you spent more time with your partner, how would your life be different? What would that change?" to which the client might answer with a higher-level goal (e.g., "Then my partner would be happier"). The same move could be used again until a goal that can't ever be completely finished is identified (e.g., "I would build intimacy in my relationship").

Another approach to identify overarching reinforcement is to use comparative framing to extract the essential quality of an action or goal. That is, you invite the client to express her preference between two or more actions or goals and then to explore the reason for this preference. For example, you might ask, "What would be more motivating to you: spending time with your partner at the grocery store or at a restaurant? Why?" to which the client might answer, "At the restaurant, because it would be more comfortable to talk." You could then follow up by asking, "Is it important to you to be able to talk with your partner? What is important about it?" targeting again hierarchical framing to extract the value from a preference toward a given action or goal.

In the spirit of this last approach, you could use coordination and distinction framing to help the client identify what is common and different among actions and goals. For example, you might ask, "What is different between spending time with your wife at the grocery store and at a restaurant?" and, if the client had also identified a desire to spend time with his partner watching television, "What is similar between being at a restaurant and watching television with your partner?" The client might then identify a preference for activities in environments that support intimacy, and eventually identify intimacy as a value.

In many cases, clients have a hard time identifying actions they are currently enjoying or would like to do. Using conditional framing to spark imagination "outside the box" can be useful in these situations. For example, you might ask, "If you had all the time in the world, what would you do with your days?" or "If you had a magical wand, what would you like to change in your life?" While the client's answers might not immediately lead to identifying a value (e.g., he might identify a goal first, such as "I would make myself rich"), you can then follow up with questions that help clients climb the hierarchical network to the higher levels of reinforcement as we described earlier. It is also possible to use deictic framing (perspective taking) to reconnect clients with past sources of reinforcement or to help them find inspiration from other people, such as role models or even fictional characters that move them. For example, you might ask, "Can you think of a time in your life when you felt in harmony with yourself, even for a short moment? What were you doing then?" (shift of temporal perspective) or "Who is someone that inspires you? If you were this person, what would be important in your life?" (shift of personal perspective).

## Building Intrinsic Reinforcement

Hierarchical framing is also key to intrinsic reinforcement because it is the kind of symbolic relation that turns an action into something reinforcing in and of itself. Instead of finding satisfaction from outcomes (i.e., a conditional relation between action and consequence), the person who frames her actions as part of a value, and focuses on the process or the journey (i.e., a hierarchical relation between action and values), is able to find meaning and purpose simply by engaging in the action.

Thus, to help a client find intrinsic reinforcement in valued actions, you need to shape the client's ability to build frames of hierarchy between actions and values. For example, if a client seems focused on the outcome of an action, such as having fun if she spends time with a friend, you might ask her to also connect spending time with her friend with a higher, more abstract purpose, such as intimacy or curiosity. The point is not to eliminate the satisfaction that can be found in having fun, but to avoid relying solely or mainly on sources of reinforcement that are not completely in the client's control. If the client connects spending time with her friend to intimacy, whether she has fun or not won't change that it was a meaningful action.

Other key types of framing can be used to remove the influence of extrinsic reinforcement in the client's exploration and clarification of values. Notably, you can use opposition or distinction framing to test whether an action would still be reinforcing if the outcome disappeared. For example, you could ask, "If nobody showed appreciation for your contribution, would you still do it?" (targeting in particular the influence of social reinforcement here) or "Imagine you go out with your friend and she is not in a good mood that day, so spending time with her turns out not to be fun. Would you still find it meaningful to spend time with her?" These types of questions can either rapidly lead the client to identify the values linked to these actions or help the client keep exploring what intrinsic sources of reinforcement could be found there. In other cases, these tests can lead to abandoning an action altogether if the client realizes that it is not meaningful (e.g., a client might quit her job because she realizes that she chose to do it in the first place as a way of pleasing her parents).

An alternative approach consists of disconnecting extrinsic reinforcement from any given action. If extrinsic reinforcement doesn't depend on any specific action, then the client can't choose actions based on extrinsic reinforcement and thus must find other sources of motivation. For example, you might ask, "If everybody loved you no matter what you self-disclosed, what would you want to say about yourself?" Extrinsic reinforcement is thus put in systematic coordination with any kind of self-disclosure, and the client can now explore what she wants to say about herself that is meaningful to her.

Often, clients struggle to identify intrinsic sources of reinforcement because they have learned to connect only with extrinsic reinforcement. Social approval is a particularly powerful source of influence on people's behavior. The freedom that is brought by removing this kind of influence can also be confusing and scary at times. In that case, you must help the client become more aware of what she appreciates outside the extrinsic source of reinforcement, for example using mindfulness and gratitude techniques.

## Building Positive Reinforcement

Building positive reinforcement in values work relies particularly on coordination framing, simply because coordination is how we put things together. In positive reinforcement, an event is added to the context of the action. Formulating values through positive reinforcement thus consists of adding a source of overarching and intrinsic reinforcement to the context of action. For example, if a client is focused on negative sources of reinforcement, such as the relief of back pain after exercising in the long term, you could encourage her to explore what might also be there if she exercises (e.g., "improving health" or "self-care"). Here also, it is important to note that values work is not meant to eliminate negative reinforcement but to add a layer of positive reinforcement—hence, the use of the word "also" in our example.

Metaphors (analogical framing) are also useful to help clients identify and build positive reinforcement in values work. For example, if a client expresses motivation to work less to decrease stress in her life, you could ask, "Imagine that stress was a piece of furniture you didn't like in your home. What will you put in that free space instead?"

While helping the client connect with sources of positive reinforcement, it is useful to notice signs that the client is experiencing more vitality (e.g., smiles, gestures, postures, and words that reflect a sense of well-being, excitement, or growth). You can also help the client notice these signs so that in the future they will become a marker of valued living.

## Challenges

While clinical RFT has the advantage of bringing more precision, flexibility, and natural flow to the therapeutic process, it also involves certain challenges. As with other approaches based on functional processes rather than topographical techniques and protocols, a major difficulty is to define interventions specifically enough so they can be evaluated and implemented as evidence-based practices. Clinical RFT interventions are described functionally rather than topographically. No words said by the therapist are helpful in and of themselves. The therapist must target certain types of framing (e.g., hierarchical/inclusion framing for values work and self-as-context), but these types of framings are not activated by any given questions, metaphors, or exercises *per se*. For example, a therapist helping a client to explore values hierarchically connected to her actions could ask, "Why is it important to you?" or "What does this action contribute to?" or "What is essential about doing that?" All these questions look different, but from the perspective of the therapist, they are all cues meant to evoke the client's hierarchical framing. Whether they will actually do so remains to be assessed as the client responds to the question. For example, a client could respond by talking about a value (e.g., the action is meant to connect with intimacy), which demonstrates hierarchical framing, or by talking about an outcome (e.g., the action is meant to get recognition from others), which demonstrates conditional framing. Thus, no specific word (or gesture, image, posture) is guaranteed to evoke a specific type of framing. And nothing the client says or does is intrinsically a sign that he is framing in a certain way.

Approaching language as a behavior from a functional contextual perspective also implies that we must be careful not to reify it. It is, for example, tempting to think that when a client has been able to name a value and an action that connects her to a value, all she will need to do is engage in the action to be connected to this value and find meaningful purpose. She now "has" a value. However, we would be missing that the process of building and connecting to meaning and purpose relies on the production of a symbolic behavior: *valuing* (augmenting, in RFT terms). The action in and of itself won't be meaningful if the client doesn't also engage in valuing, at least at an implicit level (e.g.,

"I'm spending time with my partner because I value intimacy"). The therapist must thus target relevant relational frames and make sure they are well developed in the client's repertoire before considering that she has reached the therapeutic goal (see Villatte, 2016, for an analysis of in-session assessment in contextual behavioral therapy).

The functional contextual process-based nature of clinical RFT represents a challenge for training therapists as well. Therapists must be able to apply RFT principles in the moment, not just while reflecting on a case outside the session. For a long time, RFT has been used in ACT to explain how humans develop psychological inflexibility and to provide some conceptual basis to clinical interventions. As RFT is progressively becoming a genuine guide in the therapeutic process, trainers and supervisors must find ways to make RFT accessible to clinicians without taking away its functional contextual nature (Villatte, Villatte, & Hayes, 2017). Can clinicians learn to apply RFT principles based on function and context without going through years of multiple exemplar trainings in one-on-one supervision? What is the right level of precision for an RFT analysis to be useful and not burdensome? How much knowledge in RFT must clinicians acquire? And how can we make sure that thinking with RFT will not interfere with the natural flow of a conversation? Much research is warranted to answer these questions. In my experience as a practitioner and trainer, RFT does not get in the way of the relationship. Instead, it helps clinicians become more fluid and experiential without using exercises. They become more able to use a variety of techniques, precisely because they are able to think functionally rather than topographically. They can be precise, as when targeting the three dimensions of reinforcement in values work described earlier; but they can also spontaneously engage in a conversation without necessarily thinking of the types of framing they are using at each moment.

## Research Support

A significant advantage of linking clinical practice more closely to RFT principles than to ACT terms is that basic research can inform interventions in the therapy room more directly. In this regard, clinical RFT relies on a substantial and ever-growing corpus of RFT research touching on a great variety of topics (see O'Connor, Farrell, Munnelly, & McHugh, 2017, for a review of RFT research). We now have a relatively good understanding of how the types of framing are acquired and how they transform the function of stimuli. Research on the use of framing in assessment and interventions is still at its early stage, but several studies have started to show promising results. At the core, these studies typically test the effect of instructions designed to activate different types of framing in the context of developing awareness, distancing from distressing events, or values-based motivation (e.g., Eswara-Murthy, Villatte, & McHugh, 2019; Foody, Barnes-Holmes, Barnes-Holmes, & Luciano, 2013; Luciano et al., 2011). The main limitation of this kind of research is that the verbal history of the participants is not controlled for. However, the advantage is that findings are more directly applicable to clinical work because natural language is used in the experiment. For example, in a recent study comparing the effects of conditional and hierarchical framing on motivation (Eswara-Murthy et al., 2019), we found that participants who received instructions framing their task as part of a process rather than as a condition of an outcome had better performance and higher perceived self-efficacy, willingness, and comfortableness, and this effect was transferred to performance on a different task.

RFT research on the microcomponents of using clinical metaphors is also starting to produce data directly relevant to clinical work. For example, Sierra, Ruiz, Florez, Riano Hernandez, and Luciano (2016) showed that metaphors that include physical similarities between the target (the client's issue) and the source (the metaphorical situation) have more impact. Other studies have begun to use text analysis identifying types of framing and rules to explore the extent to which they might be predictors of relevant behaviors (e.g., Belisle, Paliliunas, Dixon, & Tarbox, 2018; Styles & Atkins, 2016, 2018). This kind of research is particularly relevant to clinical assessment, as therapists might become able to rely more precisely on markers of progress in the language of their clients.

## Future Directions

Future research needs to extend the developing corpus by systematically studying the effect of different types of framing in a variety of clinically relevant contexts. In the area of values work, for example, techniques described in this chapter could easily be tested in the lab and in clinical settings by building instructions aimed at shaping positive, overarching, and intrinsic symbolic reinforcement (the study by Eswara-Murthy et al., 2019, is a step in this direction). Other research needs to be conducted on the effect of training clinicians to use RFT principles. As cognitive behavioral therapies are increasingly moving toward a process-based paradigm (Hayes & Hoffman, 2018), the contribution of clinical RFT to the training of flexible therapists might become more obvious. Even a functional contextual approach like ACT is not safe from drifting toward topographical protocols if it is not well grounded in the philosophy and basic principles of contextual behavioral science and RFT. It is my hope that this area of research and application will keep growing in the near future.

## References

Barnes-Holmes, Y., Boorman, J., Oliver, J. E., McEnteggart, C., & Thomson, M., (2018). Using conceptual developments in RFT to direct case formulation and clinical intervention: Two case summaries. *Journal of Contextual Behavioral Science, 7,* 89–96.

Belisle, J., Paliliunas, D., Dixon, M. R., & Tarbox, J. (2018). Feasibility of contextual behavioral speech analyses of US presidents: Inaugural addresses of Bill Clinton, George W. Bush, Barack Obama, and Donald Trump, 1993-2017. *Journal of Contextual Behavioral Science, 10,* 14–18.

Dahl, J. C., Plumb, J. C., Stewart, I., & Lundgren, T. (2009). *The art and science of valuing in psychotherapy: Helping clients discover, explore, and commit to valued action using acceptance and commitment therapy.* Oakland, CA; New Harbinger Publications.

Eswara-Murthy, V., Villatte, M., & McHugh, L. (2019). Investigating the effect of conditional vs. hierarchical framing on motivation. *Learning and Motivation, 65,* 33–42.

Foody, M., Barnes-Holmes, Y., Barnes-Holmes, D., & Luciano, C. (2013). An empirical investigation of hierarchical versus distinction relations in a self-based ACT exercise. *International Journal of Psychology & Psychological Therapy, 13*(3), 373–388.

Gil-Luciano, B., Ruiz F. J., Valdivia-Salas S., & Suárez, J. C. (2016). Promoting psychological flexibility on tolerance tasks: Framing behavior through deictic/hierarchical relations and specifying augmental functions. *The Psychological Record, 66,* 1–9.

Hayes, S. C., & Hoffman, S. G. (Eds.). (2018). *Process-based CBT: The clinical and core clinical competencies of CBT.* Oakland, CA: Context Press.

Hayes, S. C., Barnes-Holmes, D., & Roche, B. (Eds.). (2001). *Relational frame theory: A post-Skinnerian account of human language and cognition.* New York, NY: Plenum Press.

Hayes, S.C., Villatte, M., Levin, M. & Hildebrandt, M. (2011). Open, aware, and active: Contextual approaches as an emerging trend in the behavioral and cognitive therapies. *Annual Review of Clinical Psychology, 7,* 141–168.

Hooper, N., Saunders, S., & McHugh, L. (2010). The derived generalization of thought suppression. *Learning and Behavior, 38*(2), 160–168.

Luciano, C., Ruiz, F. J., Vizcaíno-Torres, R. M., Sánchez-Martín, V., Gutiérrez-Martínez, O., & López-López, J. C. (2011). A relational frame analysis of defusion interactions in acceptance and commitment therapy. A preliminary and quasi-experimental study with at-risk adolescents. *International Journal of Psychology and Psychological Therapy, 11,* 165–182.

McHugh, L., & Stewart, I. (2012). *The self and perspective taking: Contributions and applications from modern behavioral science.* Oakland, CA: New Harbinger Publications.

McHugh, L., Stewart, I., & Almada, P. (2019). *A contextual behavioral guide to the self: Theory and practice.* Oakland, CA: New Harbinger Publications.

Monestes, J. L., & Villatte, M. (2015). Humans are the selection criterion in psychological science, not "reality": A reply to Herbert and Padovani. *Journal of Contextual Behavioral Science, 4,* 210–211.

O'Connor, M., Farrell, L., Munnelly, A., & McHugh, L. (2017). Citation analysis of relational frame theory: 2009-2016. *Journal of Contextual Behavioral Science, 6,* 152–158.

Sierra, M. A., Ruiz, F. J., Florez, C. L., Riano Hernandez, D., & Luciano, C. (2016). The role of common physical properties and augmental functions in metaphor effect. *International Journal of Psychology & Psychological Therapy, 16,* 255–279.

Styles, R., & Atkins, P. (2016). Measuring self and rules in what people say: Exploring whether self-discrimination predicts long-term wellbeing. *Journal of Contextual Behavioral Science, 5,* 71–79.

Styles, R., & Atkins, P. (2018). Measuring perceptions of self and others in what people say: A replication and extension of the functional self-discrimination measure. *Journal of Contextual Behavioral Science, 9,* 45–52.

Törneke, N. (2010). *Learning RFT: An introduction to relational frame theory and its clinical applications.* Oakland, CA: New Harbinger Publications.

Törneke, N. (2017) *Metaphor in practice: A professional's guide to using the science of language in psychotherapy.* Oakland, CA: New Harbinger Publications.

Villatte, M. (2016). Evaluating in-session therapist and client behaviors from a contextual behavioral science perspective. In R. Zettle, S. C. Hayes, D. Barnes Holmes, & T. Biglan (Eds.), *Handbook of contextual behavioral science.* Chichester, UK: Wiley Blackwell.

Villatte, M., Villatte, J. L., & Hayes, S. C. (2016). *Mastering the clinical conversation: Language as intervention.* New York, NY: The Guilford Press.

Villatte, M., Villatte, J. L., & Hayes, S. C. (2017). A reticulated and progressive strategy for developing clinical applications of RFT. *The Psychological Record,* 1–5.

# CHAPTER 4

# Recent Conceptual and Empirical Advances in RFT
## *Implications for Developing Process-Based Assessments and Interventions*

Yvonne Barnes-Holmes

Ciara McEnteggart

Dermot Barnes-Holmes

*Department of Experimental, Clinical and Health Psychology, Ghent University*

## Overview

Behavioral science has always concerned itself with the processes of learning, adaptation, and behavioral change. Until the late 1960s or early 1970s, a widely held assumption was that these behavioral processes, broadly speaking, were common to both nonhumans and humans. This assumption was reflected in the earliest translational research associated with behavioral psychology. The famous study by Watson and Rayner (1920) in which they created and "treated" a phobia in a young child using the processes of classical conditioning and extinction, which Pavlov (1897, 1902) had identified and studied using dogs, provides a clear-cut example. Other examples, of course, abound in the literature, including the study of learned helplessness (Seligman, 1974), inhibition (Wolpe, 1958), and fear generalization (Lashley & Wade, 1946), each of which has been used in experimental analogs of both human and nonhuman "psychopathology." The continuity assumption, at the level of psychological processes, from animals to humans has not been without value, but it remains just that—an assumption, not an empirical fact.

While many scientists assume that there are differences between human and nonhuman psychological processes (e.g., Chomsky, 1959; Pinker, 1994; Premack, 2007; Sidman, 1994; Wilson, Hayes, Biglan, & Embry, 2014), highly regarded cutting-edge, process-oriented clinical research fails to grapple meaningfully with these differences. For example, recent work by Craske and colleagues on an inhibitory learning approach to maximizing the impact of exposure therapy (Craske, Treanor, Conway, Zbozinek, &

Vervliet, 2014) draws heavily on basic research conducted with nonhumans (e.g., Bouton, 1993). The underlying assumption thus appears to be that psychotherapy should be based on, and needs to target, inhibitory learning processes that are common to both human and nonhuman species. In pointing to the work of Craske, we are not questioning its quality or effectiveness, and indeed we applaud Craske's focus on processes in developing therapeutic interventions. But we believe that a more complete process-based approach to human psychological suffering and its treatment should be informed by research that has sought to understand the lines of fracture that separate animal and human psychological processes. The current chapter will attempt to present an overview of this work.

## Relational Frame Theory

In recent years, our research group has been seeking to develop and extend relational frame theory (RFT) so that it connects more directly with the types of clinical issues and concerns with which therapists grapple (see Barnes-Holmes, D., Barnes-Holmes, Y., & McEnteggart, 2019; Barnes-Holmes et al., 2018). In doing so, we have begun to conceptualize psychological events for verbal humans as involving a constant behavioral stream of relating (R), orienting (O), and evoking (E), summarized as ROEing (pronounced "rowing").* In very simple terms, *relating* refers to the myriad complex ways in which language-able humans can relate stimuli and events; *orienting* refers to noticing or attending to a stimulus or event; and *evoking* refers to whether a noticed stimulus or event is appetitive, aversive, or relatively neutral. The three elements of the ROE are not entirely separable units of analysis, but work together in virtually every psychological act emitted by a verbally able human.

For illustrative purposes, imagine you are about to enter a forest with a tour guide who warns you, "Watch out for snakes with red and yellow stripes because they are quite aggressive and also highly venomous." If you understand the warning, you may conceptualize it as involving an instance of *relating* (e.g., relating snakes with particular properties to danger), which may increase the likelihood that you will *orient* toward any unusual movement on the ground in the forest that could be a snake, followed by an appropriate *evoked* reaction, such as backing away, freezing, or beating it with a stick if you perceive the moving object to be a snake with red and yellow stripes. In effect, your reaction to the snake in the forest is conceptualized as involving the three elements of the ROE.

It is important to understand that the three elements of the ROE do not necessarily interact in a linear or unidirectional manner, but are dynamical. Thus, for example, an orienting response may produce relating, which then leads to an evoked response. Imagine you entered the forest without hearing any warning about snakes. You might be

---

\* Although the current chapter does not cover all of the basic concepts in RFT, the ROE is in essence an RFT concept. However, the concept of the ROE is broader than the concept of a frame in RFT, in that the ROE aims to capture the most basic to the most complex patterns of arbitrarily applicable relational responding (see below and Barnes-Holmes, D., Barnes-Holmes, Y., Luciano, & McEnteggart, 2017, for further details).

less likely to orient toward snake-like movements, but if you did notice a snake you may engage in some relational activity, such as emitting the self-generated rule "better safe than sorry" and withdrawing slowly. In this latter case, orienting led to relating, which led to evoking.

The examples of ROEing we have just provided are adaptive in that they help the individual to avoid a potentially lethal snake bite. But we can easily generate less adaptive examples of ROEing from common clinical interactions. Imagine a husband who is possessive and jealous with respect to his new wife and insists that they never vacation in places where she has spent time with previous partners. The husband's verbal knowledge (*relating*) that his wife had spent time in a particular location with a former partner thus *evokes* a response to that location as aversive, in part because it increases *orienting* responses toward his own intense feelings of jealousy.

The "solution" might be for the couple to avoid vacationing in any of these locations. The avoidance strategy may "work," at least temporarily, if the couple chooses to go somewhere "new" and they enjoy their vacation, in part because the husband experiences few, if any, feelings of intense jealousy while they are away. But ultimately, this "solution" will fail because it is impossible to avoid all of the stimuli that increase the likelihood that he will orient toward the feelings of jealousy related to his wife's past, particularly given the highly abstract and arbitrary nature of relating behavior within the ROE.

You may note in the foregoing example that we highlight a feeling or private event (i.e., jealousy) as a stimulus toward which an individual may orient and, indeed, which they may find aversive. In making this claim, we are not indicating that the ROE should be seen as a mentalistic concept, unless of course you wish to criticize Skinner's (1945) concept of private events as also inherently mentalistic. Indeed, the Skinnerian concepts of private events and sense of self have been elaborated considerably within RFT. The details of this elaboration are beyond the scope of the current chapter, but we will briefly consider how the self fits into the concept of the ROE before continuing.

## The Verbal Self and the ROE

The verbal self, as defined by RFT, is best thought of as a dynamical and complex relational network. Specifically, a young child needs an advanced level of derived relational responding in order to establish and refine a verbal self through interactions with the verbal community (Barnes-Holmes, D., Barnes-Holmes, Y., Roche, & Smeets, 2001). Furthermore, the self-referential terms (e.g., "I," "me," "self," "mine," the child's name) come to participate in a complex network of relational responses, some of which are more constant than others. For example, the statement or network "I am older than my brother but younger than my sister" is unlikely to change once it is established, whereas other self-related networks are more "fluid" (e.g., "Today I feel really sick, but tomorrow I might feel better"). In this sense, it is useful to think of the verbal self as lying at the very center of a vast and undulating web of derived or arbitrarily applicable relations, some of which almost never change, and others that emerge and disappear as determined by a host of contextual cues and variables.

Once a verbal self is established in the behavioral repertoire, it becomes a stimulus or ongoing event that participates in virtually every ROE. The vast majority of these ROEs may be seen as relatively trivial in the grand scheme of things, but the verbal self remains a participant in such acts. For example, the relating, orienting, and evoking that occur in the act of switching off a bedroom lamp before going to sleep could be seen as extremely trivial, but it is still a "verbal you" who turns off the lamp to achieve some outcome (e.g., a good night's sleep). Other ROEs, of course, may be seen as far more fundamental and are clearly self-focused. For example, the relating, orienting, and evoking that occur in the act of taking an overdose to end one's life could be seen as an attempt to escape, in a very permanent and final way, the very essence of the verbal self. In any case, the constant and iterative daily cycle of ROEing, from the most trivial to the most fundamental of human acts, could be seen as creating what philosophers and others have called a sense of purpose or meaning to one's life.

The concept of the ROE is designed to provide a general conceptual unit of analysis, based on RFT, that aims to capture the distinct way in which most humans navigate their psychological worlds. In a broad sense, the ROE defines human "acts of meaning" that are made possible only through the evolution of human language and our learning of a specific language through our ongoing interactions with the verbal communities in which we reside. The complexities involved in learning to engage in such acts of meaning are far from simple, and we have been working on an RFT-based framework for conceptualizing and analyzing the dynamics involved in human acts of meaning, namely the hyper-dimensional multi-level (HDML) framework.

The HDML is an extension of the multi-dimensional multi-level (MDML) framework (Barnes-Holmes et al., 2017). The HDML replaces the first M ("multi") with H ("hyper") in order to emphasize the relating *and* functional properties of acts of meaning, as defined within the ROE itself. To appreciate the shift in emphasis that the HDML framework involves, we will first focus on the relational properties of the framework, and then explain how the orienting and evoking functions of the ROE are incorporated into the MDML, thus yielding what we now refer to as the HDML. In this sense, the MDML and the HDML are more or less the same framework, but the latter contains additional foci (i.e., orienting and evoking functions) that were not explicitly contained in the MDML, which was very much focused on relating.

The HDML framework, similar to the MDML, specifies five levels of relational responding: mutual entailing, relational framing (the simplest type of relational network), relational networking, relating relations, and relating relational networks. *Mutual entailing* refers to the bidirectional nature of verbal relations (e.g., if A is more than B, then B is less than A). *Relational framing,* at its simplest, involves a combination of two mutually entailed relations (e.g., if A is more than B and B is more than C, then A is more than C). *Relational networking* involves combinations of different patterns of relational framing (e.g., if A equals B, and B equals C, and C is more than D, and D is more than E, then E is less than A, B, C, and D). *Relating relations* involves, in essence, relating a mutually entailed relation to another mutually entailed relation (e.g., if A is more than B, and in a separate relation C is more than D, then the relationship between the two relations [A is more than B, and C is more than D] is the same). Relating relational networks is similar to relating relations, except that it applies to separate relational frames or separate complex relational networks.

In addition, the framework conceptualizes four dimensions for each of these five levels: coherence, complexity, derivation, and flexibility. *Coherence* refers to the extent to which current relational responding is broadly consistent with previous patterns of relational responding (whether they are directly trained or derived). For example, if you are told that A is larger than B, the mutually entailed response B is smaller than A would be deemed relationally coherent. *Complexity* refers to the detail or density of a pattern of relational responding, including the number or types of relations in a given relational network. For example, the mutually entailed relation of sameness would be considered less complex than a comparative relation because the former involves only one relation (same), but the latter involves two (more and less) relations (e.g., A equals B entails B equals A, but A is more than B entails B is less than A). *Derivation* refers to the number of times a derived response has been emitted; the first response is high in derivation because it is being derived entirely from a trained relation, but thereafter derived responding gradually acquires its own history and is, therefore, less and less derived relative to the initial relation that was trained. For example, having been told that A is more than B, the first time you derive that B is less than A the response is highly derived because it is based entirely on the first premise. But as you repeatedly derive B is less than A, that response acquires its own history and becomes less and less derived from the first premise. *Flexibility* refers to the extent to which patterns of derived relational responding may be influenced or changed by contextual variables (e.g., when trained baseline relations are reversed). For example, imagine one day you learn that A is more than B and you derive that B is less than A. On a subsequent day, you learn that A is less than B (and thus B is now more than A). Your ability to derive this new relationship, which does not cohere with the original relation, requires flexibility. Within the MDML framework (now the HDML), each of the five levels intersects with each of the four dimensions, thus yielding a total of twenty units of experimental analysis, which, it has been argued, emphasize the highly dynamical nature of derived relational responding involved in human language and cognition (see figure 4.1).

In the foregoing explanation, the MDML framework appears to focus largely on the relating or entailing properties of the units of analysis, while the ROE, as described previously, contains relating *as well as* functional properties of events (i.e., orienting and evoking). To reflect this, any pattern of relational responding captured within the twenty analytic units of the HDML framework also involves orienting and evoking functions. As just one example of how orienting, evoking, and relating combine synergistically in the analysis of a human psychological act, imagine that you are walking on a hot day through a shopping area while visiting a new city and you have not had anything to drink for a few hours. As a result, you may find yourself noticing, or *orienting* toward, an advertisement for ice cream in a shop window, which then *evokes* a strong appetitive response for actual ice cream, and the emission of a relevant *relational network,* such as "I'll stop here and go in and buy myself some ice cream." The synergistic interactions of these three components for each of the twenty units of the HDML framework are represented in each cell of figure 4.1 by the inverted "T" shape. The vertical line represents the relative value of orienting functions from low to high, and the horizontal line represents the relative value of evoking functions from extremely aversive (on the far left) to extremely appetitive (on the far right). Within the context of the ROE, these functions impact, and are impacted by, the relational properties highlighted within each of the twenty units of the HDML framework. And virtually any contextual variable may be involved in influencing the dynamical interplay among the three properties within or across cells.

## Description of the ROE for Assessment and Treatment

The HDML framework can help clinicians conceptualize ROEs or acts of meaning in the context of psychological suffering, its assessment, and its treatment. Consider again the example of the jealous husband who avoids going on vacation with his wife to locations she visited with previous partners. Imagine that the husband goes to see a psychotherapist for help with his intense jealousy. Early in therapy, the following dialogue takes place.

*Client (C):*      I have become obsessively jealous about my wife's previous lovers.

*Therapist (T):*   Do you feel jealous all of time?

C:      Oh yes, the jealousy never goes away—it dominates my every waking hour.

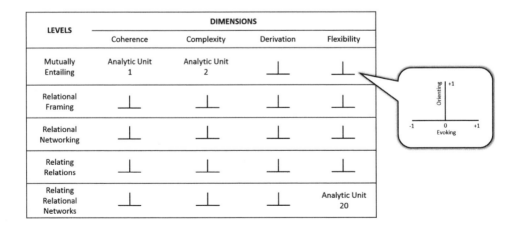

Figure 4.1. A hyper-dimensional multi-level (HDML) framework.

T:          How long have you felt like this?

C:          Almost from the first day I met my wife—she has always been very open and honest about her past life. And although we've been married for a few years now, my jealous feelings seem to be getting worse rather than better.

T:          Why do you think you are so jealous?

C:          I don't know really, I just am. I try hard not to be, but I just can't help it.

Within the framework of the HDML, we could conceptualize this therapeutic interaction as follows. The husband's first statement, "I have become obsessively jealous…," involves mutually entailing the verbal self (i.e., words and terms, such as "I," "self," and the husband's name) with "jealous." His next statement, "…the jealousy never goes away…," suggests that the relational responding is *high* in coherence in the sense that it coheres strongly with virtually all other self-statements, and it also suggests a very strong orienting response toward jealousy (because it never goes away).

His answer to the question about how long he has felt this way ("Almost from the first day I met my wife") suggests that the relational responding is also *low* in derivation, because he has been focused on his jealousy for years (e.g., orienting toward jealousy is well established). When asked why he is so jealous, the reply "I don't know really, I just am. I try hard not to be, but I just can't help it" suggests that the relational responding is *low* in complexity and *low* in flexibility. In the interest of brevity, the foregoing interpretation focuses simply on the four dimensions of the HDML framework, rather than the intersections between the dimensions and the levels of relational responding. In general, however, it seems likely that therapeutic interactions, such as the one described, often involve relational networking, relating relations, and relating relational networks (see Barnes-Holmes et al., 2019).

You can appreciate the relative precision the HDML framework provides in the assessment of psychological suffering when you consider how subtle differences in the husband's responses might be interpreted. Imagine that when the therapist asked, "Do you feel jealous all the time?" he had replied, "No, I can see many reasons not to be jealous and that I am just being stupid when I feel that way." This could suggest responding that is *low* in coherence (rather than *high*) and that orienting toward jealousy was not always particularly strong, because it is inconsistent with other examples of his relational networking with regard to his wife. Imagine also that after being asked how long he had felt this way, the husband had responded, "I only started feeling really jealous in the past few months" (rather than "Almost from the first day…"). Such a response could be interpreted as relatively *high* in derivation, because it emerged only recently in his relational responding. It may also indicate that the orienting function of jealousy is increasing, but only recently. Imagine also if he had provided a list of reasons why he is so jealous (rather than simply saying, "I just am"). For example, if he had said, "My mother and father divorced when I was young because my mother had an affair, and my first wife cheated on me, and I never really understood women anyway," the relational responding may be seen as relatively *high* rather than *low* in complexity. Finally, imagine if in response to the therapist's last question, "Why do you think you are so jealous?" the husband had replied calmly, "Maybe I'm just the jealous type and I need to learn how to deal with this." This response would suggest relational responding that is relatively *high* in flexibility (i.e., because the husband is willing to consider new ways of behaving).

In the foregoing discussion, we have offered various interpretations of the husband's hypothetical responses by focusing on the *entailing* or *relational* properties of the HDML framework, with some references to functional properties, in terms of the orienting functions of jealousy. But ROEs require focusing also on the *evoking* (functional) properties of relational responding. To reflect this, any pattern of relational responding captured within the twenty analytic units of the HDML framework involves orienting *and* evoking functions. As we shall see, focusing on the evoking functions within the ROE is particularly important in directing the ongoing functional analyses of the client's verbal behavior (in previous publications, we have referred to this as "verbal functional analysis"; see Barnes-Holmes et al., 2018).

Having identified jealousy as the core verbal stimulus presented by the client, we of course interpret this stimulus as lying at the center of a complex relational network. In the therapy work we described above, we assessed the relational and orienting functions of this network, but it is also essential to explore the appetitive or aversive evoking functions of the network. In this sense, we are exploring the client's ROEing (relating, orienting, and evoking) with respect to the "jealousy" network. Paradoxically, jealousy (the network) may have some appetitive, and not just aversive, evoking functions. For example, the husband's reporting that the problem is jealousy, although distressing in itself, may facilitate avoidance of a more complex, long-established issue, such as a fear of rejection.

During the course of the verbal assessment, it becomes apparent to the therapist that the client is relatively comfortable in discussing jealousy as a problem. It is therefore important for the therapist to continue to explore the jealousy network with a view to identifying areas of the networks or related networks that are less comfortable for the client. This might start out with the therapist asking questions such as "Why do you think jealousy plays such a strong role in your life?" If the client appears somewhat confused, becomes more reflective, or even struggles to engage with the questions, the therapist may seek to probe relational networks that may be related to jealousy but possess evoking functions that are more aversive (S-). For example, the therapist might ask the client, "What if your jealousy feels like it might protect you from *rejection* because it means that you always know what your wife is up to, and that way you won't get a nasty surprise?" If the suggestion of rejection evokes what appears to be a relatively strong aversive reaction in the client, the therapist may pursue this network and/or this reaction.

In summary, focusing on the evoking functions of jealousy allows the therapist to separate out the appetitive (S+) and aversive (S-) functions of this type of self-labeling.

That is, "jealousy" may have less aversive functions than "rejection." Indeed by describing himself as "jealous," the husband is able to avoid the more accurate (functionally speaking) description of his behavior as involving fear of rejection. To simplify this, we might refer to "jealousy" and related self-evaluations as the S+ networks (with both aversive and appetitive functions), while referring to "fear of rejection" as the S- networks (with largely aversive functions). Relatively speaking, this makes it possible that the husband's engagement with the S+ networks actually serves to reinforce avoidance of the S- networks. In therapy, we use ongoing verbal functional assessments of the evoking functions of specific relational networks to guide our first steps toward dealing with the S+ (e.g., jealousy) networks because clients engage with these more readily, and thus the therapist's move in this direction will seem less confrontational. We are nonetheless cautious that engagement with S+ networks likely continues to facilitate the avoidance-evoking functions of the S- networks.

In grappling with the contrasting evoking functions of the jealousy-versus-rejection networks, the therapist may assist the client to relate the two networks, which involves operating at the highest level of the HDML framework. The assumption here would be that these networks have rarely, if ever, been related in this way, and thus the level of derivation would be very high, while coherence (in terms of coordination) between the two networks would be very low. Relating the relational networks as coordinates would ideally serve to transform the orienting and evoking functions of both jealousy and rejection. Specifically, talking about jealousy would actualize some of the aversive functions of rejection, and thus orienting toward rejection would increase, and its aversive functions would decrease. For example, the therapist might say something like "Have you ever thought that your jealousy might actually make your wife want to reject you, because maybe it makes you almost impossible to love?" The purpose here is not to berate the client for being jealous or for fearing rejection, but to encourage him to engage with the highly aversive functions of his fear of rejection. In doing so, when he finds himself orienting toward jealousy in the natural environment, this also serves to evoke some of the functions of the rejection network. For instance, the therapist might suggest the following: "The next time that jealousy shows up, you might try to notice that jealousy is just a decoy for the more painful heart of the problem that is the fear of being rejected." In doing so across sessions, the husband in this case would be encouraged to communicate openly with his wife at the very moments he feels jealous. For example, instead of engaging in the previous jealousy-based behaviors (e.g., a barrage of questions as soon as the wife comes through the door), he could simply say something to her like "This is one of those times when I just feel really rejected and instead of being jealous about it, I just wanted to tell you honestly about how I really feel inside." In so far as this would enhance the honesty and intimacy within their relationship, it may also serve to reduce the aversive functions of talking about rejection.

# Research Support

In conceptualizing therapy, both assessment and treatment, as outlined in the example above, the current chapter attempts to present an example of the very cutting edge of our efforts to develop a language that connects the basic laboratory research with the practice of doing actual therapy in the clinic. This has been the most challenging task of our careers and is very much a work in progress that only commenced in earnest over three years ago. The highly technical concepts we are currently working with and which appear in this chapter (i.e., the MDML and HDML frameworks and the ROE) have emerged directly from basic experimental research that is only just appearing in published peer-reviewed articles (Finn, Barnes-Holmes, Hussey, & Graddy, 2016; Finn, Barnes-Holmes, & McEnteggart, 2018; Harte, Barnes-Holmes, D., Barnes-Holmes, Y., & McEnteggart, 2017, 2018; Kavanagh, Barnes-Holmes, D., Barnes-Holmes, Y., McEnteggart, & Finn, 2018; Kavanagh, Roelandt, et al., 2019; Leech, Barnes-Holmes, & McEnteggart, 2017; Leech, Bouyrden, Bruijsten, Barnes-Holmes, & McEnteggart, 2018). At this point, therefore, the manner in which we are connecting this basic experimental work and its application in therapy is at its very early stages, although we have begun to run workshops that present this work in its clinical context. There is at present no directly relevant clinical research that demonstrates the way in which we are approaching therapy—that is, employing concepts that emerge from basic experimental RFT research—improves upon therapy that is less firmly rooted in this conceptual foundation.

# Future Directions

On balance, much of the clinical work, including supervision and workshops, that we have engaged in over many years is broadly consistent with what we have presented here. What is new is an ongoing thoughtful attempt to continue to refine and develop the basic theory, conceptually and empirically, along with the development of clinical assessment and therapy as a reticulating exercise. In this context, we anticipate the most important challenge will be to train both basic researchers and clinicians in a way that will advance the work in a meaningful manner. Perhaps even more critically, it will be important to test the extent to which this training generates a vibrant program of ongoing basic research and also improves upon therapeutic practice in terms of precision in assessment and treatment. As such, we acknowledge that what we have offered here is tentative and exploratory. But in our view, only in pursuing such a research agenda will the aspiration of a process-based approach to psychological suffering, firmly rooted in basic behavior-analytic concepts, be fully realized.

# References

Barnes-Holmes, D., Barnes-Holmes, Y., Luciano, C., & McEnteggart, C. (2017). From the IRAP and REC model to a multi-dimensional multi-level framework for analyzing the dynamics of arbitrarily applicable relational responding. *Journal of Contextual Behavioral Science, 6*(4), 434–445.

Barnes-Holmes, Y., Barnes-Holmes, D., & McEnteggart, C. (2019). Narrative: Its importance in modern behavior analysis and therapy. *Perspectives on Behavioral Science (Special Issue on Narrative).*

Barnes-Holmes, Y., Barnes-Holmes, D., Roche, B., & Smeets, P. M. (2001). The development of self and perspective-taking: A relational frame analysis. *Behavioral Development Bulletin, 10*(1), 42–45.

Barnes-Holmes, Y., Boorman, J., Oliver, J. E., Thompson, M., McEnteggart, C., & Coulter, C. (2018). Using conceptual developments in RFT to direct case formulation and clinical intervention: Two case summaries. *Journal of Contextual Behavioral Science (Special Section on "Conceptual Developments in Relational Frame Theory: Research and Practice"), 7,* 89–96.

Bouton, M. E. (1993). Context, time, and memory retrieval in the interference paradigms of Pavlovian learning. *Psychological Bulletin, 114*(1), 80.

Chomsky, N. (1959). A review of B.F. Skinner's Verbal Behavior. *Language, 35*(1), 26–58.

Craske, M. G., Treanor, M., Conway, C. C., Zbozinek, T., & Vervliet, B. (2014). Maximizing exposure therapy: An inhibitory learning approach. *Behaviour Research and Therapy, 58,* 10–23.

Finn, M., Barnes-Holmes, D., Hussey, I., & Graddy, J. (2016). Exploring the behavioral dynamics of the implicit relational assessment procedure: The impact of three types of introductory rules. *The Psychological Record, 66*(2), 309–321.

Finn, M., Barnes-Holmes, D., & McEnteggart, C. (2018). Exploring the single-trial-type-dominance-effect on the IRAP: Developing a differential arbitrarily applicable relational responding effects (DAARRE) model. *The Psychological Record, 68*(1), 11–25.

Harte, C., Barnes-Holmes, Y., Barnes-Holmes, D., & McEnteggart, C. (2017). Persistent rule-following in the face of reversed reinforcement contingencies: The differential impact of direct versus derived rules. *Behavior Modification, 41*(6), 743–763.

Harte, C., Barnes-Holmes, D., Barnes-Holmes, Y., & McEnteggart, C. (2018). The impact of high versus low levels of derivation for mutually and combinatorially entailed relations on persistent rule-following. *Behavioural Processes, 157,* 36–46.

Kavanagh, D., Barnes-Holmes, Y., Barnes-Holmes, D., McEnteggart, C., & Finn, M. (2018). Exploring differential trial-type effects and the impact of a read-aloud procedure on deictic relational responding on the IRAP. *The Psychological Record, 68*(2), 163–176.

Kavanagh, D., Roelandt, A., Van Raemdonck, L., Barnes-Holmes, Y., Barnes-Holmes, D., & McEnteggart, C. (2019). The on-going search for perspective-taking IRAPs: Exploring the potential of the natural language IRAP. *The Psychological Record.*

Leech, A., Barnes-Holmes, D., & McEnteggart, C. (2017). Spider fear and avoidance: A preliminary study of the impact of two verbal rehearsal tasks on a behavior-behavior relation and its implications for an experimental analysis of defusion. *The Psychological Record, 67,* 387–398.

Leech, A., Bouyrden, J., Bruijsten, N., Barnes-Holmes, D., & McEnteggart, C. (2018). Training and testing for a transformation of fear and avoidance functions using the implicit relational assessment procedure: The first study. *Behavioural Processes, 157,* 24–35.

Lashley, K. S., & Wade, M. (1946). The Pavlovian theory of generalization. *Psychological Review, 53,* 72–87.

Pavlov, I. P. (1897, 1902). *The work of the digestive glands.* London, UK: Griffin.

Pinker, S. (1994). *The language instinct.* New York, NY: William Morrow & Co.

Premack, D. (2007). Human and animal cognition: Continuity and discontinuity. *Proceedings of the National Academy of Sciences, 104*(35), 13861–13867.

Seligman, M. E. P. (1974). Depression and learned helplessness. In R. J. Friedman and M. M. Katz (Eds.), *The psychology of depression: Contemporary theory and research* (pp. 83–126). Washington, DC: Winston-Wiley.

Sidman, M. (1994). *Stimulus equivalence: A research story.* Boston, MA: Authors Cooperative.

Skinner, B. F. (1945). The operational analysis of psychological terms. *Psychological Review, 52*(5), 270–277.

Watson, J. B., & Rayner, R. (1920). Conditioned emotional reactions. *Journal of Experimental Psychology, 3,* 1–14.

Wilson, D. S., Hayes, S. C., Biglan, A., & Embry, D. D. (2014). Evolving the future: Toward a science of intentional change. *Behavioral and Brain Sciences, 37*(4), 395–416.

Wolpe, J. (1958). *Psychotherapy by reciprocal inhibition.* Stanford, CA: Stanford University Press.

# CHAPTER 5

# Becoming More Versatile (VRSCDL)
## *Using Evolutionary Science to Suggest Innovations in ACT*

Steven C. Hayes

Cory E. Stanton

Brandon T. Sanford

Stuart Law

Janice Ta

*University of Nevada, Reno*

## Overview

Contextual behavioral science (CBS; Hayes, Barnes-Holmes, & Wilson, 2012) is a wing of behavioral science that studies whole organisms acting in and with a context that is considered historically and situationally. It views behavioral development as a variation, selection, and retention process within the lifetime of individuals and small groups through contingencies of reinforcement and contingencies of meaning (established by relational learning) and across lifetimes through social and cultural processes—both for the organisms being studied and for the scientists studying them. Stated that way, it seems that CBS and evolutionary theory have always gone together, and in an abstract sense that may be the case.

Despite the fact that these two fields have been nested conceptually, that is not the case historically. It is not for want of trying. Skinner's explicit vision was that behavioral science should be seen as part of a larger science of evolution. He noted that "the whole story will eventually be told by the joint action of the sciences of genetics, behavior, and culture" (Skinner, 1988, p. 83), and he consistently pushed for behavioral ideas to be seen as derived from evolutionary principles, and for contingencies of reinforcement to be accepted as a legitimate evolutionary strand in its own right (Skinner, 1981).

Most evolutionists of the time saw it differently. As the gene-centric vision of the modern synthesis held sway, an interest in open processes of learning and change became suspect, and seeking behavioral principles that applied across tips of evolutionary branches looked naïve, or even contradictory to evolutionary thought.

In hindsight, the disconnection between functional contextual behavioral thinking and evolutionary thinking is a history of miscommunication, misunderstanding, and missed opportunities (e.g., Hayes, Sanford, & Chin, 2017). It is worth noting that functional contextual thinkers who embrace evolutionary thought were not limited to Skinner, and some of them are known to evolutionists (Honeycutt, 2011), even if their larger points are still being assimilated. Ironically, these same researchers have not been fully appreciated by behaviorists. Zing-Yang Kuo, for example, is a known evolutionist who developed an approach he called "behavioral epigenesis," which he explicitly linked to radical behaviorism (1967, p. 65). Kuo defined behavioral epigenesis as "a continuous developmental process from fertilization through birth to death, involving proliferation, diversification, and modification of behavior patterns both in space and in time, as a result of the continuous dynamic exchange of energy between the developing organism and its environment, endogenous and exogenous" (1967, p. 59). Kuo appreciated the importance of behavioral principles but correctly thought that a complete account also needed to deal more directly with genetic, morphological, biophysical, and biochemical factors without ever slipping into the nature-nurture dichotomy, which he viewed as false. In other words, he thought learning principles were far too small of a set of principles to allow us to predict or influence the evolution of behavior. That criticism restrained the impact of Kuo on behavior analysis despite the clear connection of his work to behavioral thinking, very much as Skinner's focus on reinforcement restricted his impact on evolutionary science despite his explicit attempts to link the fields.

In the modern era, this entire territory is now being reexamined. The idea of multidimensional and multilevel evolutionary processes is becoming far more widespread as the impact of the full mapping of the human genome is felt. As we will explain below, it is now obvious that genetic structures cannot be evaluated in isolation from other dimensions and levels of evolution.

When evolutionary principles are adjusted to fit a more integrated perspective, not only is evolutionary theory strengthened, but it is made more applicable to applied behavioral domains. This chapter is meant as a kind of beginning "proof of concept" of that suggestion as it applies to acceptance and commitment therapy (ACT; Hayes, Strosahl, & Wilson, 2012), but first it is necessary to review evolutionary theory so as to focus on the key principles that can then be applied.

## Behavior and the Extended Evolutionary Synthesis

For decades evolutionary science has been under the sway of the modern synthesis, which integrated Darwinian natural selection, Mendelian inheritance, and population dynamics in a gene-centric perspective in which genes produced phenotypes, which were then selected by the environment, culling genes in a perpetual cycle. In recent years full genomic analysis on large numbers of people failed to adequately account for heritable traits (Maher, 2008), proving false simple genetic causality. As gene-centrism has begun to fade, an extended evolutionary synthesis (EES; Laland et al., 2015) has become more central by adding variation, selection, and retention processes that work in concert with genetic selection and inheritance. At least four interacting streams of evolution need to be tracked as part of an EES: genetic, epigenetic, behavioral, and symbolic (Jablonka & Lamb, 2005). We now know, for example, that heritable traits can be more fully accounted for by analyzing ways that epigenetic processes such as methylation of cytosine alter gene expression by making it harder to transcribe genes, and how inherited or sought-out environments alter selection pressure, leading to phenotypic developments (e.g., niche construction and selection), and how cultural practices impact such processes. Instead of simple genetic fittedness, "inclusive inheritance" applies to all of these dimensions, which are considered as a system (Danchin et al., 2011). In other words, modern evolutionary thought is now multidimensional, and behavior changes within the lifetime of the individual fit within the overall system.

It is also now clear that selection operates on smaller and larger levels of organization simultaneously, and for that reason evolutionary thought needs to be multilevel. Selection at higher levels of organization can become dominant when competition at the higher level is central and selfishness at low levels is held in check (Wilson & Wilson, 2007). Major evolutionary transitions happen precisely at these tipping points. For example, mitochondria are part of an ancient cooperative system in eukaryotic cells: nucleated cells can do more as a cooperative collection than separately, provided the selfish interests of mitochondria (which have different DNA that can only pass along the maternal line) can be held in check. Selfishness at lower levels of organization is never eliminated—only constrained. Even after billions of years, for example, mitochondria sometimes trick plants into reproducing only females ("male cytoplasmic sterility"). In successful major evolutionary transitions, systems at the group or higher level of organization detect and dampen such selfishness at the lower level, such as is the function of the immune system in eliminating precancerous cells. In other words, modern evolutionary thought is multilevel.

Taken together, these advances in modern evolutionary thought set the stage for behavioral science to play a central role. This can be exemplified by briefly considering the three concepts of niche selection, niche construction, and social learning (Schneider, 2012). *Niche selection* refers to the ability to seek out certain environments over others. *Niche construction* refers to long-lasting changes in environments based on behavior such as building nests, dams, and webs; digging burrows; and creating chemical environments. These two actions (niche selection and niche construction) modify the selection pressures to which organisms are exposed, further altering their physical and behavioral phenotypes (Odling-Smee, Laland, & Feldman, 1996). For example, because the food-seeking action of flamingos digging for crustaceans is operant, they could select that niche via approach behavior—impacting selection pressures that over time led to their odd beak shapes via natural selection. Similarly, beavers inhabit a local environment comprising a dam and its internal den due to the impact of their behavior on the environment over the long term. Phenotypic adaptations that help cut down trees (large upper incisors) might now be favored over adaptations that would more directly allow the avoidance of predation (e.g., legs suited for rapid running), since the burrow protects the beavers from predation, and the trees are key to the construction of the dams. *Social learning* allows learned patterns to be repeated across lifetimes, such that learned behavior can become an "adaptability driver" by providing an end-point against which genetically and epigenetically driven adaptations can now compete via selection (Bateson, 2013). That is, a complex and effective behavioral pattern need not be assembled randomly via the slow process of genetic evolution; the rapid evolutionary process of learning can assemble the unit, and genetic and epigenetic variation can then refine it. Behavior and learning is thus a driver of evolution—for example, contingency learning is arguably responsible for the rapid increase in speciation observed in the Cambrian explosion (Ginsburg & Jablonka, 2010).

Both behavioral science and evolutionary science now know they need each other for the sake of a complete account. Behavioral psychologists are used to thinking of action as a feature of a whole organism behaving in and with a context considered historically and situationally, but that merely places behavioral science firmly in the natural sciences (Zettle, Hayes, Barnes-Holmes, & Biglan, 2016); thinking of action in a way that comports with evolutionary principles is what puts behavioral science under the umbrella of evolutionary science (Wilson & Hayes, 2018).

## VRSCDL: A "Versatile" Approach to Evolutionary Accounts

What evolutionary features are needed for ACT or any other psychological approach to be refined based on evolutionary science? There are six such features: variation, selection, retention, context, dimensions, and levels. These features enter into a well-rounded evolutionary account when used to answer Niko Tinbergen's (1963) four key evolutionary questions (Wilson, Hayes, Biglan, & Embry, 2014). We will describe these features and questions and then apply them to innovation in ACT.

An acronym to help remember these six processes is VRSCDL (pronounced as a play on the word "versatile"—as in the title of this chapter), which stands for *Variation and Retention of what is Selected in Context at the right Dimension and Level*. CBS researchers have developed VRSCDL accounts in papers on the evolution of language (Hayes & Sanford, 2014), research on language in the form of relational frame theory (Hayes et al., 2017), behavior therapy (Hayes & Sanford, 2015), and culture change (Atkins, Wilson, & Hayes, 2019; Wilson et al., 2014).

For any event to evolve it must first vary. *Variation* is initially blind, but over time, variation can occur in nonrandom ways that have been beneficial in the past. For example, some plants reproduce sexually when times are hard but reproduce by cloning when resources are plentiful. An example at the level of behavior is an extinction burst: if behavior is being reinforced it persists, but when reinforcement falls away the behavior rises rapidly in frequency or force, then shifts to previously reinforced forms of behavior (e.g., tantrums), and ultimately to novel forms of behavior, which, if reinforced, are then selected and retained.

*Selection* occurs as an interaction between the organism and environment, such that an aspect of survival or success is achieved that can impact retention of a variant that alters the further likelihood of success. In natural selection, success is a matter of life and death. For example, a gene system that helps an organism avoid predation can expect to see an increase in gene frequency in generations across time. In behavior, reinforcement is a clear example of selection. So too are contingencies of meaning in which symbolic consequences (e.g., consistency with values) maintain actions.

*Retention* refers to the probabilistic passing down, or inheritance, of selected variants or the information necessary to produce them. Retention systems vary widely across evolutionary dimensions. Genetic variations are retained in the sequences of nucleotides that make up the genotype of gametes, for example. Behavior can be retained within a lifetime via habits, or across generations via cultural practices. An example of unusual retention that has tortured many a parent is how humor is passed on from child to child within a certain age range, each of whom then "ages out" of the cultural practice. Many a parent has been surprised to recognize long-forgotten and silly knock-knock jokes that have been living in an evolutionary niche called "third grade" for many decades, largely unchanged across generations of children.

Variations are always selected and retained within a *context:* selection pressures are merely a way of speaking about contextual fit. In natural selection, the context that determines life and death outcomes for phenotypic variants is key, but because the analysis is post hoc, the skills of examining context a priori are not necessarily fully developed. A careful consideration of context is especially important for intentional evolutionary change, however, because adaptations will succeed or fail based on context. An example in behavior is the importance of natural reinforcement to maintenance. If no natural reinforcer exists for behavior established in the clinic, behavioral psychologists will predict that the behavior will likely extinguish; programming such reinforcers (e.g., through work with significant others) becomes a focus of intervention.

These principles apply across *dimensions* and streams of inheritance. For that reason, applying evolutionary principles requires thought about the specific kinds of actions of most importance (e.g., overt behavior, symbolic action, emotion, sense of self) and how they will interact as a dynamical system.

Finally, variations can succeed or fail, at different *levels* of organization, simultaneously. Variations that require selection at a higher level (e.g., social cooperation, understanding of the intentionality of others) can only be selected and retained if not excessively undermined by selection operating at a lower level. For example, successful relationship skills are best developed and maintained in the context of a concern for others—not as selfish means of social manipulation or domination.

For the VRSCDL approach to give rise to scientifically and practically mature evolutionary accounts, four key types of evolutionary questions need to be asked: those of function, history, development, and mechanisms (Tinbergen, 1963). Each applies not just to genes and physiological traits but also to behavior (Hayes et al., 2017).

Questions of *function* examine how variants alter adaptation. In the case of genetic variation, that is synonymous with the survival value of a given gene or gene system; behavioral psychologists are quite familiar with considering the functions of action, such as through functional analysis. Functions are always nested and interlinked. For example, we might examine how a reinforced behavior can contribute to genetic survival (Pinxten, Desclée, & Eens, 2016), or how contingencies of meaning that emerge from symbolic thought can alter the specific consequences that function as reinforcers. For instance, a male who becomes committed to the importance of gender equity might find that verbal domination in a small mixed gender group is no longer reinforcing.

Questions of *history* examine how a variant emerges and is retained over time; these questions can span multiple time frames and multiple organisms. A person's genotype reflects a history that can involve millions or even billions of years; cultural practices can evolve over millennia; an individual develops behaviorally within their lifetime in the context of these other histories. For example, suppose a monkey discovers that washing potatoes in a stream removes sand more so than brushing it off, but then dips the potatoes in the ocean and discovers that it adds a pleasant salty taste (Kawai, Watanabe, & Mori, 1992). As this learned behavior becomes a cultural practice and spreads through the troop, let's suppose that some in the troop begin to swim, or even to catch fish. A person could speak about the function of catching fish in the troop, but without an appreciation of history they would not know why that behavior occurs in some troops and not others (Hayes et al., 2017). Behaviorists are accustomed to this question in their focus on learning history, but examining history (or any of Tinbergen's four questions) does not alone define the analysis as evolutionary. For example, you could be interested in the role of cultural factors in human behavior without ever touching on evolutionary ideas. It is asking all of these different questions from a VRSCDL perspective that makes the account evolutionary.

Questions of *development* examine how particular traits emerge within the lifetime of the organism. In the area of behavior, relatively few features emerge in isolation of other behavioral features. For example, a child learning social skills will likely have to develop sufficient perspective taking in order to rely on social modeling to improve social performance, a child learning to open a box will need to develop hand-eye coordination, and so on.

Finally, questions of *mechanisms* examine how specific external and internal factors combine to produce particular phenotypes, physical or behavioral. At a behavioral level, a multidimensional examination of mechanisms might involve brain-behavior mechanisms, social mechanisms, symbolic mechanisms, operant learning, and so on. For example, the actual mechanisms of hand-eye coordination might involve brain circuits key to perception, fostered by reinforcement of successive acts of greater hand-eye coordination.

# Implications of an Extended Evolutionary Synthesis for ACT

Can a VRSCDL evolutionary analysis focused on Tinbergen's four questions lead to concrete suggestions about innovations in ACT? That is the challenge we set for ourselves in this chapter. We see innovations in both practice and research, but we will emphasize the former in this chapter. The following are meant as examples only—they are hardly a complete list.

## Conceptualizing Psychopathology as an Adaptive Peak

Adaptation in an evolutionary sense is not the same as "desirable" in a practical sense. Normal evolutionary processes can go awry and develop into problematic behavior (Hayes & Sanford, 2015; Snell-Rood & Steck, 2019), especially when dimensions of evolution create mismatches to the current context or when self-amplifying loops occur that are adaptive in an immediate sense but undesirable in the long term.

From a VRSCDL point of view, psychopathology refers to a set of self-sustaining biopsychosocial processes that restrict healthy variation, selection, or retention, and/or sensitivity to context, dimensions, and levels. That is, psychopathology is an adaptive peak that prevents further positive behavioral development via normal evolutionary processes. Like a person walking up a small hill, the steps are seemingly progressive but the journey will necessarily be limited. Eventually, in order to make progress, the person will have to metaphorically walk back down that hill.

Thinking of pathology and its amelioration in a multidimensional, multilevel way thus challenges the idea of psychological and behavioral problems as static syndromes or latent diseases (Hayes & Hofmann, 2017, 2018; Hofmann & Hayes, 2019). The applied benefits of thinking of psychopathology as evolution gone awry is treatment utility: all of the VRSCDL processes are modifiable and subject to experimental analysis, but they fit together as a dynamic system and thus broaden the focus of functional analysis. For example, it is an empirical fact that exposure to potentially trauma-inducing events predicts a variety of psychological problems including syndromal entities (e.g., PTSD), but a VRSCDL approach applied to questions of function, history, development, and mechanism offers a more nuanced and change-focused perspective. Exposure to trauma alters epigenes that regulate the stress response as well as survival circuits in the brain (Sherin & Nemeroff, 2011). These reactions are adaptive in an evolutionary sense, but not in a practical sense, and thus can be targeted for change. For example, we can prevent or undo some of these reactions in our clients by developing social support and psychological flexibility skills, even leading to posttraumatic growth (Hawkes et al., 2013). Thus, by seeing PTSD as a kind of adaptive peak, new targets appear and a more systemic appreciation of the problem emerges.

## Fostering Healthy Variation Across Dimensions

As clients find themselves stuck on adaptive peaks that subsequently bring them into therapy, therapists must often find a way to make approaching novel situations or emitting novel behaviors desirable, meaningful, or reinforcing. Rather than allowing the client to backslide into familiar, ineffective behavior, therapists prompt clients to seek out the unfamiliar and the novel.

A focus on healthy variability considerably broadens some classic ACT ideas. Consider emotion. In a traditional ACT perspective, the key form of emotional inflexibility is experiential avoidance, but if the issue is healthy variability to that idea, we should add the importance of undermining emotional or experiential attachment, such as clinging to relaxed mood, happiness, or self-confidence. We could usefully add emotional sampling and exploration, such as deliberately seeking out rarely experienced emotions through art or literature, to ACT methods. If a person rarely feels proud, grateful, sad, or angry, that too is a kind of emotional inflexibility, and avoidance is not the only way it could occur. People for whom feelings of caring, love, or appreciation seem shallow might usefully spend time savoring, deepening, and exploring emotional experiences.

Using techniques to broaden and build the range and depth of other kinds of experience can easily fit within a more VRSCDL approach to ACT. Much as we can use body scans to increase sensitivity to somatic sensations (Mirams, Poliakoff, Brown, & Lloyd, 2013), we might use metaphorical or brainstorming techniques to foster cognitive flexibility so as to detect subtle or previously unnoticed ideas. Flexibility in attention is built into the traditional ACT model in terms of shifting or sustaining attention, but we can also help our clients to broaden their attention (e.g., noticing all of the people in a room simultaneously) or anchor it (attending to how things relate to a given event). Attention can be focused on what is here, or what is *not* here. All of these forms of flexibility are rarely explored in ACT protocols.

Classic ACT uses changes of perspective (varying the observing locus across time, place, or person), but we can augment this with deliberate role-plays of perspective, similar to methods used in psychodrama or Kelly's "fixed role therapy." We might also expand upon the range of motivational methods used in ACT beyond classic values methods. For example, we might suggest that clients write about life plans in the voice of a hero or guide, deliberately sample new experiences (e.g., singing, zip lining), or simply do a new and kind action each day.

## Expanding to the Social or Physiological Level

Multilevel selection suggests that a focus only on the individual is a mistake. All features of psychological flexibility emerged in part socially (Hayes & Sanford, 2014), and they can all be extended socially: acceptance extends into compassion, defusion into common understanding, self into perspective, attention into group focus, values into connection, and committed action into social commitments. By deliberately expanding

ACT work into such domains as compassion and social connection, we can move ACT from an intra-individual to an inter-individual treatment to construct supportive social niches.

Social niche construction can promote positive change (Snell-Rood & Steck, 2019) and long-term patterns of action that result in durable effects across evolutionary dimensions (Kuzawa & Thayer, 2011). Clients who receive positive social support tend to do better over time, so methods to help clients develop and provide social support should routinely be included. Examples of such approaches include the successful effort to combine ACT with Elinor Ostrom's Nobel Prize winning "Core Design Principles" for small groups (Atkins et al., 2019) as well as the emerging combination of ACT with compassion focused therapy.

Extending the same multilevel approach to small units of selection suggests that routine ACT work should typically be combined with a focus on nutrition, exercise, and sleep. All levels of organization are important to an evolving whole.

## Exploring the Interaction of Psychological and Bioevolutionary Processes

Suggesting that useful psychological and behavioral indicators should be linked to the biological level and vice versa is commonplace—what is different in a VRSCDL approach is that this search is constrained to key principles and questions that allow biological data to be examined functionally and contextually.

Consider the example of polymorphism in the serotonin transporter gene (5-HTTLPR). When it was found to relate to depression, researchers wasted a considerable amount of energy chasing the chimera of a "depression gene" instead of considering the impact of this polymorphism in a multidimensional and multilevel way. It turns out that this polymorphism relates to such things as the centrality of social stimulation and support, and thus its impact on depression is moderated based on the culture and unique life history of each person (e.g., Karg, Burmeister, Shedden, & Sen, 2011). The same gene pattern that is protective in a communitarian culture or a socially supportive situation might be predictive of depression in an individualistic culture or unsupportive situation. But even that is not the whole story—such emotionally difficult culture-history-gene mismatches are more toxic in the presence of experiential avoidance, and large population studies suggest that experiential avoidance is an endophenotype for the role of polymorphism on depression (Gloster et al., 2015). This gives assessment of the genetic risk factor a practical role to play in clinical practice without assuming a kind of billiard ball causality between genes and behavior.

Epigenetic pathways are another important evolutionary dimension with clear applied implications. We know that increased mindfulness alters the epigenetic regulation of stress-related gene systems (Dusek et al., 2008). These findings suggest that testing clients for specific epigenomic patterns before and after treatment might help researchers and practitioners assess both the need for ACT and the nature of its impact.

The same applies to the neurobiological processes that change when psychological change occurs. For example, we know that a successful response to ACT is associated with changes in connectivity in the brain during emotional labeling in those with social anxiety (e.g., Young et al., 2019) and during acute pain for those with chronic pain (Jensen et al., 2012), suggesting that ACT alters the role of emotion in behavioral regulation at a neurobiological level. Many of the measures in these areas were expensive and difficult to use in the past, but that is changing. High-density EEG can inexpensively replace fMRI data today, and genetic and epigenetic assessments are becoming less expensive every month.

Using biological data as a routine part of ACT practice and research could have a major practical impact on the assessment of processes of change. The day may not be far away when monthly oral swabs and epigenomic analysis are used to assess whether ACT work is impacting a given client. Doing so inside an evolutionary framework will help ACT practitioners avoid reductionism and retain the coherence provided by a functional contextual approach.

## Promoting Retention

Purely at the psychological level, retention in behavior is produced by practice and by integrating actions into large reinforced patterns. That is a start, but evolutionary thinking expands the focus on patterns to include multiple dimensions, multiple levels, robust selection processes, and a broader consideration of context. We have covered some of this material in the four points we made above, but it is worth briefly linking these ideas to retention. For example, we can foster retention of overt behavior change in our clients by deliberately varying emotional, cognitive, and attentional states during therapy; by ensuring coherent epigenetic changes and continuing treatment if they have not yet taken hold; and by integrating behavior changes with changes at the social and physical level.

## Embracing Idiographic Assumptions

Evolutionary thinking can help ACT providers and researchers better understand how individuals can manage themselves as ecosystems. For example, evolutionary science suggests that we need to foster healthy forms of variation that produce positive development, and to ensure that healthy variations have needed levels of social support. In a global theoretical sense this is not a big change, but building the empirical basis for thinking of people as evolving systems requires massive methodological change.

Research on ACT and psychological flexibility is often based on psychometrically validated measurement, group randomized trials, and mediation or moderation assessed inside these trials. All of these are methodological mismatches to a process-focused evolutionary perspective because they seek to replace consistency and variability within the individual—as a multidimensional, multilevel longitudinal evolutionary system—with consistency and variability between such systems (i.e., group averages and between-subject error terms). It is not widely appreciated in the behavioral sciences (it is in the physical sciences), but ergodic mathematical theory long ago proved that averages *cannot* be assumed to apply to individuals once multiple dimensions are examined over time (Rose, 2017). A beehive cannot be understood by creating the concept of an "average bee" that may not represent any actual living organism. An organism cannot be understood by creating the concept of an "average cell" that may not represent any living cell. Thinking of ACT as a form of evolution science thus demands idiographic means of studying therapeutic impact inside a dynamical system (e.g., Hayes et al., 2018).

Single case designs are a beginning, but a full embrace of complex network analysis at the level of the individual seems necessary to deal with VRSCDL systems, which dictates the need for high-density longitudinal assessment and an outright replacement of psychometrics (Hayes et al., 2018). Personalized medicine and other patient-driven medical approaches are already demonstrating how models of pathology and wellness can be altered to incorporate various dimensions, levels, and contexts and thus to make better predictions (e.g., Swan, 2009).

## Future Directions

ACT, and CBS more generally, is a form of evolution science (Wilson & Hayes, 2018). Psychology is not reducible to biology, and sociology is not reducible to psychology, but functional contextual evolutionary accounts can help integrate accounts at multiple levels of analysis. A VRSCDL approach provides a potentially useful framework for creating a comprehensive science of intentional change (Wilson et al., 2014). Social and conceptual value can be realized as a result of incorporating evolutionary thinking into our work as clinicians and researchers. It is our hope that this chapter illustrates the utility of using a multidimensional and multilevel evolutionary account to foster innovation in ACT so as to help individuals get more of what they want out of life.

## References

Atkins, P., Wilson, D. S., & Hayes, S. C. (2019). *Prosocial: Using evolutionary science to build productive, equitable, and collaborative groups.* Oakland, CA: Context Press/New Harbinger Publications.

Bateson, P. (2013). Evolution, epigenetics and cooperation. *Journal of Biosciences, 38,* 1–10.

Danchin, É., Charmantier, A., Champagne, F. A., Mesoudi, A., Pujol, B., & Blanchet, S. (2011). Beyond DNA: Integrating inclusive inheritance into an extended theory of evolution. *Nature Reviews Genetics, 12*(7), 475.

Dusek, J. A., Otu, H. H., Wohlhueter, A. L., Bhasin, M., Zerbini, L. F., Joseph, M. G., . . . Libermann, T. A. (2008). Genomic counter-stress changes induced by the relaxation response. *PLoS ONE, 3,* 1–8.

Ginsburg, S., & Jablonka, E. (2010). The evolution of associative learning: A factor in the Cambrian explosion. *Journal of Theoretical Biology, 266,* 11–20.

Gloster, A. T., Gerlach, A. L., Hamm, A., Höffler, M., Alpers, G. W., Kircher, T., . . . Reif, A. (2015). 5HTT is associated with the phenotype psychological flexibility: Results from a randomized clinical trial. *European Archives of Psychiatry and Clinical Neuroscience, 265*(5), 399–406.

Hawkes, A. L., Chambers, S. K., Pakenham, K. I., Patrao, T. A., Baade, P. D., Lynch, B. M., . . . Courneya, K. S. (2013). Effects of a telephone-delivered multiple health behavior change intervention (CanChange) on health and behavioral outcomes in survivors of colorectal cancer: A randomized controlled trial. *Journal of Clinical Oncology, 31*, 2313–2321. doi: 10.1200/JCO.2012.45.5873

Hayes, S. C., Barnes-Holmes, D., & Wilson, K. G. (2012). Contextual behavioral science: Creating a science more adequate to the challenge of the human condition. *Journal of Contextual Behavioral Science, 1*(1–2), 1–16.

Hayes, S. C., & Hofmann, S. G. (2017). The third wave of CBT and the rise of process-based care. *World Psychiatry, 16*, 245–246. doi: 10.1002/wps.20442

Hayes, S. C., & Hofmann, S. G. (Eds.). (2018). *Process-based CBT: The science and core clinical competencies of cognitive behavioral therapy.* Oakland, CA: New Harbinger Publications.

Hayes, S. C., Hofmann, S. G., Stanton, C. E., Carpenter, J. K., Sanford, B. T., Curtiss, J. E., & Ciarrochi, J. (2018). The role of the individual in the coming era of process-based therapy. *Behaviour Research and Therapy.* doi: 10.1016/j.brat.2018.10.005

Hayes, S. C., & Sanford, B. T. (2014). Cooperation came first: Evolution and human cognition. *Journal of the Experimental Analysis of Behavior, 101*(1), 112–129.

Hayes, S. C., & Sanford, B. T. (2015). Modern psychotherapy as a multidimensional multilevel evolutionary process. *Current Opinion in Psychology, 2*, 16–20.

Hayes, S. C., Sanford, B. T., & Chin, F. T. (2017). Carrying the baton: Evolution science and a contextual behavioral analysis of language and cognition. *Journal of Contextual Behavioral Science, 6*(3), 314–328.

Hayes, S. C., Strosahl, K., & Wilson, K. G. (2012). *Acceptance and Commitment Therapy: The process and practice of mindful change* (2nd ed.). New York, NY: Guilford Press.

Hofmann, S. G., & Hayes, S. C. (2019). The future of intervention science: Process-based therapy. *Clinical Psychological Science, 7*, 37–50. doi: 10.1177/2167702618772296

Honeycutt, H. (2011). The "enduring mission" of Zing-Yang Kuo to eliminate the nature-nurture dichotomy in psychology. *Developmental Psychobiology, 53*(4), 331–342. doi:10.1002/dev.20529

Jablonka, E., & Lamb, M. J. (2005). *Evolution in four dimensions: Genetic, epigenetic, behavioral, and symbolic variation in the history of life.* Cambridge, MA: MIT Press.

Jensen, K. B., Kosek, E., Wicksell, R., Kemani, R., Olsson, G., Merle, J. V., . . . Ingvar, M. (2012). Cognitive Behavioral Therapy increases pain-evoked activation of the prefrontal cortex in patients with fibromyalgia. *Pain, 153*, 1495–1503. doi: 10.1016/j.pain.2012.04.010.

Karg, K., Burmeister, M., Shedden, K., & Sen, S. (2011). The serotonin transporter promoter variant (5-HTTLPR), stress, and depression meta-analysis revisited: Evidence of genetic moderation. *Archives of General Psychiatry, 68*(5), 444–454.

Kawai, M., Watanabe, K., & Mori, A. (1992) Pre-cultural behaviors observed in free-ranging Japanese monkeys on Koshima islet over the past 25 years. *Primate Report, 32*, 143–153.

Kuo, Z.-Y. (1967). *The dynamics of behavior development: An epigenetic view* (Vol. PP34.). New York, NY: Random House.

Kuzawa, C. W., & Thayer, Z. M. (2011). Timescales of human adaptation: The role of epigenetic processes. *Epigenomics, 3*(2), 221–234.

Laland, K. N., Uller, T., Feldman, M. W., Sterelny, K., Müller, G. B., Moczek, A., . . . Odling-Smee, J. (2015). The extended evolutionary synthesis: Its structure, assumptions and predictions. *Proceedings of the Royal Society of Biological Sciences, 282*(1813), 1–14.

Maher, B. (2008). Personal genomes: The case of the missing heritability. *Nature News, 456*(7218), 18–21.

Mirams, L., Poliakoff, E., Brown, R. J., & Lloyd, D. M. (2013). Brief body-scan meditation practice improves somatosensory perceptual decision making. *Consciousness and Cognition, 22*(1), 348–359.

Odling-Smee, F. J., Laland, K. N., & Feldman, M. W. (1996). Niche construction. *The American Naturalist, 147*(4), 641–648.

Pinxten, R., Desclée, M., & Eens, M. (2016). Upper secondary and first-year university students' explanations of animal behaviour: To what extent are Tinbergen's four questions about causation, ontogeny, function and evolution, represented? *International Journal of Science Education, 38*(14), 2303–2325. doi: 10.1080/09500693.2016.1239139

Rose, T. (2017). *The end of average.* San Francisco, CA: Harper One.

Schneider, S. M. (2012). *The science of consequences: How they affect genes, change the brain, and impact our world.* New York, NY: Prometheus.

Sherin, J. E., & Nemeroff, C. B. (2011). Post-traumatic stress disorder: The neurobiological impact of psychological trauma. *Dialogues in Clinical Neuroscience, 13*(3), 263–278.

Skinner, B. F. (1981). Selection by consequences. *Science, 213,* 501–504.

Skinner, B. F. (1988). Genes and behavior. In G. Greenberg & E. Tobach (Eds.), *The T. C. Schneirla conference series, Vol. 3. Evolution of social behavior and integrative levels* (pp. 77–83). Hillsdale, NJ: Lawrence Erlbaum Associates, Inc.

Snell-Rood, E. C., & Steck, M. K. (2019). Behaviour shapes environmental variation and selection on learning and plasticity: Review of mechanisms and implications. *Animal Behaviour.*

Swan, M. (2009). Emerging patient-driven health care models: An examination of health social networks, consumer personalized medicine and quantified self-tracking. *International Journal of Environmental Research and Public Health, 6*(2), 492–525.

Tinbergen, N. (1963). On aims and methods of ethology. *Zeitschr. Tierpshchol.* 20, 410–433.

Wilson, D. S. & Hayes, S. C. (Eds.). (2018). *Evolution and contextual behavioral science: An integrated framework for understanding, predicting, and influencing human behavior.* Oakland, CA: Context Press / New Harbinger Publications.

Wilson, D. S., Hayes, S. C., Biglan, A., & Embry, D. D. (2014). Evolving the future: Toward a science of intentional change. *Behavioral and Brain Sciences, 37*(4), 395–416.

Wilson, D. S., & Wilson, E. O. (2007). Rethinking the theoretical foundation of sociobiology. *Quarterly Review of Biology, 82,* 327–348.

Young, K. S., LeBeau, R. T., Niles, A. N., Hsu, K. J., Burklund, L. J., Mesri, B., . . . Craske, M. G. (2019). Neural connectivity during affect labeling predicts treatment response to psychological therapies for social anxiety disorder. *Journal of Affective Disorders, 242,* 105–110. doi: 10.1016/j.jad.2018.08.016

Zettle, R. D., Hayes, S. C., Barnes-Holmes, D., & Biglan, T. (2016). (Eds.) *The Wiley handbook of contextual behavioral science.* Chichester, UK: Wiley/Blackwell.

# SECTION TWO

# Innovative Treatment Models and Treatment Integrations

# CHAPTER 6

# The ACT Matrix

Benjamin Schoendorff

*Contextual Psychology Institute*

Fabian O. Olaz

*CIPCO and National University of Córdoba*

## Overview

The ACT matrix (Polk & Schoendorff, 2014) constitutes an original way of delivering ACT. In this chapter we hope to show how the ACT matrix can help bring simplicity and flexibility to ACT and how it can readily be shared with clients to activate a range of ACT processes. We'll sketch a history of the ACT matrix, outline new aspects, and describe a stepwise way of working with the matrix model along with some advanced strategies. We'll also sketch how the matrix maps onto basic RFT processes (Hayes, Barnes-Holmes, & Roche, 2001) and outline the extant empirical base supporting its use as a tool for delivering ACT.

### Presentation and History of the Matrix

The ACT matrix (figure 6.1) is a diagram that represents patterns of behavior (toward and away moves) with respect to different contexts (public and private). The matrix is composed of two bisecting lines. The vertical line maps out the difference between the two main contexts of experience for verbal humans: the context of external experience (experiences that others can see) and the context of inner experience (only available to the person who is experiencing it). Such discrimination is clinically helpful as it can help increase contextual sensitivity and promote more flexible behavior.

The horizontal line is the behavior line (or functional line). It maps out actions that are, broadly speaking, under (verbally mediated) aversive control, for example moving away from fear, and actions that are, broadly speaking, under (verbally mediated) appetitive control, for example moving toward a loved one. The former are termed "away moves" and the latter are known as "toward moves."

**Figure 6.1.** The ACT matrix.

The matrix diagram helps people sort their experiences and stories in such a way that their functions come into sharper focus, allowing people to evaluate behaviors in terms of workability. At the same time, it fosters perspective-taking skills. By repeatedly practicing discriminating between toward and away moves, it is hypothesized that people come to engage in more toward moves. In other words, they engage in more valued living.

The matrix diagram emerged from the work of Kevin Polk and Jerold Hambright in the United States, in conversations with Mark Webster in the United Kingdom. It first appeared in June 2009 as a way to graphically map out functional contextualism, the epistemological underpinning of ACT (Hayes, 1993) and its pragmatic "workability" criterion (Polk, Schoendorff, Webster, & Olaz, 2016). By seeking to help clients learn to interact differently with trauma memories, Kevin Polk had the idea to invite them to sort their experiences and behaviors in the matrix diagram.

Since then, the matrix has become a well-established way of delivering ACT, either as a stand-alone model or as an adjunct to other ways of delivering ACT, such as those based on the six-component psychological flexibility model. A book-length presentation of the ACT matrix as a stand-alone treatment can be found in Polk et al., 2016. This presents a six-step approach to using the ACT matrix that, in contrast to more traditional descriptions of ACT as a treatment, does not revolve around the six so-called hexaflex processes, but uses a stepwise approach that we believe is useful to increase psychological flexibility. That said, the matrix model is flexible by design and cannot be reduced to one way of working or a given number of steps or set of procedures.

The ACT matrix can help organize interventions and integrate approaches other than ACT (Polk et al., 2016). Within the ACT world, it is used in a variety of ways (see for example Turrell & Bell, 2016).

## The Matrix and Relational Frame Theory

Relational frame theory (RFT) provides a model for understanding how the matrix works. According to RFT, psychological events can acquire behavioral functions due to a process of symbolically relating stimuli in response to contextual cues, absent any direct learning history with the stimuli or any nonarbitrary similarities between them. As stimuli are related, their functions are transformed. This process is known as arbitrary applicable relational responding (AARR). AARR creates vast and complex relational networks that can drive the transformation of symbolic stimulus functions and thereby substantially influence human behavior. AARR's influence on behavior often trumps the influence of direct consequences and accounts for how humans can persist in either unworkable or valued behavior in the absence of immediate physical reinforcers.

Recently, Barnes-Holmes (2018) proposed a novel way of conceptualizing psychological events for verbal humans, summarized as the ROE-ing model (pronounced "rowing"; see chapter 4 for a detailed description). This model proposes that human beings are involved in a constant symbolic behavioral stream (or "acts of meaning") that includes three main processes: relating (R), orienting (O), and evoking (E). Relating refers to the complex ways in which humans relate stimuli and events based on AARR. Orienting refers to noticing stimuli and events. Evoking refers to the way we respond to the stimulus depending on the functions of the related events (appetitive, aversive, or relatively neutral). The three ROE elements are dynamic rather than separable units of analysis and are involved in most of our psychological responses.

Consider Alberto, a man who experiences frequent panic attacks when he leaves his home. He fears certain physical sensations that he perceives as dangerous. Alberto responds to his physical sensations by arbitrarily relating them in ways that have not been directly trained. He states, "If I have these sensations, I am going to die." Clearly Alberto has not experienced death (R). This way of relating increases the likelihood that Alberto will orient toward physical sensations with an evoked reaction. When Alberto notices (O) these sensations are present, he fears dying. To escape the possibility of having a panic attack, he starts curtailing a wide range of activities such as attending classes, visiting friends, and going shopping (E). Alberto now feels his life has no meaning and believes he can't reengage in these activities until he can eliminate his panic symptoms. Alberto evidences the three ROE aspects.

ACT seeks to weaken and transform the behavioral functions of relational networks by helping shift one's perspective on these networks. This perspective is called "psychological flexibility" and, in RFT terms, can be defined as "responding to your own responding as participating in a frame of hierarchy with the deictic 'I'" (Törneke, Luciano, Barnes-Holmes, and Bond, 2016, p. 258). The *deictic I* refers to a behavioral class that leads to a special way of framing that includes three dimensions: interpersonal, temporal, and spatial ("I-you," "now-then," and "here-there" ). These three deictic relations are at the center of a complex dynamic network of derived relations from which emerges our verbal self. This allows human beings to respond appropriately to their own behavior and to evoke specific responses toward it, as postulated by the ROE-ing model (Barnes-Holmes, 2018). Thus, this way of responding allows us to hold our inner experiences as parts of the "I" holding them at a distance of observation, which weakens the behavioral control functions of verbal antecedents and allows for other relational networks with appetitive functions to influence behaviors. Alberto, for example, can be in a better position to see his inner experiences as a part of his deictic I, giving him the chance to orient his attention to other relevant aspects of his context, including some appetitive verbal networks (values).

In therapy, we foster psychological flexibility in three main ways. First, we train clients to discriminate among the problematic behavioral functions of given networks. In our example, trying not to feel particular bodily sensations networked as "dangerous" leads Alberto to live a life that shrinks and drains of vitality.

The second strategy involves helping clients frame relational networks from a broader perspective. This is done by using AARR in specific ways. Networks are framed hierarchically as parts of one's experience as well as from the deictic perspective of I-here-now experiencing their content as there-then, thereby creating perspective. In our example, Alberto will come to notice his thoughts about panic and his avoidant behaviors as parts of his experience (rather than as causal descriptions of the world). Gradually, he'll be able to notice that he is different from what his thoughts say he is, as well as having a here-now experience of his thoughts and feelings as effectively there-then. Framed thus, the content of his thoughts and attendant feelings is experienced as being less threatening, which can help lower the aversive functions of Alberto's panic symptoms.

The third strategy consists of helping clients find their way toward valued living by constructing or strengthening relational networks that may lead to life-broadening behaviors. In effect, it encourages clients to hierarchically frame behaviors and goals as part of hierarchical networks whose topmost positions are occupied by life domains, overarching goals, and qualities of actions. In our example, the clinician will encourage Alberto to identify particular behaviors related to what's most important to him, for example, going to class to move toward getting an education and cultivating his mind.

Törneke et al. (2016) have described the above three strategies as follows: (1) discriminating functional classes of problematic behavior and the consequences of these behaviors, (2) building an alternative repertoire of framing hierarchically from the perspective of the deictic I, and (3) building appetitive consequences for patterns of future behavior.

As we have said, RFT describes metaphors as the derivation of a relation of sameness between relational networks. One aspect of the matrix is that it provides a visual metaphor for certain patterns of behavior (toward and away moves) with respect to different contexts (public and private). As we will illustrate in our following description of an ACT matrix-based treatment, we believe that the ACT matrix works as a metaphor that activates the three strategies outlined above and thus can influence the way people orient and respond to events toward increased psychological flexibility.

# Description of the Matrix

Working with the matrix starts by visually presenting the diagram and inviting clients to sort their experiences and behaviors into the four quadrants created by the two bisecting lines (figure 6.2). You can do this by opening a conversation from a stance of curiosity and open inquiry. The following questions help open this conversation.

1.  Who or what is important to you?

2.  What inner stuff can show up and get in the way of moving toward who or what is important?

3.  What do you do to move away from unwanted inner stuff? What do you usually do when these experiences control what you do?

4.  What could you do to move toward who or what is important?

As clients answer each question in turn, we write down their answers in the quadrants. We also draw a circle in the middle of the diagram and ask clients who can choose what's important to them, notice their inner obstacles, and notice if their actions are toward moves, away moves, or both. Clients readily answer, "Me."

From an RFT point of view, this first step involves hierarchical framing in which particular patterns (e.g., toward moves) are grouped together as (functionally) similar and as distinct from other patterns (e.g., away moves). By noticing these differences, the client becomes better able to coordinate behaviors in functional classes. At the same time, by noticing that they stand at the center and, so to speak, "above" the perspective mapped out by the matrix diagram, clients start practicing the behavior of observing from the perspective of a self that is not limited by experiences and behavior, but rather that provides a context for these. In more technical language, they practice framing their experience and behaviors hierarchically from the perspective of their deictic I.

After we present clients with the matrix diagram, we invite them to practice noticing toward and away moves in multiple contexts. Opportunities to cue practicing this discrimination include daily life, past events, future plans, or, even more directly, what occurs in the here and now of client-practitioner interactions (e.g., Schoendorff & Bolduc, 2014).

## Functional Analysis, Creative Hopelessness, and Hooks

The matrix is a visual model that can simplify and cue verbal functional analysis. Once clients have received some basic training in sorting on the matrix, the diagram serves as an effective tool for helping them conduct a functional analysis of problematic behavior and assess workability. You can do this in a number of ways, all serving to help clients assess which of their away moves are effective and which stand in the way of moving toward what matters. Below is an example of a dialogue with Alberto around the workability of his away moves.

Figure 6.2. The basic ACT matrix with questions.

*Therapist (T):*    Have your away moves worked to bring you relief from your panic symptoms? First let's look at how effective they have been in the short term. We have turning down invitations, drinking, surfing the Internet, watching Netflix, staying in bed, staying home, not attending class, and calling friends. We also have meditating, which you do to move away from stress, right?

*Client (C):*    Yes. Meditating is kind of hit and miss. But turning down invitations, drinking, surfing the Internet, watching Netflix, not leaving the house, not attending class definitely work. Staying in bed, not so much. Calling friends, sometimes...

*T:*    Excellent! So, a lot of these make sense as they tend to work...short term. Let's now look at how effective they have been over the long term.

*C:*    Long term? That's easy: nothing really works, or I wouldn't be here!

*T:*    Yes, that's how we can easily slip into stuck loops. Stuff shows up bottom left, we do something to move away from it, then it comes back, so we do another away move, and so forth. Now let's look at whether these away moves have helped move you toward who or what is important.

*C:*    Most move me away, but, you know, calling friends and meditating actually move me toward friendship and mental health.

*T:*    That's interesting. Would you be willing to notice, when you call friends and meditate, when you do it more as a toward move, and when more as an away move?

The therapist has helped Alberto assess workability by helping him notice those of his away moves that are workable (i.e., that can help move toward values) and those that aren't. Thus guided, Alberto can learn to notice that away moves are not in themselves "bad," but rather that some work and some don't. This kind of dialogue, which can be cued by drawing on a matrix diagram (Polk et al., 2016), helps clients discriminate classes of problematic behaviors by engaging in temporal and conditional framing. By encouraging clients to notice when they engage in the same behavior as an away move and when as a toward move, the therapist fosters bringing clients' behavior under the appetitive control of values, activating the third strategy.

This way of assessing workability offers a novel way of conducting the creative hopelessness phase of ACT. Uncovering "stuck loops" underlines unworkability, while noticing that away moves can at times be effective to move toward values can foster a more functional point of view of behavior.

Through discriminating classes of unworkable behaviors, the matrix contributes to framing hierarchically from the perspective of the deictic I rules that can function as "psychological traps" (Luciano, Valdivia-Salas, & Ruiz, 2012). You can also do this work by looking in more detail at the link between inner experience and problematic behavior. Using experiential exercises, clients can experience how their efforts to not contact thoughts and experiences that they sort in the bottom left quadrant of the matrix can paradoxically increase their frequency and intensity. You can invite clients to experience how difficult it is not to think of something in particular, say a white bear, or how when trying to not feel fear of pain or death, intense fear becomes inevitable. You can then contrast the peculiarities of inner experience with physical experience. We call this the "Two Rules:" the rule of the world of external experience, in which unpleasant experience can come to be controlled through thinking about it and trying different things, and the rule of the world of inner experience, in which the more one tries to control an experience, the more one has it. By framing these two experiential contexts as being part of two distinct networks, it becomes easier to help clients further discriminate the contexts in which the functions of their away moves multiply the frequency and intensity of unwanted experiences and, more generally, the control such experiences have on their behavior.

We next present a metaphor of hooks to help clients discriminate when they get "hooked" (by the derived functions of relational networks) into behaving differently than they would have had they not bitten the hook (i.e., responded to problematic derived functions). The goal is to help clients notice, in the present moment, the connections between the current strategies they are using and the difficulties they experience, increasing clients' sensitivity and making room for more effective behavior (Törneke, 2017). The metaphor is eminently functional, with hooks defined as "whatever makes you bite" and being hooked defined as "biting," that is, engaging in unworkable behavior. This prompts framing verbal antecedents from the perspective of the deictic I while discriminating the way we interact with our own behavior. At this point, the stage is set for moving more explicitly to the third strategy, establishing verbally constructed reinforcers for appetitively controlled behavioral patterns. This is a strategy we call *Verbal Aikido.*

## Verbal Aikido

Aikido is a based on the principle of "nonstruggling with the opponent." The purpose of aikido is blending with the energy of the attack so as to bring those involved in conflict to peace and harmony. Similarly, with ACT, the aim is not to fight with our psychological experience, but to make room for it so as to bring our experiences and behavior to peace and harmony (i.e., functional coherence in which our lives effectively move toward what matters). What we call Verbal Aikido is a way of conducting clinical conversations using a set of skills that serve to "get out of the way" of the sticky stories (derived relational networks that work as verbal contexts that evoke problematic behaviors) that our clients' minds throw at them and us.

Thus, one of the main skills in working with the matrix is what we call "Yessing." Yessing is a word we've coined to denote the practice of never contradicting clients and instead beginning responses with the words "Yes, and…" or some functional equivalent. What usually comes after the "and…" are words that aim to point to some aspect of clients' experience, bringing that experience into perspective and, often, inviting them to notice a difference.

In Yessing, the "Yes" empathically validates whatever shows up, then the "and…" gently reorients attention toward whatever else may be present, and the function of behavior. Helping clients develop psychological flexibility begins with our stance as therapists and ends when they adopt this stance and adapt it to their circumstances in the service of moving toward the life they want. Yessing, when genuine, is the heart of acceptance that increases sensitivity to context, or the capacity to notice various features of the context and to respond to what is most relevant.

One way of practicing Verbal Aikido involves taking clients' words and redirecting them into the matrix, so they can see the contexts that influence their behavior and the functions of them, strengthening their ability to frame from the perspective of the deictic I. Proficiency in Verbal Aikido requires repeated and deliberate practice.

Polk et al. (2016) present one way of practicing Verbal Aikido by means of a matrix worksheet with seven questions pointing to different aspects of a client's experience and behaviors in a given situation. Once a precise situation is identified, clients are invited to

1.  describe their five senses experience (e.g., what they could see, hear, and smell in the situation);

2.  notice any hook that showed up;

3.  identify salient bodily sensations that are present when the hook shows up;

4.  describe what they did (or would have done) in case they bit the hook;

5.  (turning to the right side of the matrix:) describe what they would have done (or did) had they engaged in a toward move;

6.  contact who or what is important to them in being able to engage this toward move in that situation; and

7.  identify what bodily sensations are most salient when they contact who or what is important to them in being able to engage in the toward move.

The precise wording of the questions is less important than the effect they have on clients, and their wording can be readily adapted.

You might also ask clients if they noticed a difference between the bodily experience of being hooked and the bodily experience of being in contact with who or what is important. This discrimination becomes all the more important when clients are able to discern that this difference is different from what is generally referred to as "feeling good" versus "feeling bad." Clients can come to notice that engaging in a toward move can feel "bad" in the short term while still carrying the "feel" of a toward move, making it experientially more appetitive than engaging in an away move.

We recently developed an exercise structured around a worksheet that can help build these networks (see figure 6.3). We present clients with a picture of a tree. The roots reach around a box in which to write the name of a person or life domain of importance. On the trunk, clients are invited to write qualities they wish their actions in relation to this person or domain of importance could embody. Clients are next invited to write on leaves actions they have already engaged in that embodied at least one of the qualities written on the trunk. Looking at his intimate relationship, Alberto wrote "Present, Loving, Supportive" as the qualities he wished his actions toward his partner to embody. This exercise can help clients frame their actions hierarchically in terms of high-level verbally constructed appetitives and foster new actions linked to these qualities and values.

## Self-Compassion and Perspective-Taking with the ACT Matrix

Clients' self-talk can be so firmly aversive and rigid that it may be difficult for them to gain sufficient perspective on their present patterns of behavior to engage in new behavior. In these cases, we invite clients to engage in more direct perspective-taking practices, including some directly aimed at fostering self-compassion. Self-compassion, commonly defined as a wish to alleviate suffering, a disposition to stay with suffering, and a recognition of common humanity (Neff, 2003) can, in more technical terms, be thought of as activating affiliative approach behavior to parts of one's experiences that would normally elicit a fight-or-flight response. In RFT terms, self-compassion is only possible if we can shift perspective on one's self and one's experience.

# Grow the life you want

**How do you grow the life you want?** In the box, write down one person or direction that is important to you.
On the trunk, write one to four qualities that are important for your actions to embody in relation to this
person/direction.
On the leaves, write actions that you have already done to move toward that person/direction.

**Figure 6.3.** The Grow the Life You Want worksheet.

We have developed a metaphor of kittens (Polk et al., 2016; Tirch, Schoendorff, & Silberstein, 2014) that serves to train self-compassion. After describing how a mother cat would instinctively move toward one of her kittens in distress and provide comfort until it's soothed, we invite clients to consider their negative self-judgments, shame, traumatic memories, or other unwanted feelings as kittens in distress. Next, we invite them to notice how they tend to receive these "kittens" before asking how the "mother cat they want to be" would receive them. Finally, we invite clients to notice how they receive their "inner kittens in distress" going forward.

As we have already pointed out, fostering shifts in perspective helps our clients increase contextual awareness and better notice the functions and relevant antecedents and consequences of their behaviors.

Shifts in perspective are central to the second strategy (helping clients frame relational networks from a deictic I perspective). As we have said, from an RFT point of view, perspective taking is based in deictic framing, so you can present clients with cues that promote particular patterns of perspective taking including temporal, spatial, and interpersonal perspective shifts. For example, clients might be cued to experience themselves (behavior and content) from different perspectives:

Temporal: "Imagine seeing yourself in that difficult past situation; what do you see?"

Spatial: "Imagine that you are seeing us from that corner over there; what do you see?"

Interpersonal: "Can you imagine yourself interacting with your guilt as if it is a little kid?"

By using the matrix diagram, we can effectively cue such perspective shifts. This can help clients develop the ability to adopt an "observer" perspective in regard to their reactions and private events, transforming the relational functions of inner experience from a deictic perspective: I-here-now noticing my behavior there-then. Responding to our inner experience as if it were there-then allows us to perceive that it is not the whole of our experience, and thus experiences are more manageable. This weakens the governance of inner experience over overt behavior and promotes relations of hierarchy in which the self is a here-now context containing there-then content (Foody et al., 2014).

To apply perspective taking to future behavior, we invite clients to have a dialogue with their future selves in an upcoming situation in which they anticipate a problematic away move. We have developed an exercise involving an exchange of text messages between the client's present and future selves (i.e., different temporal and spatial perspectives). Throughout the dialogue, we pay special attention to the emotional responses of the client's future self as they receive advice and instructions from their present self. At some point in the dialogue, we suggest that the present self send a text message to the future self that says, "I know it's hard and I'm going to be there for you." Following that affirmation, clients often report their future self experiencing a deep sense of validation. More significant, they often report having had another similar dialogue, and more often than not having been able to produce their desired toward move.

Taking someone else's perspective is part of the definition of empathy. Taking one's own perspective at a different time and place can thus help foster empathy and compassion for oneself in these other situations. Combining these different aspects of perspective taking can provide clinicians with a powerful means of training compassion and self-compassion.

## Research Support

Research on the ACT matrix has been slow to become visible, partly because the ACT matrix is considered by many as a way to deliver ACT. This has resulted in a number of studies using the ACT matrix but not referring to its use (Dindo, Marchman, Gindes, & Fiedorowicz, 2015; Dindo, Recober, Marchman, Turvey, & O'Hara, 2012; Ducasse et al., 2014; Hou et al., 2017; Huddleston, Martin, Woods, & Dindo, 2018). The matrix is now becoming increasingly visible in research, and a number of recently published studies have shown its effectiveness as a means of delivering ACT. For example, the matrix has been shown as effective for treating suicidal behavior in a randomized controlled study (RCT; N = 46) of patients who had engaged in at least one suicide attempt over the previous twelve months (Ducasse et al., 2018). In this study, in which treatment as usual (TAU) + ACT with the matrix was compared with TAU + progressive relaxation, ACT showed high acceptability and improved a number of recognized precursors of suicide, in addition to moving ACT processes. Only one participant in the matrix group compared to three in the relaxation group had attempted suicide at a three-month follow-up. Now the same researchers are rolling out the ACT matrix for a multicenter RCT involving 500 participants. A group in the US has been using one-day ACT workshops based on the ACT matrix for a range of behavioral health issues including migraines, and, most recently, for an innovative intervention aimed at reducing postoperative pain and opioid use (Dindo et al., 2018, and chapter 15 in this book).

An innovative line of research based on the ACT matrix processes has been developed at Utah State University in which participants are prompted, through a simple mobile phone app, to notice if they are engaged in toward moves or away moves at random times during the day. This simple prompt, delivered five times a day over two weeks, was found to increase the probability of engaging in toward moves by 56% (Levin, Pierce, & Schoendorff, 2017). In another study, a version of the prompting app with more details and options regarding the two main discriminations of the ACT matrix was found to be effective in improving mental health in students seeking help (Krafft, Potts, Schoendorff, & Levin, 2017).

## Future Directions

Ten years after its inception, the ACT matrix has become an established way of delivering ACT. For many clients and clinicians, it represents a simple intuitive way to grasp ACT and start working from a functional contextual point of view from the earliest stages of therapy. As a visual cue, it helps clients discriminate the broader consequences of unhelpful classes of behavior. It also helps clients practice the behavior of taking a broad perspective on their various experiences and behaviors. Finally, it helps clients relate new behaviors to meaningful personal values and engage in valued living, even in the presence of inner obstacles. We believe it is also ideally suited to clinical work as conceived from an RFT perspective and using RFT-derived clinical strategies.

There are thus many ways to use the matrix, and we hope this chapter has helped to demonstrate its broad value. No doubt the next ten years will witness the emergence of new ways of using the ACT matrix as more and more clinicians and researchers start using the model and current users discover new and varied applications for this innovative intervention model.

## References

Barnes-Holmes, D. (2018, July 10). The double edged sword of human language and cognition: Shall we be Olympians or fallen angels? [Blog Post] Retrieved from https://science.abainternational.org/the-double-edged-sword-of-human-language-and-cognition-shall-we-be-olympians-or-fallen-angels/rrehfeldtabainternational-org/

Dindo, L., Marchman, J., Gindes, H., & Fiedorowicz, J. G. (2015). A brief behavioral intervention targeting mental health risk factors for vascular disease: A pilot study. *Psychotherapy and Psychosomatics, 84*, 183–185. doi: 10.1159/000371495

Dindo, L., Recober, A., Marchman, J., Turvey C., & O'Hara, M. W. (2012). One-day behavioral treatment for patients with comorbid depression and migraine: A pilot study. *Behaviour Research and Therapy, 50*, 537e543.

Dindo, L., Zimmerman, B., Hadlandsmyth, K., StMarie, B., Embree, J., Marchman, J., . . . Rakel, B. (2018). Acceptance and commitment therapy for prevention of chronic post-surgical pain and opioid use in at-risk veterans: A pilot randomized controlled study. *The Journal of Pain, 19*, 1211–1221.

Ducasse, D., Jaussent, I., Arpon-Brand, V., Vienot, M., Laglaoui, C., Béziat, S., . . . Olié, E. (2018). Acceptance and commitment therapy for the management of suicidal patients: A randomized controlled trial. *Psychotherapy and Psychosomatics, 87*(4), 211–222. doi: 10.1159/000488715

Ducasse, D., René, E., Béziat, S., Guillaume, S., Courtet, P., & Olié, E. (2014). Acceptance and commitment therapy for management of suicidal patients: A pilot study. *Psychotherapy and Psychosomatics, 83*, 374–376. doi: 10.1159/000365974

Foody, M., Barnes-Holmes, Y., Barnes-Holmes, D., Törneke, N., Luciano, C., Stewart, I., & McEnteggart, C. (2014). RFT for clinical use: The example of metaphor. *Journal of Contextual Behavioral Science, 3*, 305–313.

Hayes, S. C. (1993). Analytic goals and the varieties of scientific contextualism. In S. C. Hayes, L. J. Hayes, H. W. Reese, & T. R. Sarbin (Eds.), *Varieties of scientific contextualism* (pp. 11–27). Reno, NV: Context Press.

Hayes, S. C., Barnes-Holmes, D., & Roche, B. (2001). *Relational frame theory: A post-Skinnerian account of human language and cognition.* New York, NY: Plenum Press.

Hill, J., & Oliver, J. (2019). *Acceptance and Commitment Coaching,* Distinctive Features. London, UK: Routledge

Hou, J. K., Vanga, R. R., Thakur, E., Gonzalez, I., Willis, D., & Dindo, L. (2017). One-day behavioral intervention for patients with inflammatory bowel disease and co-occurring psychological distress. *Clinical Gastroenterology and Hepatology, 15,* 1633–1634.

Huddleston, P. C., Martin, L., Woods, K., & Dindo, L. (2018). One-day behavioral intervention for distressed veterans with migraine: Results of a multimethod pilot study. *Military Medicine, 183,* 7/8:e184.

Krafft, J., Potts, S., Schoendorff, B., & Levin, M. (2017). A randomized controlled trial of multiple versions of an acceptance and commitment therapy matrix app for well-being. *Behavior Modification, 43,* 246–272. doi: 10.1177/0145445517748561

Levin, M. E., Pierce, B., & Schoendorff, B. (2017). The acceptance and commitment therapy matrix mobile app: A pilot randomized trial on health behaviors. *Journal of Contextual Behavioral Science, 6,* 268–275.

Luciano, C., Valdivia-Salas, S., & Ruiz, F. J. (2012). The self as the context for rule-governed behavior. In L. McHugh & I. Stewart (Eds.), *The self and perspective taking: Research and applications* (pp. 143–160). Oakland, CA: Context Press.

Neff, K. (2003). Self-compassion: An alternative conceptualization of a healthy attitude toward oneself, *Self and Identity, 2,* 85–101. doi: 10.1080/15298860309032

Polk, K., & Schoendorff, B. (2014). *The ACT matrix: A new approach to building psychological flexibility across settings and populations.* Oakland, CA: Context Press/New Harbinger.

Polk, K., Schoendorff, B., Webster, M., & Olaz, F. (2016). *The essential guide to the ACT matrix.* Oakland, CA: New Harbinger Publications.

Schoendorff, B., & Bolduc, M.-F. (2014). You, me and the matrix: A guide to relationship-oriented ACT. In Polk, K. & Schoendorff, B. (Eds.), *The ACT matrix,* (pp. 59–80). Oakland, CA: New Harbinger Publications.

Tirch, D., Schoendorff, B., & Silberstein, L. (2014). *The ACT practitioner's guide to the science of compassion: Tools for fostering psychological flexibility.* Oakland, CA: New Harbinger Publications.

Törneke, N. (2017). *Metaphor in practice. A professional's guide to using the science of language in psychotherapy.* Oakland, CA: New Harbinger Publications.

Törneke, N., Luciano, C., Barnes-Holmes, Y., & Bond, F. (2016). RFT for clinical practice: Three core strategies in understanding and treating human suffering. In R. D. Zettle, S. C. Hayes, D. Barnes-Holmes, & A. Biglan (Eds.), *The Wiley handbook of contextual behavioral science* (pp. 254–273). New York, NY: Wiley Blackwell.

Turrell, S. L., & Bell, M. (2016). *ACT for adolescents: Treating teens and adolescents in individual and group therapy.* Oakland, CA: New Harbinger Publications.

# CHAPTER 7

# Growing Up Flexibly
## DNA-V *as a Contextual Behavioral Science Approach to Working with Young People*

### Louise L. Hayes

*Centre for Youth Mental Health, The University of Melbourne & Orygen,*
*The National Centre of Excellence in Youth Mental Health*

### Joseph Ciarrochi

*Institute of Positive Psychology and Education, Australian Catholic University*

## Overview

There is a revolution coming in practical psychology (S. C. Hayes et al., 2018). The field is moving away from trademarked therapies or packages and toward evidence-based processes of change. This new approach does not assume that you are "evidence-based" only if you use the specific protocols and manualized procedures that have been previously researched. Rather, the new *process* approach focuses on how to best target and change core biopsychosocial processes in specific situations for given goals with given clients (S. C. Hayes et al., 2018). In this chapter, we describe a new process approach for children and adolescents that we believe can play an important role in this revolution.

ACT has been tested for use in treatment of adult psychopathology and then translated more broadly into most adult settings (e.g., workplaces, coaching, performance). Today there are more than 250 randomized controlled trials (RCTs) showing its effectiveness across a wide breadth of human issues. Most of these RCTs are with adults.

It is easy to fall into the trap of assuming adult ACT models fit child and adolescent development instead of utilizing the extensive theories and research on child and adolescent development to create a child-focused approach. ACT has a focus on lessening the human suffering that arises through psychological inflexibility (S. C. Hayes, Strosahl, & Wilson, 2012). The stance taken is that through culture and learning, adults often become rigid, avoidant, or afraid of their thoughts and feelings. In the face of adults' struggle with life, we use ACT to help them practice turning *toward* values and committed action to live with or lessen stress, pain, depression, psychosis, or relationship problems. To us, this is profoundly different from a developmental approach, which ought to focus on how to teach, model, and shape flexible thoughts, feelings, and actions *before* psychologically inflexible patterns have set in. We can do this by helping young people grow up with flexibility, which might be thought of as a flexible growth approach.

The model DNA-V grew from our research where we attempted to adapt ACT for use with adolescents and children (L. L. Hayes & Ciarrochi, 2015). DNA-V stands for processes of behavior that are labeled Discoverer, Noticer, Advisor, and Values/Vitality. In our training programs, trainees often expressed how difficult it was for them to use ACT processes with young people. It was not easy for them to see the processes in any way other than through an adult lens. Take values for example; trainees might attempt to elicit values in children by asking, "How do you want to move toward your value?" In our opinion, such a question works poorly with children because it demands cognitive abstraction that isn't yet on board. Without developmental models of ACT, professionals must have sufficient developmental knowledge to adapt ACT on the fly. We have often witnessed trainees using the six core processes in ACT in developmentally insensitive ways.

To demonstrate the problems we have seen, we use one example of behavior and compare what we might do with an adult and a child. This discrete example is avoidance of work for adults, compared with avoidance of school for children.

If we were working with an adult who was avoiding their workplace, we would likely begin therapy with a case conceptualization on the six core processes of ACT, looking for signs of inflexibility, and use this to build an intervention plan. We would look for fusion with thoughts and feelings, help the adult experience how this fusion impacts their work, and then practice defusion activities to lessen their grip. We might look for ways in which avoidance is reinforced while helping the adult test experientially whether their avoidance behavior is helping them to build a life of value. If they chose work as a value, we would encourage them to practice staying present at work even when they do not like it. The emphasis would be on connecting this adult with the discomfort of work by seeing the long-term value and creating self-generated rules that they can follow, such as "I want to work hard now to care for my children, so they have a good future."

By way of contrast, with a six-year-old child who avoids school, we would first need to focus broadly on the social context and then work inward. We are unlikely to begin within the child's thoughts and feelings. We might explore the child's family environment, history of attachment to caregivers, developmental history, ability to separate as an infant, and instances of fear conditioning. We would need to know if they have secure attachments to caregivers and if they have a life history of using this to broaden repertoires. We would look at how they approach life changes (e.g., did they separate before and can't separate now?). We would consider if the absence of attachment figures and avoiding class might even be adaptive; seeking the safety of caregivers is adaptive, whereas attending school at a specific age is not part of the environment of adaptation for children (Wilson, Kauffman, & Purdy, 2011). We would also accept that, for some children, separation demands a level of maturity. Next, we would consider how the school might shape their school refusal behavior. The question to investigate is "Why has attending school become aversive and staying home become appetitive?" Interventions taking a developmental perspective require a broad to narrow path, centered on safety, attachment, and maturity. Fear is a profoundly useful message, and it is wrong to ask a six-year-old child to use self-rules or insight to "overcome" their fear. Thus, in this example, we would not ask a child to move *toward* their value, which is assuming the child's language is the target for primary intervention.

Adult therapy is a sophisticated dance through language. Although we know that children are not small adults, we commonly see protocols that heavily emphasize this language dance between a young client and therapist. Examples include traditional cognitive therapy (identify, label, and alter your thinking styles), positive psychology (think optimistically), and psychodynamic therapy (investigate how your life history influences you). It is essential to note the interventions that take a developmentally focused stance, such as applied behavior analysis and attachment therapy, and we rest DNA-V on this theoretical and empirical foundation.

The above example is intended to highlight that for adults, being autonomous is often the central focus, and therefore therapy often begins *within* the individual. The younger the child, the more likely we would begin working *outside* the individual—on relationships, attachment, learning history, and the environment—and only after that consider the child's agency for change. Developmentally we know that individuation and autonomy takes fifteen to eighteen years.

Once we began to see child and adolescent interventions through a holistic developmental lens, we were startled by just how often child interventions have been adapted from adult models by making the instructions simpler, instead of creating interventions steeped in the growth of a human in their context. We argue that ACT protocols and adaptations for young people must not fall into the former category of delivering a simplified language dance. ACT is delivered experientially; we learn by stepping inside an experience. We, therefore, argue that we need theoretical models and applications that show how to intervene with developmental awareness. We can emphasize using the whole of contextual behavioral science (CBS) to create developmentally consistent models.

# Description of DNA-V: Four Processes Viewed Through Two Perspectives

DNA-V is a CBS approach to working with children and adolescents. Figure 7.1 shows the flow of science, theory, and empiricism into DNA-V as an applied approach. We do not claim DNA-V as the only way, and we are expressly not suggesting DNA-V become a package. We focus instead on processes that have substantial evidence and ways to continue researching these processes.

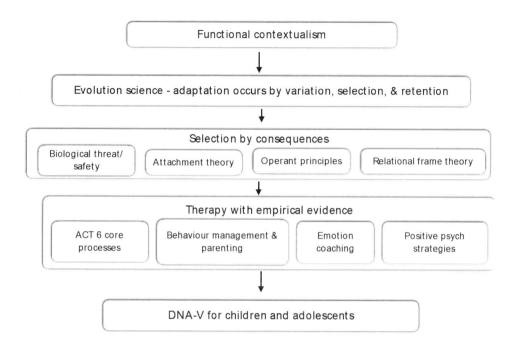

**Figure 7.1.** Assumptions, theory, and empirical evidence underpinning the DNA-V model.

At the broadest level, we draw on the streams inside evolutionary science spanning biology, behavior, learning, and cultural transmission (Jablonka & Lamb, 2006). We use the key principles from evolutionary science of variation, selection, and retention to consider adaptation in young people. Selection by consequences is also fundamental to operant principles (Skinner, 1969). When it comes to development, there can be little doubt that operant principles have helped us understand how a child's behavior is shaped contingently and how we might shape new behavior through reinforcement, punishment, imitation, and modeling (Patterson, 2002). Empirically supported evidence of behavior modification in both classrooms and parent training stand out among the very few "well established" treatments for children (Ollendick & King, 2004). Extending this to human language and symbolic thinking, relational frame theory (RFT) is also based on selection by consequences, through the principle of derived relational responding (S. C. Hayes, Barnes-Holmes, & Roche, 2001). RFT shows how language is shaped in childhood and how symbolic thoughts, such as judging and believing, are under the control of contextual factors (S. C. Hayes et al., 2001).

The DNA-V model (figure 7.2; from L. L. Hayes & Ciarrochi, 2015) comprises four processes that encapsulate behavior into broad classes; these are called Discoverer, Noticer, Advisor, and Value/Vitality. The outer circle of our model refers to the two perspectives through which we view the four processes—social context and self-context. To young people, we call these "self-view" and "social view." Social context involves learning to see other people's DNA-V (e.g., empathy) and also how social interactions and attachments shape our DNA-V behavior. Self-context involves learning to step back and see our DNA-V behaviors as our changing and evolving self, and also being able to view ourselves from different perspectives (e.g., through the eyes of a kind friend). We describe self and social as "contexts" because they can radically alter the function of D, N, A, and V (e.g., noticing might be used to build self-compassion or other compassion). Our use of context, as always in functional contextualism, is pragmatic. When we work with each of the DNA-V processes, we can take a self and/or social perspective.

## Value and Vitality—The "V"

- Process 1: Create contexts that empower young people to clarify what they value or what brings them vitality and choose value-consistent actions

At the center of DNA-V is the process of creating vitality and value. The V, as we refer to it with young people, is the heart of the model and used to connect young people to our human need for vitality, purpose, and meaning. "Vitality" involves actions that bring a sense of energy and embracing life. "Value" involves the ability to use self-talk linked to actions that over time build meaning and purpose—the ability to say, "I want my life to be about this." Value and vitality occur across six areas that support well-being: connecting with others, challenging oneself and learning, embracing the moment, giving to others, being physically active, and caring for oneself (L. L. Hayes & Ciarrochi, 2015). We use these six ways to help create self-directed language and chosen action.

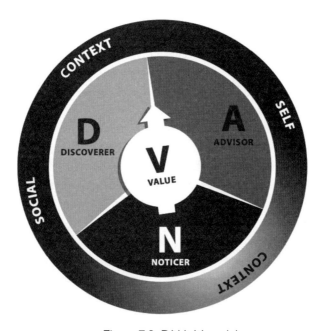

**Figure 7.2.** DNA-V model.

With DNA-V we assume that being able to identify what one values is a skill that builds across development and requires shaping by a child's verbal community. Thus, we do not assume that children and adolescents *have* values, we assume that valuing is an ongoing process. Our task is to shape it through speaking, experiencing, writing, art, and linking words to actions. We avoid adult coercion toward young people by making it explicit that values are developmentally unique to the individual and comprise qualities of action that one *chooses*. We explicitly state that working to build values is a choice, not a set of morals or rules we must follow, and importantly that values are not what adults think young people ought to do.

Procedures for shaping the "V" begin with language creation—speaking, drawing, games, imagining, poetry, creative writing, and even popular media sharing (e.g., YouTube). Each opportunity to interact with a young person should include values and vitality at some level. With children, we take a strong present-moment learning focus ("When I do this behavior, it helps me be how I want to be"). With adolescents, we aim to gradually build more of a future focus so that eventually a young person can say, "I care about this" and "I want to be doing more of this." We do this with procedures such as the Game of Life (Ciarrochi, Hayes, & Bailey, 2012), conversation cards, and six ways to well-being activities (L. L. Hayes & Ciarrochi, 2015). (Many of these procedures can be downloaded from our website at http://www.thrivingadolescent.com.) We move from talking to action by helping young people use their discoverer (see below) to test new actions that build value. We attempt to broaden repertoires by using the six ways to well-being to balance the restricted interests sometimes seen with young people (e.g., gamers challenge themselves but have few behaviors that increase "staying active"). In short, our approaches to values are like bookends; they support all the work we do on thoughts, feelings, and experiences.

It is often difficult to get young people, especially those who have been traumatized, to talk about values. They may respond to values questions with "I don't know" or a shrug of the shoulders. Talking about values may sometimes seem uncool or feel risky. To get around this issue, we start values conversations gently, with questions such as "What will we work for?" or "What do you want out of this session?" We also approach values indirectly, such as through having a conversation that orients toward values ("Who is the wisest person you know?").

Young people will often not have well-formed values statements and may even provide us with content we think is countertherapeutic ("I want to be popular. I want to leave school"); this can still be therapeutic progress. Through gentle, often indirect, values conversations, we are both forming a positive therapeutic relationship and reinforcing young people's willingness to think about value and to engage in new behaviors to discover value. As therapy progresses, we increasingly orient young people to a wider range of valued activities and to consider their value in both the short and the long term.

## Noticer

- Process 2: Help people notice inner and outer experiences, appreciate their present context, and choose responses

The noticer is the process of being aware and responding to what is going on inside us and outside us. All children are born as noticers. From birth, humans use their body and senses to seek out and connect with other humans and the physical world. Humans have evolved to detect and correct discomfort (Porges, 2011). They also learn to be aware of the needs and behaviors of other people, beginning with their closest attachments and eventually wider social connections.

Noticing is not merely a different name for the adult ACT process of being present. Instead, it involves understanding how noticing skills in young people are shaped during development. Research has shown that as children grow, their ability to tolerate the tide of emotions in themselves and others is shaped by consequences. For young people in harsh environments, sudden strong emotions are fear inducing, and they frequently respond with attempts to control or eradicate them or lash out at others (Perry, 2009).

Noticing helps us to tune into our body and detect sensations (Neumann, van Lier, Gratz, & Koot, 2010). Skilled noticers understand that all feelings and sensations are part of being human, and they do not attempt to control or eradicate feelings. Instead, they can bring feelings into their awareness and label them. We can also use noticing to tune into the external world and what it has to offer. Noticer skills involve learning to allow by being nonreactive to inner experience when a response is not needed, and this helps us to regulate our behavior in the presence of difficult emotions. When young people find themselves stuck with difficult thoughts, or responding in repeated unworkable patterns, the noticer provides a way to reconnect with the physical realm and loosen the grip of judgments, evaluations, predictions, and established repertoires of behavior. To use a car metaphor, if you are driving rapidly in the wrong direction, you might pull off on the side of the road, take a breath, and take a look around (noticer).

DNA-V procedures aim to increase flexibility and include coaching awareness of emotions and sensations, practicing pausing with mindful awareness, and responding with awareness instead of reacting. We can use experiential exercise to help a young person normalize their experience of feelings and sensations, so they come to learn that sadness, happiness, frustration, or anger are normal human experiences. We coach emotions by labeling in situ and coaching parents and teachers to reinforce this. Through metaphors, games, and practice, our young clients develop the skill of allowing sensations to come and go. The key is to help young people connect with sensations, not merely with verbal labels of sensations. We utilize a simple exercise called "AND" to do this:

**A:** Awareness of your breath. Just notice it as it flows in and out of your body.

**N:** Notice any sensations in your body. Just scan your body and notice sensations (give examples if needed, such as tension in neck and shoulders).

**D:** Describe the sensations. If you had to put a word on your sensations, what would it be (examples might include anger, anxiety, or frustration)?

We engage young people in exposure exercises that link willingness to experience difficult emotions with values and vitality. For example, let's say that during the AND exercise, a client identifies "anxiety" as a feeling that shows up when thinking about taking a difficult test. The counselor might help a young person to see that anxiety is a sensation; although uncomfortable, it is not something huge and dangerous. The key willingness question is "Are they willing to have this thing called 'anxiety' and study for the test to prepare for a future they value?"

To create flexibility in noticing our self-view, we practice taking a helicopter view and seeing that our self is all our DNA-V; that is, we are not only difficult emotions, and we do not lose our self to them. By using DNA-V as a metaphor for all of the person, we aim to loosen the "thingness" of the self and notice that our self changes. We practice mindfulness and compassionate awareness of strong feelings, such as shame, using grounding and returning to the present, validation, exposure, and home tasks such as journaling to broaden our view of our self as a noticer. With social view, we practice noticing others' feelings— being able to step in another's shoes and extend kindness and compassion. One way to do this is to use what we term "inside-outside" vision (Ciarrochi, L. L. Hayes, & Bailey, 2012), which involves a series of questions (see table 7.1) that prompt a person to look inside themselves and the other, and then look at how they appear to the other and how the other appears to them.

**Table 7.1.** Inside-Outside Vision Questions

|  | You | Other person |
|---|---|---|
| **Your inside vision** | How do I think and feel in this situation? | If I were the other person, how would I feel? |
| **Your outside vision** | How do I look on the outside? | How does this person look on the outside? |

## Advisor

- Process 3: Help people to navigate their context with language

The advisor is a metaphorical name to describe the inner voice that is often evaluating and judging ourselves and others. It involves the uniquely human ability to learn from the words of others (e.g., an elder) and thereby avoid dangerous situations and efficiently find rewarding ones. It also allows us to use reasoning to learn from the past and predict the future. The advisor saves us from trial-and-error mistakes. The advisor is contrasted to the discoverer, which *is* trial and error through experience. The advisor encompasses beliefs, rules, judgments, evaluations, problem solving, and predictions.

The task of DNA-V is to help a young person develop a flexible advisor, or the ability to use rules and evaluations when useful, and let go of such verbal processes when not useful. The advisor as a process includes defusion, just as adult ACT does, but it encompasses more than this. It also includes the growth of language skill in a child—the ability to develop language rules for navigating their world. Plus the ability to develop language rules that help young people build vitality and value and engage in experiences that broaden repertoires. Constructs that map to a flexible advisor include functional beliefs, hope, and self-esteem.

Procedures for developing flexibility in advisor behavior include normalizing the purpose of predictive thinking, which is primarily to keep us alive and safe, and therefore the focus of thinking is often negative. Teaching skilled advisors is the opposite of conventional notions in Western cultures that positive thinking is normal and desired. We use the metaphor of the advisor to help young people engage with the notion that their thoughts are something like an advisor. Just as the principal of a school has advisors who suggest how best to run the school, and a competent principal must choose which advice to listen to and which to pass over, we help young people consider their thoughts from a functional perspective, deciding if they are helpful or unhelpful in each instance. For example, a negative thought such as *I will fail my test* can be helpful if it motivates one to study, and unhelpful if it instills fear and avoidance. We can use classic ACT defusion techniques, or just practice being a DNA-V *shifter* by stepping from the advisor to the noticer to create some space and awareness of thoughts as a process. Finally, we help young people create flexible rules, test them, and change them when they are no longer helpful. One flexible rule is "Your thoughts are just like an advisor, and as a human, your task is to decide how helpful it is to follow the advice."

An essential advisor intervention involves helping young people to notice that the advisor is not in charge of their behavior. For example, you can ask young people if they experienced a time when they doubted they could do something but did it and succeeded. Thus, their advisor was generating pessimistic thoughts like *You don't have a chance,* but they were able to disregard the advisor and move their hands and feet in a way that helped them to succeed. Other advisor exercises can be experiential and straightforward. For example, have the young person sit down and say over and over to stand up, but not stand up; this is an experience of the words not controlling what they do. Finally, you could have them repeat over and over, "I can't go to the back of the room" while walking to the back of the room. All of these exercises illustrate that it is not the advisor that is in charge, but the young person.

The advisor is also viewed through both self and social context. Flexible self-view might involve having rules that say one can grow and change, or a growth mindset (Yeager & Dweck, 2012), while social view might involve the belief that others can change and grow and are not fixed by our concepts of them. Flexible self-view might include the belief that it is okay to be kind to oneself, whereas social view might include the knowledge that others also suffer and deserve kindness. With self-view we practice defusion with self rules, experiencing our advisor as a helping friend, testing out our advice, or simply stepping into a compassionate noticer. With social view, we practice not only predicting and evaluating others' behavior and motives but also testing if our verbal understandings of others are useful.

## Discoverer

- Process 4: Help young people explore in order to develop skills and resources and expand their context

The discoverer is the process of engaging in trial-and-error experiences. Once again we use a metaphorical name to capture a broad class of behaviors that include moving and manipulating our physical world to build repertoires of behavior, and to test, try, and track behaviors that lead to mastery, agency, and autonomy. The discoverer might be thought of as beginning in infancy when children learn that they can poke and push things. For example, an infant drops food off the side of her high chair, watching each time as a caregiver picks it up; she is learning that she has agency and can make things happen. She learns how many times she can drop food before her adult caregivers no longer think it is amusing (social view). Our discoverer experiences can lead to our advisor developing helpful rules (e.g., *Every time I interact with John, he insults me. I should avoid him*) or unhelpful rules (e.g., *Every time I interact with John, he insults me. I should avoid all men*). Eventually, we come to believe our self-talk, and we do not need to test and try. We use our advisor to predict instead.

The discoverer is closely tied to evolutionary theory and adapting to meet the demands of our world. Young children have adapted to learn about their physical world through play, where they learn crucial tasks of manipulating the physical environment and being part of a social group (Gray, 2009). Adolescents extend their discoverer behavior to expand their context into practicing adultlike roles. The common characteristics of adolescents across 187 cultures are risk-taking, love of novelty, sensation seeking, and changes in peer and family relationships (Schlegel & Barry, 1991). Animals in adolescence share these four characteristics (e.g., Spear, 2004). This cross-species evidence suggests that an adaptive process is occurring. Thus we argue that these risky and change behaviors are important discoverer behaviors and the key to developing independence from parents.

Interventions to build discoverer skills are numerous. One essential procedure we employ is a functional assessment, which teaches young people how to track their behaviors. Tracking helps young people (1) select those behaviors that might help to create autonomy and strengths, and (2) know which behaviors lead to vitality and value and which detract from it. For example, learning to have an opinion and speak out can build independence and a sense of value, but the very same outspoken behavior in a different context, friendships as an example, might sometimes work against building value. The key is to track how well behaviors work in a specific context. We also shape strengths with a focus on trying and testing, so the young person builds broad repertoires of behavior. We help young people test and try new things to create values too, knowing it takes time, practice, and errors to learn what they care about. Finally, in the discoverer space, they practice behaviors, set goals, and commit to action.

The simplest way to increase the discoverer skill is to teach young people to look at the consequences of their behavior and whether they link to vitality in the short term and value in the long term (depending on the age of the child). The counselor might say, "When you did that, what happened next?" and then, "Did that work for you? Did it connect to your V?"

Developing flexibility in the self-discoverer involves engaging in experiences to see that one can change and grow. The flexible discoverer can experiment, without clinging to rigid concepts that one must succeed, and can be willing to fail in the service of building strengths and value. A big component of social-discoverer interventions is getting young people to broaden and build their social groups and repertoires by doing new things. There is no possibility of them growing and learning if they keep repeating old behaviors. One exercise involves having them think about what has brought them connection in the past, across different domains of behavior, and then asking them what new things they might do in the future in each domain (see table 7.2). When working with young clients, encourage them to do something new, no matter how small, and to pay attention to what happens next. Was it fun, joyful, or meaningful?

## Research Support

There is a growing body of research supporting the use of ACT for children and adolescents. A meta-analysis involving 707 participants and twenty-one studies suggests that ACT results in improvements in symptoms, quality of life, and psychological flexibility (Swain, Hancock, Hainsworth, and Bowman, 2015). However, many of these earlier studies had weaknesses, such as small samples and nonrandomized design. More recent studies continue to provide support for the benefits of ACT for young people (for current evidence and regular updates, please see https://www.thrivingadolescent.com/dna-v-the-youth-model-of-act/scientific-publications/). For example, Hancock et al. (2018) conducted a well-powered RCT ($n = 193$ children) and showed that both ACT and CBT produced equivalent benefits in the treatment of anxiety. Faulkner, O'Dell, and Golden (2018) provided some preliminary evidence for the efficacy of the DNA-V variant of ACT and positive psychology. They found that 70% of students rated DNA-V components as "somewhat useful" to "very useful." They also found that the DNA-V intervention produced an increase in physical activity compared to the control group, but it did not produce improvements in sleep hygiene or psychological flexibility.

**Table 7.2.** Valued and Vital Experiences

| Domain | Past Things I've Valued (What things were fun, were meaningful, or made me feel alive?) | Step into the Future (What new actions can I take to get more of this in the next year?) |
|---|---|---|
| Connecting with others | | |
| Giving to others and having a positive influence | | |
| Being active | | |
| Embracing the moment | | |
| Challenging myself and learning | | |
| Caring for myself | | |
| Other | | |

There is substantial evidence for the components targeted in DNA-V, including autonomy support, value clarification, mindfulness, broadening and building behavior, emotional awareness and labeling, awareness and functional assessment of thoughts, self-compassion, empathy and perspective taking, and committed action (see Ciarrochi, Atkins, Hayes, Sahdra, & Parker, 2016) for a review. For example, the benefits of building value by avoiding coercion and harnessing adolescent passion was shown in a double-blind, randomized, placebo-controlled experiment with eighth graders (Bryan et al., 2016). The researchers compared one group of adolescents who were educated on the science of healthy eating based on its long-term health benefits (adults-control-message) with a second group of adolescents who were educated on social justice and the tactics of the food industry (adolescent-passion-message). In the latter group, healthy eating was portrayed as a way to resist adult coercion. The food choices of the two groups were monitored, and the adult-control-message group made poorer food choices than the latter adolescent-passion-message group. Thus, we argue that avoiding adultlike values and eliciting an adolescent passion for vitality and value is a critical step.

## Future Directions

We hope DNA-V can play a role in shifting the field toward process approaches for young people. As shown above, discoverer, noticer, advisor, and value and vitality are examples of evidence-based processes. The focus on process provides new constraints and freedoms. On the constraint side, the practitioner still needs to rely on evidence, and this often means not just published evidence in journals, but the evidence gathered when working with a young person in the present moment. Practitioners will ask, *What process am I putting into play? Is it working for this young person? Do I need to find another way to target the process, or do I need to target a different process right now? How do I get feedback on how things are going with the young person?*

The process approach is also freeing. The practitioner can now create interventions depending on what the situation demands. The form of the intervention is no longer the critical thing. It is the function. For example, one may create vitality or promote value clarification through art, discussion, life experiments, singing, exposure to new experiences, and appreciation of literature. The evidence-based process called "value clarification" does not have to be limited to the value clarification exercises written about in our textbook (*The Thriving Adolescent*; L. L. Hayes & Ciarrochi, 2015).

For practitioners, a process approach is like a breath of fresh air. They can finally bring the evidence base into their work in a flexible way that allows them to anchor onto the fundamental principles, process, and procedures. For researchers, this process approach may help us increase the value and efficiency of research trials. We should no longer be throwing time and money into evaluating trademarked intervention packages. There is an infinite number of ways to put processes into play, and therefore an infinite number of possible packages. There is never an end to new packages. Instead of focusing on the package level, we can focus on the process level. We believe a process-based approach to practice and research will improve intervention outcomes for youth and promote scientific progress that is more "…adequate to the challenge of the human condition" (Hayes, Barnes-Holmes, & Wilson, 2012).

# References

Bryan, C. J., Yeager, D. S., Hinojosa, C. P., Chabot, A., Bergen, H., Kawamura, M., & Steubing, F. (2016). Harnessing adolescent values to motivate healthier eating. *Proceedings of the National Academy of Sciences, 113*(39), 10830–10835.

Ciarrochi, J., Atkins, P. W. B., Hayes, L. L., Sahdra, B. K., & Parker, P. (2016). Contextual positive psychology: Policy recommendations for implementing positive psychology into schools. *Frontiers in Psychology, 7*(Oct.), 1561.

Ciarrochi, J., Hayes, L. L., & Bailey, A. (2012). *Get out of your mind and into your life for teens: A guide to living an extraordinary life.* Oakland, CA: New Harbinger Publications.

Falkner, S., O'Dell, S., & Golden, J. (2018, July). *Targeting psychological flexibility, sleep hygiene, and physical activity in high school students using DNA-V model.* Presented at the Annual Conference for the Association of Contextual Behavioral Science, Montréal, Québec, Canada.

Gray, P. (2009). Play as a foundation for hunter-gatherer social existence. *American Journal of Play, 1*(4), 476–522.

Hancock, K. M., Swain, J., Hainsworth, C. J., Dixon, A. L., Koo, S., & Munro, K. (2018). Acceptance and commitment therapy versus cognitive behavior therapy for children with anxiety: Outcomes of a randomized controlled trial. *Journal of Clinical Child and Adolescent Psychology, 47*(2), 296–311.

Hayes, L. L., & Ciarrochi, J. (2015). *The thriving adolescent: Using acceptance and commitment therapy and positive psychology to help teens manage emotions, achieve goals, and build connection.* Oakland CA: New Harbinger.

Hayes, S. C., Barnes-Holmes, D., & Roche, B. (Eds.). (2001). *Relational frame theory: A post-Skinnerian account of human language and cognition.* New York, NY: Kluwer Academic.

Hayes, S. C., Barnes-Holmes, D., & Wilson, K. G. (2012). Contextual behavioral science: Creating a science more adequate to the challenge of the human condition. *Journal of Contextual Behavioral Science, 1*(1–2), 1–16. doi: 10.1016/j.jcbs.2012.09.004

Hayes, S. C., Hofmann, S. G., Stanton, C. E., Carpenter, J. K., Sanford, B. T., Curtiss, J. E., & Ciarrochi, J. (2018). The role of the individual in the coming era of process-based therapy. *Behaviour Research and Therapy, 10*(5). doi: 10.1016/j.brat.2018.10.005

Hayes, S. C., Strosahl, K. D., & Wilson, K. G. (2012). *Acceptance and commitment therapy: The process and practice of mindful change.* (2nd ed.). New York, NY: Guilford Publications.

Jablonka, E., & Lamb, M. (2006). *Evolution in four dimensions: Genetic, epigenetic, behavioral, and symbolic variation in the history of life (Life and mind: Philosophical issues in biology and psychology).* Cambridge, MA: The MIT Press.

Neumann, A., van Lier, P. A., Gratz, K. L., & Koot, H. M. (2010). Multidimensional assessment of emotion regulation difficulties in adolescents using the difficulties in emotion regulation scale. *Assessment, 17*(1), 138–149.

Ollendick, T. H., & King, N. J. (Eds.). (2004). *Empirically supported treatment for children and adolescents: Advances toward evidence-based practice.* Chichester, UK: John Wiley & Sons.

Patterson, G. R. (2002). Etiology and treatment of child and adolescent antisocial behavior. *The Behavior Analyst Today, 3*(2), 133–144.

Perry, B. D. (2009). Examining child maltreatment through a neurodevelopmental lens: Clinical applications of the neurosequential model of therapeutics. *Journal of Loss and Trauma, 14*(4), 240–255. doi: 10.1080/15325020903004350

Schlegel, A., & Barry, H. (1991). *Adolescence: An anthropological inquiry.* New York, NY: Free Press.

Skinner, B. F. (1969). *Contingencies of reinforcement: A theoretical analysis.* Englewood Cliffs NJ: Prentice-Hall.

Spear, L. P. (2004). Adolescent brain development and animal models. *Annals of the New York Academy of Sciences, 1021,* 23–26.

Swain, J., Hancock, K., Hainsworth, C., & Bowman, J. (2015). Mechanisms of change: Exploratory outcomes from a randomised controlled trial of acceptance and commitment therapy for anxious adolescents. *Journal of Contextual Behavioral Science, 4*(1), 56–67. doi: 10.1016/j.jcbs.2014.09.001

Wilson, D. S., Kauffman, R. A., Jr., & Purdy, M. S. (2011). A program for at-risk high school students informed by evolutionary science. *PLOS ONE, 6*(11), e27826. doi:10.1371/journal.pone.0027826

Yeager, D. S., & Dweck, C. S. (2012). Mindsets that promote resilience: When students believe that personal characteristics can be developed. *Educational Psychologist, 47*(4), 302–314.

# CHAPTER 8

# Acceptance and Commitment Therapy and Exposure Exercises

Michael P. Twohig

Clarissa W. Ong

Julie M. Petersen

Jennifer L. Barney

Jeremiah E. Fruge

*Utah State University*

## Overview

Exposure therapy is one of the great psychotherapy successes. It is at the core of all empirically supported treatments for anxiety disorders. Since its development, it has undergone many procedural adjustments as well as reconceptualizations of its process of change. Exposure therapy may be going through another notable shift as a result of recent basic research on extinction and habituation, as well as applied work on their translation to applied situations. Given acceptance and commitment therapy's (ACT's) ties to basic science, these findings, as well as behavioral work on language and cognition, are guiding ways in which ACT and exposure exercises can be integrated in a theoretically logical manner. This chapter reviews this work as well as provides clinical guidance.

The roots of exposure therapy began with Mowrer's two-stage learning theory (Mowrer, 1960). Mowrer suggested fear is learned via classical conditioning; when confronted with anxiety or distress, a person will attempt to escape and reduce the anxiety, thereby strengthening that response as the anxiety-provoking stimuli is evaded. Assuming this process is repeated, the fear is gradually sustained through classical and operant conditioning. To break this cycle, the avoidance must be replaced with approach toward feared stimuli, during which habituation to the feared stimulus can occur (Mowrer, 1960).

Foa and Kozak (1986) built on Mowrer's (1960) theory with the development of emotional processing theory (EPT). EPT posits fear is stored in the brain within cognitive fear structures that contain important information about triggers and responses related to fear (Foa & Kozak, 1986). According to EPT, exposures induce emotional processing of this fear structure through habituation to the feared stimuli; after habituation, the stimuli no longer provokes fear and thereby provides new, corrective information about safety (Foa & Kozak, 1986). This new information is then incorporated into the fear structure and produces helpful, real-world changes. Foa and Kozak's (1986) theory suggests habituating to the feared stimulus will result in generalizations to other feared scenarios and permanent changes in learning.

Inhibitory learning contrasts EPT because it suggests the link between the conditioned and unconditioned stimulus never permanently disappears, regardless of habituation or any corrective learning during exposures; instead, the new learned association inhibits the previously feared association (Craske, Treanor, Conway, Zbozinek, & Vervliet, 2014). The new connection will then compete with retrieval of the fear response in the future, creating long-term gains. Thus, unlike EPT, inhibitory learning suggests habituation during and between sessions of exposure therapy does not matter; rather, this theory focuses on strength of learning and generalization. The theory of inhibitory learning is supported by laboratory research with nonhuman animals (Craske, Treanor, et al., 2014). It is important to note that all these models focus on classically conditioned fear reduction, which differs some from the model presented in this chapter.

The field of cognitive behavioral therapy (CBT) has been very effective with treatments based on these principles, especially with anxiety and obsessive-compulsive disorders (Norton & Price, 2007) and trauma-based disorders such as posttraumatic stress disorder (Schnurr et al., 2007). Additionally, exposure therapy has been explored for several other conditions, including eating disorders (Koskina, Campbell, & Schmidt, 2013), body dysmorphic disorder (BDD; Harrison, Fernández De La Cruz, Enander, Radua, & Mataix-Cols, 2016), and Tourette's disorder (Verdellen, Keijsers, Cath, & Hoogduin, 2004).

## Integrating ACT and Exposure

One issue central to applied psychology is the relationship between cognitions and behavior. Previous descriptions of exposure therapy have heavily focused on behavioral principles, but cognitions have a role as the vast majority of this work is completed with verbal humans. While EPT and cognitive theory (from CBT) are explicit about the relationship between exposures and cognitive changes, other models (e.g., inhibitory learning) have a relatively loose link to cognitive change. Findings from research have shown that cognitive change does occur as a result of CBTs for anxiety disorders (Kleim et al.,

2013), although additions of cognitive elements to behavioral therapies have not been found to result in improved outcomes (Tolin, 2009).

Relational frame theory (RFT) is a behavior analytic account of language and cognition: it provides an empirically grounded theory to guide our understanding of the relationship between cognition and overt actions. According to RFT, verbal humans do not only respond to the formal properties of stimuli, we also respond to verbally derived versions of those stimuli (relational responding). Due to our abilities to respond relationally, we respond to stimuli (internal and external) in terms of how they relate to other stimuli. The context we are in signifies how we should relationally respond to stimuli, and different contexts control what stimuli *are* and *how we should respond in their presence*. For example, someone with panic disorder can experience a fast beating heart, and the context signifies whether it is logical (exercising) or reason for concern (sitting in a lecture). The goal of therapy can be to shift what the stimulus is ("just a fast heart" or "dying"), or shift how one responds to it (escape or approach). RFT and basic research on classic and operant habituation and extinction have greatly informed the approach that ACT researchers have taken.

RFT concepts suggest we can help humans more effectively respond to stimuli by altering the verbal context in which they are experienced. We can also alter the verbal context that determines the function of verbal stimuli. Thus, ACT is much less about addressing content of any particular cognitions (or other internal experience) and more about affecting the way in which we experience stimuli in our lives. The goal for integrating ACT and exposure exercises was to use ACT to lessen the effects of internal experiences when approaching feared events, help increase the appetitive valence of approach through values exercises, and reinforce more functional behaviors. For example, when working with a client diagnosed with a phobia, the therapist would work to alter the context in which anxiety is experienced from one where "anxiety is bad," and fearful thoughts about the future are important, to a situation where anxiety is just another emotion, and thoughts are just sounds in the head. Similarly, we would work to make approaching the target stimulus more meaningful, by linking it to the client's values, than the comfort of avoiding or escaping. This approach is also consistent with human (Craske, Treanor, et al., 2014) and animal learning research (Podlesnik & Shahan, 2009) that shows once a response is learned it cannot be unlearned. Therefore, learning to respond differently to fear and anxiety may be more helpful than trying to change the fear and anxiety.

## Description of Implementing Exposure Exercises in ACT

As previously written, exposure therapy has existed since the 1960s. That original work was tied directly to operant research with pigeons (Wolpe, 1961). As the field progressed, multiple models of exposure therapy developed including behavioral, cognitive behavioral, and clinical behavioral. It is important to note that these models and related therapies grew in tandem and influenced each other. Thus, all forms of CBT (including ACT) cannot be fully distinct from other one another but do not fully overlap either (Twohig, Woidneck, & Crosby, 2013). Still, if you look at these models individually, they have specific predicted processes of change, procedures to address those processes of change, and overall goals or dependent variables.

Exposure therapies can be broken down into three key aspects: the targeted *process* of change (or what we are hoping to alter for the client), the *procedures* we use to create these changes, and the targeted *outcome* (e.g., what our main dependent variable is).

## Process of Change

The *process* of change in ACT-based exposures is psychological flexibility—the ability to be willing to experience private events (thoughts, feelings, sensations) for what they are as they occur in the present while engaging in activities consistent with values (Hayes, Luoma, Bond, Masuda, & Lillis, 2006). You might explain it to your client like this: "My hope is that we can find a new relationship with your anxiety or fear. We don't need to like it, but hopefully we can find a way to coexist with it. That way it can do what it needs while you do what you need. This will allow you to do what you care about no matter the height of anxiety or fear."

## Procedures

*Procedurally*, ACT has a specific style that is experiential and involves exercises, stories, and metaphors—all used because experiential learning is less susceptible to being rule bound and inflexible to environmental changes. ACT therapists commonly work with clients to bring up the internal experiences that will be addressed in session. For these reasons, ACT has always been an exposure-based intervention. Just as an ACT therapist would work with a client who struggles with substance use to encounter triggering stimuli related to the relevant substance, we work with clients with anxiety disorders to enter situations that occasion anxiety.

Every ACT-based exposure session begins with an assessment of the client's psychological flexibility. Based on the findings from that assessment, we engage the client with discussion, exercises, and examples with the hope of fostering psychological flexibility or at least an openness to growing more flexible. Before starting any "exposures," it is important that the client know how to and have the ability to practice psychological flexibility. If the client otherwise experiences an anxiety-provoking stimulus and does not have the skill to be present with it, the client will practice another skill, such as emotional avoidance or tolerance. We want to practice "good form" much in the same way that CBT exposures occur at a level a client can tolerate. We do not need to see movement on a measure of psychological flexibility, but loosening of language around feared stimuli and anxiety is important. We would want to hear openness ("I'm getting pushed around less by anxiety'), defusion ("I'm catching my anxious thoughts more often"), and some link to values ("Finding a way to respond to my anxiety really seems worth it for the things I want to do in life").

We have found that ACT for anxiety focuses more on acceptance, defusion, and values, with exposure exercises matching the behavioral commitments. If the therapist believes that the client is ready to practice psychological flexibility in an exposure exercise, and finds meaning in the exercise, they are free to start. They may practice the full psychological flexibility model, but sometimes we will also focus on one of the six processes of change. If an exposure exercise is going to be used as an opportunity to practice defusion (seeing inner experiences as inner experiences and nothing more), the therapist might say, "Let's go downstairs and ask the people in the coffee shop if they foresee any job openings. Obviously, you are not looking for that job, but let's practice watching all the material your mind gives you. Let's pretend we are reporters and our assignment is to watch what your mind says. I look forward to your report." Thus, we might begin behavioral commitments earlier in ACT for anxiety disorders than we might for other disorders.

At a procedural level, ACT does not need to address issues that are commonly addressed in traditional behavioral forms of exposure therapy. Specifically, we do not use SUDS (subjective units of distress scale) ratings as guides of what exposures should be completed in session or how long exposures should take. The main reason is ACT honestly teaches psychological acceptance. We do not teach tolerance—in the sense that if one allows the internal experience to be there it will eventually go away. If we truly practice acceptance, then any level of the internal experience is allowed. In session, we may ask how high the internal experience is, but that is done to guide observation, in the way we might notice the temperature. We do not need to have a certain level of anxiety in exposures, but it can be useful to notice its ebb and flow. We generally do not need to create a fear hierarchy. Even though SUDS are out of favor in general in CBT (Craske, Treanor, et al., 2014), they are still often used as a metric of treatment progress; completion of exposures with higher SUDS indicates progress. In one of our recent trials we used "willingness" scores instead of SUDS (Twohig, Abramowitz, et al., 2015; Twohig et al., 2018) so that we had matched check-ins with the client. We used the willingness scores to tell us if our target process of change was moving. If the client could maintain willingness in increasingly difficult situations, we knew we were making progress. It was a nice way to track an internal response when engaging in observable behavioral commitments. In ACT, we still need to decide on the level of the exposure exercise, but we use acceptance and values to generally determine those levels. Specifically, we want the exercise to be tied to values in some way: it may either be obvious (practicing being social for someone with social anxiety) or linked verbally (touching a garbage can for someone who struggles with germs). The level of acceptance tells us how far the client can successfully go within the exercise while still being psychologically flexible. For example, we might say, "Let's think of a way to practice being with your anxiety during the session today. Let's find something meaningful to you and at a level where you can be with the anxiety that shows up." This work could arguably be related to work based on SUDS, in that we need to know a level to start at, but one difference is that we never ask what happens to the fear or anxiety.

One similarity between ACT and other traditional behavior therapies is the stimuli and exercises that can be chosen for the exposures. Stimuli that evoke obsessions for obsessive-compulsive disorder, social interactions that may lead to embarrassment for social anxiety, feared objects for phobias, interoceptive exercises and situations that provoke agoraphobic fears for panic disorder, feared and related stimuli for posttraumatic stress disorder, and open discussions of worries for generalized anxiety disorder are all helpful exposure options. The number of actual exposures that exist are unlimited. In traditional exposures the therapist usually looks for stimuli that bring up the most distress. ACT is not opposed to that per se, but there needs to be some link to values. Thus, we find that the severity of exposures in ACT can sometimes be a little lower than in traditional exposure therapy because it can be hard to link extreme exposures to values. For all these disorders, we would also want to highlight avoidance behaviors and help the client to be aware of when those avoidance actions are about to occur or are occurring so that approach can be introduced as an option. ACT might be slightly more open than traditional behavior therapy to encourage actions that are values consistent but may not result in a high SUDS score. An ACT therapist might say:

*Therapist (T):*    Do you have any ideas of an exercise that will bring up some emotions and mind chatter but that you can also find meaning in?

*Client (C):*    We could walk outside near the playground again. You know that brings up my fears of harming someone.

T:    Sounds good. Give me the parameters:  how long, what will you do, and so on?

C:    Okay, how about fifteen minutes? We sit on those benches.

T:    What if someone talks to you? Will you respond?

C:    Sure. I will talk.

T:    Okay, give me a reason this is worth doing.

C:    I'd like to have kids someday. I guess I first need to meet someone. But all these require that I can get along around other people.

T:    Even if your mind is not always your friend?

C:    Even then.

Another large procedural adaption when doing exposure exercises from an ACT model is that there is generally more communication between the therapist and client during exposure exercises; this is aimed at determining the client's level of psychological flexibility. While sometimes one can decipher when a client is being willing versus experientially avoidant, much of the time, a conversation will give you the best information on how the client is responding to their internal events. Thus, there are many questions a therapist can ask about how clients are treating their anxiety, what they are doing with it, what it is like to have it there, and so on. Clients may also say or do things that suggest psychological flexibility. For example, a client might say, "My mind is sure saying a lot about this exercise," or, "It's funny how much this gets my heart going." Both statements show a client who is watching their thinking versus being caught up in it. A client might also show their connection to values by saying, "I was thinking about doing this exercise today because it's important to me and I find I have been avoiding it." We also give continual coaching tips to foster psychological flexibility. We have been asked whether the conversation takes the client out of the exposure, and while that is an empirical question, we argue that fostering acceptance is meant to bring the client in greater contact with their experience.

We commonly ask questions like the following during ACT-based exposures:

"Are you allowing that fear to be there or pushing it away?"

"Where would you say your willingness is?"

"Are you able to watch your thoughts or are you looking from them?"

"Give me a values-based reason to be doing this work right now."

"How in touch with the feared item are you?"

## Target Outcome

The target *outcome* of ACT-based exposures is the same as that of ACT more broadly: to help the client live the life they most desire. Pursuing idiosyncratic values is the end, and acceptance and mindfulness skills are a means to that end (Twohig, Abramowitz, et al., 2015). In other words, the ability to be open to discomfort is only useful insofar as it allows individuals to live a fulfilling life; the frequency, duration, and intensity of distress per se are less important. Therefore, the criterion for success of exposure is *acting* in personally meaningful ways in the presence of distressing stimuli—regardless of whether distress shows up, decreases (as in habituation models), or is maintained (Twohig, Abramowitz, et al., 2015). As treatment progresses, clients should get better at responding flexibly to initially repertoire-narrowing stimuli through encountering increasingly challenging situations. Ultimately, clients will generalize psychological flexibility to naturalistic situations in which distress shows up—so they can pursue the things that matter to them. The therapist can see this growth in session but can also learn about the new skills the client is engaging in by asking what the client has accomplished this week. Hopefully, the client is doing more values-based activities and showing growth in meaningful areas of life.

# Challenges

This research team has implemented exposure therapy from an ACT perspective in multiple settings over the last fifteen years (Meuret, Twohig, Rosenfield, Hayes, & Craske, 2012; Twohig, Abramowitz, et al., 2015; Twohig et al., 2018). Much of what we will provide in this section is from our personal observations, although some observations have been expressed by other experts in writing.

Interestingly, researchers have found that therapists, not clients, are afraid of using exposure therapy (Deacon, Lickel, Farrell, Kemp, & Hipol, 2013), even though it is the most supported treatment procedure for anxiety, obsessive-compulsive, and trauma disorders (Norton & Price, 2007). One reason for this is therapists' unwillingness to experience discomfort (Scherr, Herbert, & Forman, 2015), but another is that we have poorly marketed this intervention (Olatunji, Deacon, & Abramowitz, 2009). When we read some of the original behavioral exposure therapy manuals, they seemed cold. We understood and supported the work being done in those treatments, but the manuals did a poor job of portraying the kindness, compassion, and support that exposure therapists offer. Working in this field, we have come to see firsthand that countless professionals who use exposure therapy are extremely talented at it. This is important to note because we believe that even though individual therapists learn how to do exposure therapy well, much of that information is not offered in manuals.

There are two additional related challenges: it can take a long time for the client to develop psychological flexibility, and some clients do not want to do exposure exercises. If psychological flexibility is present, clients will be more willing to engage in exposures, and there is evidence to support this (Levitt, Brown, Orsillo, & Barlow, 2004; Reid et al., 2017). In one of our studies, we spent four sessions only teaching psychological flexibility before starting exposures (Meuret et al., 2012), whereas in another study we spent about half the time teaching psychological flexibility and the other half teaching exposure with response prevention (ERP) before engaging in exposures in session three (Twohig et al., 2018). Personal experience suggests that those who dropped out of therapy because they were unwilling to do exposures were too low in psychological flexibility to start the exercises, which the experimental protocol required. Thus, based on these treatment trials and clinical experience, we suggest working to foster psychological flexibility as long as needed prior to starting exposure exercises. If psychological flexibility is high, it is likely that exposures will be useful.

Another conceptual struggle involves defining when exposure therapy (or exposure exercises) is occurring and when it is not. There is substantial evidence that confronting fear- or anxiety-provoking stimuli (exposure) internally and externally and staying in their presence (response prevention) are effective at decreasing fear and anxiety in the long term as well as reducing diagnoses (Tolin, 2009). Thus, any intervention where approaching and staying in contact with the target stimulus is central to treatment can easily be seen as a form of exposure therapy, as exemplified by eye movement desensitizing and reprocessing (Jeffries & Davis, 2013). For these reasons we ran multiple studies using ACT with no formal exposure exercises, and these findings have been replicated multiple times (Twohig & Levin, 2017). These studies and related findings (Meuret et al., 2012; Twohig, Plumb Vilardaga, Levin, & Hayes, 2015) suggest psychological flexibility has an impact in the treatment of anxiety disorders sans exposure therapy. Still, the question of whether ACT is just another form of exposure therapy has been raised many times, because ACT suggests engaging in valued activities, which invariably involve confronting avoided stimuli. When we compare the proposed process of change (psychological flexibility), ACT therapeutic procedures (e.g., confronting target stimuli, practicing techniques to foster psychological flexibility), and key goals (successful living regardless of internal experience), most can see that while it overlaps with other forms of CBT, it is also a unique approach to therapy.

This final issue exists with all psychotherapy research. Specifically, humans are complex and will learn many things over the course of therapy. In ACT-based exposures, we aim to teach psychological flexibility, but it is likely the client will also learn other processes of change. For example, in one case study the client showed fast development in psychological flexibility, and only showed change in cognitive distortions toward the end of treatment (Twohig, 2009). Thus, psychological flexibility seems to have led to cognitive change. Temporality will help us understand which processes most strongly affect the outcomes and when psychological flexibility promotes other processes. Much more work illustrating which processes of change occur in ACT-based exposures is needed. Tracking processes of change throughout treatment, rather than only at pretreatment, posttreatment, and follow-up, will help us understand the order in which change occurs and how multiple processes of change affect each other.

Finally, ACT-based research has always been in a bit of a trap. We focus on building values-based actions, but because we are part of larger systems of care, standardized measures of pathology often end up being our main dependent variables. Measures of pathology tend to indicate effectiveness of ACT, but oftentimes, a notable portion of the questions on those measures focus on severity or frequency of internal events. It is likely that ACT still positively affects those measures because there are many questions on overt actions and response to internal events, and clinically we have had a lot of success by focusing on overt actions over levels of internal events. Additionally, temporally, psychological flexibility might promote natural extinction and habituation processes by teaching the client not to avoid the internal events. Thus, it is likely there will be reductions in internal responses (e.g., anxiety), but they may occur quite a bit later than the overt behavior changes.

## Research Support

To date, three case studies, nine open trials, and eleven randomized controlled trials (RCTs) have been conducted evaluating ACT plus exposure therapy. Generally, in these trials, exposures in ACT were conducted to practice willingness in the service of values rather than anxiety reduction. Findings show that ACT plus varying degrees of exposure exercises is equally effective as standard CBT for anxiety disorders.

**Social anxiety disorder (SAD).** There have been several open trials evaluating ACT for SAD. For example, Dalrymple and Herbert (2007) and Dalrymple et al. (2014) observed significant improvements in psychological symptoms, quality of life, experiential avoidance, and psychological flexibility (Cohen's $ds$ ranged from 0.30 to 2.09 across outcomes) following individual therapy using ACT and exposure with participants with SAD (N = 19) and SAD with comorbid depression (N = 38), respectively. These results were replicated in other studies using group therapy (Cohen's $ds$ ranged from 0.56 to 0.76; Block & Wulfert, 2000; Kocovski, Fleming, & Rector, 2009; Ossman, Wilson, Storaasli, & McNeill, 2006). An RCT comparing individual ACT plus exposure to CBT for SAD (N = 87) found equivalent, clinically significant improvements after treatment with response rates of 41% and 40% for ACT and CBT, respectively, at twelve-month follow up (Craske, Niles, et al., 2014).

**Generalized anxiety disorder (GAD).** Avdagic, Morrissey, and Boschen (2014) conducted an RCT comparing the efficacy of a six-week ACT-based group therapy with CBT-based group therapy for GAD (N = 38). Both groups reported significant improvements in anxiety, depression, and stress-related symptoms at posttreatment, which were maintained at three-month follow-up. Rates of reliable change were 79% at posttreatment and 60% at follow-up in the ACT group and 48% and 60% in the CBT group (Avdagic et al., 2014). Dahlin et al. (2016) evaluated the efficacy of an Internet-based, acceptance-based intervention using text, audio, and video content in an open trial (N = 14). Participants showed significant improvements in worry symptoms from pre- to posttreatment with a large effect size (Cohen's $d = 2.14$).

**Obsessive-compulsive disorder (OCD).** Most recently, an RCT comparing ERP alone and ACT plus ERP was completed with fifty-eight adults. In ACT plus ERP, most ERP methods were followed with the strong integration of ACT principles. Results were strong for both conditions, with dropout rates of 18% for ERP and 17% for ACT plus ERP, and response rates of 68% at posttreatment and 64% at follow-up in ERP, and 70% at posttreatment and 60% at follow-up in ACT plus ERP (Twohig et al., 2018).

**Panic disorder and agoraphobia.** An open trial (N = 11; Meuret et al., 2012) and an RCT (N = 43; Gloster et al., 2015) supported the effectiveness of ACT plus exposure for panic disorder. Meuret et al. (2012) found a brief ACT plus exposure therapy protocol for panic disorder without agoraphobia led to clinically significant improvements in panic symptom severity, significant increases in self-reported willingness, and reductions in avoidant behavior. Gloster et al. (2015) reported significantly greater improvement in panic disorder and agoraphobia symptoms and general functioning in ACT (which included interoceptive exercises) compared to a waitlist control condition among treatment-resistant participants with panic disorder (Cohen's $ds = 0.72$ and $0.89$, respectively).

**Mixed anxiety disorders.** An RCT comparing the results of ACT and CBT in individuals with mixed anxiety disorders (N = 128, Arch et al., 2012) demonstrated equivalent statistically significant improvements in anxiety and depression symptoms at posttreatment (within-group $ds$ ranged from 0.43 to 3.74 for ACT and from 0.43 to 3.46 for CBT). Arch et al. (2012) found the ACT group reported significantly lower clinical severity scores ($d = 1.10$), higher psychological flexibility ($d = 0.42$), and worse quality of life ($d = 0.42$) at twelve-month follow-up compared to the CBT group. Exposures were framed as opportunities to practice psychological flexibility in ACT as opposed to rational thinking and anxiety reduction in CBT.

## Future Directions

ACT and exposure therapy both originated from behavior analysis. Exposure therapy, while originally a behavioral intervention, is now most often delivered as CBT. ACT is also uniquely a behavioral and cognitive intervention, but its cognitive aspect also originates in behavior analysis. ACT focuses on fostering psychological flexibility and then practicing and enhancing it with exposure exercises. Ultimately, the client builds skills to behave effectively regardless of the inner experience. Researchers are finding that exposures done from an ACT perspective are effective, are acceptable to clients, and appear to be related to psychological flexibility. But like all other forms of CBT, ACT and ACT-based exposures are not effective for all individuals. Mediation and moderation research findings suggest the likelihood of benefits to case matching. Process-based CBT (Hayes & Hofmann, 2017) may in the future offer us guidance on how and when to use exposures from a largely behavioral, cognitive, or ACT model.

## References

Arch, J. J., Eifert, G. H., Davies, C., Vilardaga, J. C. P., Rose, R. D., & Craske, M. G. (2012). Randomized clinical trial of cognitive behavioral therapy (CBT) versus acceptance and commitment therapy (ACT) for mixed anxiety disorders. *Journal of Consulting and Clinical Psychology, 80*(5), 750–765. doi: 10.1037/a0028310

Avdagic, E., Morrissey, S. A., & Boschen, M. J. (2014). A randomised controlled trial of acceptance and commitment therapy and cognitive-behaviour therapy for generalised anxiety disorder. *Behaviour Change, 31*(02), 110–130. doi: 10.1017/bec.2014.5

Block, J. A., & Wulfert, E. (2000). Acceptance or change: Treating socially anxious college students with ACT or CBGT. *The Behavior Analyst Today, 1*(2), 1–55.

Craske, M. G., Niles, A. N., Burklund, L. J., Wolitzky-Taylor, K. B., Vilardaga, J. C., Arch, J. J., . . . Lieberman, M. D. (2014). Randomized controlled trial of cognitive behavioral therapy and acceptance and commitment therapy for social phobia: Outcomes and moderators. *Journal of Consulting and Clinical Psychology, 82*(6), 1034–1048. doi: 10.1037/a0037212

Craske, M. G., Treanor, M., Conway, C. C., Zbozinek, T., & Vervliet, B. (2014). Maximizing exposure therapy: An inhibitory learning approach. *Behaviour Research and Therapy, 58,* 10–23. doi: 10.1016/j.brat.2014.04.006

Dahlin, M., Ryberg, M., Vernmark, K., Annas, N., Carlbring, P., & Andersson, G. (2016). Internet-delivered acceptance-based behavior therapy for generalized anxiety disorder: A pilot study. *Internet Interventions, 6*, 16–21. doi: 10.1016/j.invent.2016.08.004

Dalrymple, K. L., & Herbert, J. D. (2007). Acceptance and commitment therapy for generalized social anxiety disorder: A pilot study. *Behavior Modification, 31*(5), 543–568.

Dalrymple, K. L., Morgan, T. A., Lipschitz, J. M., Martinez, J. H., Tepe, E., & Zimmerman, M. (2014). An integrated, acceptance-based behavioral approach for depression with social anxiety: Preliminary results. *Behavior Modification, 38*(4), 516-548. doi: 10.1177/0145445513518422

Deacon, B. J., Lickel, J. J., Farrell, N. R., Kemp, J. J., & Hipol, L. J. (2013). Therapist perceptions and delivery of interoceptive exposure for panic disorder. *Journal of Anxiety Disorders, 27*(2), 259–264. doi: 10.1016/j.janxdis.2013.02.004

Foa, E. B., & Kozak, M. J. (1986). Emotional processing of fear: Exposure to corrective information. *Psychological Bulletin, 99*(1), 20–35. doi: 10.1037/0033-2909.99.1.20

Gloster, A. T., Sonntag, R., Hoyer, J., Meyer, A. H., Heinze, S., Strohle, A., . . . Wittchen, H. U. (2015). Treating treatment-resistant patients with panic disorder and agoraphobia using psychotherapy: A randomized controlled switching trial. *Psychotherapy and Psychosomatics, 84*(2), 100–109. doi: 10.1159/000370162

Harrison, A., Fernández De La Cruz, L., Enander, J., Radua, J., & Mataix-Cols, D. (2016). Cognitive-behavioral therapy for body dysmorphic disorder: A systematic review and meta-analysis of randomized controlled trials. *Clinical Psychology Review, 48*, 43–51. doi: 10.1016/j.cpr.2016.05.007

Hayes, S. C., & Hofmann, S. G. (2017). The third wave of cognitive behavioral therapy and the rise of process-based care. *World Psychiatry, 16*(3), 245–246. doi: 10.1002/wps.20442

Hayes, S. C., Luoma, J. B., Bond, F. W., Masuda, A., & Lillis, J. (2006). Acceptance and commitment therapy: Model, processes and outcomes. *Behaviour Research and Therapy, 44*(1), 1–25. doi: 10.1016/j.brat.2005.06.006

Jeffries, F. W., & Davis, P. (2013). What is the role of eye movements in eye movement desensitization and reprocessing (EMDR) for post-traumatic stress disorder (PTSD)? A review. *Behavioural and Cognitive Psychotherapy, 41*(3), 290–300.

Kleim, B., Grey, N., Wild, J., Nussbeck, F. W., Stott, R., Hackmann, A., . . . Ehlers, A. (2013). Cognitive change predicts symptom reduction with cognitive therapy for posttraumatic stress disorder. *Journal of Consulting and Clinical Psychology, 81*(3), 383.

Kocovski, N. L., Fleming, J. E., & Rector, N. A. (2009). Mindfulness and acceptance-based group therapy for social anxiety disorder: An open trial. *Cognitive and Behavioral Practice, 16*(3), 276–289. doi: 10.1016/j.cbpra.2008.12.004

Koskina, A., Campbell, I. C., & Schmidt, U. (2013). Exposure therapy in eating disorders revisited. *Neuroscience & Biobehavioral Reviews, 37*(2), 193–208. doi: 10.1016/J.NEUBIOREV.2012.11.010

Levitt, J. T., Brown, T. A., Orsillo, S. M., & Barlow, D. H. (2004). The effects of acceptance versus suppression of emotion on subjective and psychophysiological response to carbon dioxide challenge in patients with panic disorder. *Behavior Therapy, 35*(4), 747–766. doi: 10.1016/S0005-7894(04)80018-2

Meuret, A. E., Twohig, M. P., Rosenfield, D., Hayes, S. C., & Craske, M. G. (2012). Brief acceptance and commitment therapy and exposure for panic disorder: A pilot study. *Cognitive and Behavioral Practice, 19*(4), 606–618. doi: 10.1016/j.cbpra.2012.05.004

Mowrer, O. H. (1960). *Learning theory and behavior.* Hoboken, NJ: John Wiley & Sons, Inc.

Norton, P. J., & Price, E. C. (2007). A meta-analytic review of adult cognitive-behavioral treatment outcome across the anxiety disorders. *The Journal of Nervous and Mental Disease, 195*(6), 521–531. doi: 10.1097/01.nmd.0000253843.70149.9a

Olatunji, B. O., Deacon, B. J., & Abramowitz, J. S. (2009). The cruelest cure? Ethical issues in the implementation of exposure-based treatments. *Cognitive and Behavioral Practice, 16*(2), 172–180. doi: 10.1016/j.cbpra.2008.07.003

Ossman, W. A., Wilson, K. G., Storaasli, R. D., & McNeill, J. W. (2006). A preliminary investigation of the use of acceptance and commitment therapy in a group treatment for social phobia. *International Journal of Psychology & Psychological Therapy, 6*(3), 397–416.

Podlesnik, C. A., & Shahan, T. A. (2009). Behavioral momentum and relapse of extinguished operant responding. *Learning & Behavior, 37*(4), 357–364.

Reid, A. M., Garner, L. E., Van Kirk, N., Gironda, C., Krompinger, J. W., Brennan, B. P., . . . André, M. C. (2017). How willing are you? Willingness as a predictor of change during treatment of adults with obsessive–compulsive disorder. *Depression and anxiety, 34*(11), 1057–1064.

Scherr, S. R., Herbert, J. D., & Forman, E. M. (2015). The role of therapist experiential avoidance in predicting therapist preference for exposure treatment for OCD. *Journal of Contextual Behavioral Science, 4*(1), 21–29.

Schnurr, P. P., Friedman, M. J., Engel, C. C., Foa, E. B., Shea, M. T., Resick, P. A., . . . Bernandy, N. C. (2007). Cognitive behavioral therapy for posttraumatic stress disorder in women. *JAMA The Journal of the American Medical Association, 297*(8), 820–830. doi: 10.1001/jama.297.8.820

Tolin, D. F. (2009). Alphabet Soup: ERP, CT, and ACT for OCD. *Cognitive and Behavioral Practice, 16,* 40–48. doi: 10.1016/j.cbpra.2008.07.001

Twohig, M. P. (2009). Acceptance and commitment therapy for treatment-resistant posttraumatic stress disorder: A case study. *Cognitive and Behavioral Practice, 16*(3), 243–252.

Twohig, M. P., Abramowitz, J. S., Bluett, E. J., Fabricant, L. E., Jacoby, R. J., Morrison, K. L., . . . Smith, B. M. (2015). Exposure therapy for OCD from an acceptance and commitment therapy (ACT) framework. *Journal of Obsessive-Compulsive and Related Disorders, 6,* 167–173. doi: 10.1016/j.jocrd.2014.12.007

Twohig, M. P., Abramowitz, J. S., Smith, B. M., Fabricant, L. E., Jacoby, R. J., Morrison, K. L., . . . Lederman, T. (2018). Adding acceptance and commitment therapy to exposure and response prevention for obsessive-compulsive disorder: A randomized controlled trial. *Behaviour Research and Therapy, 108,* 1–9. doi: 10.1016/j.brat.2018.06.005

Twohig, M. P., & Levin, M. E. (2017). Acceptance and commitment therapy as a treatment for anxiety and depression: A review. *Psychiatric Clinics of North America, 40*(4), 751–770. doi: 10.1016/j.psc.2017.08.009

Twohig, M. P., Plumb Vilardaga, J. C., Levin, M. E., & Hayes, S. C. (2015). Changes in psychological flexibility during acceptance and commitment therapy for obsessive compulsive disorder. *Journal of Contextual Behavioral Science, 4*(3), 196–202. doi: 10.1016/j.jcbs.2015.07.001

Twohig, M. P., Woidneck, M. R., & Crosby, J. M. (2013). Newer generations of CBT for anxiety disorders. In G. Simos & S. G. Hofmann (Eds.), *CBT for Anxiety Disorders* (pp. 225–250). Hoboken, NJ: John Wiley & Sons, Ltd.

Verdellen, C. W. J., Keijsers, G. P. J., Cath, D. C., & Hoogduin, C. A. L. (2004). Exposure with response prevention versus habit reversal in Tourettes's syndrome: A controlled study. *Behaviour Research and Therapy, 42*(5), 501–511. doi: 10.1016/S0005-7967(03)00154-2

Wolpe, J. (1961). The systematic desensitization treatment of neuroses. *Journal of Nervous and Mental Disease, 132,* 189–203.

# CHAPTER 9

# Incorporating Affective Science into ACT to Treat Highly Self-Critical and Shame-Prone Clients

Jason B. Luoma

Jenna T. LeJeune

*Portland Psychotherapy Clinic, Research, & Training Center*

## Overview

Research over the past three decades has shown that frequent and intense shame is related to a wide variety of problems in social and psychological functioning, including depression, PTSD, substance misuse, borderline personality, eating disorders, and suicide attempts (Cibich, Woodyatt, & Wenzel, 2016; Luoma & Platt, 2015). Furthermore, one of the problematic functions of shame is its attempts to protect the perceived fragile or "bad" self, which frequently result in social withdrawal and avoidance behaviors (Tangney, Stuewig, & Mashek, 2007), further exacerbating the social isolation and feelings of being small, helpless, or cut off that often accompany shame. Thus, interventions that target shame offer broad, transdiagnostic implications.

ACT is well suited to address broad-reaching and transdiagnostic processes of suffering such as shame. However, behavior analysis and contextual behavioral science lack a thorough basic analysis of emotion, particularly shame. Thus, we sought answers in the literature on affective science, most centrally, polyvagal theory (Porges, 2011) and related research on the role of the vagus nerve as a primary physiological conduit for modulating social engagement (Lynch, 2018). As such, this chapter offers an overview of an ACT-based intervention that incorporates findings from affective science, including basic and applied research on shame and affiliative emotions, to offer a more comprehensive approach to treating chronic shame and self-criticism.

## A Functional Evolutionary Model of Shame

Our ACT-based intervention is rooted in the idea that humans are fundamentally social creatures who are evolutionarily adapted to live in close, intimate contact with other humans. For the last two million years, we evolved primarily in small bands, typically of thirty to fifty individuals, and we are evolutionarily adapted to that context. As a result, humans' baseline state is social (Beckes & Coan, 2011), and we do not function well outside of safe, caring connections with others. Without having at least one other person we are close to, we typically function quite poorly (Lynch, 2018). For example, research on loneliness shows that feeling emotionally (not necessarily physically) separated from other people has profound effects on both mental and physical health (Hawkley & Cacioppo, 2010).

For our ancient ancestors, being part of a tribe was essential for survival. Those who got kicked out died. As a result, we evolved to be highly attuned to cues that could signal potential rejection and ostracism. Our brains continue to treat social exclusion as if it were a potentially life-threatening event, with social ostracism activating many of the same brain regions as physical pain (Eisenberger & Lieberman, 2004). As a result, we are evolutionarily prepared to be anxious in social contexts and are biased toward perceiving the social signals from others as disapproving and threatening, especially if those social signals are ambiguous. For example, neutral facial expressions are often interpreted as hostile or angry (Butler et al., 2003).

Shame evolved to warn people against behaviors that might threaten their tribe (and thus might get them ostracized) and, when activated, involves a sense that one's tribal membership is either threatened or has been lost. Shame thereby threatens our sense of belonging—we feel different from others, cut off, or otherwise unacceptable as social beings. Those who are easily or chronically threatened with shame states will find that their basic sense of belonging in the world and with others feels tenuous, weak, or nonexistent.

## Potential Prosocial Functions of Shame

Although shame is arguably one of the most painful emotions humans experience and is often perceived to be exclusively negative and problematic in the clinical literature, a functional evolutionary model of emotion suggests a more nuanced and contextually sensitive perspective on the functions of shame. Specifically, shame is thought to have evolved to regulate behavior relating to the maintenance of important group norms and moral guidelines and alert people to threats to belongingness (Keltner, Young, & Buswell, 1997; Lynch, 2018). Shame can occur in response to situations wherein a person perceives themself as failing to conform to important moral guidelines, social norms, or standards (Leach & Cidam, 2015) and, as such, can sometimes motivate attempts to repair a more positive social image through cooperative behavior (Declerck, Boone, &

Kiyonari, 2014), attempts at self-improvement (Lickel, Kushlev, Savalei, Matta, & Schmader, 2014), or prosocial behavior (de Hooge, Breugelmans, & Zeelenberg, 2008).

Shame also has signaling functions that, when the emotion is expressed in a manner appropriate to context, can elicit sympathy and cooperation from others (Keltner et al., 1997). Essentially, if people can see a way to repair a more positive sense of self, they will engage in those actions, but if this does not appear available, they will fall back on behavior aimed at escaping or avoiding the painful self-criticism and affect involved in shame (Leach & Cidam, 2015). This contextually situated view of shame, versus the uniformly negative view of shame exhibited in much of the psychology literature, is more consistent with a contextual behavioral science view of behavior in which all forms of behavior can be adaptive or maladaptive, depending upon the context and the goals involved.

## Emotion Systems, Shame, and Self-Criticism

Emotions are essential in understanding how we navigate our social worlds, communicate important information to others, and influence how they respond to us. Every emotion, including shame, can be seen as being nested within larger emotion systems. To guide our intervention, we utilize the four-system model outlined in table 9.1 and explicitly educate clients about these emotion systems in the treatment. Although other theories incorporate a different number of emotion systems—for example, compassion-focused therapy (Gilbert, 2012) emphasizes three—we have found these four groupings to be particularly relevant to the treatment of chronic shame and self-criticism. The four emotion systems can be categorized into two groups: (1) those that activate the sympathetic nervous system, thus alerting and arousing the body (i.e., the threat/defensive arousal system and the reward/drive system), and (2) those that activate the parasympathetic nervous system, thus slowing and quieting the body (i.e., the shutdown system and social/safety system).

The threat/defensive arousal system is activated when a stimulus is interpreted to signal danger or potential harm, including social threat. The reward/drive system is activated when a stimulus is interpreted to signal that something pleasurable or gratifying is available or potentially available. Both these systems are linked to the sympathetic nervous system and thereby alert and arouse the body and involve catabolizing resources and expending energy. More perfectionistic clients can often find themselves alternating between activation of the threat and reward systems, evidenced in difficulty slowing down, recuperating, relaxing, or "chilling out." The result of getting stuck in threat and reward systems is that the person becomes depleted and therefore responds in a more brittle way to ongoing events. Shame is often linked to the threat system; self-criticism functions to prevent potential rejection and ostracism, but it also activates the threat system, thus keeping people stuck in a loop of heightened threat and responding to that threat in ways that further reinforce threat-based responding.

## Table 9.1. Four Emotion Systems

| Emotion Systems That Alert and Arouse the Body (Sympathetic Nervous System) | Emotion Systems That Slow and Quiet the Body (Parasympathetic Nervous System) |
|---|---|
| **Threat/defensive arousal system**<br><br>Cue<br><br>· Danger or potential harm (including social rejection or ostracism)<br><br>Action tendency<br><br>· Urge to flee or attack<br><br>Emotions<br><br>· Anxiousness, irritation, fearfulness, anger, shame | **Social/safety system**<br><br>Cue<br><br>· Safe, loved, fulfilled, protected, or otherwise part of a tribe<br><br>Action tendency<br><br>· Desire to relax, "chill out," explore, or socialize<br><br>Emotions<br><br>· Contentment, warmth, calmness, openness, curiosity |
| **Reward/drive system**<br><br>Cue<br><br>· Something pleasurable or gratifying is available<br><br>Action tendency<br><br>· Urge to approach or pursue<br><br>Emotions<br><br>· Interest, excitement, elation | **Shutdown**<br><br>Cue<br><br>· Our life is in imminent danger<br><br>Action tendency<br><br>· Urge to give up or shut down<br><br>Emotions<br><br>· Numbness, disinterest, detachment, dissociation, intense shame |

The other two emotion systems are associated with the parasympathetic nervous system and the peripheral pathways associated with the ventral and dorsal branches of the vagus nerve (Porges, 2011). The first of these systems, the shutdown system, is cued when stimuli are interpreted as indicating an immediate threat to life. This system evolved to facilitate the conservation of energy in contexts of extreme danger in which exerting energy is unlikely to have any effect. Clinically, this emotion system is most often seen in people with past experiences of trauma, abuse, neglect, or chronic threat. A shutdown response in the context of shame is often characterized by confusion, lack of ability to put words to one's experience, dissociation, intense feelings of exposure, numbness, and clear observable signs such as postural shrinkage. Teaching clients that shame is associated with both threat and shutdown is particularly helpful for clients with these more intense shame experiences, often triggered by cues linked to past abuse.

Most people who are highly self-critical and shame prone can improve a great deal if they learn how to activate the fourth emotion system—the social/safety system. These individuals often have great difficulty relaxing, particularly when with others, and may resort to more maladaptive behaviors, such as addictive or compulsive behaviors, in order to relax. Activating the social/safety system through exposure to cues that are interpreted to indicate that they are safe, loved, fulfilled, protected, or otherwise part of a "tribe" is a major focus of treatment and will be outlined more below.

## History of Treatment Development

We began this line of work in 2002 with a grant from the National Institute of Drug Abuse to develop and test an intervention targeting shame among individuals with substance use disorders. Our initial work resulted in an open trial (Luoma, Kohlenberg, Hayes, Bunting, & Rye, 2008) and a subsequent randomized controlled trial (Luoma, Kohlenberg, Hayes, & Fletcher, 2012) of a six-hour ACT-based intervention targeting internalized shame and self-stigma among those in residential treatment for substance use disorders. The randomized controlled trial included 134 participants assigned to receive either treatment as usual (TAU) or TAU with six hours of that treatment replaced by the ACT intervention. Overall, results showed that participants receiving the ACT-based treatment for shame demonstrated lower rates of substance use at a four-month follow-up compared to those who only received TAU. Of most interest to the genesis of this intervention, though, was the process by which these changes happened. In particular, those participants who had *smaller* decreases in shame from pre- to post- treatment actually had lower rates of substance use at follow-up. Overall, we concluded that there was something unsustainable or harmful about the rapid reductions in shame found in the TAU group. We drew two main conclusions from this and other early studies (Luoma et al., 2007; Luoma et al., 2012). First, shame is the primary motivational driver behind the harm from self-stigma in addiction. Second, the finding that a greater reduction in shame predicted poorer follow-up outcomes lent further support to the idea that shame can have adaptive functions in some contexts, and that in these contexts it may be effective to target acceptance of shame rather than its elimination. Ultimately this led to attempts to develop a modular transdiagnostic intervention for people experiencing high levels of shame and self-criticism.

We have developed this treatment over the past ten-plus years, including tracking outcomes and iteratively testing different methods and strategies in both group therapy and focused individual treatment for highly shame-prone and self-critical clients. Below we provide an overview of the intervention designed for individual treatment delivery. We do not describe adaptations made for our nine-session group therapy format. You can find additional information on both approaches at https://www.actwithcompassion.com.

## Description of ACT for Shame

The intervention incorporates many of the standard ACT interventions targeting psychological flexibility processes and has five overarching strategies: (1) create a shared de-blaming platform through a collaborative case (re)conceptualization process, (2) facilitate defusion from self-critical thoughts, (3) develop psychological flexibility in response to shame via exposure to shame cues in a learning context, (4) increase repertoires of self-compassion and self-kindness, and (5) develop skills in and practice building affiliative relationships.

## Collaborative Case Conceptualization Process

The collaborative case conceptualization process includes the following four elements:

1. Development of a shared functional analysis of behavior that occurs in response to shame-eliciting contexts

2. The identification of key events and relationships contributing to shame and self-criticism

3. The identification of key events and relationships involving connection, caring, and compassion

4. Assessment using standardized measures

We think of this as a *re*-conceptualization process because clients who struggle with intense self-criticism and shame typically come into therapy with firmly held beliefs about what the problem is; the "problem" as they see it is often inherently their self. They are frequently fused with a sense of self as inadequate, damaged, broken, or otherwise deeply flawed—a self that needs to be "fixed" or in some cases destroyed. As the intense self-criticism they often experience is tied to attempts to fix what the client views as the problem (i.e., this problematic or bad self), it is often precisely the client's story of what is "wrong" and what needs to be "fixed" that is keeping them stuck in self-criticism and shame. So while it is important that the client has a sense that you see the world from their perspective, it is essential that you move beyond the client's current understanding of the presenting problem and reconceptualize the nature of their struggle.

Through this collaborative case conceptualization process, the client learns to identify central relationships and situations that may be key in the development, maintenance, or acceptance of shame and self-criticism. You may discover relationships and situations that elicit shame, which will serve as the focus of future exposure and self-compassion exercises in therapy. Alternatively, you might explore compassionate relationships and experiences to help the client contact a more self-compassionate perspective in perspective-taking exercises.

The case conceptualization process can take several sessions. Few clients have much experience talking about shame, even those who have been in extensive therapy. As such, it often takes persistent and gentle focus on the part of the therapist to begin to elicit the thoughts, feelings, and other content associated with shame. The simple act of speaking about topics and thoughts that have never been said to anyone before often fosters defusion and opens up the possibility for more flexible perspective taking and self-compassion. If shame is like a festering wound, then talking about it is like bringing light and air to the wound that allows it to heal. You can begin this opening up through the collaborative case reconceptualization process.

## Defusion from Self-Criticism

Central to this work is helping clients consider and hopefully change their relationship with themselves. For most clients who are highly self-critical and shame prone, the idea that they even *have* a relationship with themselves is a novel one. Instead, they see themselves as being like an object that is broken or damaged; it is just the "Truth" and it/they are the problem that needs to be "fixed." They do not see that the *perception* of shamefulness and brokenness is the result of a process of fusion with a self-dialogue characterized by a particular manner of relating to themselves. You can help clients begin the process of discarding this perception by building awareness of self-critical thinking.

We conceptualize self-criticism as functioning primarily as a form of experiential avoidance and fusion aimed at preventing possible rejection or ostracism. Thus, it serves to maintain patterns of avoidance that prevent effective exposure from occurring. Therefore, we target self-criticism with cognitive defusion using any relevant exercises and metaphors, especially those that involve flexible perspective taking, such as the bus metaphor or exercises that involve physicalizing.

## Exposure to Shame

The relationship between self-criticism and shame is analogous to that between anxiety and fear. In anxiety disorders, anxiety occurs when people avoid the feared stimulus, and the focus of exposure in that context is to the stimuli that evoke fear, not anxiety. Similarly, self-criticism functions to avoid social rejection and shame, and as such, in this treatment you expose clients to cues that evoke shame, not self-criticism.

Similar to other ACT conceptualizations of exposure (see chapter 8 in this volume), the main goal of exposure to shame is not the reduction of shame, but the development of more psychologically flexible responses to shame cues. Thus, you evoke shame in session and use perspective taking and other flexibility processes to help the client develop new ways of responding to themselves in this context, ideally the responses involve activation of the social/safety system. Exposure to shame cues requires purposefully eliciting shame in session, which often involves either having the client recall relevant memories (such as those involving abuse or rejection) or conducting perspective-taking exercises that elicit shame in reaction to strong self-criticism. Many of these exercises involve chair work that expands on models of two-chair work for self-criticism found in emotion-focused therapy (Elliott, Watson, Goldman, & Greenberg, 2004). In these exercises, you coach the client to move between the "critic" chair (i.e., the self-critical perspective) and the "experiencer" chair (i.e., the perspective that receives the self-criticism) while you facilitate a dialogue between the two sides.

We also use flexible perspective-taking strategies liberally to help clients develop new ways of responding to themselves. Specifically, you can foster flexibility in relation to oneself through repeated and flexible use of perspective taking involving time, place, and person frames (Luoma, Hayes, and Walser, 2017). For example, you might ask:

- (*When the client is in the experiencer chair*) "What is it like inside to hear those criticisms? Can you tell the critic how you feel when they say those things?"

- (*When the client is speaking from the critic chair*) "What is it you want for [client's name] over there?"

We also sometimes utilize a third chair to further facilitate this perspective taking. For example, we may ask the client to move to a third chair and coach them to take an outside observer perspective of their internal dialogue by saying something like the following:

- "While you are over here, can you notice that these two sides of yourself are over there (*pointing to the two empty chairs*)? Over there are two experiences that you have from time to time; one is the experience of being someone who criticizes and the other is the experience of being someone who is being criticized. But you aren't the same as those experiences. You are more like the container that can hold both of them and notice them occurring."

You might add cues with the aim of evoking more nurturing or affiliative responses. However, for many highly self-critical and shame-prone clients, their ability to engage in self-compassion is extremely limited, at least in the beginning of treatment. For these clients, asking them to take the perspective of a compassionate other, for example a friend or even the therapist, is often more effective than asking them to take a self-compassionate perspective. For example:

- "If your best friend were watching this interaction, what would they say? Would they be kind, gentle? Given this, what kind of a friend would you want to be to yourself if you got to choose?"

- "If you were me and you heard what you are saying right now, what would you be feeling?" (*often followed by therapist eventually disclosing their actual reactions*)

Alternatively, as individuals typically find it easier to extend compassion to others than to themselves, it can be helpful to tap into those established repertoires, for example:

- "Imagine your daughter were in that chair over there, feeling the way you are feeling now…how would you feel toward her?…what would you say to her?"

# Increasing Repertoires of Self-Compassion and Self-Kindness

In addition to having very limited self-compassion repertoires, people who are self-critical and shame prone have also often learned to not allow themselves to experience the openness, emotional vulnerability, and letting go of defenses associated with feeling warm and loving emotions. People might have been abused in the past when they let their guard down, they may have learned that compassion is something to mock or ridicule, or they may have simply lacked experiences of warmth in their life. Consequently, discussing experiences with compassion and kindness can paradoxically elicit a threat response, and contact with compassion and kindness cues may evoke shame, grief, and other painful emotions. Learning to treat themselves with kindness and compassion and also to let in the kindness and compassion of others is one of the main tasks of this intervention.

You can employ a range of exercises and strategies to activate more affiliative ways of responding to oneself, with a focus on activating the social/safety system. For example, you may have clients:

- Interact with themselves as a child feeling similar feelings to those felt now, as an adult

- Explore or construct chosen values toward themselves

- Write compassionate letters to themselves

- Develop plans for how to respond to self-criticism and shame when taking committed action

- Imagine the perspective of caring others, including the therapist

As loving-kindness has established effectiveness with self-criticism (Shahar et al., 2014) as well as a range of other problems (Hofmann, Grossman, & Hinton, 2011), we introduce clients to a sequence of loving-kindness meditation (LKM) practices that they are encouraged to try out. We have developed a number of strategies to help highly shame-prone clients overcome the barriers that are common in beginning LKM. These strategies include identifying phrases that are likely to be effective, identifying targets for the meditation, and offering a modified sequence of practice that begins with focusing on loving-kindness toward others.

The model transcript below illustrates how we use perspective-taking strategies to build repertoires of compassion and kindness toward oneself and activation of the social/safety system:

*Client (C):*    On nights like that I feel so incredibly lonely and empty, like I'm crawling out of my skin. I just can't stand it. The only way I can make it stop is to cut myself.

*Therapist (T):*   At those times you feel like there is nothing that will help, nothing that can soothe you. But the cutting makes it better for a little while.

C:   But then I feel so terrible after I do it because I know it's bad. I just hate being so weak and needy.

T:   So it seems like you're really stuck. In those times you feel so empty and alone, but then when you do the one thing you know how to do that helps, even for a little bit, you beat yourself up for being too weak. That's a really tough spot. How long do you think this pattern has been going on?

C:   Well, I started cutting about five years ago.

T:   And is that when the feelings of loneliness and emptiness started? Or do you remember times of feeling alone and empty before that? (*While the self-injury is the current solution, the pain the client is trying to solve through the self-injury likely goes back well before that.*)

C:   Oh no, I've felt that way since I was a little kid. But I did other things then, like I'd overeat or when I was really young I remember curling up under the covers in my bed and pretending that I was in a make-believe world.

T:   And how old were you then, when you'd be under the covers trying to escape to another world? (*The therapist is seeking to contact a specific, vivid image that can be used to facilitate the perspective taking and make the exercise more experiential.*)

C:   I don't know, maybe six or seven.

T:   Wow, so you've been suffering with this for a really long time. I'm wondering if you'd be willing to do a brief exercise with me so we can maybe see what's happening from another perspective?

C:   Sure.

T:   Okay. If you're willing, can you close your eyes for me? (*Client closes her eyes.*) Notice the feeling of your feet on the floor. Just follow the natural rhythm of your breath breathing itself, in and out. (*Therapist leads the client through a brief centering exercise.*) Now I want you to imagine that you're there on your bed in your childhood bedroom and you are your six-year-old self. Look down at your hands and notice what they look like. See what you're wearing as your six-year-old you. Feel your hair. Notice the bedding that is on your bed and what it feels like to sit on the bed. Is it hard or soft? What does it smell like in that room? What does the light look like? And see if you can hear any sounds that are going on there around you as you sit there on your bed. Are you there? Can you picture it? (*The therapist is using first-person and present-tense terms to coach the client to adopt the perspective of being the young child.*)

C:    Yes.

T:    Okay, now see if you can feel what it feels like to be this six-year-old and be so alone. You don't know what to do, you're only six. And here you are, this little first grader on this bed, in her room, all alone and feeling very empty and scared. What does it feel like to be this little girl?

C:    I feel really overwhelmed and scared.

T:    Yes. And you just want to hide under the covers and escape to your make-believe world. (*Client nods.*) Okay, so now I want you to imagine that you are standing outside your childhood house but you are the age you're at now. You're wearing what you're wearing now and you are just as you are now. You start walking into your house and you go to the bedroom you had as a child. You open the door, and you see this little six-year-old girl who looks exactly like you. You can tell she's scared and overwhelmed. She looks like she has been crying. Notice what it feels like to look at this little girl, this little first grader. How do you feel when you look at her?

C:    I feel sad for her. I want to go give her a hug.

T:    Okay, go do that. See what it feels like to go to this little scared, overwhelmed girl who is so lonely and give her a hug.

C:    It feels right.

T:    Yes, it does feel right. Okay, now you're hugging the little girl and imagine that she just kind of disappears into your chest. She becomes part of you again. Because she is a part of you. You're holding her in your heart. And now, you can notice your feet back on the floor again here. Notice your body in the chair. You can picture in your mind's eye what you will see when you open your eyes and whenever you are ready, you can open your eyes.

This is a somewhat truncated version of the exercise, which can take anywhere from about ten minutes to most of a session. However, it demonstrates how utilizing perspective-taking strategies can help build repertoires of self-compassion and self-kindness that are often severely lacking in those who experience chronic self-criticism and shame.

## Building Affiliative Relationships

In addition to working on the clients' *intrapersonal* relationships to themselves and developing new patterns of self-to-self relating, as is common in most compassion-based interventions, this intervention also directly targets the *interpersonal* relationships that can either exacerbate and maintain the cycle of shame or, alternatively, be a curative force in the individual's life. Unfortunately, shame and self-criticism often contribute to interpersonal behaviors that can trigger rejection and ostracism from others. For example, the low levels of self-disclosure found in many people who are highly self-critical can make it difficult for them to feel close to others, even someone they have known for many years (e.g., a spouse). As a result, they may feel chronically lonely. Chronic feelings of loneliness and ostracism make shame all the more likely and threatening. In addition, it is difficult for clients to maintain kind patterns of relating to themselves in the absence of others who show that they care about and value them.

Thus, an additional goal of therapy is developing interpersonal responses that signal more affiliative intentions and result in others' liking the client and wanting to be closer to them. If the client tends to do things that make others want to distance from or attack them, then you may focus on helping the client learn to interact with you in ways that elicit compassionate feelings and desires to affiliate with the client. You can then coach the client on how to bring what they are learning with you into their other relationships. Alternatively, you may develop action plans with the client to learn and practice the skills necessary to develop the kinds of relationships they need so that they have at least one person in their life with whom they feel close. Any ACT methods that relate to values and committed action in relationships may be employed to this end. In addition, we have found that focusing on developing skills related to social signaling, forgiveness, and how to accept interpersonal feedback—material we have adapted from radically open dialectical behavior therapy (Lynch, 2018)—has been very useful in helping these clients develop and maintain more satisfying, intimate, and nurturing relationships.

## Research Support

A range of pilot data supports the adaptation of ACT to work with shame and related problems like self-stigma and self-criticism (Luoma & Platt, 2015), though data on the particular adaptations described above are currently limited to pilot data on the group application (Luoma, LeJeune, & Platt, 2017). In addition to the open trial and randomized trial for self-stigma and shame already reviewed above, a handful of other studies examine how ACT might be applied to these topics. A study comparing a one-day ACT workshop to treatment as usual (TAU) for people seeking to maintain their weight loss showed that the ACT intervention resulted in reduced self-stigma, lower body mass, and improved quality of life compared to TAU (Lillis, Hayes, Bunting, & Masuda, 2009). A multiple baseline study using ACT to reduce internalized homophobia found that six to ten sessions focused on this topic resulted in large reductions in internalized homophobia, reduced distress related to sexuality, and decreases in self-stigmatizing thoughts about same-sex sexual attraction (Yadavaia & Hayes, 2012). Using a combination of ACT and compassion-focused therapy, Skinta, Lezama, Wells, and Dilley (2014) addressed self-stigma related to HIV in five HIV-positive men, with HIV-related stigma and psychological flexibility showing improvements at posttreatment. Finally, using a randomized design, a six-hour ACT workshop targeting self-compassion was compared to a waitlist for people screened to have low self-compassion (which is associated strongly with high self-criticism). The ACT treatment resulted in greater improvements, compared to the control, in distress-related variables, self-compassion, psychological flexibility, self-criticism, and positive affect, among other variables (Yadavaia, Hayes, & Vilardaga, 2014). In sum, while results are preliminary, it appears that ACT is a promising approach to self-stigma, self-criticism, and shame.

## Future Directions

Research is necessary at multiple levels to test the ideas presented in this chapter. Outcome research is needed to examine the size of the effect of this intervention on shame and self-criticism and to investigate how much targeting these difficulties affects other difficulties that are not directly targeted. Mediational and process of change studies are needed to test some of the theorized mechanisms of action, such as whether changes in the social safety responding—particularly the activity of the ventral vagal complex and the vagal nerve pathways—mediate treatment outcomes. In addition, component tests would be useful, for example, testing whether the specific version of LKM suggested for this population is more helpful than a standard LKM sequence.

Our hope is that the ideas presented in this chapter will spur further developments in scientific research and guide therapists so that people stuck in the pain and isolation of shame can find their way to kindness and compassion within themselves and a sense of belonging with others.

## References

Beckes, L., & Coan, J. A. (2011). Social baseline theory: The role of social proximity in emotion and economy of action. *Social and Personality Psychology Compass, 5*(12), 976–988.

Butler, E. A., Egloff, B., Wilhelm, F. H., Smith, N. C., Erickson, E. A., & Gross, J. J. (2003). The social consequences of expressive suppression. *Emotion, 3*(1), 48–67.

Cibich, M., Woodyatt, L., & Wenzel, M. (2016). Moving beyond "shame is bad": How a functional emotion *can* become problematic. *Social and Personality Psychology Compass, 10*(9), 471–483.

Declerck, C. H., Boone, C., & Kiyonari, T. (2014). No place to hide: When shame causes proselfs to cooperate. *The Journal of Social Psychology, 154*(1), 74–88.

de Hooge, I. E., Breugelmans, S. M., & Zeelenberg, M. (2008). Not so ugly after all: When shame acts as a commitment device. *Journal of Personality and Social Psychology, 95*(4), 933–943.

Eisenberger, N. I., & Lieberman, M. D. (2004). Why rejection hurts: A common neural alarm system for physical and social pain. *Trends in cognitive sciences, 8*(7), 294–300.

Elliott, R., Watson, J. C., Goldman, R. N., & Greenberg, L. S. (2004). *Learning emotion-focused therapy: The process-experiential approach to change.* Washington, DC: American Psychological Association.

Gilbert, P. (2012). Compassion-focused therapy. In W. Dryden (Ed.), *Cognitive Behaviour Therapies* (pp. 140–165). London, UK: Sage.

Hawkley, L. C., & Cacioppo, J. T. (2010). Loneliness matters: A theoretical and empirical review of consequences and mechanisms. *Annals of Behavioral Medicine, 40*(2), 218–227.

Hofmann, S. G., Grossman, P., & Hinton, D. E. (2011). Loving-kindness and compassion meditation: Potential for psychological interventions. *Clinical Psychology Review, 31*(7), 1126–1132.

Keltner, D., Young, R. C., & Buswell, B. N. (1997). Appeasement in human emotion, social practice, and personality. *Aggressive Behavior, 23*(5), 359–374.

Leach, C. W., & Cidam, A. (2015). When is shame linked to constructive approach orientation? A meta-analysis. *Journal of Personality and Social Psychology, 109*(6), 983–1002.

Lickel, B., Kushlev, K., Savalei, V., Matta, S., & Schmader, T. (2014). Shame and the motivation to change the self. *Emotion, 14*(6), 1049–1061.

Lillis, J., Hayes, S. C., Bunting, K., & Masuda, A. (2009). Teaching acceptance and mindfulness to improve the lives of the obese: A preliminary test of a theoretical model. *Annals of Behavioral Medicine, 37*(1), 58–69.

Luoma, J. B., Hayes, S. C., & Walser, R. D. (2017). *Learning ACT: An acceptance and commitment therapy skills training manual for therapists* (2nd ed.). Oakland, CA: New Harbinger.

Luoma, J. B., Kohlenberg, B. S., Hayes, S. C., Bunting, K., & Rye, A. K. (2008). Reducing self-stigma in substance abuse through acceptance and commitment therapy: Model, manual development, and pilot outcomes. *Addiction Research & Theory, 16*(2), 149–165.

Luoma, J. B., Kohlenberg, B. S., Hayes, S. C., & Fletcher, L. B. (2012). Slow and steady wins the race: A randomized clinical trial of acceptance and commitment therapy targeting shame in substance use disorders. *Journal of Consulting and Clinical Psychology, 80*, 43–53.

Luoma, J.B., LeJeune, J., & Platt, M. (2017). *Big heart, open wide: Overview and pilot data on a novel group therapy for people who are highly self-critical and shame prone.* Paper presentation at the Annual Conference of the Association for Contextual Behavioral Science, Sevilla, Spain.

Luoma, J. B., & Platt, M. G. (2015). Shame, self-criticism, self-stigma, and compassion in acceptance and commitment therapy. *Current Opinion in Psychology, 2*, 97–101.

Luoma, J. B., Twohig, M. P., Waltz, T., Hayes, S. C., Roget, N., Padilla, M., & Fisher, G. (2007). An investigation of stigma in individuals receiving treatment for substance abuse. *Addictive Behaviors, 32*(7), 1331–1346.

Lynch, T. R. (2018). *Radically open dialectical behavior therapy: Theory and practice for treating disorders of overcontrol.* Oakland, CA: New Harbinger.

Porges, S. W. (2011). *The polyvagal theory: Neurophysiological foundations of emotions, attachment, communication, and self-regulation (Norton Series on Interpersonal Neurobiology).* New York, NY: W. W. Norton & Company.

Shahar, B., Szsepsenwol, O., Zilcha-Mano, S., Haim, N., Zamir, O., Levi-Yeshuvi, S., & Levit-Binnun, N. (2014). A wait-list randomized controlled trial of loving-kindness meditation programme for self-criticism. *Clinical Psychology and Psychotherapy, 22*(4), 346–356.

Skinta, M. D., Lezama, M., Wells, G., & Dilley, J. W. (2014). Acceptance and compassion-based group therapy to reduce HIV stigma. *Cognitive and Behavioral Practice, 22*(4), 481–490.

Tangney, J. P., Stuewig, J., & Mashek, D. J. (2007). Moral emotions and moral behavior. *Annual Review of Psychology, 58*, 345–372.

Yadavaia, J. E., & Hayes, S. C. (2012). Acceptance and commitment therapy for self-stigma around sexual orientation: A multiple baseline evaluation. *Cognitive and Behavioral Practice, 19*(4), 545–559.

Yadavaia, J. E., Hayes, S. C., & Vilardaga, R. (2014). Using acceptance and commitment therapy to increase self-compassion: A randomized controlled trial. *Journal of Contextual Behavioral Science, 3*, 248–257.

# SECTION THREE

# Innovations with Targeted Populations and Problems

# CHAPTER 10

# Innovations in Applying ACT Strategies for Obesity and Physical Activity

## Jason Lillis
*The Miriam Hospital/Brown Medical School*

## Diane H. Dallal
*Drexel University*

## Evan M. Forman
*Drexel University*

## Overview

Obesity is one of the leading causes of preventable morbidity and mortality worldwide. More than two-thirds of US adults are overweight or obese (Flegal, Carroll, Kit, & Ogden, 2012), which poses significant health risks. Related to this, habitual moderate- to vigorous-intensity physical activity (MVPA) provides significant and wide-ranging health benefits (Haskell et al., 2007; Penedo & Dahn, 2005; Poirier et al., 2006; Reiner, Niermann, Jekauc, & Woll, 2013) and is a key factor in long-term weight control (Jakicic & Otto, 2005; Swift, Johannsen, Lavie, Earnest, & Church, 2014). However, it is estimated that only 5% of US adults meet recommended levels of physical activity when measured objectively in bouts of at least eight to ten minutes (Troiano et al., 2008).

Gold standard comprehensive behavioral interventions seek to modify eating and exercise behavior through the use of goal setting (reduced-calorie diet, increased physical activity); self-monitoring of weight, calorie intake, and physical activity minutes; environmental change strategies; problem-solving techniques; and cognitive change interventions. Standard behavioral interventions result in weight loss of roughly 7% of initial body weight (Brownell & Jeffery, 1987; Knowler et al., 2002; Wadden, Butryn, & Wilson, 2007; Wilson, 1994), producing clinically important health benefits (Espeland et al., 2007; Knowler et al., 2002), even in adults who have already acquired obesity-related illness (Dombrowski, Avenell, & Sniehotta, 2010). However, studies show that patients regain one-third to one-half of lost weight in the first year following treatment, and by three to five years posttreatment, 80% of patients have returned to or exceeded their pretreatment weight (Anderson, Konz, Frederich, & Wood, 2001; Barte et al., 2010; Jeffery et al., 2000; Perri, 1998). Furthermore, standard behavioral interventions typically include only two to three sessions on physical activity strategies (Lillis & Wing, 2014), and impact on MVPA is modest, typically falling well short of current minimum recommendations (150 minutes per week; Baillot et al., 2015).

We believe interventions that are based on, or incorporate, strategies from acceptance and commitment therapy (ACT; Hayes, Strosahl, & Wilson, 1999) are ideally suited to address current shortcomings in standard behavioral intervention. For example, ACT's values clarification and commitment strategies can align healthy behaviors with one's personal identity and values, which could significantly improve motivation to persist. Additionally, acceptance and defusion strategies can be used to increase tolerance of unwanted private experiences, such as hunger, loss of pleasure, and self-stigmatizing thoughts, that often accompany weight-control efforts. Finally, mindfulness can improve awareness of goals and decision making. In this chapter we describe how we have used ACT strategies to address weight control and physical activity, review the evidence for acceptance-based treatments in these areas, and discuss important future directions for research and practice.

# Description of Two Acceptance-Based Approaches

We have developed two separate but related approaches that integrate acceptance-based principles into gold standard behavioral weight loss interventions. We apply acceptance principles in both approaches to address problems such as dietary nonadherence, but we do so through different theorized mechanisms of change. The first approach, acceptance-based behavioral treatment (ABT), is a behavioral facilitation approach premised on the idea that the typical behavioral goals that make up standard behavioral treatment (e.g., weight loss, increased physical activity, decreased calorie intake, self-monitoring) are fundamentally sound. At the same time, the approach takes the view that the skill set that is part of standard behavioral treatment is not sufficient for navigating the particularities of human psychology in the modern environment. The second approach, values-based healthy living (VHL), comes from the stance that motivation to lose weight is often part of the problem when it is based on an agenda of avoidance and inflexibility. An alternative VHL approach aims at undermining a typical weight loss agenda and situating weight-management behaviors firmly in the context of valued living broadly defined.

These treatment approaches have generally implemented the format and intensity of standard behavioral weight loss methods. As such they tend to be conducted in small groups of approximately twelve to sixteen people, over the course of one year, and with sessions that begin weekly but decrease in frequency over time (i.e., fading contact design).

## Behavioral Facilitation Approach: Acceptance-Based Behavioral Treatment

As noted above, in ABT, we build upon standard behavioral weight loss interventions based on the assumption that, for many individuals, the core dietary and physical activity recommendations and behavioral strategies present in standard behavioral treatments are necessary but not sufficient to promote weight loss (Forman & Butryn, 2015). Specifically, we know that when individuals adhere to behavioral prescriptions in highly structured environments (such as a weight loss "camp"), they successfully achieve weight loss. However, outside of such environments, it becomes increasingly difficult to stick to dietary recommendations in the long term. One of the reasons for this difficulty is that humans have powerful biological predispositions toward consuming highly palatable, calorie-rich foods and staying at rest. Moreover, these predispositions operate in part outside of conscious awareness, so they often dictate our eating and physical activity decisions despite our best intentions. Of note, such tendencies to eat when food is available and to conserve energy when possible evolved because they were once adaptive for human survival. However, these predispositions are no longer adaptive in the modern Western environment, where tasty, high-calorie foods are universally available (e.g., from fast food restaurants, food trucks, corner stores), and labor-saving devices facilitate the ability to stay at rest (e.g., automobiles, online stores).

These factors make it exceedingly difficult to make and maintain the necessary behavioral changes to achieve weight loss. Therefore, we argue in the behavioral facilitation approach that specialized psychological skills (i.e., acceptance-based skills, described below) are also required to successfully negotiate our powerful inborn responses to internal (e.g., cognitive, emotional) and external (e.g., environmental) cues. In the behavioral facilitation approach, we apply acceptance-based principles to promote skills such as tolerating distress and forgoing pleasure, which facilitate adherence to behavioral change in the face of opposing drives. We also focus on helping individuals initiate and maintain motivation to engage in health behavior change. Namely, we present strategies to individuals under the framework that they must control what they can and accept what they can't.

### ABT FOR WEIGHT CONTROL

Below, we provide a necessarily brief clinical description of ABT for weight control, which, as you'll find, overlaps considerably with ABT for physical activity promotion, which we'll elaborate on later. Readers seeking a detailed description of the treatment protocol should reference the *Effective Weight Loss: An Acceptance-Based Behavioral Approach* clinician's guide (Forman & Butryn, 2016a) and client workbook (Forman & Butryn, 2016b).

The framework for ABT is "Control what you can; accept what you can't." This framework, which also serves as a useful mantra, asks clients to consider that there are many things we cannot change about weight control (e.g., the obesogenic food environment, tendency toward weight gain) and that our minds and bodies work in particular ways beyond our control (e.g., we will never be able to completely eliminate cravings for palatable foods or urges to remain sedentary). However, we ask clients to also bear in mind that we do have control over some aspects of weight control (e.g., behaviors we can choose to perform, including those that modify our immediate surroundings), and we should exert that control when possible.

**Control what you can.** ABT clinicians help clients recognize that a host of behaviors that are in their control increase the likelihood of eating healthfully and being physically active. These may include selecting the kinds of foods that we bring into the home and planning meals in advance. Other examples include putting extra portions in the freezer before sitting down for a meal, changing how we commute to work (e.g., biking versus driving), selecting what goes into our shopping carts, leaving our house keys in a gym locker on the way to work, and packing a lunch to take to work. We ask clients to identify such behaviors that are within their control and can increase the likelihood that they will eat healthfully, and to commit to engaging in those behaviors and establishing healthy behavior patterns.

**Accept what you can't.** ABT clinicians also help clients to understand that, even after exerting control over certain behaviors (e.g., through stimulus control, self-monitoring of food intake, planning ahead), many of the challenges of weight loss remain, and a willingness to accept these challenges is necessary for long-term success. In fact, we aim to build the core skill of *willingness,* or the ability to freely choose one's behaviors based on long-term values rather than on short-term impulses, cognitions, or emotions. We encourage clients to accept sensations and cognitions they cannot control, such as tiredness, anxiety, low motivation, hunger, cravings, thoughts about giving up, and thoughts that rationalize not meeting one's goals. Willingness to accept these experiences may take many forms, including experiencing a craving without acting on it, exercising despite being tired, or giving up the option of pleasure from an unhealthy food option. Someone with low willingness, for example, may be able to refrain from eating a palatable treat only if a good-tasting substitute is readily available to reduce urges, while another individual may be able to engage in exercise only when feeling energetic and refreshed. Enhancing willingness in ABT involves teaching clients strategies that fall into three major categories: acceptance, mindful decision making, and values-driven action.

We teach the principle of *acceptance* to help individuals tolerate the uncomfortable cravings, physiological sensations, emotions, and reductions in pleasure associated with healthful eating and exercise that occur during weight control. Acceptance helps clients recognize that (1) eating-related distress (e.g., urges to eat, hunger, feelings of deprivation) is highly likely to occur given the profound reach of today's obesogenic food environment, (2) attempting to avoid or suppress this distress is often ineffective and may even be counterproductive, and (3) one must be willing to engage in desired behaviors even in the face of such distress. We elicit acceptance of this distress by asking such questions as "What do we need to accept about the environment we live in that makes weight control challenging?" (e.g., the obesogenic environment, labor-saving devices that promote sedentary activity) and "What do we need to accept about how the mind and body work?" (e.g., biological predispositions, cravings for palatable foods). Willingness to accept such distress may also be enacted by asking a client to complete the Pick Up the Pen exercise. We ask clients to imagine that they feel so tired that they cannot pick up a pen. As clients imagine this, the clinician asks them to then pick up the pen and begin saying out loud, "I am too tired to pick up this pen," repeatedly. The goal of this exercise is to demonstrate that clients can have a thought or feeling without it being true and without having to act in accordance with it. Then, we ask clients for examples of weight-control behaviors that they think they cannot do, in order to test whether they may be willing to act in opposition to their thoughts.

*Mindful decision making* allows clients to become aware of and override their automatic decision making, a process that is heavily biased toward inborn preferences to consume high-calorie food and stay sedentary. In particular, we teach mindful decision making to decrease mindless eating and, instead, increase one's awareness, attention, and intention when making dietary choices. We encourage mindful decision making by having clients closely monitor their bodily reactions and feelings before, during, and after eating and exercise. Such self-monitoring helps clients attend to their cognitive and affective responses to eating and exercise. This training is unlike conventional mindful eating interventions in that its major focus is on helping clients make quite deliberate, "mindful" behavioral choices, including what foods to buy, when to start and stop eating, and when to start and stop exercising. Growing attuned to one's bodily reactions and feelings surrounding eating and exercise interrupts the automatic, unconscious influences on eating behavior that often lead to overeating and sedentary behavior. Another strategy we teach to facilitate mindful decision making is slowing down and paying deliberate attention to the mind's decision-making process in order to become more aware of what may be driving behavior. We ask clients to deliberately notice the internal cues (e.g., thoughts, feelings, urges) and external cues (e.g., sights, sounds, smells) that prompt clients to want to eat. For example, we may ask clients to imagine themselves as sports commentators reporting on every aspect of their decision-making process around eating; however, the speed of their voice has been placed on slow motion. We would then ask clients for specific examples of instances when they tend to mindlessly eat and then model an example of such sports commentary.

Finally, we emphasize the principle of *values-driven action*. We teach clients that "ordinary" or superficial forms of motivation are not enough to sustain weight-control behaviors; commitment to difficult behavioral goals requires connection to personal values that are important and meaningful enough to make the effort and sacrifice worthwhile. As such, we teach clients to identify and clarify their values (e.g., being a loving parent) and to keep these values in mind while making eating and physical activity decisions. One strategy to facilitate values-driven action is to ask clients to require that each eating decision they are contemplating comes with a corresponding up or down vote of an associated value. For example, a client out to dinner with his family who is considering ordering pizza would acknowledge explicitly to himself that doing so would be to vote "down" on the value of being a loving, present parent in the long term.

## ABT FOR PHYSICAL ACTIVITY PROMOTION

Beyond weight control, we have also applied ABT to promote physical activity. While the goal is not weight loss in this case, the perspective is identical to that described above. In other words, we teach clients that physical activity is often avoided or minimized because it involves (or is perceived to involve) less pleasurable or uncomfortable internal experiences. In order to meet physical activity goals, the client must learn how to psychologically accept experiences such as muscle fatigue, soreness, sweating, feeling hot, being out of breath, boredom, and urges to stop moving. Decisions to be active thus require a willingness to be in a less comfortable state for the sake of a valued goal. Finally, we help clients identify and clarify the specific values that connect to physical activity goals and make them worth pursuing, and we teach them how to have these values in mind when making physical activity decisions.

ABT for physical activity promotion uses the same interventions as ABT for weight loss. For instance, we teach clients the concepts of acceptance and willingness by having them assume and hold a "plank" position. During this exercise, clients observe and name each aspect of their internal experience (e.g., muscle tiredness, an urge to rest) but simultaneously choose, for a specified amount of time, to continue the plank position. We then provide clients with examples of challenging thoughts and feelings they may experience specific to physical activity, such as beginning a thirty-minute walk but, five minutes in, feeling tired and hot, and having a thought about how it would be better to walk on a cooler day. We teach clients how to make the decision in that moment to continue walking even while having these thoughts and feelings.

We also illustrate willingness by asking clients to differentiate between conditional ("only if") and conditionless ("even if") statements. Clients are taught that they can learn new skills if they are willing, by changing their "only if" types of responses (I will walk only if it is not hot outside) into "even if" statements (I will walk even if it is hot). We also use values clarification exercises (e.g., imagining what the client would wish loved ones to say about them in a eulogy) and strategies to utilize identified values in moments of decision making (e.g., imagining a sports broadcaster narrating the internal experiences that could initially be shaping a physical activity decision and then overriding these with a values-consistent choice).

## Values Facilitation Approach: Values-Based Healthy Living

In contrast to ABT for weight control, described earlier, values-based healthy living (VHL) situates ACT values work more centrally in the intervention. The primary goal of VHL is to foster behavior change consistent with one's personal values, as opposed to achieving a specified weight loss. Therefore, we aim to have clients align weight-management behaviors with their personal identity and values as much as possible. We see weight loss as a valid goal only insofar as it serves to empower values-consistent living broadly speaking. For example, losing weight can improve work performance, provide needed energy for parenting, improve intimacy, allow for continued engagement in desirable activities with friends, or improve longevity to witness family milestones. Weight loss absent connection to values is not an aim, and it follows then that weight-control behaviors do not have inherent value, but rather are valuable if they serve to increase values-consistent behavior.

We developed VHL in part because we observed that the goal of losing weight is often in itself a form of psychological inflexibility. Clients often report primarily avoidant motivations for losing weight, such as reducing self-judgment, being seen as more attractive or competent by others, and alleviating negative emotions. We believe that is at least one piece of the puzzle when considering the failure of traditional weight loss methods, as an agenda of avoidance and inflexibility, which can be effective in the short-term, is prone to being ineffective over the long term. Weight management is difficult and requires unnatural persistence, and thus individuals who are losing weight primarily to influence their thoughts and feelings (and the thoughts and feelings of others) are likely to find that (1) they did not lose "enough" weight to "fix" their thoughts and feelings, or (2) they lost the weight and still find themselves struggling to change unwanted thoughts and feelings. Either way, they lose persistence in health behaviors over time. VHL attempts to undermine an agenda of avoidance and inflexibility by deemphasizing the scale and strongly emphasizing the connection of weight-management behaviors to values-based living broadly defined.

Similar to ABT, VHL recognizes the practical challenges of the interaction between our biological tendencies and the obesogenic environment and employs similar acceptance-based strategies in order to facilitate values-consistent health behavior change.

Below, we provide a brief clinical description of VHL. Readers seeking a detailed description of the treatment protocol should reference our recent publications (Lillis, Dahl, & Weineland, 2014; Lillis et al., 2015; Lillis et al., 2016).

Although VHL and ABT overlap considerably, we focus here on the difference. The framework for VHL centers on the principle that healthy behavior change needs to be aligned with deeply held, personally identified values related broadly to a life well lived as defined by the client. Clients frequently present with avoidance-based sources of motivation (e.g., "to look better so people will like me more," "to have fewer judgments about myself," "to appease my spouse/doctor"), which are insufficient for long-term change. Therefore, VHL is primarily focused on helping clients clarify values, aligning healthy behavior change with those values, and providing skills for persisting in healthy behavior change in the face of cognitive, emotional, and physiological barriers.

VHL has been most frequently used in a traditional format, with small groups, weekly meetings, and a fading contact design. It can also be implemented following completion of behavioral weight loss in a workshop format, with one five-hour clinical, group-based, in-person meeting followed by email and phone call extended contact.

## VALUES CLARIFICATION

Our goals in values clarification are to help clients (a) identify important personal experiences, people, and accomplishments; (b) describe the personal importance and meaning of various behaviors and life outcomes; (c) understand how values can be used as guides for behavior; (d) learn how to prioritize different life domains and make adjustments to priorities when necessary; (e) identify desired qualities of action; and (f) link healthy behavior change to optimal functioning in other life domains.

Importantly, our protocol includes broader ACT work outside the context of weight and health behaviors, such as exploring, tracking, and committing to values-consistent behaviors generally in one's life. For example, a client might identify "being a caring and present mother" as a core value. We describe values metaphorically as directions, like traveling east, with behaviors moving either toward (e.g., spending time playing with a child) or away from (e.g., using social media on the phone in the presence of a child) the stated value.

After identifying broadly relevant values, we also ask clients to identify ways in which healthy behavior change can empower values-consistent behavior. For example, losing weight and increasing physical activity provides increased energy and mood regulation, which allow for sharper attentional focus and increased stamina for active participation in play sessions with children, while limiting the irritability that fuels parent-child conflict. In essence, health behaviors become not just about "losing weight" or "being healthier," but also about "being the parent I want to be." Thus, making a healthy food choice is now directly linked to an area of deep importance (parenting).

Values clarification is accomplished in a number of ways, including free writing, group brainstorming, and guided imagery exercises used to uncover core values. For example, we ask clients to imagine themselves in ten years and make note of what they would want to meaningfully accomplish, how they want to impact important individuals, and how they would have spent their time under ideal circumstances. Clients also write freely about the importance of various life domains and their own chosen qualities of action within those domains. Finally, we facilitate group discussion to help clients connect weight-control behaviors to these values domains, using questions such as "How will you be able to be different in X after losing weight?" or "How will eating healthier and exercising help you be more like X?"

## VALUES COMMITMENT

After identifying broadly relevant personal values and how they connect with health behavior changes, we then orient clients to committed actions. We teach clients how to (a) generate new goals from values, (b) set values-based goals, (c) implement values-based goals, and (d) evaluate whether their behavior is consistent with their personal values and goals. We accomplish this primarily through didactic presentation and group discussion. A key factor here, similar to ABT, is to teach clients to be mindful of behavior/value congruence. For example, before making a food choice, one might ask which food option moves them closer to their value of being a more present and engaged mother. The goal is to *increase the day-to-day satisfaction of engaging in healthy behaviors.*

We also ask clients to generate lists of "towards" and "away" behaviors with respect to a specific health value, such as "being healthy and active." Towards moves are both proximal (e.g., walking outside for thirty minutes, eating a healthy prepared lunch at work) and distal (e.g., obtaining proper walking shoes, shopping for healthy foods at the grocery store). The same is true for away moves (e.g., proximal: watching TV on the couch; eating a fast food lunch at work; distal: failing to schedule exercise time; sleeping in, which precludes preparation of a healthy lunch). We instruct clients to develop a hierarchy of commitments in various domains and generate specific goals linked to health and nonhealth values, with a focus on explicating the connection of health behaviors to desired outcomes in nonhealth domains. For example, a strong vocational value can be linked to healthy behavior change by explicating how reduced inflammation, improved mood, better sleep, increased energy, and more general stamina can empower clients to be more efficient at work, more effective interpersonally with coworkers, and better able to deal with challenges. In addition, clients identify potential barriers to engaging in values-consistent behaviors.

## ACCEPTANCE

Similar to ABT, VHL teaches acceptance-based skills to address barriers to behavior change. However, the focus of behavior change is more broad, focusing on values-consistent behavior in a variety of domains, as opposed to just weight change behaviors. Specifically, we teach clients how to (a) notice and distance themselves from problematic thoughts (e.g., *I just can't do this anymore!*), and (b) tolerate psychological discomfort (e.g., boredom, deprivation, anxiety) with the goal of increasing values-consistent behavior in the presence of psychological barriers. For example, clients learn to experience food urges as a transient state and tolerate them via food exposure. Clients bring in desired foods and interact with them (without eating) through clinician-guided exercises in order to become more aware and accepting of unpleasant sensations that arise from being in the presence of desired food. First, we direct clients to observe the food without touching it, noting the intensity of food urges, where they are located in the body, and any co-occurring cognitive experiences (e.g., *I must eat this!*). Next, we have clients pick up and interact with the food, noticing and cataloging any internal experiences they are having with regard to smell and texture. Throughout the exercise, we teach the recognition of the ebb and flow of food cravings and direct clients to track craving peaks and valleys, before ultimately discarding the food and making note of their reactions of the experience as a whole.

We also teach clients to become more aware of, and detached from, self-sabotaging thoughts, such as *I will always fail,* and unhelpful reasons for unhealthy behavior, like *I'm too tired,* as opposed to trying to change or eliminate them. We use a number of strategies, including metaphors (e.g., imagining your mind as the worst motivational speaker alive) and experiential exercises (e.g., the classic ACT metaphor Take Your Mind for a Walk; Hayes et al., 1999, pp.162–163).

## Challenges

As previously highlighted, standard behavioral treatment is organized around losing weight as the primary goal, which could conflict with acceptance-based methods if the overarching treatment goal is values-consistent living broadly defined. This can be especially true when clients state that they are refraining from values-based behavior (e.g., visiting family, going to the beach, being intimate with their partner) *until* they reach a specified goal weight or feeling state. This can be exacerbated if weighing at treatment meetings is utilized, as it can send an underlying message that scale achievement is the most important definer of treatment success. Possible solutions are to refrain from session weigh-ins and to add values-consistent behavior tracking in areas other than eating and exercise.

Another challenge is dealing with cue avoidance as a weight loss strategy. Standard treatment explicitly teaches clients to avoid unhealthy eating cues by keeping desired foods out of sight or out of the house entirely and by avoiding restaurants and eating-out scenarios as much as possible. A possible solution is incorporating desired foods into session and doing acceptance-based exposure work in addition to encouraging participation in values-based activities while practicing refraining from excessive eating of foods that would be detrimental to weight-control efforts.

Finally, acceptance-based methods may have a higher skill threshold to be administered, creating another potential obstacle. Although ultimately an empirical question, acceptance-based methods are less intuitive and unlikely to be run competently by dieticians or equivalent bachelor's level practitioners without significant training and supervision. A recent randomized controlled trial utilizing an integrated ACT treatment showed significantly better results when administered by experts (Forman et al., 2013). One possible solution is to develop protocols that are focused on a few key teachings, enabling more streamlined training methods. Another possible solution is the use of ongoing supervision by a more established and experienced ACT therapist.

## Research Support

Both ABT and VHL have proven successful in promoting weight control, with empirical support from several open trials and randomized controlled trials. In a preliminary test of ABT, researchers conducted a twelve-week open trial where participants lost an average of 8.1% of their initial weight (i.e., 7.9 kg) post-intervention and maintained weight losses (an additional 2.2% or 1.7 kg) over a six-month follow-up period (Forman, Butryn, Hoffman, & Herbert, 2009). In a full-scale randomized controlled trial (Forman et al., 2013), a year-long, group-based version of ABT was delivered in comparison to gold standard behavioral treatment for weight loss among 128 overweight individuals. Weight loss at eighteen months (i.e., six months posttreatment) was somewhat greater for those who had received ABT. Moreover, those who were highly vulnerable to the effect of eating cues in the environment (e.g., those with high levels of emotional eating, responsivity to food cues, and depression) lost considerably more weight in ABT. In a later, larger iteration of this study that included 190 overweight participants, individuals who received ABT lost considerably more weight (13.3%) than did those receiving standard treatment (9.8%; Forman et al., 2016). Additionally, findings revealed that changes in psychological acceptance and intrinsic motivation mediated, or explained, the advantages of ABT.

ABT approaches to increase physical activity have been shown to improve bouts of physical activity among college students when compared to educational approaches (Butryn, Forman, Hoffman, Shaw, & Juarascio, 2011). Additionally, ABT approaches resulted in increased minutes per week of MVPA in a sample of community adults who were trying to maintain clinically important levels of exercise (Butryn, Kerrigan, Arigo, Raggio, & Forman, 2018).

A pilot study of VHL for individuals who were overweight or obese and who recently reported weight loss compared a one-day ACT workshop to a waitlist control group. The study found that a greater percentage of ACT participants either lost or maintained weight (95% versus 70%), had greater improvements in quality of life, and had larger reductions in weight-related stigma and experiential avoidance at three-month follow-up (Lillis, Hayes, Bunting, & Masuda, 2009). A large-scale randomized clinical trial compared a VHL approach integrated with traditional behavioral weight loss to standard behavioral treatment (SBT) alone for 162 overweight and obese adults over twelve months of treatment with a fading contact design. The VHL-enhanced intervention improved long-term weight loss by attenuating regaining of weight after treatment was discontinued as compared to SBT (weight gain month 12 to 24: 4.6kg in VHL versus 7.1kg in SBT; $p = .005$) and a significantly higher proportion of participants in VHL achieved a 5% (38% versus 25%) and 10% (22% versus 12%) weight loss at twenty-four months (Lillis et al., 2016).

## Future Directions

Future research should address the following priorities: (1) identifying characteristics of individuals that predict success or nonsuccess in ACT/ABT interventions, (2) conducting component analyses to examine which components of ACT/ABT are active in which treatment contexts (weight loss, maintenance, physical activity), (3) using adaptive interventions that incorporate ACT/SBT to improve response to treatment (e.g., providing additional intervention or different components to initial nonresponders), (4) studying the training of nonpsychologist health interventionists, such as dieticians and exercise physiologists, in ACT/ABT, and (5) testing ACT/ABT in mobile and online contexts. Clinicians are successfully applying values- and acceptance-based principles to help improve weight control and physical activity, and these approaches will likely continue to improve in effectiveness as further innovations are made to address key barriers to persistence in health behavior change.

# References

Anderson, J. W., Konz, E. C., Frederich, R. C., & Wood, C. L. (2001). Long-term weight loss maintenance: A meta-analysis of US studies. *American Journal of Clinical Nutrition, 74*(5), 579–584.

Baillot, A., Romain, A. J., Boisvert-Vigneault, K., Audet, M., Baillargeon, J. P., Dionne, I. J., . . . Langlois, M. F. (2015). Effects of lifestyle interventions that include a physical activity component in class ii and iii obese individuals: A systematic review and meta-analysis. *PLoS ONE, 10*(4). doi: 10.1371/journal.pone.0119017

Barte, J. C. M., ter Bogt, N. C. W., Bogers, R. P., Teixeira, P. J., Blissmer, B., Mori, T. A., & Bemelmans, W. J. E. (2010). Maintenance of weight loss after lifestyle interventions for overweight and obesity, a systematic review. *Obesity Reviews, 11*(12), 899–906. doi: 10.1111/j.1467-789X.2010.00740.x

Brownell, K. D., & Jeffery, R. W. (1987). Improving long-term weight loss: Pushing the limits of treatment. *Behavior Therapy, 18*(4), 353–374. doi: 10.1016/s0005-7894(87)80004-7

Butryn, M. L., Forman, E., Hoffman, K., Shaw, J., & Juarascio, A. (2011). A pilot study of acceptance and commitment therapy for promotion of physical activity. *Journal of Physical Activity and Health, 8*(4), 516–522.

Butryn, M. L., Kerrigan, S., Arigo, D., Raggio, G., & Forman, E. M. (2018). Pilot test of an acceptance-based behavioral intervention to promote physical activity during weight loss maintenance. *Behavioral Medicine, 44*(1), 77–87. doi: 10.1080/08964289.2016.1170663

Dombrowski, S. U., Avenell, A., & Sniehotta, F. F. (2010). Behavioural interventions for obese adults with additional risk factors for morbidity: Systematic review of effects on behaviour, weight and disease risk factors. *Obesity Facts, 3*(6), 377–396. doi: 10.1159/000323076

Espeland, M., Pi-Sunyer, X., Blackburn, G., Brancati, F. L., Bray, G. A., Bright, R., . . . Look, A. R. G. (2007). Reduction in weight and cardiovascular disease risk factors in individuals with type 2 diabetes: One-year results of the Look AHEAD trial. *Diabetes Care, 30*(6), 1374–1383.

Flegal, K. M., Carroll, M. D., Kit, B. K., & Ogden, C. L. (2012). Prevalence of obesity and trends in the distribution of body mass index among US adults, 1999–2010. *Journal of the American Medical Association.*

Forman, E. M., & Butryn, M. L. (2015). A new look at the science of weight control: How acceptance and commitment strategies can address the challenge of self-regulation. *Appetite, 84*, 171–180.

Forman, E. M., & Butryn, M. L. (2016a). *Effective weight loss: An acceptance-based behavioral approach, clinician guide.* Oxford, UK: Oxford University Press.

Forman, E. M., & Butryn, M. L. (2016b). *Effective weight loss: An acceptance-based behavioral approach, workbook.* Oxford, UK: Oxford University Press.

Forman, E. M., Butryn, M. L., Hoffman, K. L., & Herbert, J. D. (2009). An open trial of an acceptance-based behavioral intervention for weight loss. *Cognitive and Behavioral Practice, 16*(2), 223–235.

Forman, E. M., Butryn, M. L., Juarascio, A. S., Bradley, L. E., Lowe, M. R., Herbert, J. D., & Shaw, J. A. (2013). The mind your health project: A randomized controlled trial of an innovative behavioral treatment for obesity. *Obesity, 21*(6), 1119–1126. doi: 10.1002/oby.20169

Forman, E. M., Butryn, M. L., Manasse, S. M., Crosby, R. D., Goldstein, S. P., Wyckoff, E. P., & Thomas, J. G. (2016). Acceptance-based versus standard behavioral treatment for obesity: Results from the mind your health randomized controlled trial. *Obesity, 24*(10), 2050–2056.

Haskell, W. L., Lee, I. M., Pate, R. R., Powell, K. E., Blair, S. N., Franklin, B. A., . . . Bauman, A. (2007). Physical activity and public health: Updated recommendation for adults from the American College of Sports Medicine and the American Heart Association. *Medicine and Science in Sports and Exercise, 39*(8), 1423–1434. doi: 10.1249/mss.0b013e3180616b27

Hayes, S. C., Strosahl, K., & Wilson, K. G. (1999). *Acceptance and commitment therapy: An experiential approach to behavior change.* New York, NY: The Guilford Press.

Jakicic, J. M., & Otto, A. D. (2005). Physical activity considerations for the treatment and prevention of obesity. *American Journal of Clinical Nutrition, 82*(1), 226S–229S.

Jeffery, R. W., Drewnowski, A., Epstein, L. H., Stunkard, A. J., Wilson, G. T., Wing, R. R., & Hill, D. R. (2000). Long-term maintenance of weight loss: Current status. *Health Psychology, 19*(1), 5–16. doi: 10.1037//0278-6133.19.Suppl1.5

Knowler, W. C., Barrett-Connor, E., Fowler, S. E., Hamman, R. F., Lachin, J. M., Walker, E. A., . . . Diabetes Prevention Program Research Group. (2002). Reduction in the incidence of type 2 diabetes with lifestyle intervention or metformin. *New England Journal of Medicine, 346*(6), 393–403.

Lillis, J., Dahl, J., & Weineland, S. M. (2014). *The diet trap: Feed your psychological needs & end the weight loss struggle using acceptance and commitment therapy.* Oakland, CA: New Harbinger Publications.

Lillis, J., Hayes, S. C., Bunting, K., & Masuda, A. (2009). Teaching acceptance and mindfulness to improve the lives of the obese: A preliminary test of a theoretical model. *Annals of Behavioral Medicine, 37,* 58–69.

Lillis, J., Niemeier, H. M., Ross, K. M., Thomas, J. G., Leahey, T., Unick, J., . . . Wing, R. R. (2015). Weight loss intervention for individuals with high internal disinhibition: Design of the Acceptance Based Behavioral Intervention (ABBI) randomized controlled trial. *BMC Psychology, 3*(1), 17.

Lillis, J., Niemeier, H. M., Thomas, J. G., Unick, J., Ross, K. M., Leahey, T. M., . . . Wing, R. R. (2016). A randomized trial of an acceptance-based behavioral intervention for weight loss in people with high internal disinhibition. *Obesity, 24*(12), 2509–2514. doi: 10.1002/oby.21680

Lillis, J., & Wing, R. (2014). Behavioral strategies in weight management. In R. F. Kushner & D. H. Bessen (Eds.), *Treatment of the obese patient* (2nd ed.). New York, NY: Springer Science.

Penedo, F. J., & Dahn, J. R. (2005). Exercise and well-being: A review of mental and physical health benefits associated with physical activity. *Current Opinion in Psychiatry, 18*(2), 189–193. doi: 10.1097/00001504-200503000-00013

Perri, M. G. (1998). The maintenance of treatment effects in the long-term management of obesity. *Clinical Psychology-Science and Practice, 5*(4), 526–543.

Poirier, P., Giles, T. D., Bray, G. A., Hong, Y. L., Stern, J. S., Pi-Sunyer, F. X., & Eckel, R. H. (2006). Obesity and cardiovascular disease: Pathophysiology, evaluation, and effect of weight loss. An update of the 1997 American Heart Association Scientific Statement on obesity and heart disease from the Obesity Committee of the Council on Nutrition, Physical Activity, and Metabolism. *Circulation, 113*(6), 898–918. doi: 10.1161/circulationaha.106.171016

Reiner, M., Niermann, C., Jekauc, D., & Woll, A. (2013). Long-term health benefits of physical activity: A systematic review of longitudinal studies. *BMC Public Health, 13,* 813. doi: 10.1186/1471-2458-13-813

Swift, D. L., Johannsen, N. M., Lavie, C. J., Earnest, C. P., & Church, T. S. (2014). The role of exercise and physical activity in weight loss and maintenance. *Progress in Cardiovascular Diseases, 56*(4), 441–447. doi: 10.1016/j.pcad.2013.09.012

Troiano, R. P., Berrigan, D., Dodd, K. W., Masse, L. C., Tilert, T., & McDowell, M. (2008). Physical activity in the United States measured by accelerometer. *Medicine and Science in Sports and Exercise, 40*(1), 181–188. doi: 10.1249/mss.0b013e31815a51b3

Wadden, T. A., Butryn, M. L., & Wilson, C. (2007). Lifestyle modification for the management of obesity. *Gastroenterology, 132*(6), 2226–2238. doi: 10.1053/j.gastro.2007.03.051

Wilson, G. T. (1994). Behavioral treatment of obesity: Thirty years and counting. *Advances in Behaviour Research and Therapy, 16*(1), 31–75. doi: 10.1016/0146-6402(94)90002-7

# CHAPTER 11

# Contextual Behavioral Science Interventions to Address Racism

Jonathan W. Kanter
*University of Washington*

Mariah Corey
*University of Washington*

Katherine Manbeck
*University of Washington*

Daniel C. Rosen
*Bastyr University*

## Overview

Contextual behavioral science (CBS) asserts that we, clinicians and researchers, are not qualitatively different from those we seek to help, that psychological processes are normative. Simply put, we are all in the same boat.

When those psychological processes cause suffering in others rather than in ourselves, however, it is easy to distance ourselves from them and push them away. Perhaps nowhere is this difficulty more apparent than in the case of racism (e.g., Hayes, Niccolls, Masuda, & Rye, 2002). Yet an emerging science and new language of racism, including terms such as *implicit bias* (Greenwald, Poehlman, Uhlmann, & Banaji, 2009), *colorblindness* (Neville, Awad, Brooks, Flores, & Bluemel, 2013), and *microaggressions* (Sue et al., 2007), has turned our understanding of racism toward racist processes that occur normatively in society. To effectively deal with and ultimately move past them, we cannot and should not push them away.

We believe CBS has much to offer with respect to understanding and intervening on racism. Our fundamental assumption, that the processes underlying racial bias are normative, is consistent with trends in the field and facilitates empathic validation of those harmed by the processes *and* empathic joining with those doing (and committed to reducing) the harm. Our priority to define variables as human actions-in-context provides clear mechanisms to help those engaging in harmful behaviors who want to change (Hayes, Barnes-Holmes, & Wilson, 2012). Furthermore, we have developed evidence-based techniques for how to stay engaged in change efforts even when one feels bad (Levin, Hildebrandt, Lillis, & Hayes, 2012), which is inevitable for most White people as the dialogue on racism increasingly turns toward the self.

In this chapter, we describe our recent efforts to develop a CBS understanding of, and interventions that target, the processes implicated by the new language of racism. Consistent with trends from the diversity training industry, in which most anti-racism interventions are single-day workshops for groups of individuals defined by a common organizational or situational context (e.g., employees, health professionals, students), the innovations we describe are public-facing, workshop interventions. Also consistent with these trends, we center our work on the concept of microaggressions. We place less emphasis on the construct of implicit bias (a social-cognitive construct defined as non-conscious, automatic negative attitudes and stereotypes that influence cognition, emotion, and behavior), as our CBS view prioritizes constructs defined as actions-in-context that may be more amenable to intervention. CBS values point us toward not only decreasing microaggressions, but increasing valued, prosocial outcomes, including increased expressions of accurate empathy and increased social connectedness in interracial relationships.

## Understanding Microaggressions

Microaggressions are "brief and commonplace daily verbal, behavioral, and environmental indignities, whether intentional or unintentional, that communicate hostile, derogatory, or negative racial slights and insults to the target person or group" (Sue et al., 2007; p. 273). Research indicates these experiences are significant and distressing for people of color, and—while the content of this chapter is focused primarily on microaggressions committed by White people against Black people—microaggressions are experienced across various minoritized groups and settings (reviewed in Wong et al., 2014). We believe that the analyses and interventions offered herein are applicable wherever oppression and discrimination between groups defined by differential power and privilege occurs.

Our research has explored the phenomena of microaggressive likelihood in White people and reached an important conclusion: the more likely a White person is to engage in microaggressions, the more likely they are to score higher on other, validated indicators of racism (Kanter et al., 2017). This finding establishes that people of color are justified in claiming that microaggressions are experienced as acts of racism and are not easily dismissed as innocent, innocuous behaviors (cf., Lilienfeld, 2017).

# Four Psychological Processes Underlying Microaggressions

Our research also has explored the psychological processes underlying the delivery of microaggressions. Although not exhaustive, we have uncovered four related but distinct types of microaggressions: colorblindness, objectifying, explicit negative attitudes and stereotypes, and anxiety and avoidance (for a full description, see Kanter et al., 2018).

## COLORBLINDNESS

The most common microaggression is *racial colorblindness,* involving a denial of race and racism on the basis that one should ignore interracial divisions and view each person solely as an individual, or find common humanity rather than focus on any differences between us (Neville et al., 2013). Racial colorblindness, while strongly correlated with wanting to believe the world is fair and unbiased, produces denials of racism and a host of biased behaviors (Neville et al., 2013). Examples of colorblind microaggressions include "I don't think of Black people as Black," "Everyone suffers, not just Black people," and "All lives matter."

Through our CBS lens, colorblindness is rule-governed behavior: a coherent verbal network of "if-then" rules (e.g., "If I do not notice race, then I cannot be a racist"). This is learned during development in response to social norms and adopted by many White people, who then follow these rules as a way of adhering to social norms (e.g., pliance) and appearing nonracist/nondiscriminatory. In this way, colorblind verbal behavior is likely reinforcing in the short term, provided one determines that one is following the rule regardless of the actual impact on people of color. These rules may be particularly problematic in some cultural contexts, such as Evangelical faith communities, where colorblindness is seen as an expression of God's will and pliance with such rules likely is very strong (Emerson & Smith, 2000).

## OBJECTIFYING

The second microaggression is *objectifying,* in which a White person's attention is hooked by the racially distinct features of a person of color, and their responding is dominated by these cues. Objectifying microaggressions include "Where are you from?" (e.g., to an Asian person) and "Can I touch your hair?" (e.g., to a Black woman with African-style hair braiding).

Objectifying is evidence for the futility of colorblindness. In fact, the hooking of attention to the racial features of one's partner in an interaction happens automatically, in as little as a tenth of a second (Ito & Urland, 2003). These features serve as powerful contextual cues for behavior whether one likes it or not, and behavior that is directed by such differences is often experienced as disconnecting and harmful by the recipient independent of the actor's intent.

## EXPLICIT NEGATIVE ATTITUDES AND STEREOTYPES

The third microaggression involves expressions of explicit negative attitudes and stereotypes about people of color that lack empathy and perspective taking. Examples include "A lot of minorities are too sensitive," "Black people should work harder to fit in to our society," and, in response to a young Black male wearing a hoodie, "That guy looks like a thug and can't be trusted."

These problematic responses are deeply ingrained and tied to core features of identity for many White people. For White children, "White" as an ingroup category, tied to the self, forms quickly (Bar-Haim, Ziv, Lamy, & Hodes, 2006), in a frame of opposition with "Black" as an outgroup. Most White children are raised in all-White or mostly all-White environments without significant exposure to Black communities through which one actually comes to know and understand the lived experiences of Black people (Cox, Navarro-Rivera, & Jones, 2016 ). This, combined with near constant exposure to negative racial stereotypes and images in media and society, produces a likelihood to negatively stereotype Black people and difficulties with empathy and perspective taking.

From the perspective of relational frame theory, such relational learning can be quite arbitrary, allowing for largely inaccurate and harmful distinctions to be learned. The result for White people is a complex, relational network of negative associations with "Black," such as lazy, dangerous, and unintelligent, with automatic functional transformations that produce a host of aversive emotional responses. All of this learning is essentially arbitrary in that it is learned through multiple direct and indirect verbal relations rather than direct experiential contact with Black people (Hayes et al., 2002).

## ANXIETY AND AVOIDANCE

Intergroup anxiety is defined as an overarching, cross-situational anxiety response to an outgroup when anticipating or engaging in intergroup interactions (Stephan & Stephan, 1985). When negative stereotypes are cued by contextual features, such as a Black person's face, functional transformations occur and racial anxiety is elicited. In this context, racial anxiety is seemingly inevitable and normative. We know, for example, that when interacting with Black people, most White people demonstrate hyperactivations of the amygdala (Chekroud, Everett, Bridge, & Hewstone, 2014).

Microaggressions related to racial anxiety and avoidance include crossing the street to avoid walking past a Black man, leaving the room during a conversation about race, and staying quiet in an interaction with a Black person to avoid saying something offensive. Aversive emotions, such as shame and guilt related to being privileged, may also be experienced by White people during interracial interactions, and result in similar avoidance behavior.

In these moments, while racial anxiety is automatically elicited, our context also supports the emergence of strong, aversive responses to these elicited responses. White people learn that being anxious around Black people is bad and itself an indicator of being racist, leading to more anxiety or shame in response to the original feeling of anxiety.

The situation seems perfectly poised to generate experiential avoidance (EA) around race or racial issues. Similar to how EA is generally defined (Hayes, Wilson, Gifford, & Follette, 1996, p. 1154), we may define race-based EA as an unwillingness to contact private experiences stimulated by racial differences, such as negative racial stereotypes and anxieties, and taking steps to avoid these experiences and the contexts that occasion them. Thus, some White people may avoid dialogues on race or racism, spaces in which interactions with people of color are likely, and any suggestions that they may be, or appear to be, racist. Like general EA, we suggest that race-based EA persists because it is negatively reinforcing in the short term (i.e., aversive experiences are temporarily reduced or avoided), even though it is damaging with respect to living a value-driven life (i.e., becoming less racist) in the long term because doing so requires at times openness to aversive experiences. Colorblindness can be seen as an explicit articulation of rules for race-based EA.

Microaggressions are the primary behavioral manifestations of multiple forms of racism in interracial relationships, including colorblindness, negative stereotypes, objectifying, and fear and avoidance. As discussed next, addressing microaggressions requires addressing fundamental psychological processes that fuel racism, including issues of identity, perspective taking, defusion, acceptance, values, and committed action.

# Description of CBS Interventions to Address Racism

In this section, we describe how several CBS intervention techniques may be adapted and employed in the context of interventions to reduce microaggressions. For example, these techniques may be applied in "diversity trainings" in organizational settings, collegiate workshops designed to educate students about bias and help diverse students connect with each other, or workshops for medical providers or mental health practitioners to improve their cultural competence and culturally responsive care.

## Addressing Negative Racial Thoughts and Feelings with ACT Processes

Diversity workshops often try to raise awareness of negative stereotypes and encourage people to eliminate them. In our view, this is a recipe for race-based EA and likely will lead to suppression attempts that will backfire, making these thoughts more frequent and more behaviorally impactful (Wegner, Schneider, Carter, & White, 1987).

CBS suggests that the problem is not the occurrence of negative racial thoughts and anxieties, it is how they dominate and control one's behavior. Thus, our trainings focus on contact with the present moment, defusion, and acceptance. Rather than trying to disrupt, change, avoid, or suppress race-based thoughts or anxieties, attendees learn to experience them more gently, with distance, and with less functional impact on behavior, thereby increasing psychological flexibility to access values-based actions and reduce harm to others.

## THE CASE OF WILLARD

Consider a hypothetical workshop participant, Willard, a seventy-year-old retired liberal White man. In his youth, he was active during the original civil rights movement and attended protests and rallies, but he has done little to keep pace with changes in the language and science of racism. He donates money to nonprofit social justice organizations and considers himself nonracist. But Willard has had very little genuine exposure to and intimate connections with people of color, and when interacting, he becomes anxious that he will say something racist. This at times paradoxically causes him to do the very thing he is scared of.

For example, Willard recently met a Black man, Mike, at the library. He immediately noticed that he was Black and had a minor anxiety response. If the response could have been given words, it would have said, "He's Black! Don't say anything racist!" This immediately (and paradoxically) cued relational networks related to Blackness and racism, and—although they were talking about the weather—at a pause in the conversation, Willard quickly changed the subject, mentioned that he noticed Mike was Black, and asked what he thought of the local team's playoff chances in the upcoming football season. Willard's behavior in this interaction had features related to objectifying, avoidance, and explicit negative stereotypes, and might have been experienced as microaggressive by Mike.

## CONTACT, DEFUSION, AND ACCEPTANCE INTERVENTIONS

A variety of well-known contact, defusion, and acceptance techniques can be adapted and implemented in the context of anti-racism interventions for people like Willard. These techniques include mindfulness techniques that encourage Willard to explore negative racial thoughts and racial anxiety in an accepting and nonjudgmental fashion (e.g., Leaves on a Stream, the Physicalizing exercise); metaphors that encourage Willard to practice interacting with negative racial thoughts and feelings "from a distance" or in ways that disrupt normative contexts that support tight relations between thoughts, feelings, and behavior; and word repetition tasks that produce extinction, through repeated exposure, of the behavioral functions that co-occur with negative racial thoughts.

For example, in our workshops we employ a simple mindfulness exercise to help attendees better notice the negative racial thoughts and anxieties that might occur outside of awareness and control behavior when interacting with a person of color. First, we lead participants through a traditional eyes-closed mindfulness meditation that facilitates nonjudgmental contact with the present moment without a focus on racial themes (e.g., notice the sound of the facilitator's voice, the feel of one's body in one's clothes, one's breathing, heartbeat, any thoughts and feelings that arise). Then, maintaining gentle, mindful contact with the present moment, we introduce racial themes. Participants open their eyes and view a series of pictures of people of color in different settings (e.g., in a law office, on a street corner in front of a corner grocery, at a police station). We encourage participants to notice, with more exquisite attention and openness than is typical, any negative stereotypical thoughts and emotions that may be elicited by the pictures, as follows:

> See if you can nonjudgmentally observe how your mind and body react to this image, with the same open, gentle attention that you gave to my voice, your breath, your heartbeat, your other thoughts and feelings. Perhaps you can observe these reactions gently, with compassion and acceptance…

After the exercise, attendees discuss how it might apply in their lives. Willard would be encouraged to consider that such an exercise, if practiced over time, could produce new contact, defusion, and acceptance skills that could improve his ability to connect with people of other races, without relying on stereotypes.

## Addressing Colorblindness with ACT Processes

Self-as-context and perspective-taking interventions may be broadly applicable to address racist processes. Here we discuss how they are employed to reduce colorblindness and increase empathy for people of color.

### THE CASE OF KYM

Consider another hypothetical workshop participant, Kym, a thirty-seven-year-old White church-going woman, mother of three, who considers herself nonracist. She was taught by her parents and her church that "we are all God's children," and she tries to treat everyone equally. Kym believes deeply that the world is just and fair and racial colorblindness is one of her core values. However, she gets visibly anxious when interacting with people of color and makes efforts to either end these interactions quickly or avoid them altogether. She is not aware of when she makes Black people nervous as a result of her own visible anxiety (e.g., she does not make eye contact, blinks frequently, hesitates before speaking) or that her behavior is experienced as unfriendly and untrustworthy by most Black people.

### SELF-AS-CONTEXT INTERVENTIONS

We all typically hold our conceptualized selves tightly and feel threatened when the content is threatened. Thus, Kym may need to strengthen self-as-context, which involves developing a more expansive and flexible *observer self* that is less tied to specific content (e.g., through the chessboard metaphor, or the Observer Self exercise).

For example, we might employ a simple "Who Are You?" exercise with Kym. In this exercise, we ask participants the question "Who are you?" and participants respond by completing the sentence "I am…" After each response, we reply, "Thank you," pause, and then ask, "Who are you?" again. This is repeated to the point that participants begin to experience their responses as somewhat arbitrary and to discover that their experience of self is more flexible than expected. The goal is to meaningfully experience "I just am" as the ultimate response.

After a generic version of this exercise, we may tailor it to content that is specific to colorblindness. We encourage participants to provide "I am…" responses in the context of their nonracist beliefs and values, such as "I am colorblind," and "I am nonracist," alternating with "I am…" responses that are the opposite, such as "I am occasionally anxious and uncomfortable around people of color" and "I am not able to fully ignore the color of a person's skin." Discussion centers on how these responses are incompatible at the level of self-as-content but not incompatible at the level of self-as-context. For example, we might employ a chessboard metaphor with colorblind "I am…" responses represented by the white pieces and the alternative "I am…" responses represented by the black pieces, and encourage the participants to view themselves as the board that holds all the pieces rather than fusing solely with either the black or white pieces.

## PERSPECTIVE-TAKING INTERVENTIONS

Helping Kym to develop a more flexible experience of self, centered on self-as-context, also facilitates opening to the possibility that the world is presently unjust and unfair, promoting empathy and perspective taking toward people of color (rather than colorblindness and denial of racism). A stronger sense of self-as-context loosens rigidly held oppositions such as "I" and "you" and "White" and "Black" and allows participants to develop a more diffuse sense of self in which they experience commonalities without colorblindness, and differences without stereotyping.

We developed a "What if It Was All True?" meditation/contemplation to encourage this process. After a brief orienting to breath, body, and the present moment, the contemplation begins with an invitation to consider something so personally painful that participants instinctively push it away and try not to think about it:

> We all have things in our lives that are too hard to think about. Maybe your child has real challenges. Maybe your partner is cheating on you. Maybe you or a loved one is sick and scared that you may not get to live as long as you planned, and hoped. If you are willing, conjure up a life experience that is too hard to usually think about. You can't stand it. Consider this possibility—this might happen. This might be true. Maybe life will not work out the way we hope, the way we dream. Maybe life is unfair.

We encourage participants to approach this content from the perspective of an observing self, not pushing the content away but holding it lightly, safely, with defusion, acceptance, and compassion. Then, the content of the contemplation shifts to consider a hypothetical Black woman, Michelle. We ask participants to explore how they may be similar to Michelle:

> …You probably both share a desire to make a difference in this world, you both have hopes and dreams about life, you both care deeply about your families, your friends…

Then, we encourage participants to explore the fundamental, hard-to-accept racism in Michelle's life:

> What if, at a fundamental level, her life experience has been so unfair, and so unlikely to be fixed, that it is actually physically uncomfortable for you to really let yourself feel it? What if her experience, the racism in her life, is as bad as the thing you don't want to believe about your life, because you want to believe the world is fair? That things will work out. But it already exists for her—it is already true.

We provide specific examples, with vivid details, to contemplate, and the contemplation ends with the question:

> What if Michelle wants to connect with you about these aspects of her life, but she is not sure if she can tell you these things, because she isn't sure you will believe her? She is scared you will react in a colorblind or dismissive way. But what if it is all true?

Overall, the goal is to help participants recognize that colorblindness has been an important aspect of identity in the past, and to experience that aspect of identity as content that can be explored and observed safely, without fusion, from a distance. Then, with this flexibility, participants explore the painful feelings of being a White person living in a fundamentally unfair, racist society with acceptance. Through these processes, we aim to improve empathy and perspective taking around the lived experiences of people of color.

## Facilitating Social Connectedness with ACT Processes

The exercises described above are not an end in themselves, but function in the service of improved, value-directed behavior in interracial interactions. Most diversity trainings involve racially mixed groups of participants who attend for different reasons, but both White and Black participants typically enter with shared values around authentic, compassionate interactions and connections. We can harness these values by encouraging workshop participants to engage in courageous committed actions during the workshop that facilitate authentic, intimate interracial exchanges and the development of social connectedness, which produces more positive outgroup attitudes among both Black and White people (Davies, Tropp, Aron, Pettigrew, & Wright, 2011).

To facilitate social connectedness, we invite participants to engage in a sequence of interracial interpersonal exercises. These exercises integrate intergroup contact theory (Pettigrew & Tropp, 2006) with the dominant psychological science model on how intimate relationships form, known as the interpersonal process model (Reis & Shaver, 1988), and with techniques developed within functional analytic psychotherapy (Holman, Kanter, Tsai, & Kohlenberg, 2017).

## INTERGROUP CONTACT

Research on intergroup contact theory demonstrates that contact between groups promotes positive attitudes and reduces prejudice between those groups (Pettigrew & Tropp, 2006). This is the case especially under certain conditions such as when the contact is structured, involves exchanges that both parties see as equitable, and is explicitly supported by the authorities of the larger institution of which participants are members.

## THE INTERPERSONAL PROCESS MODEL

In diversity workshops, however, people of color are typically asked to vulnerably disclose experiences of racism, and White people are asked to listen passively. If the goal is to increase empathy and genuine social connectedness rather than simply teach, this is problematic. Such exchanges are not equitable. According to the interpersonal process model, equity in close and trusting relationships involves *reciprocity: both* members of the dyad must engage in vulnerable self-disclosure (Sprecher, Treger, Wondra, Hilaire, & Wallpe, 2013), and *both* must respond well to each other's disclosures (Reis & Clark, 2013). When this full process occurs, closeness develops. This is found across multiple relationship types including interracial relationships (e.g., Davies et al., 2011). According to this research, if White participants join in the vulnerable disclosures rather than simply bearing witness, Black participants will feel more trust and safety, and White participants will feel more empathy and have improved perspective taking.

## FUNCTIONAL ANALYTIC PSYCHOTHERAPY

To facilitate reciprocal intimate exchanges in our workshops, we have modified exercises used to train therapists in functional analytic psychotherapy (FAP). FAP is a CBS intervention that centers clinician responses to clients' vulnerable behaviors using structured experiential exercises (Kanter, Tsai, Holman, & Koerner, 2013), with applications for racially diverse dyads (Miller, Williams, Wetterneck, Kanter, & Tsai, 2015). In one FAP training exercise, participants form small groups (e.g., four to six individuals) and take turns briefly (e.g., six minutes) sharing their personal life histories, while the others in the group listen and respond with empathy and understanding. For diversity workshops, we try to have equal numbers of Black and White participants in each small group.

In ACT terms, participation in these exercises may be framed as opportunities for valued, committed actions around developing cross-group connections. Participants, when telling their life histories, are encouraged to share not simply autobiographical facts, but more vulnerable events that have shaped who they are, in the service of connecting. Other possible exercises include sharing stories of grief, betrayal, and discrimination, as well as positive memories.

All of the previous workshop learning comes into play in these connection exercises. We encourage participants to pay exquisite attention, with defusion and acceptance, to any distracting thoughts and emotions that might arise, while either sharing or listening. We prompt them not to push away these reactions, but to simply notice and gently focus on their values and goals for the interaction, which are to share their story and to respond with understanding, validation, and caring.

### OTHER COMMITTED ACTIONS

Other FAP and ACT exercises can be adapted to this setting to engage in values work and committed actions around connecting with diverse others. For example, toward the end of the workshop, we encourage participants to develop and share personal "mission statements." In this exercise, participants consider their personal values that were operative during the workshop: *Why are they here? What is important to them about this work?* Then, they consider their experiences and what they learned over the course of the workshop, and write these down in a personally meaningful way. Next, they consider and write down specific actions that they can take, consistent with their values and what they learned during the workshop, that would keep these changes alive in their lives.

Following this, participants volunteer to stand up and share what they are committing to. Finally, participants share specific appreciations for others with whom they have interacted during the workshop. These appreciations can be particularly meaningful moments where participants are able to celebrate and extend the connections they have made. As a whole, we focus on identifying, reinforcing, and generalizing actions that can be sustained outside of the workshop setting.

# Challenges

The psychological processes described throughout this chapter arise during the workshop experience, making it challenging for both participants and facilitators. For many White people, the work is hard and the natural tendency is to distance from it. White people may engage in microaggressions and exhibit fear, avoidance, defensiveness, denial, and outright hostility (Sue, Rivera, Capodilupo, Lin, & Torino, 2010), and White facilitators are not immune to these impulses in charged workshop moments. Black people may enter the workshop fearing the worst from the White people involved, and these fears are often justified. Furthermore, viewing racist behavior as resulting from normative psychological processes may be difficult to tolerate for people of color who are understandably offended by these behaviors. It is unreasonably burdensome to ask them for compassion and empathy in moments in which offenses are experienced.

In our experience, it takes a lot of clinical skill, humility, self-awareness, and sensitivity to navigate this terrain, and we do not always get it right. Facilitators try for a balance that feels equitable, which reinforces successive approximations in White participants, giving them space to grow and not be perfect, while appreciating the needs of the people of color to have their experiences heard and validated and to have even subtle microaggressions addressed. White facilitators face the concern that, by overly validating the anxieties and difficulties that White participants have around engaging with this material, they may be validating their fragility (Diangelo, 2011) or "whitewashing" racism. Black facilitators may worry that their priority to be direct about racism and privilege may result in negative evaluations (Boatright-Horowitz & Soeung, 2009) and being negatively stereotyped as hostile or aggressive by White participants. Facilitators must lean in to these challenges, do the work themselves, and be prepared to engage defusion, acceptance, and self-as-context processes as an ongoing stream, applied to both the self and others, as the workshop proceeds.

## Research Support

Several converging lines of evidence provide empirical support for the ideas in this chapter. First, many of the ACT component processes discussed herein have received empirical support in lab-based, experimental studies (Levin et al., 2012). While none of this research has targeted racism specifically, if the CBS conceptualization is correct, the processes should apply across multiple domains and the generalization to racist content is reasonable.

Several studies have investigated the effects of interventions that combine ACT components on various forms of prejudice, including counselors' prejudice toward their clients with substance abuse issues (Hayes et al., 2004) and racial and ethnic prejudice among college students (Lillis & Hayes, 2007). These studies show positive effects on relevant processes, such as decreased distress associated with prejudiced thoughts and increased psychological flexibility, and these effects may be strongest among those who enter the interventions with lower levels of psychological flexibility to begin with (Masuda et al., 2007).

We recently evaluated our workshop approach in several studies. These included a six-hour intervention to increase connectedness among Black and White undergraduate students, a six-hour intervention to improve White medical student provider empathy in interactions with Black patients, and a five-hour intervention to decrease political polarization and improve connectedness between conservative and liberal college students

(Manbeck et al., 2018). In all cases, improved connectedness between workshop participants was evident immediately after the interventions and one month later (when measured). We found that these changes generalized as improved attitudes toward the outgroup in general for the college-student racism workshop but not for the college-student politics workshop. Furthermore, when measured, we found a decreased likelihood of microaggressing among White participants after the interventions.

## Future Directions

We find this work to be challenging, innovative, and meaningful. It is challenging and innovative in that the basic CBS frame, to not try to get rid of negative racial thoughts and feelings, may be misinterpreted as an acceptance of racism itself. To clarify, we do not believe that racism should be tolerated, but that acceptance of private events is required in the service of long-term behavioral, and even societal, change. Both our personal experiences, and our scientific findings, give us optimism. Our hope, and the meaning in the work, is that this CBS approach to intervening on racism may decrease harmful racist behaviors by White people and improve quality of life and other important outcomes for people of color and White people alike.

There are many future directions to explore. Much as lab-based experimental component process research has facilitated the development and evaluation of the full ACT model (Levin et al., 2012), similar research on the component processes described in this chapter may clarify and maximize the effectiveness of intervention packages in this specific context. Workshop interventions that combine component processes may be evaluated with larger samples, in different contexts, and against different comparison conditions.

A major focus of our work, race-based EA, has not been adequately explored as an intervention target by mainstream researchers, and it is not often a focus of mainstream interventions. We think this is a mistake, likely a function of lack of knowledge of most diversity trainers and researchers about anxiety and avoidance. CBS researchers and clinicians, who have a more nuanced and sophisticated understanding of EA, need to step up, have their voices heard, and conduct this important work. Without addressing this key functional process, interventions are likely to be less effective, and race-based EA evoked during workshops may disrupt other learning.

To date, only a handful of CBS intervention researchers have turned toward racism as a topic of interest. We hope this changes and that this chapter facilitates this change in some small way. Racism is one of humanity's greatest challenges, and CBS, from its philosophical roots, scientific methods, and community values, is poised to make great contributions.

# References

Bar-Haim, Y., Ziv, T., Lamy, D., & Hodes, R. M. (2006). Nature and nurture in own-race face processing. *Psychological Science, 17*(2), 158–163. doi: 10.1111/j.1467-9280.2006.01679.x

Boatright-Horowitz, S., & Soeung, S. (2009). Teaching white privilege to white students can mean saying good-bye to positive student evaluations. *American Psychologist, 64*(6), 574–575. doi: 10.1037/a0016593

Chekroud, A. M., Everett, J. A. C., Bridge, H., & Hewstone, M. (2014). A review of neuroimaging studies of race-related prejudice: Does amygdala response reflect threat? *Frontiers in Human Neuroscience, 8*(179). doi: 10.3389/fnhum.2014.00179

Cox, D., Navarro-Rivera, J., & Jones, R. P. (2016). Race, religion, and political affiliation of Americans' core social networks. *Public Religion Research Institute.* https://www.prri.org/research/poll-race-religion-politics-americans-social-networks/

Davies, K., Tropp, A., Aron, A., Pettigrew, T. F., & Wright, F. C. (2011). Cross-group friendships and intergroup attitudes. *Personality and Social Psychology Review, 15*(4), 332–351. doi: 10.1177/1088868311411103

Diangelo, R. (2011). White fragility. *International Journal of Critical Pedagogy, 3*(3), 54–70.

Emerson, M., & Smith, C. (2000). *Divided by faith: Evangelical religion and the problem of race in America.* Oxford, England: University Press.

Greenwald, A. G., Poehlman, T., Uhlmann, E., & Banaji, M. R. (2009). Understanding and using the Implicit Association Test: III. Meta-analysis of predictive validity. *Journal of Personality and Social Psychology, 97*, 17–41.

Hayes, S. C., Barnes-Holmes, D., & Wilson, K. G. (2012). Contextual behavioral science: Creating a science more adequate to the challenge of the human condition. *Journal of Contextual Behavioral Science, 1*, 1–16.

Hayes. S. C., Bissett, R., Roget, N., Padilla, M., Kohlenberg, B. S., Fisher, G., . . . Niccolls, R. (2004). The impact of acceptance and commitment training and multicultural training on the stigmatizing attitudes and professional burnout of substance abuse counselors. *Behavior Therapy, 35*, 821–835. doi: 10.1016/S0005-7894(04)80022-4

Hayes, S. C., Niccolls, R., Masuda, A., & Rye, A. K. (2002). Prejudice, terrorism, and behavior therapy. *Cognitive and Behavioral Practice, 9*, 296–301.

Hayes, S. C., Wilson, K., Gifford, E., & Follette, V. (1996). Experimental avoidance and behavioral disorders: A functional dimensional approach to diagnosis and treatment. *Journal of Consulting and Clinical Psychology, 64*(6), 1152–1168. doi: 10.1037/0022-006X.64.6.1152

Holman, G., Kanter, J. W., Tsai, M., & Kohlenberg, R. (2017). *Functional Analytic Psychotherapy made simple: A practical guide to therapeutic relationships.* Oakland, CA: New Harbinger Publications.

Ito, T., & Urland, G. (2003). Race and gender on the brain: Electrocortical measures of attention to the race and gender of multiply categorizable individuals. *Journal of Personality and Social Psychology, 85*(4), 616–626. doi: 10.1037/0022-3514.85.4.616

Kanter, J. W., Rosen, D. C., Manbeck, K. E., Kuczynski, A. M., Corey, M. D., & Branstetter, H. M. L. (2018). Using contextual-behavioral science to understand racism and bias. In M. T. Williams, D. C. Rosen, & J. W. Kanter (Eds.), *Eliminating race-based mental health disparities: How to address inequities and barriers in clinical practice.* Oakland, CA: New Harbinger.

Kanter, J. W., Tsai, M., Holman, G., & Koerner, K. (2013). Preliminary data from a randomized pilot study of web-based functional analytic psychotherapy therapist training. *Psychotherapy, 50*(2), 248–255. doi: 10.1037/a0029814

Kanter, J. W., Williams, M. T., Kuczynski, A. M., Manbeck, K., Debreaux, M., & Rosen, D. (2017). A preliminary report on the relationship between microaggressions against Black people and racism among White college students. *Race and Social Problems, 9*(4), 291–299. doi: 10.1007/s12552-017-9214-0

Levin, M. E., Hildebrandt, M. J., Lillis, J., & Hayes, S. C. (2012). The impact of treatment components suggested by the psychological flexibility model: A meta-analysis of laboratory-based component studies. *Behavior Therapy, 43*(4), 741–756. doi: 10.1016/j.beth.2012.05.003

Lilienfeld, S. (2017). Microaggressions: Strong claims, inadequate evidence. *Perspectives on Psychological Science, 12*(1), 138–169. doi: 10.1177/1745691616659391

Lillis, J., & Hayes, S. C. (2007). Applying acceptance, mindfulness, and values to the reduction of prejudice: A pilot study. *Behavior Modification, 38,* 389–411.

Manbeck, K. E., Kanter, J. W., Kuczynski, A. M., Fine, L., Corey, M. D., & Maitland, D. W. M. (2018). Improving relations among conservatives and liberals on a college campus: A preliminary trial of a contextual-behavioral intervention. Unpublished manuscript: University of Washington.

Masuda, A., Hayes, S. C., Fletcher, L. B., Seignourel, P. J., Bunting, K., Herbst, S. A., Twohig, M. P., & Lillis, J. (2007). The impact of acceptance and commitment therapy versus education on stigma toward people with psychological disorders. *Behaviour Research and Therapy, 44,* 2764–2772.

Miller, A., Williams, M. T., Wetterneck, C. T., Kanter, J. W., & Tsai, M. (2015). Using Functional Analytic Psychotherapy to improve awareness and connection in racially diverse client-therapist dyads. *The Behavior Therapist, 38,* 150–156.

Neville, H. A., Awad, G. H., Brooks, J .E., Flores, M. P., & Bluemel, J. (2013). Color-blind racial ideology theory, training, and measurement implications in psychology. *American Psychologist, 68*(6), 455–466. doi: 10.1037/a0033282

Pettigrew, T. F., & Tropp, L. R. (2006). A meta-analytic test of intergroup contact theory. *Journal of Personality and Social Psychology, 90*(5), 751–783.

Reis, H. T., & Clark, M. S. (2013). Responsiveness. In J. Simpson & L. Campbell (Eds.), *The Oxford Handbook of Close Relationships* (pp. 400–423). New York, NY: Oxford University Press. doi: 10.1093/oxfordhb/9780195398694.013.0018

Reis, H. T., & Shaver, P. (1988). *Intimacy as an interpersonal process.* In S. Duck, D. F. Hay, S. E. Hobfoll, W. Ickes, & B. M. Montgomery (Eds.), *Handbook of personal relationships: Theory, research and interventions* (pp. 367–389). Oxford, England: John Wiley & Sons.

Sprecher, S., Treger, T., Wondra, J. D., Hilaire, N., & Wallpe, K. (2013). Taking turns: Reciprocal self-disclosure promotes liking in initial interactions. *Journal of Experimental Social Psychology, 49*(5), 860–866. doi: 10.1016/j.jesp.2013.03.017

Stephan, W. G., & Stephan, C. W. (1985). Intergroup anxiety. *Journal of Social Issues, 41*(3), 157–175. doi: 10.1111/j.1540-4560.1985.tb01134.x

Sue, D. W., Capodilupo, C., Torino, G., Bucceri, J. M., Holder, A. M. B., Nadal, K. L., & Esquilin, M. E. (2007). Racial microaggressions in everyday life: Implications for clinical practice. *American Psychologist, 62,* 271–286.

Sue, D. W., Rivera, D. P., Capodilupo, C. M., Lin, A., & Torino, G. C. (2010). Racial dialogues and White trainee fears: Implications for education and training. *Cultural Diversity and Ethnic Minority Psychology, 16*(2), 206–13. doi: 10.1037/a0016112

Wegner, D. M., Schneider, D. J., Carter, S., III, & White, L. (1987). Paradoxical effects of thought suppression. *Journal of Personality and Social Psychology, 53,* 409–418.

Wong, G., Derthick, A. O., David, E. J. R., Saw, A., & Okazaki, S. (2014). The what, the why, and the how: A review of racial microaggressions research in psychology. *Race and Social Problems, 6*(2), 181–200. doi: 10.1007/s12552-013-9107-9

# CHAPTER 12

# Innovations in ACT for Cancer

## Joanna J. Arch

*Department of Psychology and Neuroscience, University of Colorado Boulder*
*Division of Cancer Prevention and Control, University of Colorado Cancer Center*

## Joel N. Fishbein

*Department of Psychology and Neuroscience, University of Colorado Boulder*

## Alex Kirk

*Department of Psychology and Neuroscience, University of Colorado Boulder*

## Overview

Imagine you feel out of sorts and visit your doctor. Imagine the worried look on their face when they refer you to an oncologist to check you out. Imagine stepping into an oncology office for the first time and, not long thereafter, receiving a diagnosis of cancer—a word you connect to death. Within days, you are marked to receive terrifying things: surgery that removes a major body part; radiation that forces you into uncomfortable positions and risks triggering secondary cancers; and chemotherapy that exhausts you, causes brain fogginess, and leaves you feeling ill and unable to work or care for others fully. This is many people's experience of cancer. After this, if you are lucky, you are declared to have "no evidence of disease." But the possibility of cancer recurrence lurks in the background.

Amazingly, many people treated for cancer do surprisingly well. However, a sizable minority of cancer survivors bear an enduring mental health burden from cancer, and a decade after treatment, cancer survivors report elevated anxiety relative to controls (Mitchell, Ferguson, Gill, Paul, & Symonds, 2013). Individuals with metastatic solid tumor cancer, which is often incurable, face eventual death from cancer along with, in many cases, uncomfortable physical symptoms and unending treatment.

From the perspective of what ACT offers, why does all of this matter? First, encountering a potentially life-limiting disease can force people to reevaluate what matters most in the midst of changed realities, eliciting existential or spiritual concerns that most behavioral approaches are not designed to address. In contrast, ACT's focus on values and committed action helps people to explore what matters most and to align their actions and decisions with their values. Though notable meaning-focused interventions for people with metastatic cancer exist (e.g., Breitbart et al., 2012), none directly target avoidance of unwanted internal experience—unwanted feelings, thoughts, memories, physical sensations (Angiola & Bowen, 2013)—a process shown to underlie psychological suffering and the psychological disorders most common among cancer patients (Hayes, Wilson, Gifford, Follette, & Strosahl, 1996). In contrast, ACT aims to increase a sense of life meaning *and* reduce internal avoidance, representing a new and potentially more powerful intervention for adults with cancer.

Second, fears of cancer recurrence or death from metastatic cancer can be realistic, and such medical outcomes are often uncontrollable. Traditional cognitive behavioral therapy (CBT) for elevated fear and anxiety is designed to address fears about relatively harmless objects and situations such as panic symptoms, talking with strangers, or reimagining a trauma that has already happened. But the consequence of dying from cancer can lead to outcomes such as orphaning one's children, destroying a family's sole source of income, or abandoning a disabled loved one who has nobody else to care for them— seemingly unbearable possibilities that do not reflect the minimal-harm situations that CBT is designed to evaluate. In the face of circumstances that cannot be controlled or wholly influenced, ACT *allows for* distress, helping people to acknowledge and sit with pain and loss *and* to live meaningfully. Similarly, ACT's acceptance stance may be particularly suitable for addressing other common realities of cancer, including learning to live with missing, disfigured, or damaged body parts; facing the reality that your cancer can recur or progress at any time; or feeling so overwhelmed by treatment-related fatigue that you cannot get out of bed in the morning. In summary, ACT offers a compelling approach to address the emotional and physical circumstances faced by many individuals with cancer.

## Description of ACT in Practice with Cancer Patients

One challenge of applying ACT in cancer populations is addressing the diverse experiences of people with cancer. For example, patients with curable disease may have difficulty adjusting back into a daily routine after active treatment ends and living with the uncertainty of whether cancer will return. In contrast, patients with incurable disease may struggle to decide what to do with their remaining time and to make decisions about end-of-life care. To address this diversity, we use two central, well-known ACT tools across our interventions for cancer populations: the Passengers on the Bus metaphor (Hayes, Strosahl, & Wilson, 1999) and the matrix (Polk & Schoendorff, 2014, and chapter 6 in this book), which we call the "Compass" to align with the Passengers metaphor. We supplement these classic tools with tailored exercises and adapt the format, length, and content of the intervention to the particular population.

In two case studies we illustrate how ACT can be flexibly applied, using individual and group intervention formats, to address the needs of different cancer populations.

# Case Study 1: Individual ACT for Early-Stage Breast Cancer

Donna is a sixty-four-year-old divorced woman who works part time. She has two adult children, three young grandchildren, and a close group of friends. Donna was diagnosed with curable, early-stage breast cancer and was treated with surgery, chemotherapy, and radiation. After these treatments, she began a multiyear course of daily anti-hormonal medication to prevent cancer recurrence.

Now that intensive cancer treatment was over, Donna, like a sizable minority of patients, felt upset. She remained easily fatigued and mentally foggy, and worried constantly about whether her cancer would come back. This worry caused her to lose sleep, and consequently she was often tired at work. Donna also feared that people saw her as "deformed" because she had a mastectomy and had decided not to undergo reconstruction surgery. She found that spending time with her grandchildren and friends and volunteering at the library, activities she had cherished before treatment, were less enjoyable now. While engaging in these activities, she ruminated on how "things will never be the same as they were before cancer."

Donna was referred to our service a few months after completing treatment for cancer because she sought help with anxiety about her life not being back to normal, fears about cancer recurrence, and difficulty reengaging in activities she had enjoyed before treatment. During intake, the therapist learned that Donna was experiencing fusion with thoughts that her life should be the same as it was before cancer. Her language indicated low levels of acceptance and compassion toward her new life circumstances; for example, she said that "things *should* go back to how they were before" and "I'm too deformed to be in public." She engaged in avoidance, such as declining phone calls and friends' invitations. When with family or friends, she struggled to stay present with them. At intake, the therapist administered the Valued Living Questionnaire (VLQ; Wilson, Sandoz, Kitchens, & Roberts, 2010) and learned that her most important valued domains included family, friends, work, and volunteering, but that she was only modestly engaging in behaviors consistent with her values.

To help Donna reengage with her life and address her pattern of experiential avoidance, the therapist began Session 1 by using the Compass to explore her values, committed actions, and barriers to committed action. The therapist drew the Compass and helped Donna to distinguish between internal and external behaviors and how they moved her toward and away from her values (see figure 12.1). Of note, "away moves" also function to move people away from uncomfortable internal experiences. In our work among people with cancer, however, we choose to emphasize the "moving away from values" function of away moves because we have found that both patients and providers more readily relate to this framing. We have also found it valuable to reorient the Compass to place values and toward moves on the top, and internal struggles and away moves on the bottom. This allows us to draw lines connecting values with specific toward moves linked to them, and connecting sources of internal struggles with specific away moves linked to them.

One theme of this session was recognizing the costs of "away moves":

*Therapist:*    Sometimes what moves us away from our values is what we experience on the inside—like fears, worries, beliefs, or feelings. Do those ever get in the way for you?

*Donna:*    (*long pause*) Hmm, that's a tough question.

*Therapist:*    How so?

*Donna:*    Well, when I have thoughts about how hard the past year has been, I just try to push them away. They make me sad.

*Therapist:*    That's a really common thing that people do. Do those thoughts come up when you're trying to do things that are important to you, like being with your grandkids?

*Donna:*    Almost always. I think that's part of my problem. I can't enjoy being with my grandkids when all I can think about is how different they are now, and how much I missed!

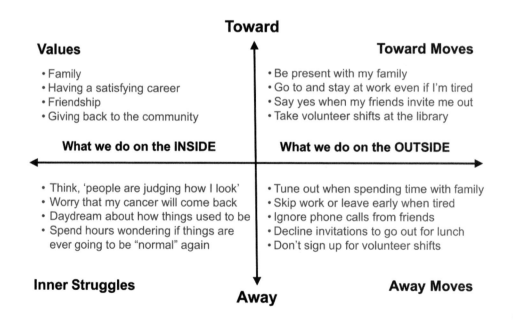

**Figure 12.1.** Donna's Compass.

In Sessions 2 through 4, the therapist focused on increasing Donna's willingness to contact the present moment and open up to her internal experience, using guided mindfulness exercises in session and as homework to help Donna notice and accept, rather than push away, challenging thoughts. One especially effective in-session strategy was acting out the Tug-of-War ACT metaphor (Hayes et al., 1999) using a sturdy scarf. Donna noticed that pulling on the scarf was much like her experience with thoughts about people judging her appearance: "The more I try to yank those thoughts out of my mind, the harder they yank back. It's exhausting." The therapist also had Donna track her daily toward and away moves, with an attitude of compassion for her away moves. Donna then committed to practicing small toward moves each week that she had previously avoided and to troubleshoot barriers to doing them.

Building on the tug-of-war metaphor, in Session 5, the therapist introduced the Passengers On The Bus metaphor to practice acceptance, mindfulness, and defusion by having Donna envision driving a bus toward the values she had identified on her Compass sheet, with unruly passengers attempting to divert her. Using colored pens, Donna illustrated who her unruly passengers were. One passenger, "Not Normal Norma," was a severe woman who shouted things like "Your life will never be the same again…YOU will never be normal again!" Then, the therapist moved the therapy room furniture so that Donna could pretend to drive the bus, with the therapist in the back acting as her passengers. Donna initially struggled to drive when her passengers were speaking to her. With coaching, she was eventually able to use her mindfulness and acceptance skills to stay focused on driving. Toward the end, she said, "Norma, you might actually be right, my life isn't the same as it was before cancer and it might not ever be the same. But talking back to you isn't making it normal, it's making it worse! So I'm going to keep driving."

By Session 7, Donna was more engaged with her family and friend group, and she had reached out to the library about resuming her volunteer work there. At this point, her most prominent concern was her constant worry about her cancer coming back. She was still losing sleep worrying about this, and would occasionally miss work due to fatigue from sleep loss. When invited to reflect on what she most deeply feared, she conceded she was especially afraid of "having to do all that treatment over again, and that it will be even worse than before." She would quickly push this thought out of mind. The therapist acknowledged how challenging this thought was and how much it brought up for her, bringing a compassionate stance toward her experience. The therapist decided to use the Acceptance of Emotions exercise (Harris, 2009) to help Donna open up to the feelings accompanying this thought. During the exercise, which the therapist recorded, Donna became tearful as she contacted an overwhelming sense of fear and sadness that arose when she opened up to the thought. Afterward, she admitted how challenging it was to allow her feelings to surface without pushing them away. Yet she also felt relief at facing her most feared thought and greater kindness toward herself once she contacted the intensity of what she was facing. With encouragement, Donna agreed to try the exercise again for homework, using the recording.

In the following few sessions, Donna reported that she continued to worry about cancer recurrence, but that she was "making more space for the thoughts." The therapist spent the final sessions reviewing her progress. Upon termination, Donna's VLQ scores indicated that she was acting much more consistently in her valued domains of family, friendship, and work, relative to pretreatment. She was spending more time with friends and family, and she reported that she was able to stay present and enjoy that time more. She was also missing less work and sleeping better. Donna began treating the urge to miss work when fatigued as "just another passenger" while also acknowledging shifts in her body's needs, such as a need to go to bed earlier, focus on one thing at a time, limit her "to do" list, and be gentle with herself. She was taking occasional volunteer shifts at the library and planned to increase her role there as she grew stronger. Overall, Donna was accepting rather than avoiding distressing thoughts about cancer and its effects on her life and was reengaged in the activities that mattered most to her.

In many ways this treatment matches classic ACT protocols. However, you'll notice some key themes that are important to attend to in the context of cancer, including worrying about cancer coming back, adjusting to changes in roles and physical capabilities, coping with treatment-related disfigurement, and benefitting from a gentle compassionate stance toward the self in the midst of the real threats and physical symptoms that cancer can impose. Each of these can be targeted with typical ACT methods. We also emphasized key exercises we found particularly applicable for cancer patients. In response to reports that the cognitive effects of cancer treatment can make it more difficult to remember lots of new skills or those with too much complexity, we limit the number of exercises and offer them in a straightforward and experiential manner.

## Case Study 2: Group ACT for Advanced Cancer Patients

Group therapy is often recommended in working with cancer patients because of (1) the critical role of mutual support from other patients, and (2) the opportunities it affords to facilitate acceptance based on the shared experience of cancer, and to model, elicit, and reinforce ACT processes more generally, when skillfully moderated. Group interventions are also highly common due to the limited resources available for ongoing, one-on-one therapy in most cancer care settings.

Our group consisted of seven patients, all diagnosed with incurable cancer, including stage IV breast, lung, and colon cancer. Patients ranged from forty-nine to seventy-seven years old and included five women, three of whom identified as White and non-Latina, and two of whom identified as multiracial and Latina. Patients were referred to treatment by social workers within the oncology practice network based on screenings that showed high distress. The group was led by two of us (a clinical social worker and a psychologist, both trained in ACT) and included an online daily check-in using a webpage we developed for this purpose. The online check-in reinforced and extended ACT skills learned in group sessions to daily life, for example, having people note whether they were struggling with a thought or feeling/sensation, and selecting a "defusion" (for thoughts) or "acceptance/mindfulness" (for feelings/sensations) exercise to practice briefly in that moment.

In Session 1, we began with brief introductions and then introduced the Compass on a whiteboard in the therapy room. Group members volunteered examples of away moves, such as "skipping family events because I am in pain," and toward moves, such as "texting or emailing friends if I can't physically visit them." For homework, we asked group members to complete their own Compass and to track their toward and away moves, using worksheets distributed in the group, supplemented by the online daily check-in. Particularly given the context of metastatic cancer, we discussed the importance of noticing away moves (or a lack of toward moves) with self-compassion, stating, "If sometimes all you can do is stay in bed, that's completely okay. Just notice with compassion that you're doing your best in that moment."

In Sessions 2 and 3, we continued to help patients examine their values, commit to enacting small valued actions, and track toward and away moves each day using the online daily check-in. We began each session with a brief mindfulness meditation. Then, in an "opening circle," we reviewed the valued actions that participants (and group leaders) committed to in the previous week, discussed what facilitated or got in the way of doing them, troubleshooted, and committed or recommitted to enacting a valued action in the coming week. After the opening circle, we introduced experiential practices and metaphors to facilitate mindfulness, acceptance, and defusion. Given that many participants experienced chronic pain, one eyes-closed exercise we used was compassionately noticing physical sensations experienced as uncomfortable or painful, noting the stories the mind generated about them, lightly labeling them as "stories," and gently returning to the sensation.

In Session 4, we began by introducing the Passengers on the Bus metaphor and providing time for participants to personify difficult thoughts, images, and feelings as passengers. This included selecting names, sketching images for them, and writing down what their passengers typically said. Camilla, a group member, came up with a passenger named "Grim Reaper," who personified her fears about dying (see figure 12.2)—a common passenger among those with metastatic cancer. Jon, another group member, identified "Mr. Homeless," who embodied his fear of his family losing their home because, due to cancer, he was no longer able to work and provide financially for them.

We then invited group members to role-play the part of the driver and the passengers. The volunteer driver, Camilla, began driving toward her value of family, with passengers shouting, "What's the point? You won't be around for your family soon anyway!" The other group members and group leaders coached her to practice mindfully acknowledging what her passengers were saying and her reactions to them while keeping her focus on driving. Like most participants we have had in our groups, Camilla found that the Grim Reaper passenger was especially difficult to cope with, as evident in this dialogue:

**Figure 12.2.** Bus with passengers depicted by Camilla and Jon.

| | |
|---|---|
| *Jon:* | (*acting as the Grim Reaper*) Camilla, what's the point? Soon, you won't be around for your family anyway. You're abandoning them! |
| *Camilla:* | (*starts crying, unsure how to respond, and stops driving*) |
| *Therapist:* | Can anyone here relate to having Camilla's passenger? (*Nearly everyone raises their hand.*) It's natural to want to give up when we hear those words. Who can help Camilla respond to the Grim Reaper? |
| *Group member 1:* | I have that same passenger and I hate him! |
| *Therapist:* | Yes, he really tries to bully us into giving up on living life, to give up doing what we care about. (*gently*) How well is that working for moving toward your value of family? |
| *Camilla:* | (*tearfully*) Not well. |
| *Therapist:* | What would it look like to acknowledge the Grim Reaper, make space for the emotions he triggers, and eventually allow yourself to keep driving? |
| *Camilla:* | I'm not sure. |
| *Group member 2:* | Maybe try that thing where we put our hands on our hearts and breathe into the feeling? |
| *Camilla:* | (*puts hand on heart, closes eyes, takes a few breaths, tears up a little*) |

| | |
|---|---|
| *Therapist:* | I can see you're really opening up to those feelings. Can you drive while remaining open to those feelings? |
| *Camilla:* | I think so…if I open my eyes I can… *(begins driving again)* |
| *Jon:* | Actually, you might as well drive this bus right back to the hospital instead. You'll just get sick again and need another round of chemo. |
| *Camilla:* | *(suddenly angry)* Urghhh! I can't handle him. *(turns around to face him)* It's hard enough to drive this bus without you shouting horrible stuff in my ear! I don't know how I'm supposed to drive when you won't be quiet! Maybe it's not worth trying if I'm just going to die anyway. |
| *Therapist:* | I can appreciate why you feel that way. And I'm wondering, if you wait for the Grim Reaper to be quiet before you drive toward family, how long will you be waiting? |
| *Camilla:* | …I'll be waiting forever. |
| *Therapist:* | Sadly, yes. *(gently)* So which do you choose: living your life or waiting forever for the Grim Reaper to be quiet? |

For the rest of the session, we and the group members helped Camilla to practice defusing from the Grim Reaper. Afterward, we debriefed by asking Camilla and the participants who acted out her passengers or witnessed the exercise what it was like for them. Then, a few other patients practiced driving their buses as well. We continued emphasizing shared themes among patients' passengers to cultivate a sense of common humanity and acceptance. For home practice, participants completed a new online check-in that focused on identifying which passengers were present that day, noticing how they approached them, and selecting an ACT skill to practice in that moment if helpful. For Session 5, we practiced more by giving other group members the opportunity to experience driving their bus in the face of their passengers.

Advance care planning (ACP) includes (a) designating someone to make medical decisions when a patient becomes too ill to do so, (b) clarifying values and wishes that are most important to the patient, (c) completing a living will that reflects those values and wishes, and (d) indicating preferences for end-of-life care (e.g., decisions about interventions such as artificial resuscitation and preferences about dying at home or in a hospice facility versus in the hospital). Unfortunately, many people with metastatic cancer never engage in ACP (Narang, Wright, & Nicholas, 2015). Given its focus on values, acceptance, and committed action, we view ACT as a well-matched framework for facilitating engagement in ACP. If you help a patient engage in ACP, it is important to know the ACP guidelines and resources for your country and region and to coordinate with the patient's health care providers.

In the final two group sessions (Sessions 6 and 7), we asked patients to consider how their values inform their advance care planning (ACP) and how engaging in ACP could represent a toward move. We explained the steps of ACP, emphasizing to patients the importance of officially designating someone to make medical decisions should they be unable to do so themselves, and communicating ahead of time what care they wish to receive. We provided patients with the legal paperwork to execute some of their ACP decisions with their families and health care providers. We draw heavily on flexible perspective taking to have patients imagine what they would need to know if they served as someone else's medical decision maker. One patient shared:

> For a long time, I had been avoiding talking with my husband about me not being around anymore. But I realized that I can take care of my family by preparing them for the end. So my toward move this week was talking with my husband about being my medical decision maker, and how important it is for me to pass in my own bed, not in a hospital, with him by my side.

As this case study illustrates, we draw on ACT to help patients with metastatic cancer live as fully as possible with the time that remains; to cope with radical loss, fear, and uncertainty; and to help ensure that their bus keeps moving in valued directions even if they become too ill to drive it themselves.

# Challenges

Cancer is a complicated context for intervention. Cancer comes in over 100 types, each with different stages or levels of severity. Some are easy to treat and others remain deadly; many lie in between. Treatment is evolving faster in cancer than in nearly any area of medicine. Treatment side effects can affect brain functioning and mental health, but there are so many different treatments, that assessing side effects remains challenging, and for newer treatments, the full side effects may not yet be well known. Newer treatments such as the immunotherapies can dramatically change a patient's prognosis overnight and, along with it, the psychological sequelae of the disease. By having basic knowledge about cancer and the issues that commonly affect patients, and by anticipating common barriers to treatment, therapists can be prepared for—and address—challenges that may arise.

## Common Challenges Facing Clients with Cancer

Therapists should be aware of the range of relevant issues facing patients, including (but not limited to) difficulties communicating treatment preferences to loved ones and health care providers, grieving what cancer has stolen, coping with uncertainty, fearing that prolonged treatment or dying will overburden loved ones, not wanting to "give up" or disappoint others and stop treatment with a poor risk/benefit ratio, and difficulties changing poor health habits that affect certain cancers. Particularly in the context of metastatic or recurrent cancer, providers should be prepared for quick dramatic changes in health status along with patients abruptly not being able to continue psychotherapy.

We recommend that therapists receive a basic education in cancer, cancer treatment, and prognosis and have regular communication with cancer care providers. Further, although we may be prepared to help a person with stage IV cancer face death, they may not be aware that they are dying or will die from cancer in the future. A surprising number of people with cancer do not know their prognosis; thus, gaining the patient's understanding of their disease, what caused it, and how they expect to fare, is essential.

## ACT-Related Barriers and How to Address Them

In cancer contexts, numerous barriers relevant to ACT can arise; here, we briefly touch on seven barriers we have encountered frequently.

First, the complex neurocognitive side effects of treatment commonly known as "chemobrain" can affect dimensions of concentration, executive functioning, and memory. Simplifying ideas, doing experiential exercises, reviewing topics frequently, and taking breaks can help. Second, common treatment and cancer side effects such as intense fatigue and physical pain/neuropathy can present barriers to pursuing values-driven behavior. Such barriers require psychological flexibility for both patients and therapists to creatively brainstorm manageable alternatives to pursuing values while acknowledging the loss involved in not being able to pursue values in the same way as before. Third and similarly, if significant pain is present, in our experience, body-focused mindfulness can initially spike perceived pain levels for some patients because they are being asked to focus on physical sensations. We have found that flexible perspective taking in meditation can be helpful, for example, imagining the pain is like a big rock in the middle of a much larger lake and inquiring, "Can you acknowledge and explore the rock while also experiencing the broader space around it?"

Fourth, people with metastatic cancer often experience distressing thoughts and beliefs ("When I die, my kids won't have a dad") that are true, valid, and devastating to contemplate. We have seen patients with incurable cancer whose parent died of the same disease when the patient was a child, with the patient now repeating this loss for their own children. If a person is haunted by such thoughts, it can be highly invalidating to jump straight to cognitive defusion. Instead, we invite patients (and therapists) to sit with the thought or image and open up to the feelings and action tendencies that arise alongside it, cultivating compassion and acceptance, and practicing defusion chiefly when such thoughts and beliefs impede valued action.

Fifth, a common frustration among cancer survivors who have finished treatment is "Why aren't I back to normal yet?"—a sentiment often echoed by family, friends, and colleagues. Such frustration calls for a strong emphasis on education, self-compassion, and self-care to help people thrive amidst the physical and mental aftereffects of cancer and cancer treatment.

Sixth, the public metaphor for cancer in the US is a war metaphor, as in the "war on cancer," "fighting cancer," and "defeating cancer." This mindset can be helpful for some, but particularly if a person is "losing the war" with incurable cancer, this metaphor can obstruct acceptance. Addressing fears that facing a difficult prognosis means "defeat" or "giving up" can be critical if the war metaphor is rigidly fused with "at any cost" or blocks valued action. Returning to workability and values can prove helpful here.

Finally, in our experience, people with cancer and cancer survivors have a strong collective need to connect with one another by sharing stories about their cancer. Cancer remains a stigmatized condition, particularly among young and middle-age adults. Sharing stories about one's cancer can reduce stigma and increase a sense of shared humanity and acceptance in the face of a common struggle, particularly if the stories are mutual and transformative. In ACT groups, we found that we needed to set aside more time than expected to allow patients to share with one another. The emphasis on cognitive defusion in ACT, if adhered to rigidly, can disrupt this storytelling process—though of course remains valuable for disrupting stories that keep people stuck.

## Research Support

While relatively new in its application to cancer populations, ACT has yielded initially promising effects on psychological distress, quality of life, and physical health outcomes (Gonzalez-Fernandez & Fernandez-Rodriguez, 2018).

### Psychological and Quality of Life Outcomes

Because of the significant co-occurrence of cancer and internalizing symptoms (Nakash et al., 2014), ACT in cancer contexts has been regularly applied to address anxiety, depression, and general distress as well as quality of life. A single-arm, multiple-baseline study showed significant improvement with moderate to large effect sizes for anxiety and depression symptoms, fear of cancer recurrence, and cancer-related trauma symptoms following a seven-week group ACT intervention for cancer survivors experiencing anxiety (Arch & Mitchell, 2016). This study also found improvements in life meaning, manageability, and comprehensibility by three-month follow up. Another single-arm study evaluating nine weeks of individual ACT treatment for patients at different stages of cancer treatment and survivorship (Feros, Lane, Ciarrochi, & Blackledge, 2013) showed similar results, with significant improvements in general distress, quality of life, and psychological flexibility, each with medium to large effect sizes.

The results of these single-arm studies have been largely replicated in randomized clinical trials to date. For example, an early small trial of a twelve-session individual ACT intervention for women with late-stage ovarian cancer showed significantly superior outcomes on all reported measures following ACT relative to a classic cognitive behavioral therapy-derived intervention (called treatment as usual, or TAU; Rost,

Wilson, Buchanan, Hildebrandt, & Mutch, 2012), including for distress and quality of life. A very large, recent clinical trial comparing telehealth ACT to TAU among colorectal cancer survivors (Hawkes, Pakenham, Chambers, Patrao, & Courneya, 2014) found no significant differences in distress outcomes between groups but found that ACT led to greater improvements in posttraumatic growth, spirituality, and cancer-specific quality of life than TAU.

Although beyond the scope of this chapter, as mindfulness represents a facet of the ACT hexaflex, it is worth mentioning for interested readers that an impressive body of work demonstrates the efficacy of mindfulness meditation-based approaches in cancer populations (e.g., Carlson et al., 2013).

## Health-Related Outcomes

Work with cancer patients often entails a greater focus on health behaviors and physical outcomes in light of preventing cancer recurrence or worsening, and to improve health. In a large trial among colorectal cancer survivors (Hawkes et al., 2013), relative to usual care, ACT (delivered in telephone coaching sessions) led to greater increases in moderate physical activity, improved body mass index, and lower dietary fat intake. The small single-arm study of cancer survivors experiencing anxiety found that group ACT improved physical pain and fatigue/vitality outcomes (Arch & Mitchell, 2016). Though these results are promising, more research is needed.

## Change Processes

Multiple studies have measured ACT processes or mechanisms of change in cancer populations. The large randomized trial of ACT-based telehealth among colorectal cancer survivors (Hawkes et al., 2014) found that acceptance and mindfulness mediated the relationship between the interventions (ACT, TAU) and posttraumatic growth, spirituality, and physical well-being at six-month follow-up. In the randomized trial of ACT versus TAU for women with ovarian cancer, improvements in active planning and mental disengagement mediated the relationship between treatment condition and the primary outcomes of distress and quality of life (Rost et al., 2012). Finally, our single-arm trial for survivors experiencing anxiety (Arch & Mitchell, 2016) suggested that cancer-specific psychological flexibility predicted subsequent improvement in most outcomes. As such, the literature to date indicates core ACT processes as likely mechanisms of change within ACT for cancer populations. Future work identifying the most accurate measures to use in assessing such processes would be beneficial.

## Brief Summary of Research

In summary, extant ACT studies in cancer populations (see Gonzalez-Fernandez & Fernandez-Rodriguez, 2018) have largely focused on posttreatment cancer survivors.

With the notable exception of the large ACT telehealth trial for colorectal cancer survivors, most studies have been small or uncontrolled. Findings from extant studies remain promising; however, larger randomized controlled trials are now needed to more rigorously evaluate the potential of ACT-based interventions in cancer populations.

## Future Directions

In the US, most adults with cancer are treated in the community rather than at academic cancer centers; thus, a critical future direction is increasing the sustainable uptake of ACT interventions in community settings. At least three innovations signify promising future directions for community implementation. First, the largest trial to date of an ACT intervention in cancer ($n = 410$ colorectal cancer survivors; Hawkes et al., 2013) relied on brief telehealth sessions to successfully change multiple health behaviors related to prevention of cancer recurrence, which enables clinicians to reach cancer survivors beyond their geographic area. Future work should build on this success and evaluate whether targeted outcomes in other cancer populations can be improved through ACT telehealth. Second, our own work has strategically trained onsite clinical social workers in community oncology care settings to deliver ACT group interventions (Arch & Mitchell, 2016). This approach relies on existing staff and staff roles to implement ACT in community settings, increasing the potential for long-term sustainability and scalability. Third, to address low rates of online-only intervention completion, we have begun developing and testing hybrid interventions that integrate in-person and online components. The in-person components facilitate face-to-face connection among patients, offer professional provider contact for ACT skill building, and provide accountability for completing the online components. The online components reinforce skills learned in person, help participants apply them to daily life, and increase the dose of the intervention without increasing provider time or patient travel demands. Building upon these and numerous other innovations outlined in this book will help us to reach the large community of adults with cancer or a history of cancer who are distressed, and to leverage our growing knowledge to benefit those with serious health conditions more broadly.

## References

Angiola, J. E., & Bowen, A. M. (2013). Quality of life in advanced cancer: An acceptance and commitment therapy view. *The Counseling Psychologist, 41*(2), 313–335.

Arch, J. J., & Mitchell, J. (2016). An acceptance and commitment therapy group intervention for cancer survivors experiencing anxiety at reentry. *Psycho-Oncology, 25*(5), 610–615.

Breitbart, W., Poppito, S., Rosenfeld, B., Vickers, A. J., Li, Y., Abbey, J., . . . Cassileth, B. R. (2012). Pilot randomized controlled trial of individual meaning-centered psychotherapy for patients with advanced cancer. *Journal of Clinical Oncology, 30*(12), 1304–1309.

Carlson, L. E., Doll, R., Stephen, J., Faris, P., Tamagawa, R., Drysdale, E., & Speca, M. (2013). Randomized controlled trial of mindfulness-based cancer recovery versus supportive expressive group therapy for distressed survivors of breast cancer. *Journal of Clinical Oncology, 31*(25), 3119–3126. doi: 10.1200/JCO.2012.47.5210

Feros, D. L., Lane, L., Ciarrochi, J., & Blackledge, J. T. (2013). Acceptance and Commitment Therapy (ACT) for improving the lives of cancer patients: A preliminary study. *Psychooncology, 22*(2), 459–464. doi: 10.1002/pon.2083

Gonzalez-Fernandez, S., & Fernandez-Rodriguez, C. (2018). Acceptance and Commitment Therapy in cancer: Review of applications and findings. *Behavioral Medicine,* 1–15. doi: 10.1080/08964289.2018.1452713

Harris, R. (2009). *ACT made simple.* Oakland, CA: New Harbinger.

Hawkes, A. L., Chambers, S. K., Pakenham, K. I., Patrao, T. A., Baade, P. D., Lynch, B. M., . . . Courneya, K. S. (2013). Effects of a telephone-delivered multiple health behavior change intervention (CanChange) on health and behavioral outcomes in survivors of colorectal cancer: a randomized controlled trial. *Journal of Clinical Oncology, 31*(18), 2313–2321. doi: 10.1200/JCO.2012.45.5873

Hawkes, A. L., Pakenham, K. I., Chambers, S. K., Patrao, T. A., & Courneya, K. S. (2014). Effects of a multiple health behavior change intervention for colorectal cancer survivors on psychosocial outcomes and quality of life: A randomized controlled trial. *Annals of Behavioral Medicine, 48,* 359–370.

Hayes, S. C., Strosahl, K. D., & Wilson, K. G. (1999). *Acceptance and commitment therapy: An experiential approach to behavior change.* New York, NY: Guilford Press.

Hayes, S. C., Wilson, K. G., Gifford, E. V., Follette, V. M., & Strosahl, K. (1996). Experiential avoidance and behavioral disorders: A functional dimensional approach to diagnosis and treatment. *Journal of Consulting and Clinical Psychology, 64*(6), 1152–1168.

Mitchell, A. J., Ferguson, D. W., Gill, J., Paul, J., & Symonds, P. (2013). Depression and anxiety in long-term cancer survivors compared with spouses and healthy controls: A systematic review and meta-analysis. *The Lancet Oncology, 14*(8), 721–732.

Nakash, O., Levav, I., Aguilar-Gaxiola, S., Alonso, J., Andrade, L. H., Angermeyer, M. C., . . . Scott, K. M. (2014). Comorbidity of common mental disorders with cancer and their treatment gap: Findings from the World Mental Health Surveys. *Psychooncology, 23*(1), 40–51. doi: 10.1002/pon.3372

Narang, A. K., Wright, A. A., & Nicholas, L. H. (2015). Trends in advance care planning in patients with cancer: Results from a national longitudinal survey. *JAMA Oncology, 1*(5), 601–608. doi: 10.1001/jamaoncol.2015.1976

Polk, K. L., & Schoendorff, B. (2014). *The ACT matrix: A new approach to building psychological flexibility across settings and populations.* Oakland, CA: Context Press.

Rost, A. D., Wilson, K., Buchanan, E., Hildebrandt, M. J., & Mutch, D. (2012). Improving psychological adjustment among late-stage ovarian cancer patients: Examining the role of avoidance in treatment. *Cognitive and Behavioral Practice, 19*(4), 508–517. doi: 10.1016/j.cbpra.2012.01.003

Wilson, K. G., Sandoz, E. K., Kitchens, J., & Roberts, M. (2010). The Valued Living Questionnaire: Defining and measuring valued action within a behavioral framework. *The Psychological Record, 60*(2), 249–272. doi: 10.1007/BF03395706

# CHAPTER 13

# ACT Innovations for Dangerous Weight Control
## *Anorexia Nervosa and ED-DMT1*

Rhonda M. Merwin

*Duke University Medical Center*

## Overview

Anorexia nervosa (AN) is recognized as the most lethal mental health condition (Papadopoulos, Ekbom, Brandt, & Ekselius, 2009). Deaths are related to the medical complications of starvation, but a substantial number of people with AN also die by suicide, highlighting the profound suffering of these individuals (Arcelus, Mitchell, Wales, & Nielsen, 2011). Recently, an even deadlier variant of extreme maladaptive weight control has emerged: ED-DMT1 (eating disorder in diabetes mellitus, type 1; Criego, Crow, Goebel-Fabbri, Kendall, & Parkin, 2009). To illustrate, a Danish nation-wide study of psychiatric cases indicated a mortality rate of 7.3 (per 1,000 person-years) for individuals with AN and 34.6 for individuals with AN who also had type 1 diabetes (T1D; Nielsen, 2001). Of concern, individuals with ED-DMT1 may underutilize insulin for weight control (Merwin et al., 2015; Merwin et al., 2018). This behavior is reinforced by dramatic weight loss, but it also can be immediately life threatening (resulting in the unfettered release of ketones into the bloodstream that turns the blood acidic) and per-petuate diabetes-related micro- and macro-vascular damage and disease (Nathan & Group, 2014).

There are no empirically supported treatments for adults with AN (Brockmeyer, Friederich, & Schmidt, 2017). For adolescents with AN, family-based treatment (FBT; as manualized by Lock, LeGrange, Agras, & Dare, 2001) has accumulated significant empirical evidence, but many individuals treated with FBT have suboptimal outcomes (Lock, 2015). Individuals with ED-DMT1 are likewise without evidence-based treatment options (Goebel-Fabbri, 2009). Past studies suggest conventional treatments for anorexia and bulimia nervosa are less effective for individuals with T1D (e.g., Peveler & Fairburn, 1992) and do not appear to decrease insulin restriction or improve hemoglobin A1c (HbA$_{1c}$; an index of average blood glucose [BG] over three months).

The complexity of maladaptive weight control makes it challenging to treat. Intervention must be swift to avoid life-threatening complications, at the same time that the client may be attached to weight/weight loss behaviors and thus ambivalent about change. Separation of the individual from the eating disorder (ED) is essential but diffi-cult. Low weight and severe caloric restriction also have a significant impact on individuals' cognitive and emotional faculties. Biological adaptations to starvation—such as hypometabolism, increased rigidity or stereotypy, and decreased interest in things other than food—perpetuate entrenchment in the ED and may make it impossible to intervene without external supports (such as parents or family members). Among individuals with T1D, erratic BG may cause mood instability and cognitive dysfunction. Intervention among individuals with T1D must also be sensitive to the fact that relinquishing the ED means facing a chronic illness that provides near constant reminders about the possibility of future negative health outcomes and early mortality, no matter how well the condition is managed.

This chapter describes treatment innovations for dangerous maladaptive weight control. I begin with a novel formulation of EDs (as maladaptive self-regulation), which may have some advantages over traditional cognitive behavioral therapy (CBT) and previous acceptance and commitment therapy (ACT) approaches that focus more narrowly on the distressing thoughts and feelings about the body that individuals with EDs are preoccupied with (and attempt to avoid). This is followed by innovative intervention strategies for individuals with EDs based on this formulation. Finally, I describe innovations in treatment structure and delivery for these high-risk populations, including a separated family treatment for adolescents with AN and the use of mobile technology to facilitate real-world behavior change among adults with ED-DMT1. Interventions are informed by over twelve years of experience treating these individuals in a major medical center and ongoing basic behavioral and applied research.

# Description of a Novel ACT-Based Approach to Dangerous Weight Control

Traditional CBT views EDs as "cognitive disorders" characterized by a distorted view of the body (or the importance of maintaining a particular body weight) and an ED filter that biases perspective on the world (Fairburn, 2008). While this approach can be helpful, it may also lead to a caricature of EDs as individuals who want to be thin and will do anything to achieve their weight goal. This not only belies the long history of AN (that far predates the "thin ideal"), but also fails to account for the fact that a phobic fear of fatness is *not* observed universally, cross-culturally, or among all individuals with AN in Western cultures (Lee, Ho, & Hsu, 1993). Further, by overemphasizing the content of ED cognition (i.e., typical thoughts of individuals who engage in dangerous weight control), treatment may neglect how these preoccupations function for the individual.

Over the past decade, my colleagues and I have developed an alternative model that may parsimoniously explain the range of behavior observed in AN and guide ACT-based intervention (Merwin et al., 2011; Merwin, Zucker, & Wilson, 2019). AN may be understood as verbally mediated, punitive self-regulation in which actions are determined by rigid rules that neglect the individual based on what is "good" or "right." Rules prioritize work and performance and guide not only eating and exercise (e.g., "Don't eat more than

500 calories a day") but also academic and occupational pursuits (e.g., "Don't stop until it is perfect") and social interactions (e.g., "Always put others first," "Don't burden others"). Body weight is *only one* marker of success (or failure) that individuals with AN use to evaluate themselves and their performance.

In the short term, this behavior is reinforced. Rules decrease uncertainty and increase predictability and control. Rules provide clear parameters for behavior and concrete markers regarding whether expectations are met. Extreme "self-discipline" also results in conventional measures of success (i.e., outward achievements) that are visible and valued by other people. These experiences stand in stark contrast to the feelings of discomfort or failure individuals with AN may feel at other times or in other situations, such as when trying to navigate amorphous social interactions or, in the case of T1D, when trying to manage their BG and diabetes.

While this approach to managing themselves has benefits, it comes at a cost. Because their behavior is not dynamically matched to the demands of the situation, individuals with AN live in a state of profound physical and emotional deprivation. This is most obvious in the wasting of their body; however, it can also be observed in a lack of meaningful connection to other people and to the activities they pursue. By increasing psychological flexibility, individuals with AN may adopt a more flexible and attuned approach to managing themselves and their behavior and be better able to meet their physical and emotional needs.

Although individuals with AN sometimes engage in more disinhibited behavior (e.g., eating indiscriminately and purging), we focus our formulation on the rigid, restrictive aspect of AN (and EDs more generally) because it is this rigidity that is central to the phenomenology, and it sets conditions for disinhibition (via severe caloric deficits or the abstinence-violation effect; Polivy & Herman, 1985).

## Intervention Innovations

We have developed a variety of intervention innovations based on our formulation of AN and other forms of extreme weight control. In this section, I provide detailed examples of specific strategies that we have developed and that you might try in practice (see Merwin, Zucker, & Wilson, 2019, for a book-length description).

### THE PARENTING METAPHOR

Parenting styles in childrearing provide a metaphor for the central problem and the solution: to move from rigid, punitive self-regulation to an approach that is respectful, flexible, and responsive to one's needs—or *authoritative* self-parenting. You can leverage this metaphor to set the course for treatment, organize behavior change goals, and track progress. The parenting metaphor also serves the additional function of eliciting a behavioral repertoire of kindness and compassion by putting the individual in a frame of coordination with a child who needs to be responded to, protected, or cared for.

Baumrind (1991) first described parenting styles that are now common vernacular in working with families or parents. Styles vary along two dimensions: (1) demands or expectations and (2) warmth. Both can be high or low, the intersection of which creates four distinct "styles" (adapted from Baumrind, 1991): *authoritative* (high expectations, high warmth), *authoritarian* (high expectations, low warmth), *permissive* (low expectations, high warmth), and *neglectful* (low expectations, low warmth). While these approaches reflect parenting of children, they might also reflect the style or approach that individuals adopt to managing themselves and their own behavior.

Individuals with AN (or other EDs of maladaptive weight control) have adopted an authoritarian style of self-parenting, imposing rules that are insensitive to the person and their needs, and demanding obedience (sometimes punishing behavior that is out of bounds). In the domain of eating and weight control, this may look like restricting eating though hungry or forcing exercise though tired or in pain. In other domains, it may look like always putting others' preferences before their own or avoiding things that are joyful or pleasurable, if nonproductive. For some individuals with EDs, this rigid approach to managing themselves and their behavior will give way to moments of overly permissive self-parenting in which they relinquish all limits (e.g., eating in a disinhibited manner or engaging in boundless procrastination). However, rather than see this as a signal of the need to allow greater ease in their typical self-management, they are likely to respond to these transgressions punitively, setting stricter and harsher limits.

Below are two sample dialogues that leverage the self-parenting metaphor in treatment to highlight that overcontrol is the problem and suggest there may be an alternative.

In the first dialogue, the client is presenting with AN and a history of suicidal ideation. This interaction takes place early in therapy, but after a present and compassionately curious conversation about the way in which restriction and weight loss (and the client's broader approach to managing themself with rigid, punitive overcontrol) has and has not been helpful.

*Therapist (T):*    You have been doing exactly what society says will lead to a good life: "Work hard, really hard. Be the best. Be perfect. Your needs don't matter… In fact, if you need to rest that just means you are lazy, weak…pathetic…" And I hear you saying that in many ways, this has been working… You make the marks. You lose weight, you feel like you look the part… (*pause*) It makes sense that you keep doing it… (*pause*) It's an incredibly human thing to do.

*Client (C):*    Everyone complimented me when I first started losing weight… (*pause*)

*T:*    And yet…

*C:*    (*knowing sigh*)

*T:*    …Sometimes you wish that you could die… (*pause*)

C:      It's tedious, you know... Everything must be counted. Accounted for. And nothing is ever good enough really. I used to be able to stop at eight miles...now I have to do sixteen or I feel terrible about myself...

T:      The demands are unrelenting... (*pause*) And never in kindness. Never very nice to yourself.

C:      (*makes a face; communicating distrust in being kind to oneself*)

T:      In some ways, managing yourself and your behavior is like parenting...you are deciding what limits to set for yourself...how you will treat yourself, how you will respond to your needs. There are lots of different ways to parent... (*takes out paper and creates the four quadrants of the intersection between high and low demands and warmth and gives overview of parenting styles*) It seems that you are like an authoritarian self-parent...beating yourself into submission... I wonder if you can imagine treating a younger version of yourself, or a young person you know, in this way... Like: "I don't care if you are tired or hungry. Run. Keep Running. Why are you so lazy... You are a waste of space..."

C:      (*quietly reflective, long pause*)

T:      What if there is another way? Like, could you imagine...being another kind of parent to yourself... as a choice?

C:      I have no idea how to do that...and I am afraid that I would just eat whatever... and... (*trails off*)

T:      I hear you, it's scary...and completely different than the way in which you have been operating. It brings up fear. A lot of fear. And thoughts that you can't be controlled without the harsh rules and clamping down...

In the next dialogue the client is presenting with maladaptive eating and weight control in the context of T1D. The client fluctuates between food restriction and overeating without giving themself insulin.

C:      It's like, "Don't eat carbs, no desserts, etcetera." It is the only way that I can manage my diabetes.

T:      And so you follow these rules...but sometimes you break free...totally free... there are no limits at all. And when you do that, then you don't give insulin...

C:      (*affirms*)

T:      When we are younger, our parents or caregivers have a major role in setting limits for our behavior and meeting our needs... Over time, we take on this responsibility. It becomes our job to cue in and know what we need...we essentially self-parent… There are lots of ways to do this… (*takes out paper and creates the four quadrants of parenting styles and describes them*)

T:    What kind of parent are you?

C:    (*discusses*)

T:    Yeah, it sounds like you move between authoritarian and permissive parenting. What would it be like to live in this other space (*points to the authoritative quadrant*)—respectful, responsive, attuned…? It starts by giving yourself permission to have some of the things you enjoy sometimes…greater flexibility…in managing yourself and your diabetes.

C:    (*fearful/unsure expression*)

T:    I know you are afraid of what will happen if you are more flexible or responsive to your needs, including the need to have your preferences taken into account… and I wonder if you would be willing to try it and see what happens—see what happens without the punitive *over*control that has you, or your body, screaming out at times…?

## DISCRIMINATING ED VOLUME

ED content (e.g., thoughts about eating or the need to lose weight) is compelling, particularly when it occurs in the context of emaciation. It may be tempting to challenge these thoughts. Clients might also view the content and truth of these thoughts as the central issue. Clearly articulating how attachment to eating and body weight concerns functions for the individual guides intervention. You can elucidate the function of eating and weight preoccupation (as well as the broader system of punitive overcontrol) by identifying the historical context in which it emerged. In addition to careful interviewing, we often create a timeline of onset, exacerbation, and relative remittance of dieting or overexercise to identify functional relationships. Typically, this reveals that eating and weight preoccupation emerged when the individual was feeling uncertain, overwhelmed, or out of control (in their life or body), or following experiences that challenged their competence or likeability (e.g., a perceived failure or rejection).

Events that elicit these (or similar) emotional experiences in daily life will compel increased preoccupation with eating and weight control in the moment. In treatment, these moments are opportunities for the client to practice acceptance of unwanted internal experiences.

We use the metaphor of "ED volume" to train clients to discriminate momentary changes in the intensity of their eating and weight preoccupation. By observing variation in the ED volume (across hours, days, or weeks), the client learns how the ED might function to direct their attention away from painful emotions. Teaching clients to monitor ED volume also serves other therapeutic purposes. It functions as defusion (as clients treat the ED as a collection of thoughts, feelings, or urges that they can be curious about, describe, or otherwise interact with), and it strengthens the observer self, which is experienced as separate and distinct from this content. The dialogue below illustrates how the therapist might direct the client's attention to the broader emotional context of increased eating and weight preoccupation. In this example, the client is describing a recent situation with her sister.

C:    I was trying to tell her that I didn't want to go, and she just turned away from me.

T:    What was that like for you?

C:    (begins to fidget, puts pillow on lap) I can't stand my legs… my thighs are disgusting…

T:    I am wondering what was happening right before your attention went to the size of your thighs? What did you notice—thoughts, feelings, body sensations?

C:    (describes discomfort)

T:    It seems, at that moment, the ED was trying to protect you from this feeling—give you something else on which to focus your attention…? (pause) Just allowing yourself to know this, and to know what that initial experience was, is an act of willingness…

Later, near the end of session:

T:    That moment when you covered your thighs… How loud was the ED? If you were to give it a volume rating where one is a whisper and ten is a bullhorn in your ear…?

C:    Eight

T:    Would you be willing to monitor the ED volume over the next week, and when it is loud…like today…take a few notes about what is going on in and around you…at that moment, and the moments before? This will provide us with information, but it is also a practice in allowing…allowing yourself to be aware of your feelings.

Clients can also practice monitoring between sessions by completing a diary card whenever they notice a significant change in eating and weight preoccupation (See table 13.1). Initially, clients may need help identifying antecedents beyond the most proximal ED "trigger." For example, clients may be aware of a proximal and concrete event that increased weight preoccupation (e.g., trying on clothes), but not the deeper feelings or the events that sensitized them to this experience in the first place (e.g., an uncomfortable social interaction or feelings of failure earlier in the day). Simply identifying or acknowledging the unwanted feelings that turned their attention toward body weight or shape is itself an act of willingness. Over time, the client may practice allowing feelings for greater durations or in novel ways.

### Table 13.1 ED Volume Diary Card

| ED Volume (0–10) | Date/Time | Situation | Other Thoughts & Feelings | Events Earlier in the Day That Might Have Impacted Mood |
|---|---|---|---|---|
|  |  |  |  |  |

## PREDICTING AN EXTINCTION BURST

When clients begin to challenge their rigid rules and take risks (e.g., eating or resting more, asking for what they need), they are likely to experience a temporary exacerbation in distress. In the realm of eating and weight control, this will be experienced as *more intense* ED thoughts and feelings and may even take the form of self-abuse (e.g., *You are so disgusting* [*fat and lazy*]). This may be worsened by detectable body changes (e.g., weight gain during renourishment; edema following increased insulin). Helping clients predict that the ED will initially become "louder" and "more insistent," as in the example below, is useful in creating distance and helping the individual stay the course or maintain committed action.

T:    As you start to eat more, you may notice that AN will get louder, more insistent. I know this might seem as though things are getting worse, but often this is a good sign. It means that you are not simply going along with its demands. You are choosing for yourself—so it's giving you the sales pitch or trying to bully you into making a different choice…

We can also expect that if you continue to work to restore and repair your body, you will experience a different kind of discomfort, such as bloating. This is when it is most important to continue to take steps forward—if you want to get to the other side. Like trudging through a swamp, if you retreat, you start over on the bank and have to come through this place again…

## MEETING NEEDS

In the past, clients' behavior has often been determined by punitive rules of what they "should" or "ought" to do. Treatment helps them move to a more responsive, attuned way of managing themselves, in which behavior is more respectful of the individual, their feelings and needs, and the circumstances or situation.

Clients practice acknowledging what they are feeling (i.e., "This is sadness") and identifying the need that the feeling might convey (e.g., the need for comfort or social support). Taking action to meet needs is not to make the feeling go away (although it might), but rather to be a respectful, responsive caretaker. With regard to hunger/satiety, this process occurs in stages. Early in treatment, the individual might practice being responsive to their needs by eating or dosing insulin as prescribed by a treatment team (with the individual's preferences taken into account). Later, as weight normalizes, the individual will begin to practice attunement with their hunger/satiety.

We explicitly describe the adaptive value of emotions (or other motivational states) as communication to others and to oneself. We also train discriminating direct experience of a signal from the body from judgment or evaluation of it. Clients repeatedly practice identifying their feelings and the needs that they convey (see the online supplement at http://www.newharbinger.com/43102 for an example worksheet from Merwin et al., 2019).

Difficulties identifying emotions and emotional experiences are common among individuals with EDs. For some clients, the metaphor of a scientist or an investigator collecting data can be useful. Clients start with the known element of experience (e.g., heaviness or turning of the gut) and then observe other internal and external events to arrive at a hypothesis about what they are feeling. Clients might then ask themselves, *What do people need when they feel this way?* By assuming a dispassionate or mindful observer perspective, the client may be able to be more cognitively flexible in the presence of unwanted emotions.

As clients accumulate self-knowledge (e.g., learn what they are feeling and need), they are also in a better position to clarify personal values. By engaging in value-guided behavioral activation, the client may create patterns of activity incompatible with AN.

## Innovations in Structure and Delivery

When individuals are starved, or in the case of T1D, have chronically high BG, cognitive and emotional changes may make it exceedingly difficult to reverse their condition without additional support outside of session. Clients may also need help generalizing skills to the natural environment or to new situations. I describe two innovations to facilitate this: (1) integrating parents or the family with adolescents or young adults with AN, and (2) engaging mobile technology to deliver intervention in the home environment for ED-DMT1 clients. These innovations are situated within our full treatment protocols that build on the novel formulation and treatment strategies previously described.

## COMBINING ACT WITH FBT FOR ADOLESCENT AN

Historically, parents and families of individuals with AN were viewed as instrumental to the development of their child's condition and excluded from treatment. However, in the 1980s, the family-based treatment (FBT) approach was developed. This model included parents in treatment by taking an explicitly nonetiological approach to AN and focusing on present-day management of ED behaviors. The core intervention of FBT was raising parental awareness of the seriousness of the child's condition and having parents assume temporary responsibility for feeding their child and restoring weight. Later, control over eating was passed back to the adolescent, who was assumed to resume a normal developmental trajectory. FBT was instrumental in integrating parents and empowering them to disrupt patterns of restrictive eating that they may have previously been instructed to ignore. From studies of FBT, it became clear that including parents was helpful (particularly in the early stages of intervention) and could more quickly reverse the physical impact of AN. FBT, however, offered little additional skill development for the parents or the adolescent, and while FBT works well for some adolescents, many have suboptimal outcomes (Lock, 2015), and some clients may do better in a separated family format (Eisler et al., 2000). The relapse rate for AN is also high, highlighting the importance of addressing the root issue (i.e., the functional significance of eating and weight preoccupation), rather than just the physical manifestations.

Combining ACT with FBT, we developed an intervention for adolescent AN that increases parent and adolescent psychological flexibility to facilitate immediate and longstanding behavior change: acceptance-based separated family treatment (ASFT; Merwin, Zucker, & Timko, 2013; Merwin et al., 2019; Timko, Zucker, Herbert, Rodriguez, & Merwin, 2015). Parents and adolescents are seen separately for the majority of treatment, with conjoint sessions periodically and at the end of treatment. Parents not only block restriction and facilitate food exposure (as in FBT) but also help the adolescent practice approach-based coping in the moment. This approach makes behavior-change plans (i.e., strategies for increasing food intake) explicit and addresses parents' psychological barriers (e.g., fear that their child will get worse) with acceptance, mindfulness, and values clarification. This occurs at the same time that the adolescent is learning how the ED functions in their lives, practicing openness to internal experiences, and authoring personal values to establish more adaptive patterns of behavior. In the latter half of treatment, adolescents practice treating themselves and their needs with more kindness and respect and pursuing things that are meaningful, even if not predictable and well controlled.

**Framing AN as avoidant coping.** I provide two dialogues that illustrate how you might orient parents to AN and how it functions for their child. The key message is that AN (or rules) has helped their child cope with emotional discomfort by either (1) creating order and structure in a world that is overwhelming or (2) giving them something to feel good about.

In this example, the therapist is talking to a parent about the way in which AN provides structure and helps their child feel less overwhelmed in decision making.

T:    Have you ever been to a café with a huge menu—tons of choices? If you don't eat meat or dairy, you can just eliminate whole sections of this menu. For your daughter, the world is like this and it is overwhelming. There are tons of possibilities and every decision feels monumental and of consequence. AN simplifies things by dramatically reducing her choices. Rather than twenty different options, there is just one. It's Tuesday, she must run. There is something wonderfully comforting in that…she can feel confident she is making the right decision. Taking away these rules, it feels like the whole world comes barreling in and there are infinite options…and the potential to "mess up" or choose the wrong thing.

In this next example, the therapist is talking to a parent about how AN helps their child escape insecurities using the metaphor of a magic cloak.

T:    Your child has found a magic cloak. When she puts it on, all her fears and insecurities go away. She feels protected and safe (from judgment), and good about herself and what she is accomplishing. She can hold her head up and walk around the world. The idea of giving this [AN] up is terrifying to her. It feels as though this would take away the one thing that has made things a little better… made it a little easier to live inside her own skin.

**Family meeting.** A "family meeting" resets the context, establishing a tone of warm boundaries (on the ED) with contingencies. It also allows the parents an opportunity to model acceptance or willingness for deeply held personal values.

Here, the therapist is modeling a family meeting for parents. The interaction continues with the parents "taking a turn" and processing thoughts and feelings that arise as they imagine saying this to their daughter.

T:    It might sound something like this: "You, your health and well-being are the most important thing to us…Up until now, we have been either quiet or upset… out of our own fear and distress…and we can see how that has not been helpful to you…that we have lost you more to the ED…and that is not what we want to be about… We love you too much. So we are going to make a plan, as a family… about how best to help you nourish your body, which has become depleted… We would like to start by discussing ballet and the conditions under which it is safe for you to go…"

**Observing emotional waves.** Having a child who is restricting food is extremely painful. Parents might experience an array of feelings, including fear and uncertainty, sadness, guilt, shame, and anger or frustration. We teach parents to observe their emotions as waves (that rise and fall and rise again) and to stay firmly planted on the shore of their values. Highlighting how parents' emotional experience (e.g., uncertainty, loss of control) parallels that of their child can increase willingness to allow this emotional discomfort as it offers them a window in (and a point of connection) to their child and their child's experience.

We also teach parents to observe *their child's* ED waves, which many manifest as yelling about the use of oil or butter, saying hurtful things to their parents about being made to eat, or distress about how their body looks or feels. We encourage parents to treat their child's waves as a signal (or "flare") indicating that their child is experiencing uncomfortable emotions.

We also remind parents that their child's waves may temporarily get bigger as the child defies AN (i.e., breaks rules and begins to nourish their body). It can be useful to help parents appreciate that what they are witnessing is a reflection of their child's internal experience: "When your child eats more than AN wants them too, AN has a temper tantrum inside your child's head, sometimes yelling and screaming at them, or calling them names. It will be helpful to remember this when your child is behaving in a way that is difficult, such as saying you are an awful parent for making them eat. In these moments, your child is experiencing fear, guilt, or shame. Validation and warm, consistent boundaries will help them through." This helps the parents stay the course, maintain compassion, and experience their child as separate and distinct from the ED in the most difficult moments. (An additional description of the ASFT protocol is provided in Merwin et al., 2013, and Timko et al., 2015. See also Zucker, 2006.)

## COMBINING ACT WITH MOBILE APP TECHNOLOGY FOR ADULTS WITH ED-DMT1

Dysregulated eating and maladaptive weight control are surprisingly common among individuals with T1D. A recent study found a cumulative probability of developing an ED among young women with T1D to be 60% by age twenty-five. ED behaviors among T1D patients include dietary restriction and binge eating, as well as the unique behavior of omitting insulin to lose weight. Most have postulated that the prevalence of dysregulated eating and weight control in T1D is due to T1D exacerbating conditions that spawn EDs in the general population (e.g., increased attention to food choices, weight gain with the initiation of insulin therapy; Goebel-Fabbri, 2009). However, the fact that conventional treatments are less effective for T1D patients suggests unique factors associated with living with T1D.

Individuals with T1D survive by self-administering insulin multiple times a day to keep BG in a normal range. Failure to control BG has severe consequences, including early and severe diabetes-related medical complications (e.g., retinopathy, neuropathy) and increased risk of premature death. However, at any given moment, BG is the result of a confluence of factors, some of which are not completely under the individual's control, or may never be fully known (e.g., stress, illness). Thus, even the most valiant attempts to take insulin as prescribed may produce an undesirable result (BG above the target range). As a result, individuals with T1D may experience frequent feelings of failure and powerlessness. The situation is further exacerbated by the profuse evaluative language of T1D management. For example, BG and HbA$_{1c}$ are often characterized as "good/bad" (as is their diet) and individuals with T1D are told to "correct" their BG when it is high.

To manage this situation, individuals with T1D may adopt one of two strategies: either (1) try to clamp down more (implement rigid rules and demand that their BG cooperate) or (2) reject T1D management outright and focus instead on weight (which is much more controllable, particularly with insulin omission).

We developed an innovative treatment, iACT, for ED-DMT1. Treatment combines individual ACT sessions with a mobile app used in between sessions. The primary aim of treatment is to help patients adopt a more flexible approach to managing themselves and their diabetes and tolerate the uncertainty and distress inherent in living with T1D. Individuals practice taking a less rigid and punitive approach to T1D and its management (e.g., not berating themselves for perceived imperfections) and giving themselves permission to eat and to meet their other physical and emotional needs. Treatment also aims to shift the reinforcement contingencies to favor approaching T1D in daily life by pairing T1D management with patients' deeply held personal values.

The app is included to enhance skill acquisition and generalization. It contains interactive features that increase patients' in-the-moment awareness of internal experience and behavior patterns. It also delivers ACT-based interventions when an individual endorses unwanted thoughts or feelings, cueing acceptance, defusion, and mindfulness and using personal values as a guide. Patients are able to set achievable goals for behavior change, and T1D is recontextualized with T1D-specific messages of humor, compassion, and strength to promote radical acceptance and encourage approach behavior. The app was built on the infrastructure of Recovery Record, an existing mobile app designed to help individuals with EDs (without diabetes), but was modified based on our research to meet the needs of this specific patient population/clinical problem (see figure 13.1).

## Research Support

Our research team evaluated the ASFT protocol described in this chapter in a pilot open trial with forty-seven adolescents with AN and their families (Merwin et al., 2013; Timko et al., 2015). Nearly half of the adolescents met criteria for full remission at end-of-treatment, approximately 30% met criteria for partial remission, and 21% were not improved. ASFT may have unique benefits or processes of change, relative to FBT. Results are promising for an initial trial.

We also piloted iACT with twenty-six adults with T1D with maladaptive eating and weight control. Treatment consisted of twelve weekly sessions and three additional sessions of reduced frequency with app use in between sessions. Thus far, twenty individuals

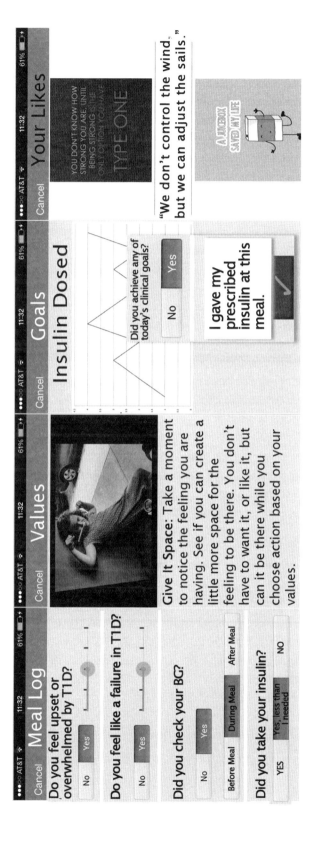

**Figure 13.1.** *Screenshots of primary app features.* **1.** Logs for self-monitoring thoughts, feelings, and T1D management and ED behaviors (restriction, bingeing). **2.** Personalized values images are presented with ACT skills when individuals endorse emotional distress. **3.** Goal progress focuses on momentary choices aligned with personal values (rather than outcomes not completely in the individual's control, such as BG or HbA$_{1c}$). **4.** T1D is recontextualized with messages of strength, humor, and compassion that the user may "like" for later review.

have completed treatment, and we have seventeen post-assessments available for analyses. Participants evidenced clinically significant improvements in diabetes self-management ($d = 1.00$) and diabetes distress ($d = 1.46$). Participants also reported greater acceptance of distressing thoughts/feelings about diabetes ($d = .99$), which correlated with lower $HbA_{1c}$ at end-of-treatment (Spearman's rho = .57). Among participants with suboptimal glycemic control, $HbA_{1c}$ was significantly improved at end-of-treatment ($p < .05$). Final results are forthcoming.

## Future Directions

The evidence for using ACT with eating disorders is still preliminary. A total of fourteen studies have been conducted, with seven specifically targeting AN. Only one study (which I reported here) has evaluated the use of ACT with ED-DMT1. Thus, more research is sorely needed. In our treatments, we have tried to explicitly tie interventions to well-articulated conceptual models of dangerous weight control. These models will need to be tested (with process metrics) and refined accordingly. Treatment development should also continue to explore how mobile technology can be leveraged to facilitate behavior change in the moment. Strategies that help increase clients' awareness of how they are relating to their thoughts and feelings might be particularly useful (for example, prompting, "To what extent are you fused or entangled with this thought?" "To what extent are you fighting this feeling?").

In this chapter, I described innovations in the treatment of dangerous weight control, focusing on two populations at high risk: individuals with AN and individuals with ED-DMT1. Both of these groups have limited (or no) empirically supported treatment options. Preliminary evidence supports the usefulness of ACT, as delivered with these innovations, and the hope is that this will encourage additional treatment development.

## Acknowledgements

This research was supported by grants from the National Institutes of Health (R21 MH085975, PI: Timko; 09-U01-013, PI: Merwin; R01 DK089329, PI: Merwin, R21 DK106603, PI: Merwin). The author wishes to acknowledge colleagues who contributed to the evolution of this work: Nancy L. Zucker, PhD, Duke University; Ashley A. Moskovich, PhD, Duke University Medical Center; Lisa K. Honeycutt, LPC, Duke University Medical Center; and C. Alix Timko, PhD, Children's Hospital of Philadelphia. The author also wishes to thank Jenna Tregarthen and the Recovery Record Development Team for their work adapting the mobile application for type 1 diabetes.

# References

Arcelus, J., Mitchell, A. J., Wales, J., & Nielsen, S. (2011). Mortality rates in patients with anorexia nervosa and other eating disorders. A meta-analysis of 36 studies. *Archives of General Psychiatry, 68*(7), 724–731.

Baumrind, D. (1991). To nurture nature. *Behavioral and Brain Sciences, 14*(3), 386–387.

Beck, A. T. (1979). *Cognitive therapy of depression.* New York, NY: Guilford Press.

Brockmeyer, T., Friederich, H.-C., & Schmidt, U. (2017). Advances in the treatment of anorexia nervosa: A review of established and emerging interventions. *Psychological Medicine,* 1–37.

Bruch, H. (1982). Anorexia nervosa: Therapy and theory. *The American Journal of Psychiatry, 139*(12), 1531–8.

Colton, P. A., Olmsted, M. P., Daneman, D., Farquhar, J. C., Wong, H., Muskat, S., & Rodin, G. M. (2015). Eating disorders in girls and women with type 1 diabetes: A longitudinal study of prevalence, onset, remission, and recurrence. *Diabetes Care, 38*(7), 1212–7.

Criego, A., Crow, S., Goebel-Fabbri, A. E., Kendall, D., & Parkin, C. (2009). Eating disorders and diabetes: Screening and detection. *Diabetes Spectrum, 22*(3), 143–146.

Eisler, I., Dare, C., Hodes, M., Russell, G., Dodge, E., & Le Grange, D. (2000). Family therapy for adolescent anorexia nervosa: The results of a controlled comparison of two family interventions. *The Journal of Child Psychology and Psychiatry and Allied Disciplines, 41*(6), 727–736.

Fairburn, C. G. (2008). *Cognitive behavior therapy and eating disorders.* New York, NY: Guilford Press.

Goebel-Fabbri, A. E. (2009). Disturbed eating behaviors and eating disorders in type 1 diabetes: Clinical significance and treatment recommendations. *Current Diabetes Reports, 9,* 133–139.

Lee, S., Ho, T. P., & Hsu, L. G. (1993). Fat phobic and non-fat phobic anorexia nervosa: A comparative study of 70 Chinese patients in Hong Kong. *Psychological Medicine, 23*(4), 999–1017.

Lock, J. (2015). An update on evidence-based psychosocial treatments for eating disorders in children and adolescents. *Journal of Clinical Child & Adolescent Psychology, 44*(5), 707–721.

Lock, J., Le Grange, D., Agras, W., & Dare, C. (2001). *Treatment manual for anorexia nervosa: A family-based approach.* New York, NY: Guilford Press.

Merwin, R. M., Dmitrieva, N. O., Honeycutt, L. K., Moskovich, A. A., Lane, J. D., Zucker, N. L., . . . Kuo, J. (2015). Momentary predictors of insulin restriction among adults with type 1 diabetes and eating disorder symptomatology. *Diabetes Care, 38*(11), 2025–2032.

Merwin, R. M., Moskovich, A. A., Honeycutt, L. K., Lane, J. D., Feinglos, M., Surwit, R. S., . . . Batchelder, H. (2018). Time of day when type 1 diabetes patients with eating disorder symptoms most commonly restrict insulin. *Psychosomatic Medicine, 80*(2), 222–229.

Merwin, R. M., Timko, C. A., Moskovich, A. A., Ingle, K. K., Bulik, C. M., & Zucker, N. L. (2011). Psychological inflexibility and symptom expression in anorexia nervosa. *Eating Disorders, 19,* 62–82.

Merwin, R. M., Zucker, N. L., & Timko, C. A. (2013). A pilot study of an acceptance-based separated family treatment for adolescent anorexia nervosa. *Cognitive and Behavioral Practice, 20*(4), 485–500.

Merwin, R. M., Zucker, N. L., & Wilson, K. G. (2019). *ACT for anorexia nervosa.* New York, NY: Guilford Press.

Nathan, D. M., & Group, D. E. R. (2014). The diabetes control and complications trial/epidemiology of diabetes interventions and complications study at 30 years: Overview. *Diabetes Care, 37*(1), 9–16.

Nielsen, S. (2001). Epidemiology and mortality of eating disorders. *Psychiatric Clinics of North America, 24*(2), 201–214.

Papadopoulos, F. C., Ekbom, A., Brandt, L., & Ekselius, L. (2009). Excess mortality, causes of death and prognostic factors in anorexia nervosa. *The British Journal of Psychiatry, 194*(1), 10–17.

Peveler, R. C., & Fairburn, C. G. (1992). The treatment of bulimia nervosa in patients with diabetes mellitus. *International Journal of Eating Disorders, 11*(1), 45–53.

Polivy, J., & Herman, C. P. (1985). Dieting and binging: A causal analysis. *American Psychologist, 40*(2), 193–201.

Timko, C. A., Zucker, N. L., Herbert, J. D., Rodriguez, D., & Merwin, R. M. (2015). An open trial of acceptance-based separated family treatment (ASFT) for adolescents with anorexia nervosa. *Behaviour Research and Therapy, 69*(0), 63–74.

Zucker, N. (2006). *Off the CUFF: A parent skills book for the management of disordered eating.* Durham, NC: Duke University Medical Center.

# SECTION FOUR

# Innovations in Implementing ACT

# CHAPTER 14

# Implementing ACT in a Partial Hospitalization Program

Kristy L. Dalrymple

Catherine D'Avanzato

Theresa Morgan

*Department of Psychiatry, Lifespan Physicians Group*

*Department of Psychiatry and Human Behavior,*
*Alpert Medical School of Brown University*

## Overview

Partial hospitalization programs (PHPs) are increasingly common in the United States (Neuhaus, Christopher, Jacob, Guillaumot, & Burns, 2007). PHPs provide daily intensive treatment but allow patients to return home each evening, therefore maintaining important contact with independence and valued living (Block & Lefkovitz, 1991). PHPs vary in treatment-day duration, but they typically last several hours and include diagnostic evaluation, group therapy, individual therapy, case management, and medication management. They are a cost-effective alternative to inpatient hospitalization: a "step up" in treatment from outpatient, or a "step down" from inpatient providing a smoother transition to outpatient settings.

Although PHPs are an increasingly utilized service, they are underrepresented in the research literature compared to inpatient or outpatient settings. Despite this relative paucity, evidence supporting PHP level of care is generally positive. Compared to inpatient care, PHPs are equally or more effective (e.g., Priebe et al., 2011) and result in faster improvement in mental state (Marshall et al., 2001). Patients also report higher levels of satisfaction with care in PHPs compared to inpatient programs (e.g., Horvitz-Lennon, Normand, Gaccione, & Frank, 2001).

PHPs have several unique features and challenges compared to outpatient treatment; thus, certain adaptations in the delivery of psychosocial treatment within PHPs may be necessary to maximize outcomes. In this chapter, we describe the PHP treatment setting and ways that acceptance and commitment therapy (ACT) may be a particularly useful treatment model for PHPs. We review specific ways of adapting ACT for this setting based on our development of the Acceptance and Mindfulness-Based Adult Partial Hospitalization Program at Rhode Island Hospital (RIH). This program is an ongoing clinical research program; therefore, we also describe ways that clinical research is integrated within this setting and how it guides further program development.

# Development of the Acceptance and Mindfulness-Based Adult PHP at RIH

When the opportunity arose to restructure the PHP at RIH, the ACT therapeutic model seemed to be a natural fit based on its tenets. We asked ourselves these critical questions to facilitate the program development process, including:

- How do we combine group and individual treatment to ensure that ACT principles are consistently applied throughout the program?

- How should the content be structured (e.g., address all core processes, or focus on only a few)?

- How do we make the treatment program more flexible for real-world purposes yet maintain fidelity to the ACT model?

- How do we integrate research into this clinical program?

You may want to consider similar questions when developing an ACT-based program within an intensive treatment setting.

## Overview of the Program

A typical day at the PHP consists of an individual therapy session, four therapy groups (see figure 14.1), and a medication-management session with a psychiatrist. The average length of stay is approximately seven to ten days, but it varies widely (from a few days to three months). Average daily census is approximately forty-five patients, covering the full spectrum of psychiatric diagnoses including psychotic, mood, anxiety, substance use, impulse control, and borderline personality disorders. Individuals represent diverse ethnic, racial, gender identity, sexual orientation, education, and socioeconomic backgrounds. Over half of our patients have no degree past high school, and ages range from eighteen to eighty-nine.

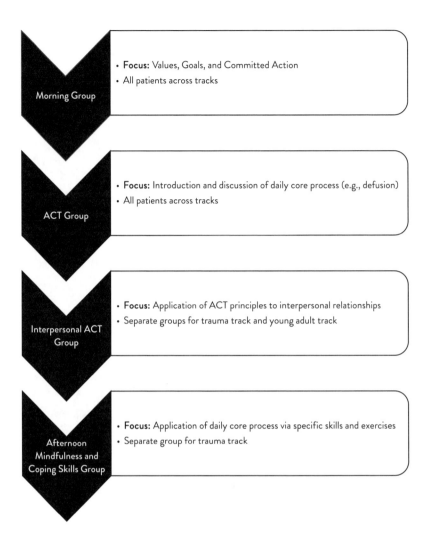

**Morning Group**
- **Focus:** Values, Goals, and Committed Action
- All patients across tracks

**ACT Group**
- **Focus:** Introduction and discussion of daily core process (e.g., defusion)
- All patients across tracks

**Interpersonal ACT Group**
- **Focus:** Application of ACT principles to interpersonal relationships
- Separate groups for trauma track and young adult track

**Afternoon Mindfulness and Coping Skills Group**
- **Focus:** Application of daily core process via specific skills and exercises
- Separate group for trauma track

**Figure 14.1.** Structure of the partial hospital treatment day groups.

## Challenges in the PHP Setting

Patients in PHPs tend to experience greater severity/acuteness of symptoms and functional impairment compared to outpatients. Therefore, you need to adjust treatment strategies to address patients' acute crises and provide sufficient motivation for behavior change at a time when discomfort is at a peak. Because heterogeneity in PHPs is common, designing interactive groups that are of utility to all patients presents a significant clinical challenge. Treatment in PHPs is brief yet intense; thus, you may need to adjust the breadth, depth, and "dosage" of the therapeutic content. For example, you may need to prioritize skills or concepts introduced, given the brief length of stay. PHPs typically involve an ongoing enrollment process, with individuals being admitted to and discharged from the program each day, which can present challenges regarding therapeutic content. In light of this, you should consider designing interactive groups that are helpful to patients at varying points of their PHP admission.

PHPs tend to be multidisciplinary, including staff from psychiatry, psychology, social work, and other mental health disciplines, which can lead to challenges with coordinating care across providers who may have different theoretical perspectives. This extends beyond discharge from the PHP, as patients ultimately return to outpatient providers who may have different theoretical perspectives. Therefore, you may need to adapt treatment delivery to support varied disciplines and optimize a team approach to care.

## How ACT Is Poised to Address These Challenges

Evidence for the larger ACT model has been well documented (e.g., A-Tjak et al., 2015; Twohig & Levin, 2017) and supports the efficacy of ACT in treating complex presentations in a wide variety of settings. Its transdiagnostic focus makes it especially well suited for the PHP setting in which the patient population is highly heterogeneous and comorbid.

Valuing in ACT may be particularly helpful for PHP patients to identify personally meaningful life directions and build patterns of behavior that can continue to be fostered in outpatient treatment. Valuing is an important motivating factor for behavior change, and it is compatible with other therapeutic modalities that may be used by outpatient therapists following discharge. The emphasis on increasing willingness to experience discomfort while building patterns of values-consistent behaviors can be useful in this type of setting where patients are experiencing acute distress, as it validates their experience while also providing them with tools for coping with discomfort. Combined with an intensive, yet safe, treatment environment, patients have ample opportunity to practice new behaviors as they increase acceptance around the discomfort that will likely arise.

The ACT model is flexible in that no component process is required as a "beginning point," and thus patients may theoretically derive benefit from any process-based group regardless of order of administration. Therefore, patients are not precluded from joining treatment at any time, which can alleviate the challenge of ongoing enrollment in PHPs. This is particularly useful for designing interactive groups that maximize outcomes in a setting where heterogeneity prevails.

## Description of ACT Adaptations in a PHP Setting

We adapted our ACT program in several ways to overcome challenges and better fit a PHP setting. In this section we review the specific adaptations, which you may wish to consider when adapting ACT for intensive treatment settings. We first explain how to structure and plan content of therapy groups within a rolling admissions program, then discuss the tailoring of group content to challenging patients with diverse concerns and levels of functioning. We also discuss ways to modify ACT for individual therapy within intensive treatment settings to meet the challenges of brief, frequent sessions.

## Modifying ACT for a Group Format

To embrace the flexibility of the ACT model, we elected to forego a highly structured manual for delivering group content. Instead, we developed a flexible manual with a small sample of group session outlines for each of the six ACT core processes. Our therapists draw from these sample outlines in preparing group sessions, yet they have the flexibility to develop alternative content by substituting metaphors and exercises of their own.

To address the challenge of rolling admissions, we designate one ACT core process of the day as the focal point of the day's group content. The daily core process rotates on an approximately seven-day cycle in a fixed order, so that patients receive content on each of the core processes within a seven-day typical length of stay. We also integrate self-compassion and interpersonal effectiveness skills into the topic rotation based on our prior experience and clinical research showing that patients benefit from these skills. The morning ACT group and afternoon Mindfulness and Coping Skills group are paired with respect to the designated daily core process. We introduce the core process in the morning ACT group, and the afternoon skills group applies the core process via specific exercises that allow hands-on experience implementing skills such as mindfulness, defusion, observer-self, and acceptance.

For example, on mindfulness day we start the morning ACT group with a general discussion of what defines mindfulness and why it is important. We then may conduct a Mindfulness Quiz experiential exercise with questions on sights and sounds patients can recall observing throughout the unit (e.g., "What is in the photo hanging in the waiting room?"). We normalize how common it is to miss such observations in the present moment and elicit the group's input on why this is (e.g., spending most of their time ruminating on the past or future) and the pros and cons (e.g., how this pulls them away from valued directions). We end the morning ACT group by comparing mindfulness to mindlessness and discussing how mindfulness can be helpful in addressing the patients' presenting concerns (visit http://www.newharbinger.com/43102 for a sample outline). In the afternoon Mindfulness and Coping Skills group, we then conduct a hands-on mindfulness exercise (e.g., body scan). We invite patients to discuss their experience during the exercise, including comparing it to their default mode of attention, addressing obstacles and challenges that arose, and addressing questions.

Our flexible group manual allows us to accommodate patients with lengths of stay beyond seven days; the therapist team uses a topic log to record and plan group content to avoid repeating the same metaphors or exercises. On mindfulness day, for example, the group therapist notes in the topic log that a body scan was done so that we would select a different mindfulness exercise (e.g., mindfulness of breath) the next time that mindfulness comes up in the topic rotation. Thus, while patients with longer lengths of stay will repeat core processes, we can introduce new material to ensure that group content engages patients at all points in treatment.

There are several things to consider when deciding whether or not to structure your program to focus on one core process of the day. One important advantage is that it allows us to track which core processes have been covered to ensure all patients, regardless of length of stay, receive adequate coverage of ACT content. This structure also allows for greater repetition of concepts within the day, which may help patients to better absorb and implement the material. Similarly, it allows therapists to better integrate group content into individual therapy sessions (e.g., referring back to exercises introduced in earlier groups). This may be particularly helpful for programs with high patient census and large multidisciplinary teams, in which patients are subdivided into multiple groups or tracks that are running simultaneously.

A potential disadvantage of designating one core ACT process of the day is that this may reduce flexibility to highlight multiple core processes simultaneously during a given group session. We recommend considering the following strategies to mitigate these concerns. Using the mindfulness day example, although we are designating mindfulness as the process of the day, we frequently discuss how mindfulness relates to other core processes such as acceptance and values (e.g., during the body scan, discussing how mindfulness involves willingness to experience uncomfortable emotions and relinquish control of thoughts). In addition, daily individual therapy session content does not need to be structured around the core process of the day, allowing flexibility to alternate between core processes or discuss multiple processes simultaneously.

The flexible manual approach also plays a critical role in tailoring group content to meet the needs of patients with diverse functioning levels and problems. Some metaphors and activities, or methods of delivering them, tend to work better with particular functioning levels and/or presenting concerns. A flexible approach allows us to plan group material in consideration of the needs of the current milieu, which is continually changing in the PHP setting. For instance, we have found that particular patient groups vary in their experience level with mindfulness and meditation, their level of engagement, and other factors, and thus particular exercises tend to work better with some groups than others. As opposed to using fixed group outlines (e.g., always conducting the body scan exercise on mindfulness day), the flexible manual approach allows us to better match particular mindfulness exercises to the milieu at hand.

We meet twice weekly as a team and informally during each day, and recommend doing so to review patients and discuss challenges that arise in the milieu. For example, if the morning ACT group leader senses a low level of engagement and willingness in the group, they may alert the afternoon Mindfulness and Coping Skills group leaders, who have the flexibility to choose an exercise that may be less challenging (e.g., a brief physical grounding exercise). In sum, based on our experiences, we recommend that you consider designating a core process of the day around which to plan group content, while also allowing therapists to choose from a broad range of group outlines based on frequent input from the team about the needs of the current milieu.

## Modifying ACT for Individual Sessions in an Acute Care Setting

PHP patients attend daily thirty-minute therapy sessions, in contrast to the typical weekly forty-five-minute sessions in outpatient treatment. The brief length of stay requires rapid case conceptualization and treatment planning, typically completed within the first one to two days of treatment and revised as needed based on input from the multidisciplinary team. A typical patient presents to our program with multiple concerns, including posttraumatic symptoms, interpersonal and emotion regulation difficulties, depression, and co-occurring anxiety disorders. A goal of the first two sessions is to identify core transdiagnostic processes that we hypothesize may be contributing to difficulties in functioning and living according to values. Due to the short-term nature of intensive care settings, we recommend that providers, in collaboration with the patient, strive to identify and prioritize one or two targets for treatment (e.g., is the patient's social anxiety or posttraumatic stress currently interfering the most?). Initially, we may hypothesize that the patient's avoidance of trauma reminders is the principal target, but through consultation with group leaders we may receive input on the patient's interpersonal behaviors in group that should be prioritized.

The substantial proportion of patients presenting to PHPs with serious suicidal ideation, hopelessness, and significant functional impairment compounds the challenge of achieving meaningful change in a short time. In initial sessions, creative hopelessness plays an important role in raising awareness of the unworkability of avoidance and control strategies and in building motivation for change. For example, the Chinese Handcuffs exercise (Hayes, Strosahl, & Wilson, 1999, p. 105) has worked well in individual sessions with patients with diverse functioning levels and presenting concerns. This experiential exercise helps with initiating a discussion about avoidance behaviors, exploring short- versus long-term costs of particular behaviors, and harnessing distress to build motivation for change.

We also tailor exercises to problem and functioning level by creating multiple formats of handouts for behavioral monitoring or homework (e.g., revising handouts for patients at lower functioning levels to be more concrete). With the Chinese Handcuffs exercise, for example, we modified the standard version of a form used in our outpatient work by further simplifying the language for patients who had difficulty understanding. For individual sessions, we recommend selecting handouts tailored to particular patients (whereas for group therapy with patients with diverse functioning levels, we recommend starting with the simplified version, thus allowing all patients to benefit). We also recommend preceding abstract experiential exercises with concrete instructions about how the exercise may relate to the patient's concerns and providing frequent summaries of key points throughout the session. You may also wish to use a whiteboard and other visuals to summarize key points.

We regularly integrate behavioral exercises into individual sessions, which often requires modifications to fit the population and abbreviated daily session structure.

Exposure exercises help to build willingness and defusion skills for patients presenting with primary goals to target various types of anxiety. Exposure in a PHP setting often is shorter in duration than in traditional outpatient therapy; however, ACT's emphasis on achieving a clearly defined behavioral goal that furthers movement toward values, rather than within-session habituation, is an advantage in the PHP setting. For example, for a patient with social anxiety, we might integrate brief exposure work in individual therapy by setting a goal to speak in the morning group session. Afterward in the brief individual therapy session, we check on whether the patient met their behavioral goal (speaking in group), how this related to values, and what the patient learned from this exercise (e.g., handling anxiety better than expected). The PHP setting allows frequent and varied opportunities to reinforce behavior change, including daily therapy sessions and exposure homework in groups. Patients' individual providers (e.g., psychiatrist and therapist) consult with one another and with group leaders to reinforce this exposure process. Using the social anxiety example, we might ask the group leader for feedback on how the patient did speaking in group and incorporate that in the follow-up individual therapy discussion. As another example, a patient with posttraumatic stress working in individual sessions on in-vivo exposures to crowded public places may be invited to sit in the center during group sessions near unfamiliar people or away from the exit. We also incorporate written exposure exercises for posttraumatic stress into individual sessions, which can be delivered in an ACT-consistent way in a brief, daily intensive format as an alternative to traditional imaginal exposure.

## Developing Specialty Tracks

Another important decision point is how presenting problems should factor into designing groups. Although ACT's transdiagnostic focus can address this challenge, our experience has been that some patients benefit from groups tailored to their presenting concerns. We addressed this need through the creation of specialty tracks, consistent with others who have developed therapist guides that integrate additional content specific to a presenting problem (e.g. Walser & Westrup, 2007). Currently, specialty tracks are available to patients with (1) trauma-related concerns, (2) young adult concerns, and (3) borderline personality disorder and emotion regulation difficulties. Patient satisfaction surveys and focus groups informed our decision to establish specialty tracks, and patients commented that they benefit from the ability to connect with others with similar experiences and therapy content focused on their concerns.

All patients, regardless of presenting concern, attend general group programming such as the same morning group on values clarification and committed action (see figure 14.1). For up to two of the four daily groups, patients either split off into their specialty track or attend an analogous general track group. For instance, patients in the trauma track attend the same morning group with general track patients but attend a track-specific coping skills group in the afternoon. This afternoon group covers the same ACT content as the general track, while allowing for modification of exercises and more tailored discussion of trauma-related concerns. Modifications to mindfulness exercises in this group include allowing the option of eyes-open mindfulness, reducing the length of meditation exercises, or opting for mindfulness of physical sensations or sensory stimuli in the environment over exercises focused on mindfulness of thoughts (Walser & Westrup, 2007, p. 32). Patients in the personality track attend their own morning ACT group, with the same content as the general track but tailored specifically to their needs. We have modified this group to integrate elements of dialectical behavior therapy (Linehan, 1993) with ACT, based on prior work in this area (Morton and Shaw, 2012). For example, when defusion is the core process of the day, skills might be used to label experiences such as fear of abandonment or mood swings as "that's my BPD" to increase awareness and decrease struggle with these experiences. Patients in the young adult track attend their own interpersonal ACT group, tailored to address their needs during an important developmental period (e.g., how to effectively relate to their parents as they are developing their independence).

## Maintaining Consistency Within a Multidisciplinary Team

Each patient meets daily with a therapist and psychiatrist; thus, steps are needed to ensure that care is delivered as consistently as possible with the ACT model across providers. Psychiatrists practicing based on a medical model often emphasize the role of biology and may be more likely to attribute improvements in symptoms and functioning to medication. Patients may then become fused with beliefs that their symptoms must improve, perhaps by finding the right medication, before engaging in valued activities. In contrast, therapists often emphasize internal attributions for change, as patients may be more motivated to engage in committed action when attributing improvement to behavioral choices.

We rely on three key strategies to promote consistency within the team. First, we invite providers across disciplines to participate jointly in training opportunities to become more familiar with ACT. Opportunities include workshops for current staff, outside speaker presentations on ACT (e.g., ACT for psychosis), local/regional ACT trainings, and a department-wide ACT peer consultation meeting. Second, it has been helpful to raise concerns about inconsistency in weekly team meetings. When patients are engaging in therapy-interfering behaviors, members of the treatment team or other staff may inadvertently reinforce these behaviors. We have found that discussing these issues openly among all team members ensures a clear and consistent conceptualization of the interfering behaviors, which then facilitates use of more effective behavioral strategies. Third, frequent one-on-one consultations between providers on patients' care teams have played a critical role in identifying and addressing potential discrepancies to arrive at a more consistent treatment plan. In addition to consulting at formal weekly meetings, we recommend that psychiatrists and therapists consult briefly on a daily basis or as needed to discuss shared patients. If a therapist is doing exposure work with a patient, for example, we have found it beneficial for the therapist to notify the psychiatrist to ensure that consistent messages are being given to the patient during the exposure process (e.g., reminding the patient that increased momentary anxiety will occur with exposure, and abstaining from as-needed medication or other substances to allow for exposure to work fully).

# Integrating Research into an ACT PHP Program

At the inception of our program in 2013, we were unable to identify any studies examining the use of ACT specifically in PHPs. And since that time, only one such article has emerged, reporting a study of ACT in a specialized day treatment setting for treatment-resistant patients with personality disorders (Chakhssi, Janssen, Pol, Van Dreumel, & Westerhof, 2015). Therefore, in addition to providing a beneficial clinical service, our aim was to collect data to contribute to the literature on the effectiveness of PHPs and the application of ACT in this setting. We also anticipated using our data to adapt and improve our clinical work in the PHP setting. Thus, once the clinical program was established, we developed the infrastructure for our clinical research program within the PHP. Even if you do not plan to publish findings on outcomes, when developing a clinical program we recommend collecting some data to guide further refinement of the program and ensure that patients are benefitting from the program. We provide examples of how we have integrated research into our program, should you decide to develop an ACT program in an intensive treatment setting.

## Feasibility of Integrating Clinical Research into Clinical Care

We began the clinical-research integration with obtaining Institutional Review Board approval to collect data from patients undergoing treatment at a PHP. We now employ six research assistants who track and coordinate recruitment of patients, data collection, and maintenance of the databases. Providers also facilitate recruitment and data collection (e.g., obtaining informed consent at intake, collecting daily measures from patients during their individual sessions), and providers interested in being more heavily involved in research collaborate on developing and refining research procedures and disseminating results. By embedding research procedures into the clinical workflow, we have created a culture of participation in clinical research on the part of both patients and staff.

The majority of our therapists use daily measures in treatment, and we found that results from daily measures were requested regularly in our interactions with insurance companies. Furthermore, regulatory agencies are increasingly requiring documentation of the use of validated outcome measures on a daily basis. Therefore, we recommend assessing psychiatric symptoms (e.g., depression, anxiety) daily. Initially, we assessed ACT processes, functional impairment, and coping only at intake and discharge.

Although providers were aware of how to interpret and track symptoms over time, not all providers regularly included process work such as values or acceptance in their assessments. To address this issue, we designed and implemented a daily ACT process measure, using items from existing scales where possible and creating items when scales did not exist (e.g., for self-as-context). This scale serves a clinical purpose as well; several patients reported using it to assess how they are doing each day. Thus, the very act of assessing these core processes orients patients to important areas for change and sends an important message about our program focus. We recommend daily assessment of processes in addition to symptoms, as this can provide useful clinical information and opportunities for scientifically studying changes in proposed core processes over time.

## Preliminary Results from an ACT PHP Program

In this section, we provide some preliminary results from our clinical-research PHP program to provide examples of what types of data can be collected and how it can be used. We have collected data on outcomes for the purposes of ensuring that the program is effective for patients and to contribute to the literature on the effectiveness of PHP programs. In addition, we have collected satisfaction data to guide refinement of the program.

### INITIAL OUTCOMES

We enrolled 84.8% (750/881 patients) into clinical research within the first two years of the program. Of the first 750 consented patients, nearly 70% completed treatment as recommended by their treatment team (n = 516), over an average of 8.2 days (SD = 3.9). Patients who completed treatment reported significant decreases in depression and anxiety from intake to discharge (Cohen's $d$ from 0.78 to 1.26, indicating large effects). Quality of life and functioning also increased significantly from intake to discharge (Cohen's $d$ from .75 to 1.13, indicating large effects). ACT processes changed too, albeit more modestly: the largest change was for valuing, which increased by 30% over the course of treatment (Cohen's $d$ = .90). Psychological inflexibility also dropped by 20% from intake to discharge (Cohen's $d$ = .76).

### PATIENT SATISFACTION WITH AN ACT PHP PROGRAM

We assessed patient satisfaction for each daily group for a period of several months (see the online supplement "Examples of Patient Satisfaction Scales" at http://www.newharbinger.com/43102). Patients provided ratings on a Likert-type scale ranging from 0 (not at all) to 6 (extremely) for four questions: usefulness of the session, satisfaction with the content, satisfaction with the presenter, and comprehension of the content. Satisfaction for all groups was very high (means from 4.6 to 5.1), and patients reported the highest satisfaction and perceived utility for the interpersonal ACT group. Patients reported the lowest satisfaction and utility for the morning values group. Nonetheless, satisfaction was high overall, with no groups being rated lower than 4.5 on average for both satisfaction and utility.

We used this satisfaction data to inform decisions about group content. For example, the morning values group was shortened and restructured to include more written exercises. Subsequent to this change, satisfaction increased in this group. We piloted a brief, daily meditation group, which was well received as indicated by satisfaction surveys and thus became a part of daily care. Because we tracked the designated daily core process of each group, we were able to assess patient comprehension and usefulness of group content. Analyses indicated lower levels of comprehension, self-reported satisfaction, and usefulness for the core process of self-as-context, with no significant differences found between the five remaining core processes. Therefore, we decided to retain but decrease the frequency of self-as-context in the group topic rotation, while integrating discussion of self-as-context into groups on mindfulness and defusion in ways that simplified the material. The therapists also met as a team to discuss modifications to presenting self-as-context to help patients better absorb the material.

We also administered satisfaction surveys at discharge to assess patients' experience with program components cumulatively across their admission (see the online supplement "Examples of Patient Satisfaction Scales" at http://www.newharbinger.com/43102). Ratings were on a scale from 0 (not at all satisfied) to 4 (extremely satisfied). Patients reported the highest satisfaction with individual therapy sessions (mean = 3.75, SD = .58). Didactic and interpersonally focused ACT groups were also rated highly (all means > 3) for satisfaction. Consistent with the postgroup ratings described above, the morning values group was rated somewhat lower compared to other groups (mean = 2.89). Nonetheless, this rating indicated that patients were "moderately" to "very" satisfied with the morning values group overall. Finally, over 70% of patients indicated they would "definitely recommend the program to a friend or family member."

## Adapting Clinical Research Processes over Time

Consistent with our principles of workability and flexibility, we made several changes to the clinical research process over time. For instance, we incentivized clinicians to obtain informed consent from patients by linking objective measures of consent rates (or documented nonconsent) to annual staff raises, increasing our enrollment rate to over 90%. We also implemented a more structured process to get data from treatment teams to our research assistants, decreasing the rate of missing data that is endemic to naturalistic clinical settings. We created a form for the treatment team to track collection of daily measures, both to serve as a reminder to the treatment team and to aid the research assistants in matching the measures to the corresponding treatment day to facilitate coding in the database.

# Future Directions for Research

Results of our research thus far have been promising, but it is crucial to conduct further research on outcomes and processes to demonstrate the clinical utility of ACT in this level of care. Challenges exist in conducting psychotherapy research in routine practice settings, such as ethical concerns related to randomizing patients to treatment, and lack of financial/infrastructure resources. Nonetheless, naturalistic studies on outcomes in PHPs can complement results from more tightly controlled clinical trials. Below are some ideas that we have explored, which may be useful for you to consider if you are developing a clinical-research intensive ACT program.

While it is difficult to use comparison conditions in this setting, we could examine outcomes in a more creative manner via the specialty tracks. We cannot randomize patients to the general track or the trauma track, for example, but often there is a waitlist to move patients to the trauma track given the high demand for this service. We can use this as a waitlist design proxy, by comparing outcomes for patients who are on the waitlist for the first few days to those who receive care on the trauma track beginning on treatment day one. Maintenance of outcomes post-discharge also is an important area of inquiry, as this period is a crucial time to intervene due to a high risk of relapse and rehospitalization (Zeeck, Hartmann, & Kuhn, 2005). We now offer aftercare outpatient groups, and we could collect data to compare follow-up outcomes between patients who attend aftercare groups and those who do not. We also assess process variables at intake, at discharge, and daily, which allows us to examine changes in ACT processes over the course of the program and whether these processes serve as mediators or moderators of outcomes.

We have considered examining issues related to staff training and fidelity, especially as our program continues to expand. Methods for monitoring fidelity in clinical trials are often too cumbersome for use in a routine clinical setting. However, we have developed a proxy for this by creating a patient self-report measure to assess the degree to which patients have retained messages that are consistent with the ACT model. We currently are validating this measure and will use it both for research and clinical purposes to monitor fidelity and make adjustments to program content as necessary.

# Future Directions for Clinical Adaptations

Although we already have made several changes to the program since its inception in 2013, we will continue to expand and evolve the program based on the literature and our own research findings. Potential areas for future adaptations might include continuing to add to the rotation of daily core processes based on the literature and satisfaction of patients, as we did with adding self-compassion and interpersonal effectiveness. Other specialty tracks could be added as our program continues to grow. For example, due to the recent opioid epidemic and the strong evidence base for the use of ACT with chronic pain patients (Hughes, Clark, Colclough, Dale, & McMillan, 2017), we could add a specialty track for patients experiencing comorbid chronic pain.

In conclusion, the partial hospital setting poses certain challenges, including how to provide effective treatment in a short period of time, to patients with a wide variety of presenting problems and functioning levels, and in collaboration with a multidisciplinary team. The ACT model may be particularly poised to address these challenges, based on its transdiagnostic focus and flexible approach. Within our own program, we have found that strategies such as using flexible manuals for group therapy and designating a core process theme for the day have helped to ensure that important ACT processes are addressed in ways that are engaging for patients regardless of presenting problem, functioning level, or point of treatment stay. In addition, we have utilized weekly team meetings and frequent "curbside" consultations between treatment team providers to maintain consistency regarding case conceptualization and treatment planning. Finally, we have created a culture of clinical research in our program; this provides us with data to ensure that treatment approaches are effective for patients, and it aligns with our values of engaging in processes of program refinement/improvement and evidence-based practice.

# References

A-Tjak, J. G. L., Davis, M. L., Morina, N., Powers, M. B., Smits, J. A. J., & Emmelkamp, P. M. G. (2015). A meta-analysis of the efficacy of acceptance and commitment therapy for clinically relevant mental and physical health problems. *Psychotherapy and Psychosomatics, 84*, 1–36.

Block, B. M., & Lefkovitz, P. M. (1991). American Association for Partial Hospitalization standards and guidelines for partial hospitalization. *International Journal of Partial Hospitalization, 7*, 3–11.

Chakhssi, F., Janssen, W., Pol, S. M., Van Dreumel, M., & Westerhof, G. J. (2015). Acceptance and commitment therapy group-treatment for non-responsive patients with personality disorder: An exploratory study. *Personality and Mental Health, 9*, 345–356.

Hayes, S. C., Strosahl, K. D., & Wilson, K. G. (1999). *Acceptance and commitment therapy: An experiential approach to behavior change.* New York, NY: The Guilford Press.

Horvitz-Lennon, M., Normand, S. T., Gaccione, P., & Frank, R. G. (2001). Partial versus full hospitalization for adults in psychiatric distress: A systematic review of the published literature (1957–1997). *American Journal of Psychiatry, 158*, 676–685.

Hughes, L. S., Clark, J., Colclough, J. A., Dale, E., & McMillan, D. (2017). Acceptance and commitment therapy (ACT) for chronic pain: A systematic review and meta-analyses. *Clinical Journal of Pain, 33*, 552–568.

Linehan, M. M. (1993). *Cognitive-behavioral treatment of borderline personality disorder.* New York, NY: The Guilford Press.

Marshall, M., Crowther, R., Almaraz-Serrano, A., Creed, F., Sledge, W., Kluiter, H., . . . Tyrer, P. (2001). Systematic reviews of the effectiveness of day care for people with severe mental disorders: (1) Acute day hospital versus admission; (2) Vocational rehabilitation; (3) Day hospital versus outpatient care. *Health Technology Assessment, 5*, 1–75.

Morton, J., & Shaw, L. (2012). *Wise choices: Acceptance and commitment therapy groups for people with borderline personality disorder.* Melbourne, Victoria: Australian Postgraduate Medicine.

Neuhaus, E. C., Christopher, M., Jacob, K., Guillaumot, J., & Burns, J. P. (2007). Short-term cognitive behavioral partial hospital treatment: A pilot study. *Journal of Psychiatric Practice, 13,* 298–307.

Priebe, S., McCabe, R., Schutzwohl, M., Kiejna, A., Nawka, P., Raboch, J., . . . Kallert, T.W. (2011). Patient characteristics predicting better treatment outcomes in day hospitals compared with inpatient wards. *Psychiatric Services, 62,* 278–284.

Twohig, M. P., & Levin, M. E. (2017). Acceptance and commitment therapy as a treatment for anxiety and depression. *Psychiatric Clinics of North America, 40,* 751–770.

Walser, R., & Westrup, D. (2007). *Acceptance & commitment therapy for the treatment of post-traumatic stress disorder & trauma-related problems: A practitioner's guide to using mindfulness & acceptance strategies.* Oakland, CA: New Harbinger.

Zeeck, A., Hartmann, A., & Kuhn, K. (2005). Psychotherapy in a day clinic: Results of a 1.5 year follow-up. *The Psychiatric Quarterly, 76,* 1–17.

# CHAPTER 15

# One-Day ACT Workshops for Patients with Chronic Health Problems and Associated Emotional Disorders

## Lilian Dindo

*Baylor College of Medicine*
*Center for Innovations, Quality, and Effectiveness*

## Aliza Weinrib

*Pain Research Unit, Department of Anesthesia and Pain Management*
*General Hospital, University Health Network*
*Department of Psychology, York University*

## James Marchman

*Department of Psychological and Brain Sciences, University of Iowa*

## Overview

People with chronic illness often lead lives of quiet desperation (Thoreau, 2008). Though their suffering can be severe and their lives circumscribed, they do not seek behavioral health services and don't see themselves as having problems that could be addressed by behavioral means. Over time, their frustration with illness and disability mounts, isolation increases, and the possibility of living rich and rewarding lives seems ever more remote. For 20% of these patients, clinical anxiety and depression develop (Evans et al., 2005; Merikangas et al., 2007). Significant illness-driven distress can exacerbate existing disease, and avoidant behaviors such as reduced adherence to medical treatments can follow (DiMatteo, Lepper, & Croghan, 2000; Merikangas et al., 2007).

Traditional interventions (e.g., twelve sessions of individual psychotherapy) are often not feasible or appealing to these patients. With practical barriers and competing priorities, nearly 40% of patients terminate outpatient psychotherapy after the first or second visit (Wierzbicki & Pekanik, 1986). A treatment that fails to retain patients long enough to achieve benefit cannot be considered a "gold-standard" treatment, even if it shows positive effects in randomized controlled trials (Najavits, 2015).

What if another way forward is possible? What if we could reach these patients in one-day workshops, transform their stance toward their pain and suffering, and plant seeds of commitment to values-driven, rewarding lives? Our workshop approach aims to do this by addressing some the barriers to effective care discussed below (see table 15.1). In this chapter, we describe our approach, which has been honed over approximately sixty workshops—each followed by qualitative feedback interviews—over eight years. We experientially teach the whole of the ACT model in one encounter, aiming for substantial and lasting change.

### Table 15.1 The One-Day Workshop Addresses Barriers to Care

| Intervention Component | Barrier Addressed | How It Will Be Addressed |
|---|---|---|
| Implemented in primary or specialty care clinics | • Veterans not presenting to mental health clinics <br><br> • Stigma <br><br> • Cost | • Primary care and specialty care physicians actively involved in recruitment <br><br> • Intervention held in primary care or specialty clinic setting |
| One-day treatment delivered as a workshop | • Time constraints <br><br> • Treatment adherence and completion <br><br> • Stigma | • Repeated weekly visits not needed <br><br> • Full treatment obtained in one day <br><br> • Labeling as workshop more acceptable and less stigmatizing |
| ACT treatment model | • Significant comorbidity of medical and distress-based conditions <br><br> • Difficulties with social/ occupational functioning <br><br> • Stigma | • Transdiagnostic, unified approach for comorbidity <br><br> • Less focus on mental illness and greater focus on acceptance and enhanced engagement in life |

## Workshop Components

We believe there are three important components to the workshop format, and each may have power to induce therapeutic change. Together, they are particularly potent.

### PATIENT EDUCATION

Patients often have surprisingly little understanding of their illness, the rationales of its treatment, and their own ability to influence its course. Each workshop therefore includes one hour of illness education designed by a specialist in the medical condition of interest. This includes discussion of causes and course of the condition as well as common treatments or medications with their side effects and risks. We provide authoritative informational handouts for patients to take home to review. Throughout the workshop we refer to this information and how the ACT concepts are relevant.

## SOCIAL SUPPORT

Not only does the group format conserve institutional resources, the social support offers important advantages. Groups generally consist of five to ten participants sharing their common experiences, providing patients with a sense that they are not alone and, further, that their struggles are not due to personal weakness, but rather are natural consequences of being human beings. In a study using social support as a control condition, our control participants showed significant improvements in mood and quality of life (Dindo, Recober, Turvey, & Calarge, in preparation).

## PSYCHOLOGICAL FLEXIBILITY TRAINING

ACT is a process-focused intervention designed to promote *psychological flexibility*. The psychologically flexible individual is able to pursue valued goals and directions even in the presence of painful internal experience. The ACT therapist encourages clients to explore and clarify their values; to "show up" to life in the present moment; to be mindful of thoughts, feelings, and action potentials without having to act on them; to willingly accept the unwanted feelings that are inevitably elicited by taking difficult actions; and to cultivate the habit of taking committed actions in line with fundamental values and goals. Our aim is to help participants learn and practice the skills needed to live with engagement and vitality and without unnecessary suffering.

## Guidelines for ACT Workshops

Here are some principles we keep in mind as we conduct these workshops:

**Embody the model.** Don't just talk about psychological flexibility, embody it from moment to moment (you don't need to be perfect—being human is the order of the day). Remain open and vulnerable while behaving professionally; self-disclose when it is clinically useful, being careful not to make the session about you and your problems.

**Principles come first.** The goal from moment to moment is to move the processes in the direction of greater psychological flexibility. Though we tend to choose from a repertoire of exercises (see the supplemental handout, "Commonly Used ACT Metaphors and Experiential Exercises for the One-Day Workshop," available at http://www.newharbinger.com/43102, for a common list of exercises used in this setting), we are more devoted to being as effective as possible with each particular set of patients than we are to standardization of our protocol.

**Invite willing participation.** Encourage and facilitate everyone's involvement, but honor the choice of anyone unwilling to participate. There is no pressure on the patients, ever, to do or commit to anything.

**Being compassionate means validating *and* "ripping off the bandage."** Remember they're doing the best they can with the resources they have; we're here to help them develop more resources. Don't try to protect them from inevitable pain; instead, show that you have faith in their ability to make dramatic changes in their lives even in the presence of difficulty or pain.

**Keep it productive.** People living with chronic illness have suffered a lot and typically want to share their story with other group members. We compassionately review how past fix-it efforts have led to feeling increasingly "stuck" (creative hopelessness) and consistently bring the focus back to ACT processes.

**Have fun.** Humor and well-timed irreverence can be powerful tools for defusion. One aspect of group work we find especially useful (and fun!) is the opportunity to play with live metaphors (e.g., Life Line described below; Bus Driver).

# Description of the One-Day ACT Workshop Curriculum

At the beginning of the day, we (1) inform group members about the schedule for the day, (2) ask them to be open and respectful of each other and to keep private information confidential, (3) gently encourage them to get involved and to ask questions, and (4) give them a short summary of the scientific evidence for ACT. Once we have done this, we proceed with the training, as outlined below.

## Setting the Stage with Values-Focused Introductions

We have developed a particular way to begin with introductions. Each therapist gives their name and identifies one person or valued domain that is important to them (e.g., a child). Each participant in turn states their name, then answers the questions "How long have you had [the chronic illness]?" and "Who and what is important to you?" We record the participant's answers to the second question on the right side of a large whiteboard. After each person provides at least one example, we ask if there is anything missing from the list. We devote a few minutes to fleshing out the list so the most common and important valued domains are included. We then state, "This is what our day is going to be about—the people and things in our lives that mean the most to us and how we can build our lives around what's important."

This opening exercise results in a list of valued domains on the board for all to observe, placing values at the center of our work. It also allows the group members to recognize and appreciate that they share values such as family, friends, health, intimate relationships, and community, which bind us together as human beings. The list remains on the board for the entire day, so we can regularly refer to it. Beginning the workshop in this manner orients the conversation from the very start toward cultivating a life worth living.

## BIG LIFE and small life

Next, we write "BIG LIFE" on the board next to the list of valued domains. We ask, "What are some words to describe a BIG, FULL LIFE? What would you be doing or experiencing?" We give examples such as "adventure" and "love." If participants say "health" or "anxiety-free," we respond, "If you had better health, what would you do more or less of?" or "Which of these things on the board would you more actively engage with if you had freedom from anxiety?"

We also introduce the idea that difficult emotions are part of living a big, valued life. We may ask, "Who in this group has children? Is that stress-free? Is it sometimes painful and scary? Is having children still worthwhile?"

Next we write "small life" on the left side of the board and ask, "What are some words to describe a small, unfulfilling life?" Words that frequently come up include "stagnant," "boring," "depressing," "alone," "constricted," and so on.

A BIG LIFE is associated with meaning and vitality, *and* it can also be scary and difficult at times. A small and constricted life is associated with demoralization and unhappiness, but it may *feel* safe. "BIG LIFE" and "small life" are not static places, of course. Each moment, we are faced with choices that will either expand our lives and make them richer or contract our lives and make them poorer. As we talk about this we play with a Hoberman sphere, an expanding and contracting ball.

## The ACT Matrix

The ACT matrix, developed by Polk and colleagues (Polk & Schoendorff, 2014; Polk, Schoendorff, Webster, & Olaz, 2016), provides the framework for discussing ACT processes in didactic presentations and practicing in experiential exercises. The matrix is presented in detail elsewhere (see chapter 6); here we will highlight key points of our adaptation (see figure 15.1).

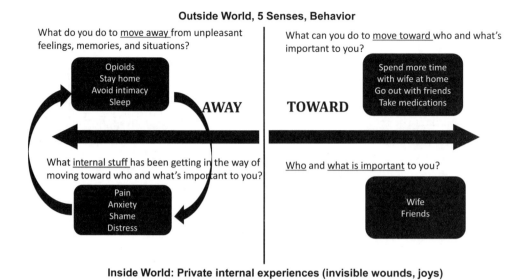

**Figure 15.1.** The ACT matrix provides the framework for the one-day ACT workshop.

## THE VERTICAL LINE

We introduce the inside world/outside world vertical line. We have found the follow-ing points to be critical:

- Our interpretations (Inside World) are distinct from our sensory experiences (Outside World), yet we often treat our interpretations as if they are facts ("I'm too sick to do X").

- We all have different thoughts and feelings based on our individual histories.

- We have relatively little control over what shows up *inside* (thoughts/feelings/body sensations) and more control over our overt behavior and where we place our attention.

- The ways we change things in the outside world don't work so well with the internal world.

- We often spend a lot of time in the "inside world" and lose touch with the "outside world." This can lead to lack of vitality.

## THE HORIZONTAL LINE

We then introduce the toward/away horizontal line of the matrix, as follows:

We now want to distinguish two types of actions, *toward* moves and *away* moves. Imagine I see a boy running across a playground. I could describe how he's running, how fast, what direction, but what I don't know is *why* he's running. He could be running to meet a friend. We would call this a *toward* move. He's moving toward his friend. Or he could be running from the bully who threatened to beat him up. That would be an *away* move. I can't tell by looking whether it's an away move or a toward move, but he certainly can tell. And it makes a lot of difference to the kid! It feels good to run toward something you want, but it doesn't feel so good to run from something that scares you.

## WORKING WITH THE RIGHT SIDE OF THE MATRIX

We give a personal example of a value and a valued action, then ask participants to do the same.

*Therapist (T):*    John, you said your family is important to you. What is something you could do that would move you toward being the kind of person you want to be with your family?

*Patient (P):*    My family is important to me, so I could eat better and check my blood sugar regularly so I am well enough to do fun things together.

At this point we are not asking for a commitment. We are practicing making the connection between some voluntary behavior and a value, and we don't want to inhibit that by implying they are expected to do it.

One basic premise of ACT is this: if we are able to really know and feel in our bones what is important to us, and if we can solidly link these values to a particular pattern and quality of behavior, then *engaging in that behavior becomes intrinsically reinforcing* (Hayes, Strosahl, & Wilson, 2012; pp. 92–94). Values-based behavior is satisfying even if it's hard; it seems and feels *right* although it may feel "*bad*." Our goal is to help people live vital lives of meaning and purpose, so we emphasize *chosen values* and the intentional actions that instantiate them.

## MOVING TO THE LEFT SIDE OF THE MATRIX

We now introduce the concept of internal obstacles that get in the way of values-based actions.

*T:*    Say you need to go talk to your boss about a situation you know is going to upset her, maybe make her angry. There's no physical barrier between you and her office, no armed guard. What might stop you?

*P:*    I'd be afraid she'd get mad at me.

*T:*    Great! Fear might show up. Let's write that down (*writes "Fear" in the lower left quadrant*). What else?

We encourage the group to give us a number of thoughts, feelings, judgments, memories, and so on that might get in the way of values-based actions. We write them on the board (lower left), putting thoughts in quotation marks. Next, we ask for examples of away moves.

*T:*    Now let's list some of our away moves. What might you do to try to control or get away from anxiety?

*Ps:*   Watch TV. Take a pill. Drink. Sleep. Have sex. Go to the gym. Facebook or Snapchat or Twitter. Work longer and harder. Email. Listen to a relaxation tape. Recite affirmations. Search the Internet for self-help books. Clean. Work on a hobby. Meditate. Go for a run. Stay home from work. Call my mom. Go shopping.

We collect a good sample of experiential avoidant behaviors, labeling them as away moves. Notice that we are not focused solely on away moves related to the medical problem.

We highlight the commonality of these unwanted internal experiences and away moves with lighthearted questions (e.g., "Is there anyone here who doesn't know what we mean by shame?" "Raise your hand if you've never felt guilty." "Is there anyone here who hasn't tried to distract themself to fix/eliminate/numb their pain?"). We hope patients grasp that these all are part of the same pattern: when there's stuff inside I don't like, it's normal to try to get rid of it, but ultimately efforts to control and eliminate are usually futile if not counterproductive.

At this point, we're keeping things pretty generic. We want to get the basic model established without making it too personal. Later we invite individuals to work with specific issues in their lives. This has been billed as a workshop, not group therapy, so there is no expectation that anyone get deep into personal issues unless they choose to.

## Examining the Consequences of Away Moves

We now turn explicitly to questions of workability as suggested in Polk et al. (2016). We ask group members to rate each away move (works, doesn't work, neutral) for each of these three questions:

1.  How does a particular away move work in terms of short-term relief?

2.  How does it work in the long term in the sense of eliminating the aversive experience for good?

3.  How does it work in terms of enabling you to move toward who and what is important to you?

Example:

T:     How does drinking work for relieving your social anxiety in the short term?

P:     It's great. A few drinks, no more anxiety. I'm the life of the party.

T:     How does it work in the long run, as a permanent solution?

P:     It doesn't. I feel worse the next day and I still get anxious the next time.

T:     How does it work in terms of moving toward who and what is important?

P:     I would say it helps me make friends but makes it harder to be productive at work. Also, my health. My doctor says I'm damaging my liver.

Recognizing the positive consequences of away moves acknowledges them as not crazy but normal and understandable. This validation makes it easier to move to the next step of showing how the seductive power of experiential avoidance can lead to "stuck loops" (Polk et al., 2016). With avoidance—like with an addictive drug—the more you use it, the more likely you are to use it again.

T:     Imagine I find myself face-to-face with something I'm afraid of. I turn away and feel immediate relief. The next time, I avoid it even sooner. Sooner yet the next time. The thing I fear becomes even more frightening and "dangerous." Over time I get better and quicker at avoiding it and anything that reminds me of it. Taking medications reminds me of my illness, so I "forget" to take the medicine or get the prescription filled. Or I find great excuses for avoiding going out in public because of my irritable bowel symptoms or not doing my rehab exercises. If I'm a really skilled avoider, I may avoid noticing I'm avoiding.

       Now, minds doing what minds do, I come to feel that the fear itself is dangerous. What had been the indicator of danger now has itself become a thing to fear! So, I try to suppress the fear, drink, use drugs, push it down, berate myself for being weak or a coward. Yet the very efforts not to feel the feelings create more suffering. Eventually I have made huge parts of the world off limits, and unfortunately, those parts are where some of the most rewarding possibilities reside.

As we discuss this, we use various diagrams and metaphors (e.g., Tug of War; Struggling in Quicksand; Man in the Hole; Baby Tiger; Lie Detector; Holding the Ball Under the Water) to describe how struggling against unwanted internal experience is not just futile, but leads to greater suffering. The ability to pursue valued goals and directions even in the presence (*especially* in the presence) of painful emotions, troubling thoughts, and the strong motivation to escape or avoid is the essence of mental health from an ACT perspective and our explicit outcome goal.

We're then ready to address willingness and acceptance more directly.

T:    If avoidance doesn't work in the long term, what's the alternative?

*(Silence)*

P:    We're screwed. I guess we just have to live with it, like everybody says.

T:    What about relating to it differently, not fighting it? What if we just allowed it to be what it is? What if we willingly have the discomfort and still do what matters?

We're offering an alternative: willingness to carry uncomfortable experiences along as we move toward the activities and people that matter. Living a life of purpose involves pain and discomfort, a poignant insight for people suffering from serious or chronic medical conditions (see figure 15.2).

Thus, we are communicating the following points: "Away moves" work very well in the short term by leading to immediate relief of internal difficult experience. Unfortunately, away moves do not lead to long-term relief of the internal difficult experience. In fact, avoidance often leads to more avoidance, more difficulties, and greater distance from valued living. The alternative is willingness to experience difficulty while moving toward what matters.

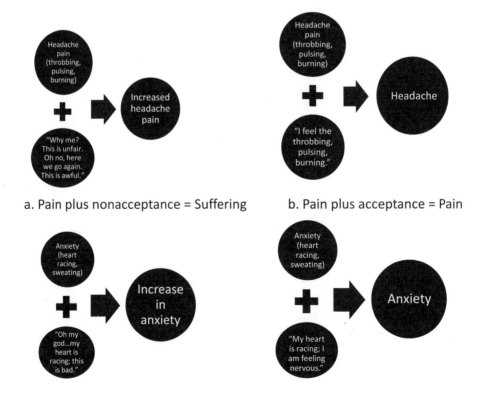

Figure 15.2. The difference between pain and suffering.

## Practicing Defusion

We have touched on the basic skills of (1) connecting with chosen values, (2) choosing actions that embody those values, (3) stepping back and taking perspective on our experience, (4) noticing the internal obstacles that get in the way of acting on values, and (5) discriminating moves on the basis of their function (away/toward). Throughout the workshop we've been practicing defusion informally by responding to thoughts in ways not based on their literal meaning.

We may turn now to more specific defusion exercises, including the classics like repeating thoughts in funny voices, singing the thought, saying "I'm having the thought *I can't take it anymore.*" A favorite exercise that also gets us active is to have everyone walk around the room in a circle while saying "I can't walk," and other statements that contradict the ongoing behavior. This "silly" exercise sometimes has powerful effects as individuals experience directly and mindfully that these are just words and they don't have to be obeyed.

## Taking Time for a Personal Example: The Life Line Exercise

We have reviewed the ACT model, didactically and experientially, with the group as a whole. We now focus on one volunteer in more detail and conduct the Life Line exercise. Here is a fictionalized example:

P:    These headaches have ruined my life. I never know when one will hit. I've tried all kinds of medications. My doctor keeps telling me I'll just have to live with them. I'm spaced out on the drugs about half the time and mostly sleep and watch TV.

T:    When we talked earlier about managing migraines medically, did that give you any ideas?

P:    Yeah. We've been doing it wrong. I need to talk to the doc but I don't know if she'll do anything different. I'll take some of this material in with me and see what she says.

T:    Excellent. I think you're here because you hope to get your life back. Would you be willing to come up here in front of the room?

        *(Patient does and gives a little background. He's divorced and most bothered by the fact he's pulled away from his daughter and rarely sees her. Therapist writes "Daughter" in the lower right quadrant of the matrix, then asks patient to talk about her. He talks for a few minutes but is unemotional and seems resigned to not having a relationship.)*

T:    Would you tell me about when she was little?

P:    I was so excited when she was born. I used to just look at her and think about how beautiful she was. (*He's more emotional.*)

T:    As you talk, I can see how special she is to you, how sad you are about this. Do you remember a time when she was little and you held her and talked to her?

P:    Yeah. I used to hold her in my hands like this (*demonstrates*) and I would look in her little face and tell her how much I loved her. That I was her daddy and I would always take care of her (*starts to tear up*).

T:    Is it okay if I touch you on the arm? (*Patient nods. Therapist puts hand on patient's elbow, showing support but not comforting or reassuring. Therapist takes a few minutes to talk about the child, amplifying the feeling of loss and the longing for reconnecting on a deep level with his daughter.*)

T:    If you made the decision to get back into your daughter's life in a really meaningful way, what might be a step to do that? (*points to upper right quadrant of the matrix*)

P:    Arrange to take her for a weekend and do something fun. My ex would be okay with that. She would like the break and she's been complaining about me not seeing her.

T:    Would that mean calling and talking to her and her mother about this?

The patient agrees, so the therapist sets up an exercise, beginning by making an X on the whiteboard at eye level, and then leading the patient to the opposite side of the room where they turn to face the board. The members of the group are silent and watching intently.

T:    The mark I made on the board represents that phone call. You're standing here preparing to make the call. What shows up inside?

P:    I can't do it.

T:    You have the thought, *I can't do it.* Good. (*Therapist writes the thought on a sticky note, places the note on the floor a few inches in front of the patient, and stands next to him.*) Now I'd like you to say that thought out loud then take a step toward that note. (*Patient does so.*)

T:    What do you feel right now?

P:    Kind of scared.

T:       (*Writes "Scared" on a sticky note and places it on the floor. Stands next to the patient and puts hand on his elbow.*) I would like you to feel that scared feeling, and when you really have it, look up in the direction of your daughter, take a breath, and take the next step.

P:       (*Waits a moment, then sighs and takes the step*) Wow, this is hard.

T:       Maybe too hard (*then gently turns the patient to the side, away from the board*). You don't have to do it. How's this? Tell me what you feel now.

P:       Not so good. Disappointed in myself. A little sick to my stomach.

T:       So what do you want to do?

P:       Turn back toward my daughter.

T:       Okay. (*turns him back toward the board*) Notice how that feels. Is it different?

P:       Yeah. It still feels hard. My heart's beating a little faster. But it feels better.

We continue this, step by step, putting each thought, feeling, or memory that shows up on a sticky note and having the patient step forward. At last he nears the board and hesitantly reaches out and touches the X. This is often an emotional and memorable moment for everyone in the group.

In this physicalized metaphor, we have value front and center, with the entire episode being about commitment to values-based action. Defusion is reflected in writing the thought on the note then taking a step that violates the thought's command. Acceptance is noticing the feelings that arise, attending to them, and then taking the next step in the presence of the feeling. We also ask him to notice how toward and away moves feel. All this is occurring while fully present and mindful.

## Perspective Taking and Choosing

As we continue, we select metaphors and exercises that match the needs of our group (see the supplemental handout, "Commonly Used ACT Metaphors and Experiential Exercises for the One-Day Workshop," at http://www.newharbinger.com/43102). We take care to touch on perspective taking, particularly distinguishing self from illness and noticing self is bigger than and contains the illness. As an exercise in choosing, we hold out both hands:

T:       In one hand, you have this difficult illness. And you stay home, avoid interacting, keep to yourself, and medicate so you don't feel the pain. You are not engaged in much around you, but it feels safer. In this *other* hand, you have this difficult illness. *And* you choose to go out and spend time with people that matter. You keep up with activities that you have always enjoyed. It's hard at times and painful. In both hands, you have the illness; which one do you choose?

We let the patient sit inside that question.

## Concluding the Workshop

At the end of the workshop, we do two exercises, Passengers on the Bus and Stand and Commit, which we will comment on briefly below.

### PASSENGERS ON THE BUS

Near the end of the session, we do Passengers on the Bus, a fun and memorable exercise to summarize the themes of the day. We have a volunteer be the driver heading in the direction of a specific values-based action, and have each member of the group be a thought or feeling that shows up to oppose that action. Each member goes up to the driver and expresses the thought they represent and urges the driver to turn to the right or left. We may go through several rounds, coaching the driver to respond in various ways, including doing what the passenger says, arguing with the passenger, and throwing the passenger off the bus. We note that when they did these things, they took their eyes off the road and lost control of the bus. Finally, we have the driver simply nod to the passengers while staying focused on the road and continuing to drive toward the goal.

### STAND AND COMMIT

We end our workshops with a Stand and Commit exercise. First, therapists model the task. Each person is invited to stand up and finish the following sentences:

What I care about is _____.

What I've been doing is _____.

I'm through with that. I'm going to _____.

## Challenges

With a single-day workshop, we get one shot with each set of patients. Flexibility is essential. Deep familiarity with the ACT model is needed to work in a principle-based manner, rather than depending on a protocol that tells you what to do and when to do it. Therapists must be willing to commit to the training and practice to develop this level of skill in ACT.

Doing this work requires cooperation and support from physicians to refer patients and encourage them to attend. The illness education component of our workshops works best with the enthusiastic involvement of a specialist with up-to-date knowledge of the medical condition at hand. Physicians are acutely aware that psychological factors are an important part of the picture with these chronic conditions, and the positive outcome of our initial project with migraine sufferers resulted in part from the encouragement and participation of a neurologist headache specialist. As our initial results became known in the community, other medical providers approached us about doing something with their patients. This led to the work with cardiovascular risk, irritable bowel syndrome, and postsurgical pain and opioid issues. It may take persistence to find the right medical partner, but once a match is made, it is a highly rewarding experience for all parties.

# Research Support

We were inspired to test the efficacy of a one-day ACT workshop by the work of Gregg and colleagues (Gregg, Callaghan, Hayes, & Glenn-Lawson, 2007), who randomized eighty-one patients with *type 2 diabetes* to either (a) seven hours of diabetes education or (b) four hours of education plus three hours of ACT. Three months following the intervention, patients who had received the combined intervention exhibited lower blood glucose levels than those in the education group, and the changes in blood glucose were mediated by increased acceptance and improved self-care behaviors.

One-Day Acceptance and Commitment Training workshops (five to six hours in a single session)** by our group have been found to provide the following benefits:

- Clinically depressed *migraine* sufferers (Dindo, Recober, Marchman, O'Hara, & Turvey, 2014; Dindo, Recober, Marchman, Turvey, & O'Hara, 2012) in an ACT plus migraine education workshop experienced significant improvements in headache frequency, severity, and medication use in comparison to treatment as usual (TAU). Depression and disability also improved significantly.

- Individuals at *high cardiovascular disease risk* with comorbid anxiety (Dindo, Marchman, Gindes, & Fiedorowicz, 2015) attending an ACT plus education workshop showed improved quality of life, anxiety, and depression in comparison to a TAU group. Of note, the effect of the intervention increased at each follow-up visit.

- People living with *inflammatory bowel disease* (IBD) plus depression and anxiety (Hou et al., 2017) reported significantly less distress at three-month follow-up than at baseline, and self-reported IBD symptoms were reduced.

- Patients who underwent *orthopedic surgery* (Dindo et al., 2018) without complications reported earlier postsurgical pain cessation (fifty-eight days) when

---

** It is worth noting that the median number of sessions for psychotherapy is around five, so our workshop patients get about as much treatment in one day as the typical outpatient gets in weekly therapy.

exposed to a presurgical one-day ACT workshop compared to patients random-ized to TAU (eighty-seven days). At seven weeks post-op, 29% of the ACT group were taking opioids, in comparison to 52% of the TAU group.

Other researchers have found evidence supporting one-day ACT workshops:

- People living with *multiple sclerosis* (Sheppard, Forsyth, Hickling, & Bianchi, 2010), a disease with no known cure, had reduced depression and impact of pain on behavior along with improved quality of life.

- Individuals living with *obesity* (Lillis, Hayes, Bunting, & Masuda, 2009) had greater improvements in body mass at three-month follow-up compared to a waitlist control, and quality of life and distress improved.

Although much research remains to be done, this is indeed a promising beginning.


# Future Directions

For interventions to be truly successful, they must be both effective and disseminated. We are encouraged by the early success of these one-day group interventions and hope this chapter will serve to assist fellow practitioners and researchers to bring these work-shops to other settings in the name of reducing suffering and increasing valued living in behaviorally underserved medical populations.

Future investigation could explore whether the entire ACT treatment package is needed to enhance psychological flexibility or whether specific ACT principles should be highlighted more for particular clinical problems. For some patients, more follow-up, support, and behavior shaping may be needed. For example, we found that patients who have postsurgical complications do not respond as well to the one-day workshop as those without complications, and we believe they may need additional ACT postsurgically.

The life experience of a distressed person with chronic illness often follows a familiar arc. In the presence of an *acute* illness or problem, seeking treatment and relief is normal and appropriate. If patients find that their first attempt is unsuccessful, they naturally keep trying to find something that works—they may change doctors, look for specialists with the latest techniques, search the Internet for medical breakthroughs, or try experi-mental drugs, herbal remedies, or acupuncture. To cope with pain and fatigue, they may stop exercising, withdraw from activities, depend on medications, or engage in other efforts to get relief. These are all reasonable and rational responses—up to a point. But when the problem is intractable, persistent efforts to fix the unfixable—while avoiding healthy behaviors that have become difficult—result in an impoverished life narrowly focused on struggling with the illness. In cultivating psychological flexibility, ACT helps people loosen their attachment to the fruitless struggle, accept the unchangeable with some degree of equanimity, and develop skills to engage more fully in meaningful and valued life activities, even in the presence of discomfort. As patients' lives become more about the people and activities that truly matter, life satisfaction grows while the illness takes up relatively less mental and emotional energy. Learning this in a brief group intervention delivered with lightness and compassion is the goal and promise of One-Day Acceptance and Commitment Training.

# References

DiMatteo, M. R., Lepper, H. S., & Croghan, T. W. (2000). Depression is a risk factor for noncompliance with medical treatment: Meta-analysis of the effects of anxiety and depression on patient adherence. *Archives of Internal Medicine, 160*(14), 2101–2107.

Dindo, L., Marchman, J., Gindes, H., & Fiedorowicz, J. (2015). A brief behavioral intervention targeting mental health risk factors for vascular disease: A pilot study. *Psychotherapy and Psychosomatics, 84*(3), 183–185. doi: 10.1159/000371495

Dindo, L., Recober, A., Marchman, J., O'Hara, M. W., & Turvey, C. (2014). One-day behavioral intervention in depressed migraine patients: Effects on headache. *Headache, 54*(3), 528–538.

Dindo, L., Recober, A., Marchman, J. N., Turvey, C., & O'Hara, M. W. (2012). One-day behavioral treatment for patients with comorbid depression and migraine: A pilot study. *Behavior Research and Therapy, 50*(9), 537–543. doi: 10.1016/j.brat.2012.05.007

Dindo, L., Recober, A., Turvey, C., & Calarge, C. (in preparation). Randomized controlled trial of 1-day ACT compared to education and support for patients with migraine and depression.

Dindo, L., Zimmerman, M., Hadlandsmyth, K., St Marie, B., Embree, J., Marchman, J., . . . Rakel, B. (2018). Acceptance and commitment therapy for prevention of chronic post-surgical pain and opioid use in at-risk veterans: A pilot randomized controlled study. *Journal of Pain.*

Evans, D. L., Charney, D. S., Lewis, L., Golden, R. N., Gorman, J. M., Krishnan, K. R., . . . Valvo, W. J. (2005). Mood disorders in the medically ill: Scientific review and recommendations. *Biological Psychiatry, 58*(3), 175–189. doi: 10.1016/j.biopsych.2005.05.001

Gregg, J. A., Callaghan, G. M., Hayes, S. C., & Glenn-Lawson, J. L. (2007). Improving diabetes self-management through acceptance, mindfulness, and values: A randomized controlled trial. *Journal of Consulting and Clinical Psychology, 75*(2), 336–343. doi: 10.1037/0022-006X.75.2.336

Hayes, S., Strosahl, K., & Wilson, K. (2012). *Acceptance and commitment therapy: The process and practice of mindful change.* (2nd ed.). New York, NY: Guilford Press.

Hou, J. K., Vanga, R. R., Thakur, E., Gonzalez, I., Willis, D., & Dindo, L. (2017). One-day behavioral intervention for patients with inflammatory bowel disease and co-occurring psychological distress. *Clinical Gastroenterology and Hepatology, 15*(10), 1633–1634. doi: 10.1016/j.cgh.2017.05.022

Lillis, J., Hayes, S. C., Bunting, K., & Masuda, A. (2009). Teaching acceptance and mindfulness to improve the lives of the obese: A preliminary test of a theoretical model. *Annals of Behavioral Medicine, 37*(1), 58–69. doi: 10.1007/s12160-009-9083-x

Merikangas, K. R., Ames, M., Cui, L., Stang, P. E., Ustun, T. B., Von Korff, M., & Kessler, R. C. (2007). The impact of comorbidity of mental and physical conditions on role disability in the US adult household population. *Archives of General Psychiatry, 64*(10), 1180–1188. doi: 10.1001/archpsyc.64.10.1180

Najavits, L. M. (2015). The problem of dropout from "gold standard" PTSD therapies. *F1000Prime Reports, 7,* 43. doi: 10.12703/P7-43

Polk, K., & Schoendorff, B. (Eds.). (2014). *ACT matrix: A new approach to building psychological flexibility across settings and populations.* Oakland, CA: New Harbinger Publications, Inc.

Polk, K. L., Schoendorff, B., Webster, M., & Olaz, F. (2016). *The essential guide to the ACT matrix: A step-by-step approach to using the ACT matrix model in clinical practice.* Oakland, CA: Context Press/New Harbinger.

Sheppard, S., Forsyth, J., Hickling, E., & Bianchi, J. (2010). A novel application of acceptance and commitment therapy for psychosocial problems associated with multiple sclerosis. *International Journal of MS Care, 12,* 200–206.

Thoreau, H. D. (2008). *Walden.* Oxford, UK: Oxford University Press.

Wierzbicki, M., & Pekanik, G. (1986). The relationship between expected and actual psychotherapy treatment duration. *Psychotherapy (Chic), 23,* 532–534.

# CHAPTER 16

# Implementing ACT Online

Raimo Lappalainen

Päivi Lappalainen

*Department of Psychology, University of Jyväskylä*

## Overview

In the last few years, new and innovative ways to deliver acceptance and commitment therapy (ACT) have emerged. In addition to traditional face-to-face forms of therapy, ACT has been delivered through written self-help materials including books and manuals, and, lately, via Internet- and mobile-based interventions. This chapter will give an overview of ACT-based Internet-delivered interventions developed and tested during the last ten years. We will also provide examples of how they can be applied in clinical practice.

### Development of Web-Based ACT Interventions

The history of our innovation, Internet-based ACT interventions, goes back to early 2000 and started with research and practice of brief psychological interventions. The catalyst for the development of brief interventions was twofold. First, growing evidence showed that brief interventions with very few treatment sessions can create significant psychological changes in people with mental health or other life adjustment issues (e.g., Bryan, Morrow, & Appolonio, 2009). Second, practice contexts were changing and conventional multisession treatments were not realistic and affordable in these new settings. Research funding was scarce and the lack of ACT practitioners forced us to start investigating how ACT could be delivered in brief formats and by unexperienced psychology students as therapists. The ACT approach seemed ideal for brief interventions for various reasons. Among others, ACT offers a good motivational tool (values), and its core concepts are easily understood even by non-mental health professionals.

Results and experiences of a series of brief face-to-face ACT interventions, such as a ten-session (Lappalainen et al., 2007) and four-session (Kohtala, Muotka, & Lappalainen, 2017) ACT protocol, inspired us to test whether a six-session protocol based on ACT could be transferred to the Internet. Internet-based cognitive behavioral therapy (ICBT) had already been proven to be a highly effective treatment for a range of conditions (e.g.,

Andrews, Cuijpers, Craske, McEvoy, & Titov, 2010), but research on web-based ACT was scarce. In addition, the Internet was rapidly expanding and becoming more accessible through portable devices, such as mobile phones. ACT combined with the Internet would provide the possibility to reach out to people who would otherwise not be able to receive treatment and provide a new, cost-effective tool to promote psychological flexibility and well-being. Internet-based treatment may reduce the barriers experienced in conventional face-to-face treatment, such as long distances, stigma, and the inconvenience of scheduling and making appointments.

## Six-Session Web-Based ACT Components

Over the last ten years, we have developed approximately twenty web-based ACT programs for a variety of conditions, each building upon the previous one. The leading principle has been to build upon experiences from previous studies and data when developing a new web-based program. A six-session treatment protocol *formed* the *basis* of the web-based ACT interventions, including the following main phases:

1. Assessment: a face-to-face, phone, or videoconference session including interview and case formulation

2. Web-program: 5–6 weeks with short, written weekly coach-provided feedback via the web, or, alternatively, 10–12 weeks with short written feedback every other week

3. A closing face-to-face, phone, or videoconference session with assessment interview

# Description of Internet-Based Interventions in Practice

In this section we will illustrate how Internet-based interventions can be applied in clinical practice. We will also provide practical examples for how Internet-based ACT treatment can be introduced and delivered to clients. It should be noted that the effects of Internet-delivered treatments are larger when therapists provide some form of support (Lappalainen, Langrial, Oinas-Kukkonen, Tolvanen, & Lappalainen, 2015); therefore, a so-called blended or guided self-help approach is strongly recommended.

## Assessment

Ideally, Internet-based treatment starts with a live meeting with the client. If face-to-face assessment is not possible due to long distances or other reasons, an alternative way to assess the client is via a phone or videoconference meeting. In our model, assessment includes (1) questionnaires measuring symptoms, quality of life, and ACT-related processes; (2) an assessment interview; and (3) case formulation based on the interview. The length of the assessment session is usually forty-five to sixty minutes.

## Case Formulation Model

We conduct case formulation using focused assessment questions, such as the Love, Work, Play, and Health Questions and the Three Ts (see Strosahl, Robinson, & Gustavsson, 2012), and based on these questions we construct a problem list. In addition, we use the functional analytic clinical case model (FACCM; Haynes & O'Brien, 2000), which is a vector-graphic tool to describe the concerns of the client, the background of these concerns, their importance, and in which way these problems interact with each other (see figure 16.1). The hand-drawn lines in figure 16.1 indicate that these issues are probably important for this particular client and could be assessed more closely; these areas could also be the focus of the therapist's feedback during the web intervention. The case formulation provides the possibility to assess factors that contribute to psychological inflexibility (e.g., avoidance behaviors, fusion with evaluating thoughts, unclear life direction). We send the case formulation to the client via email or mobile phone or place it in the shared feedback area in the web program. In the final face-to-face phone or videoconference meeting, we return to this case formulation and discuss whether the client's situation has changed.

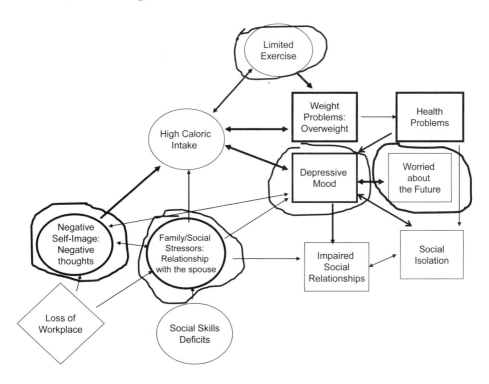

**Figure 16.1.** The case formulation.

## Introducing the Web-Based ACT Intervention

The first face-to-face interview provides a good chance to communicate about the aims and guidelines for the web-based treatment, such as how the treatment works, what is expected from the client, the timetable, home assignments, and feedback. The therapist (also referred to as the coach) may begin by describing the empirical evidence of web-based interventions and by motivating the client by describing some of the advantages with web-based treatments, as we illustrate below:

### INTRODUCING WEB-BASED ACT TREATMENT

*Therapist (T):*    In our treatment we'll combine face-to-face, in-person meetings with a web-based ACT program. There is a large number of studies showing that Internet-based treatments can be effective for many clinical issues. Often they have equal effects compared to traditional treatments. In addition, most clients are very satisfied with the programs.

### DESCRIBING THE ADVANTAGES OF WEB-BASED ACT TREATMENTS

*T:*    Web-based treatments have *a number of* advantages. Many clients appreciate saving time and money by not having to travel for in-person meetings. In addition, you are able to access the program at a convenient time and you can work at your own pace. The program is available for you all the time. If you do not understand the content of the modules at the first reading, you can go back and study that module again. This type of treatment is also personal and private. The platform is secured, which means that you can safely write and post your assignments. No one except me has access to your personal folder.

One of the disadvantages is that this type of treatment includes less in-person contact. However, I will be in contact with you weekly (or every two weeks) and give you written feedback on your assignments.

## Clear Communication Guidelines

To keep the client engaged and motivated, it's essential to tell them exactly what is expected of them and when. It is important, for instance, to familiarize the client with the web-based intervention during the first session by describing the purpose and the content of the program and by demonstrating how to use the program. Just providing the address to the web-program without further demonstration of the usage may increase noncompliance and risk for drop-out. Access to a computer or a tablet is a must during the initial session so that you can show the client the actual program directly. Clear deadlines for the completion of home assignments are important. If you want to make sure the client follows the treatment as expected, provide them with a timetable for the treatment and home assignments (see table 16.1).

Introduce the timeline as follows:

T:    You'll find the schedule of the treatment program below. You'll have one week (or two weeks) to complete each module. You'll get access to a new module every (or every other) Monday.

## Table 16.1. Treatment Schedule with Home Assignments: An Example

| Timetable of the Treatment Program* | | |
|---|---|---|
| **Week 1** | Jan 1–2 | Face-to-face session: assessment interview |
| **Week 1–2** | Jan 1–13 | The 1st module is open: read the content, listen to exercises, watch the videos, and answer the questions.<br><br>Complete and send your home assignment by January 14 at the latest. Your therapist will give you feedback by January 15–16. |
| **Week 3–4** | Jan 14–27 | The 2nd module is open: read, listen, watch, and answer the questions. Complete and send your home assignment by January 28 at the latest. Your therapist will give you feedback by January 29–30. |
| **Week 5–6** | Jan 28–Feb 10 | The 3rd module is open: read, listen, watch, and answer the questions. Complete and send your home assignment by February 11 at the latest. Your therapist will give you feedback by February 12–13. |
| **Week 7–8** | Feb 11–Feb 24 | The 4th module is open: read, listen, watch, and answer the questions. Complete and send your home assignment by February 25 at the latest. Your therapist will give you feedback by February 26–27. |
| **Week 9–10** | Feb 25–March 10 | The 5th module is open: read, listen, watch, and answer the questions. Complete and send your home assignment by March 11 at the latest. Your therapist will give you feedback by March 12–13. |
| **Week 11–12** | March 11–March 24 | The 6th module is open: read, listen, watch, and answer the questions. Complete and send your home assignment by March 25 at the latest. Your therapist will give you feedback by March 26–27. |
| **Week 13** | March 25–31 | Face-to-face session: we will meet for the final session. We will make an appointment later via the platform. |

* This treatment schedule is based on a program that is spread out over twelve weeks.

## COMMUNICATING GUIDELINES FOR THE ONLINE INTERVENTION

T:    We are going to have two face-to-face meetings during this treatment, one at the beginning and one at the end of the intervention. Between these two meetings you'll work independently on the online program. We'll have written contact via the online program weekly (or every other week). You'll have weekly (or every other week) home assignments and I'll give you feedback when you have completed them. If needed, we may also have telephone contact or even a face-to-face meeting during the treatment. Here you'll find instructions for how the program works, including the schedule for treatment (*show the client the instructions on the computer or table*).

## FAMILIARIZING THE CLIENT WITH THE ONLINE INTERVENTION

T:    Don't worry if you do not remember everything I say, you'll find all that information on the information sheet. You'll find the program here (*show the client the web page at https://headsted.co.uk/main on the computer or tablet*; note that these programs are available at a cost). This is actually a skills-training program. It increases your skills to identify what matters to you or what is important for you in your life. It also teaches skills for how to handle unpleasant or difficult thoughts and emotional reactions. The program is based on a therapy model called acceptance and commitment therapy, and it has been developed and evaluated by behavioral experts. This program includes six modules. I am expecting you to invest one week (or two weeks) in each module.

Let us now look at how to use the first module… As you can see, you'll find text, video, audio exercises, a web diary, and a discussion group. Please read the texts, watch the videos, and listen to the exercises. Here you'll find your personal diary, and this link goes to a discussion group if you feel like sharing your experiences with others. And note: each module ends with a home assignment where you'll get a task to reflect on something related to the module's theme, or a task to apply a particular skill in your daily life.

It is very important that you work through the program and invest time in it. Based on our experiences and results, most people benefit from the program, but it is like taking a medication. If you are not taking the pill consistently, even the best medicine will not have any impact. "The pill" in this case is the program. We have seen that most people need to spend about one hour on the program per week. However, you can work in small doses, such as fifteen minutes at a time. One more thing that is really important, as in all skills training, is that you apply the methods in everyday life. I recommend you try out the exercises and apply them as often as possible—they are so simple that you can do them anywhere and at any time. The more you practice, the more you get. What you do actively will create changes in your life.

## Home Assignments

Home assignments are typically short essay-type exercises—relevant to each week's theme—that the client writes and places in their own folder in the treatment platform, or sends via email. The purpose of home assignments is to encourage learning and practicing skills in one's daily life and to report on experiences and outcomes to the coach. Providing flexibility with home assignments may have a negative impact on treatment outcome. In other words, when clients are allowed more time to complete their home assignments, they may improve less (Paxling et al., 2013).

### INTRODUCING HOME ASSIGNMENTS

T:     If you scroll down you'll find the home assignments for the first module... In this box you can write your reflections or responses to the home assignments. I can see your reflections and I will respond to them on a weekly basis (or every two weeks). I am expecting you to post your home assignments in general by Monday, and I will give you feedback on Tuesday or Wednesday. Please check the treatment timetable for when you are expected to post your assignments. If I have not received your reflections by the given date, I will send a reminder to your phone or email.

The home assignment takes the following form: We instruct clients, first, to read a text highlighting the week's ACT process, and then, to complete the experiential exercises included in the module by listening or reading, reflect upon questions arising from the weekly process, and write a short reflection based on their experiences. For example, in the first module of the web-based program focusing on *Values,* we instruct clients to read about values, watch the video provided, conduct daily exercises described in the module, write a short essay reflecting on the exercises, and place the report in their personal folder in a secured encrypted platform. Below is an example of a home assignment.

### SAMPLE ASSIGNMENT

1.    Reflect on your life values and formulate them. Choose one or more areas of life (listed below) and values that are important for you right now. Write down your thoughts here.

**Family and parenting:** How would you like to be in these relationships, as mom/dad/partner/sister/brother/daughter/son, and so on?

**Friends:** Are you the friend you want to be? How would you like to be in those relationships?

**Leisure time:** What do you find joy in doing? What would be really fun?

**Work:** What type of work would you like to do? What gives you a sense of meaning when it comes to work?

**Health and well-being:** What does good health and well-being mean to you? How do you take care of yourself?

**Other areas:** Feel free to choose a life area that is meaningful to you.

2.  ACT! Which small step could you take today that could move you a step closer to what you value in life? Do it! My steps are:

```
┌─────────────────────────────────────────────────┐
│                                                 │
│                                                 │
│                                                 │
└─────────────────────────────────────────────────┘
```

## ASSIGNMENT FEEDBACK

The client receives written feedback from their personal coach generally within forty-eight hours. Feedback consists mainly of encouragement, answers to questions, and suggestions for possible additional exercises suited to each participant's situation. We have also used semistructured feedback, which means that our coaches receive a feedback prototype that they may edit and adapt according to the client. An example of semistructured feedback for module 1: Values is provided below.

Dear Kate,

(*Place a greeting here and say something about how the client has succeeded, for instance:*) Hope you are doing well today! I am really glad that you have gotten started with the program.

During these first two weeks you have been reflecting on important questions, such as how you want to live your life and what matters most to you. You mentioned, for example, that

_____ (*insert what the client has written*) is important to you. Also, you seem to value _____ (*insert what the client has written*).

I am glad that you have also had time to *give* some *thought* to what little steps you could take toward what you really care about. And, most importantly, you have applied what you planned (*if that is the case*). What did you notice? I am sure that if you continue with these small steps, it will make a difference in your life.

In the following two weeks you'll have the opportunity to continue with small steps toward a more balanced life.

(*Place final words of encouragement here, for instance:*) Good luck with the next step! Let's keep in touch! I hope to hear from you again in two weeks' time.

Yours, Anna

## Content of the Web-Based ACT Treatment

Along with text material, web-based treatment programs usually consist of audio and video files, chat forums, discussion groups, and other interactive elements. We have also used cartoons and games. Treatment should preferably be delivered in modules within a fixed time span. Most available web-based programs consist of six to fifteen modules of different length and follow a specific structure. Our ACT-based programs consist usually of five to six modules based on the processes of ACT: (1) values, (2) value-based actions, (3) present moment, (4) watching one's thinking, and (5) acceptance (including self-compassion; see table 16.2). Thus, each module introduces a set of skills and strategies related to each topic to be practiced offline during and between the modules. Participants are instructed to follow one module per week or, alternatively, per two weeks. In some programs we went from a five- or six-week program to a ten- or twelve-week program as a result of feedback from the study participants who perceived the program as too stressful.

The web-based program consists of text highlighting each ACT process, along with experiential exercises and metaphors based on ACT that can be downloaded as MP3 recordings. We also offer videos providing information on ACT processes and examples to clarify its concepts. Participants also have access to a web diary and a discussion group (see table 16.2). It goes without saying that the readability and structure of the text material is crucial. Texts need to be compact and easy to understand and provide clear instructions for home assignments. Too much material may lead to complex treatment programs that clients may perceive as too condensed and stressful, which may, in turn, impact client adherence and result in drop-out.

**Table 16.2.** Overview of Internet-Based ACT Treatment Components

| Treatment phase (bold text) and content (light text) | Information, rationale, and assignment of the week | Examples of exercises in each module |
|---|---|---|
| **Face-to-face, telephonic, or videoconference session 1:** | Questionnaires; assessment through discussion or structured interview questions for case formulation (Haynes & O'Brien, 2000) | |
| Assessment | Short introduction to the web program with instructions and schedule of the treatment program | |
| | Form for value work provided | |
| **Week 1: Choose your values!** | Text of the week: Creative hopelessness, values | Experiential exercises, including 8 audio recordings such as Attending Your Own Funeral, Half a Year to Live, Passengers on the Bus |
| | Video: What Are Values in Life? | |
| | Several exercises | |
| | Automated reminder via phone or email (optional) | |
| Weekly assignment and feedback from coach via platform | Value analysis: Reflect and write about your values | |
| | A second automated reminder if assignments have not been returned by given date | |
| **Week 2: Take action!** | Text of the week: Value-based actions | The same exercises as above |
| | Video: What Are Value-Based Actions? | |
| | Exercises | |
| Weekly assignment and feedback from coach via platform | Take action: Choose actions based on your values | |
| **Week 3: Live here and now!** | Text of the week: Be present, live here and now. | Experiential exercises, including 8 audio recordings such as Follow Your Breath, Mindful Sitting, Mindful Eating |
| | Video: What Is Mindfulness? | |
| | Exercises | |

| Weekly assignment and feedback from coach via platform | Practice mindfulness exercises and mindfulness in everyday life<br><br>Take action: Choose another value-based action | |
|---|---|---|
| **Week 4: Self-as-context** | Text of the week: Different stories about myself: What story are you telling yourself?<br><br>Video: The Art of Observing<br><br>Exercises | Experiential exercises, including 3 audio recordings, such as Observer, Leaves on a Stream |
| Weekly assignment and feedback from coach via platform | Retell your story and write about it<br><br>Practice experiential exercises<br><br>Take action: Choose another value-based action | |
| **Week 5: Watch your thinking!** | Text of the week: Watch your thinking!<br><br>Video: Gaining a New Perspective<br><br>Exercises | Experiential exercises, including 5 audio recordings, such as Milk, Milk, Milk; The Little Man |
| Weekly assignment and feedback from coach via platform | Practice exercises related to cognitive defusion<br><br>Take action: Choose another value-based action | |
| **Week 6: Accept your feelings and thoughts; accept what you cannot change** | Text of the week: What do I need to accept?<br><br>Video: What Is Acceptance?<br><br>Exercises | Experiential exercises, including 1 audio recording, such as Stone on a Beach, The Child |
| Weekly assignment and feedback from coach via platform | Observer-exercise<br><br>Reflect and write about: What do I need to accept?<br><br>Take action: Choose another value-based action | |
| **Final face-to-face, telephonic, or videoconference session** | Review and summary of the experiences obtained during the intervention<br><br>Planning of the follow-up period based on what has worked during the intervention<br><br>Continue with mindfulness exercises and value-based actions | |

## Therapist Support

Therapist support can be provided via email (preferably in a secure system), telephone calls, text messages, or a shared, secure portal to which both therapist and client have access. Two of the therapist's main tasks are to motivate the client to work with the online program and to provide feedback during the course of the program. The therapist provides written feedback, and, ideally, spends about ten to twenty minutes on support and feedback weekly or every other week, depending on the spacing of the modules. While the type of support may not play such an important role, it is essential to make it clear to the client that there is a person behind the treatment program. Compliance with treatment increases when the client knows that there is a person "watching over" them, expecting them to work through the program. Too much contact, on the other hand, may decrease the client's self-efficacy (Bendelin et al., 2011).

## The Closing Session

An interview at the end of the treatment, along with clear deadlines for treatment, has been found to impact client adherence and decrease drop-out (Nordin, Carlbring, Cuijpers, & Andersson, 2010). During the closing session the therapist can summarize the observed experiences: what has been learned, what has changed, and so on. The therapist and the client may return to the case formulation and use it as a basis for a closing discussion. We recommend setting a follow-up meeting, to take place either by phone or in person. Below is an example of what a therapist might say during a closing session.

T:    I noticed when investigating these questionnaires that you filled in, and when reading your reflections while you were working on the program, that your mood has improved and there seem to be other positive changes as well. What have you done? Could we make a list of those things that you have observed or learned?

## Clinical Tips

If you have never implemented an online intervention, here are a few key points and tips that might help you:

- Get familiar with one or two web-based treatment programs. You do not need to know the program in every detail. Use the program by yourself for some time and plan how you'd introduce it to the client.

- Have an in-person meeting at the beginning and end of the program or arrange a live meeting via telephone call or videoconference. Start with a case formulation, addressing also ACT-related processes. Explore client motivation and potential barriers for Internet treatment. Make sure you have access to a tablet or a computer to present the program to the client. Provide the client with a timetable and instructions for using the program.

- Use home assignments that help the client to reflect and digest the material emotionally and engage in value-based activities. Give clear instructions and set deadlines for home assignments and feedback.

- Consider secure alternatives for correspondence with the client. Home assignments and feedback could be handled via a shared feedback area in the web program to which both the therapist and the client have access. In this way, all correspondence with a client is saved in one place.

- To improve clients' adherence to the treatment program, explore the mode of communication that would work best for the client regarding your weekly (or every other week) support. Incorporate phone, WhatsApp, Zoom, Skype, or similar modes of communication in the intervention. In case of noncompliance, prompt the client via text messages or phone calls.

## Challenges

Even though web-based interventions have been shown to be effective and are generally well accepted by clients, there are several challenges. The first challenge is determining for whom Internet-based interventions work. So far, attempts to find predictors of treatment outcome have been limited, and it is difficult to draw clear conclusions regarding for whom Internet-based treatment is suitable and beneficial. Available research indicates that computer skills have little or no impact on treatment success (Hedman, Carlbring, Ljóttson, & Andersson, 2014). There are some indications that Internet treatment works best with slightly older people and people able to take responsibility for their treatment (Hedman et al., 2014). Predictors of positive outcome in Internet-based treatment include having fewer comorbid conditions, having a stable economic situation, being employed, and being in a relationship (Hedman et al., 2014). When investigating barriers for use, we have seen, among other factors, that motivation of the client and treatment credibility may play important roles.

Internet-delivered treatment is often based on text materials and written correspondence between client and therapist, which may imply that proficiency with verbal fluency is an essential factor in clients. Therefore, it has been suggested that Internet-delivered treatment may best suit those who are used to reading, writing, and applying the relevant skills to themselves. However, this does not mean that web-based interventions work only for highly educated people. We have worked with individuals with various disabilities, and our experience is that web-based treatments work—the challenge is finding an appropriate treatment approach for these individuals. For instance, they may need extra support from a professional who goes through the program in close collaboration with them. To minimize the risk of unsuccessful Internet treatment, you should explore the client's reading and writing habits, learning disorders, and possible other barriers the client may face. To prevent these difficulties related to written language, we have considered using voice messages instead of written assignments.

Based on our experiences, the challenge in many cases is not how to motivate the client to take part in web-based ACT treatment, but rather how to motivate professionals to implement Internet-based interventions. Therapists may be uncertain whether they possess appropriate skills to provide Internet-based ACT therapy. However, the professional qualification of the therapist providing the web-based intervention seems to be of less importance. Support may also come from a nonclinician and require less therapeutic skill than in face-to-face-delivered therapies. For instance, we have received very good results with psychology students as coaches. The standardized ACT protocol has been easy for the students to learn, and in association with supervision, students have been able to provide weekly feedback to clients after only a brief training in ACT.

## Research Support

Internet-delivered ACT-based treatments have been investigated for a number of conditions, such as depressive symptoms, tinnitus, chronic pain, fibromyalgia, and smoking cessation, as well as for enhancing college students' well-being and undergraduate students' academic performance. Some examples of these studies are presented below.

### Health Issues

Internet-delivered ACT and cognitive behavioral therapy (CBT), in a guided self-help format (Hesser et al., 2012), were equally effective for global tinnitus severity, and they were significantly better than a monitored Internet discussion forum (d = 0.68–0.70). Regarding chronic pain (Trompetter, Bohlmeijer, Veehof, & Schreurs, 2015), 28% of those receiving Internet-based guided self-help ACT showed general clinically relevant improvement in pain interference, as well as in pain intensity and depression (compared to 5% of those receiving an Internet-based expressive writing intervention or a waiting list control condition). Also, web-based ACT for smoking cessation among smokers with depressive symptoms has shown promising results (Jones et al., 2015). A pilot study by Hoffmann, Rask, Hedman-Lagerlöf, Ljótsson, and Frostholm (2018) showed that web-based ACT may be a feasible treatment for health anxiety.

### Depressive Symptoms and Anxiety

Brown, Glendenning, Hoon, and John (2016) conducted a review of ACT-based web interventions for mental health and well-being, and concluded that web-based ACT was effective in the management of depressive symptoms (d = 0.24). However, this review included only ten randomized controlled studies. Pots et al. (2016) found significant reductions in depressive symptoms following the web-based ACT intervention, compared with the control group (d = 0.56) and the expressive writing intervention (d = 0.36). Further, Lappalainen et al. (2014) compared the effectiveness of a supported six-week web-based ACT intervention including two face-to-face meetings and weekly written feedback for depressive symptoms to a six-week face-to-face ACT intervention. Both ACT-based interventions affected not only depressive symptoms but also general health, life satisfaction, and psychological flexibility. Interestingly, a tendency for better outcomes was observed in the web-based ACT group compared to the face-to-face condition (18-month follow-up, d = 0.23). A similar six-week web-based ACT intervention without face-to-face contact was offered to participants with depressive symptoms (Lappalainen et al., 2015). Compared to the waiting list control, web-based ACT produced significant improvements in depressive symptoms, psychological flexibility, mindfulness, and thought suppression (d = 0.53–0.83). Dahlin et al. (2016) investigated the effects of a nine-week therapist-guided Internet-based treatment program for generalized anxiety disorder (GAD) based on acceptance-oriented behavior therapy. The treatment was effective compared to a waiting list control condition, with moderate to large effect sizes on symptoms of GAD (d = 0.70–0.98) and depression (d = 0.51–0.56).

## Well-Being

Räsänen, Lappalainen, Muotka, Tolvanen, and Lappalainen (2016) showed that web-based ACT including two face-to-face sessions and weekly online written feedback enhanced psychological, emotional, and social well-being; reduced symptoms of depression and stress; and improved self-confidence and mindfulness compared to a waiting list control group (d = 0.46–0.69). College students with psychological problems were offered web-based ACT and compared to a waitlist condition (Levin, Haeger, Pierce, & Twohig, 2017). Relative to those on the waitlist, participants receiving ACT improved on overall distress, general anxiety, social anxiety, depression, academic concerns, and positive mental health (d = 0.47–0.78). Results of another study suggest that web-based ACT may be well suited for promoting adolescents' well-being in the school context (Puolakanaho et al., 2018). Compared to normal support from the school, the supported ACT-based web intervention resulted in a small but significant decrease in overall stress (d = 0.22) and an increase in academic buoyancy (d = 0.27; Puolakanaho et al., 2018). An ACT-based web-intervention was offered without therapist contact for adults with sleeping disturbances (Lappalainen, Langrial, Oinas-Kukkonen, Tolvanen, & Lappalainen, 2019). Significant positive improvements were seen for quality and duration of sleep, sleep-related dysfunctional beliefs and attitudes, depressive symptoms, and thought suppression (d = 0.21–0.53) compared to the waitlist control. Finally, web-based ACT has shown positive initial results in promoting well-being among parents of children with chronic conditions, with large between-group effect sizes of d ≥ 0.80 for burnout, depression, and anxiety symptoms, as well as the mindfulness skill of acting with awareness (Sairanen et al., 2019).

## Future Directions

In the future, we predict that different types of web and mobile ACT interventions will become more common, and they will be combined in different ways with existing face-to-face treatments. Combined treatment formats such as live group or individual sessions combined with Internet treatment programs will be more common, and we believe the Internet will be used in some way in nearly all future treatments. For example, we will use online self-observation methods and other technological solutions that work on phones and other mobile devices, and data and information will be transferred from these devices directly to the therapist so it is available before the live or virtual meeting with the client.

Within the coming years, web-based programs taking advantage of artificial intelligence will be developed. Artificial intelligence allows us to handle large amounts of data collected from previous interventions or while the client is actually using the program. For example, an online intervention could individually adapt to the observed changes in symptoms and psychological flexibility while the client is using the program. Also, different types of data collection tools and behavioral assessment procedures will be developed and incorporated into the programs. At the moment, there is a large interest in developing different types of environmental momentary assessment (EMA) and environmental momentary intervention (EMI) applications and models. In these models, assessment data can be collected via smartphones and the intervention can be delivered to the client in small doses during a day, or automated feedback can be given based on the assessment data. As an example, Levin, Haeger, and Cruz (2018) tested EMI that tailored the ACT content based on a participants' in-the-moment check-in responses, and found that compared to a nontailored version, the tailored version improved outcomes.

Research on process-based interventions will inform the development of web-based and mobile interventions. Mobile interventions will be built more on evidence-based processes, which will give more detailed information on key elements of successful treatment elements. In the future, relational frame theory (RFT) will increasingly influence the development of mobile interventions. In addition, web and mobile interventions, in order to improve adherence, will utilize elements such as games and virtual reality. There are already ongoing pilot trials investigating how games and RFT dialogues can be combined to improve adherence of school children and influence their psychological flexibility. Different types of online ACT interventions have been well accepted by the users and have shown promising results in a variety of clinical areas. They are excellent tools when providing evidence-based services.

# References

Andrews, G., Cuijpers, P., Craske, M. G., McEvoy, P., & Titov, N. (2010). Computer therapy for anxiety and depressive disorders is effective, acceptable and practical health care: A meta-analysis. *PLoS ONE, 5,* e13196.

Bendelin, N., Hesser, H., Dahl, J., Carlbring, P., Zetterqvist Nelson, K., & Andersson, G. (2011). Experiences of guided Internet-based cognitive-behavioural treatment for depression: A qualitative study. *BMC Psychiatry, 11,* 107.

Brown, M, Glendenning, A., Hoon, A.E., & John, A. (2016). Effectiveness of web-delivered acceptance and commitment therapy in relation to mental health and well-being: A systematic review and meta-analysis. *Journal of Medical Internet Research,18,* 8:e221. doi: 10.2196/jmir.6200.

Bryan, C. J., Morrow, C., & Appolonio, K. K. (2009). Impact of behavioral health consultant interventions on patient symptoms and functioning in an integrated family medicine clinic. *Journal of Clinical Psychology, 65,* 281–293. doi: 10.1002/jclp.20539

Dahlin, M., Andersson, G., Magnusson, K., Johansson, T., Sjögren, J., Håkansson, A., . . . Carlbring, P. (2016). Internet-delivered acceptance-based behaviour therapy for generalized anxiety disorder: A randomized controlled trial. *Behaviour Research and Therapy, 77,* 86–95. doi: 10.1016/j.brat.2015.12.007

Haynes, S. N., & O'Brien, W. (2000). *Principles and practice of behavioral assessment.* New York, NY: Springer.

Hedman, E., Carlbring, P., Ljóttson, B., & Andersson, G. (2014). *Internetbaserad psykologisk behandling. Evidens, indikation och praktiskt genomförande.* Stockholm: Natur och Kultur.

Hesser, H., Gustafsson, T., Lundén, C., Henrikson, O., Fattahi, K., Johnsson, E., . . . Andersson, G. (2012). A randomized controlled trial of internet-delivered cognitive behavior therapy and acceptance and commitment therapy in the treatment of tinnitus. *Journal of Consulting & Clinical Psychology, 80,* 649–661.

Hoffmann, D., Rask, C. U., Hedman-Lagerlöf, E., Ljótsson, B., & Frostholm, L. (2018). Development and feasibility testing of Internet-delivered acceptance and commitment therapy for severe health anxiety: Pilot study. *JMIR Mental Health, 5*(2), e28.

Jones, H. A., Heffner, J. L., Mercer,L., Wyszynski, C. M., Vilardaga, R., & Bricker, J. B. (2015). Web-based acceptance and commitment therapy smoking cessation treatment for smokers with depressive symptoms. *Journal of Dual Diagnosis, 11*(1), 56–62 doi: 10.1080/15504263.2014.992588

Kohtala, A., Muotka, J., & Lappalainen, R. (2017). What happens after five years?: The long-term effects of a four-session acceptance and commitment therapy delivered by student therapists for depressive symptoms. *Journal of Contextual Behavioral Science, 6,* 230–238. doi: 10.1016/j.jcbs.2017.03.003

Lappalainen, P., Granlund, A., Siltanen, S., Ahonen, S., Vitikainen, M., Tolvanen, A., & Lappalainen, R. (2014). ACT Internet-based vs face-to-face? A randomized controlled trial of two ways to deliver Acceptance and Commitment Therapy for depressive symptoms: An 18-month follow-up. *Behaviour Research & Therapy, 61,* 43–54. doi: 10.1016/j.brat.2014.07.006.

Lappalainen, P., Langrial, S., Oinas-Kukkonen, H., & Lappalainen, R. (2019). ACT for sleep - Internet-delivered self-help ACT for sub-clinical and clinical insomnia: A randomized controlled trial. *Journal of Contextual Behavioral Science.*

Lappalainen, P., Langrial, S., Oinas-Kukkonen, H., Tolvanen, A., & Lappalainen, R. (2015). Web-based acceptance and commitment therapy for depressive symptoms with minimal support: A randomized controlled trial. *Behavior Modification, 39*(6), 805–834. doi: 10.1177/0145445515598142

Lappalainen, R., Lehtonen, T., Skarp, E., Taubert, E., Ojanen, M., & Hayes, S. C. (2007). The impact of CBT and ACT models using psychology trainee therapists: A preliminary controlled effectiveness trial. *Behavior Modification, 31,* 488–511.

Levin, M. E., Haeger, J., & Cruz, R. A. (2018). Tailoring acceptance and commitment therapy skill coaching in-the-moment through smartphones: Results from a randomized controlled trial. *Mindfulness.*

Levin, M. E., Haeger, J., Pierce, B. & Twohig, M. P. (2017). Web-based acceptance and commitment therapy for mental health problems in college students: A randomized controlled trial. *Behavior Modification, 41,* 141–162.

Nordin, S., Carlbring, P., Cuijpers, P., & Andersson, G. (2010). Expanding the limits of bibliotherapy for panic disorder: Randomized trial of self-help without support but with a clear deadline. *Behavior Therapy, 41*(3), 267–276.

Paxling, B., Lundgren, S., Norman, A., Almlov, J., Carlbring, P., Cuijpers, P., & Andersson, G. (2013). Therapist behaviours in internet-delivered cognitive behaviour therapy: Analyses of e-mail correspondence in the treatment of generalized anxiety disorder. *Behavioural and Cognitive Psychotherapy, 41,* 280–289. doi: 10.1017/s1352465812000240

Pots, W. T., Fledderus, M., Meulenbeek, P. A., ten Klooster, P. M., Schreurs, K. M., & Bohlmeijer, E. T. (2016). Acceptance and commitment therapy as a web-based intervention for depressive symptoms: Randomised controlled trial. *British Journal of Psychiatry, 208*(1), 69–77. doi: 10.1192/bjp. bp.114.146068

Puolakanaho, A., Lappalainen, R., Lappalainen, P., Muotka, J., Hirvonen, R., Eklund, K., . . . & Kiuru, N. (2018). Reducing adolescent stress and enhancing academic buoyancy using a brief web-based program based on acceptance and commitment therapy: A randomized control trial. *Journal of Youth and Adolescence, 48,* 287–305. doi: 10.1007/s10964-018-0973-8

Räsänen, P., Lappalainen, P., Muotka, J., Tolvanen, A., & Lappalainen, R. (2016). An online guided ACT intervention for enhancing the psychological wellbeing of university students: A randomized controlled clinical trial. *Behaviour Research and Therapy, 78,* 30–42. doi:10.1016/j. brat.2016.01.001

Sairanen, E., Lappalainen, R., Lappalainen, P., Kaipainen, K., Carlstedt, F., Anclair, M., & Hiltunen, A. (2019). Effectiveness of a web-based Acceptance and Commitment Therapy intervention for wellbeing of parents whose children have chronic conditions: A randomized controlled trial. Manuscript submitted for publication.

Strosahl, K., Robinson, P., & Gustavsson, T. (2012). *Brief interventions for radical change: Principles and practice of focused acceptance and commitment therapy.* Oakland, CA: New Harbinger Publications.

Trompetter, H. R., Bohlmeijer, E. T., Veehof, M. M., & Schreurs, K. M. G. (2015). Internet-based guided self-help intervention for chronic pain based on Acceptance and Commitment Therapy: A randomized controlled trial. *Journal of Behavioral Medicine, 38,* 66. doi: 10.1007/ s10865-014-9579-0

# CHAPTER 17

# Adapting Acceptance and Commitment Therapy to Diverse Cultures

## Akihiko Masuda

*University of Hawaii at Manoa*

## Overview

As is the case with many psychosocial interventions (e.g., Messer & Gurman, 2011), acceptance and commitment therapy (ACT; Hayes, Strosahl, & Wilson, 2012) originated in individual and group psychotherapy settings in Western culture. Since its inception in the early 1980s (Hayes, 1984, 2015), ACT has been shaped into diverse forms (e.g., individual psychotherapy, group therapy, workshop, bibliotherapy, and e-therapy) to facilitate adaptations to various clinical and applied contexts (e.g., independent practice, managed care settings, outpatient clinics, inpatient care, counseling, outreach, community, and organizations). Today, this shaping process remains ongoing and active (Hayes, Barnes-Holmes, & Wilson, 2012; Hayes, Levin, Plumb-Vilardaga, Villatte, & Pistorello, 2013).

For the past decade, ACT also has been widely disseminated across the globe, including various applied settings in Asia, Africa, Oceania, Central America, and South America. This global-level dissemination effort is galvanized in part by a rapidly growing body of evidence that points to ACT as a unified procedure of change (A-tjak et al., 2015; Atkins et al., 2017). More specifically, ACT is now considered as an *evidence-based procedure* for adults with depression, anxiety, chronic pain, substance and alcohol use problems, and potentially many other clinical and applied concerns.

The dissemination and adaptation efforts of evidence-based procedures to diverse sociocultural contexts are important. However, many behavioral health scholars and practitioners caution about such efforts, especially when these procedures are transported to novel contexts where their clinical effectiveness has not yet been fully examined (Cardemil, 2010; Hall, 2001; Hall, Yip, & Zárate, 2016; Hwang, 2006). Common questions raised include (a) whether a given evidence-based procedure is practiced effectively in *its original forms* with clients from different sociocultural backgrounds (e.g., non-Western society), (b) whether key concepts and strategies in an evidence-based procedure are biased toward social norms supported by a particular culture (e.g., individualism, autonomy), (c) under what circumstances cultural adaptation of an evidence-based procedure is required, (d) when it is required, how the cultural adaption of a given therapy is done, and (e) what would be a guiding and unified model of cultural adaptation and multicultural competency. Carefully examining these questions can help clarify the fundamental understanding of what ACT is (for) and how we may best conceptualize and practice ACT for the "prediction-and-influence" of greater behavioral adaptation across diverse populations with diverse issues.

As discussed extensively elsewhere (e.g., Cardemil, 2010; Hall, 2001; Hall et al., 2016), the effective cultural adaptation of an evidence-based procedure, such as that of ACT, is not necessarily an easy task. Furthermore, a hasty transportation and adaptation of ACT may fall short of its intended outcomes, or may even cause harm (Hall, Hong, Zane, & Meyer, 2011; Hayes, Muto, & Masuda, 2011). For this reason, the present chapter offers some insights that can be used when adapting ACT to new clients, new treatment settings, or new cultural contexts. To begin, I briefly present the extant literature of cultural competency and cultural adaptation to orient readers to this very topic. Subsequently, in comparison to a content-focused treatment adherence and cultural adaptation approach, I will present a functional contextual account and its application to the understanding and practice of ACT, cultural competence, and cultural adaptation. Finally, I will present examples of how effective cultural adaption of ACT can be done *functionally and contextually* (Hayes et al., 2011; Hayes & Toarmino, 1995; Masuda, 2014a, 2016).

## Cultural Competency and Cultural Adaptation: Historical Background

A given evidence-based procedure found to be effective in a given sociocultural context (e.g., White Americans with depression in the US) is not necessarily effective in other sociocultural contexts (e.g., Asian Americans with depression in the US; Cheng & Sue, 2014; Hall, 2001; Sue, 1998, 1999). Despite its unified nature and its large body of empirical support (Atkins et al., 2017; Hayes, Strosahl, et al., 2012), ACT is no exception.

In behavioral science literature, *cultural competence* and *cultural adaptation* of treatment are two major constructs that highlight the importance of delivering an effective treatment equally to clients from diverse sociocultural backgrounds. At a psychological level of analysis, cultural competence generally refers to *clinicians' skill sets* for effectively working with diverse groups of individuals (Sue, Zane, Hall, & Berger, 2009; Whaley & Davis, 2007). These behavioral repertoires typically include, but are not limited to, rapport building, cultivating a therapeutic relationship, assessment, case conceptualization, and treatment delivery (Sue et al., 2009; Whaley & Davis, 2007). Cultural adaptation refers to a strategic adjustment of existing evidence-based treatment protocols that "consider language, culture, and context in such a way as that it is compatible with the client's cultural patterns, meanings, and values" (Bernal, Jiménez-Chafey, & Domenech Rodríguez, 2009, p. 362). For example, culturally adapting an English-written ACT protocol to a Japanese client may include translating the protocol into Japanese, modifying and tailoring therapeutic exercises in the protocol to this Japanese client (e.g., the use of the word "tea" instead of "milk" for the Milk-Milk-Milk defusion exercise), and setting up treatment goals (e.g., genuine contribution to a collective whole, balanced with personal autonomy) while taking into consideration contingencies that operate within this Japanese client's sociocultural context (Masuda, 2016; Masuda, Muto, Hayes, & Lillis, 2008).

## Functional and Contextual Adaptation of ACT

From a functional contextual perspective (Hayes, Long, Levin, & Follette, 2013; Hayes et al., 2011), not all accounts of cultural competency and cultural adaption are equally adequate. More specifically, proponents of ACT argue that cultural competency and cultural adaptation must be understood and practiced functionally and contextually (Hayes, Long, et al., 2013; Hayes et al., 2011; Masuda, 2016, 2014b). This means that a given therapeutic approach (a) is guided by a functionally and contextually informed case conceptualization of psychological flexibility (see Hayes, Strosahl, et al., 2012, pp. 103–141), (b) identifies target behavioral processes in terms of relevant behavioral domains (e.g., form, frequency, intensity, situations where they occur) and their relevant contextual variables (e.g., antecedents, consequences, and competing behaviors), (c) develops a treatment plan, and (d) implements and adjusts therapeutic work based on its workability in both short-term (e.g., moment-by-moment, within-session) and longer-term (e.g., final treatment) goals. In other words, the adaptation of ACT is a continuous and ongoing interplay between the client and the therapist done functionally and con-textually. That is, an ACT-consistent cultural adaptation must diverge from a strict con-tent-based understanding of cultural competency and cultural adaptation (Masuda, 2014a, 2016; Whaley & Davis, 2007).

A major shortcoming of content-focused treatment adherence and cultural adapta-tion is that the *topographical presentation* (contents) of a given therapeutic work (e.g., act of a therapist, metaphors, experiential exercises) itself does not determine its workability (Masuda, 2016). Rather, the workability of a given therapeutic work is determined by the culturally shaped and established interaction between the client and the therapist (Hayes, Strosahl, et al., 2012, pp. 142–143). For example, the Passengers on the Bus metaphor (Hayes, Strosahl, et al., 2012, pp. 250–252) works only if clients are able to intuitively and experientially relate the narrative within the metaphor (e.g., how the bus driver responds to difficult passengers) to the clients' present experience (how they relate to their difficult thoughts and feelings), and then draw some wisdom from it (the awareness that they can respond to difficult private events openly without reacting to them). For some clients, the Passengers on the Bus metaphor is effective in evoking such wisdom immediately, but for others (e.g., affluent clients who have never used a public transportation system, includ-ing a bus, or clients who live in a remote area where community members are not disrup-tive to others), doing so is extremely challenging. This may be in part because these individuals may not have the sufficient sociocultural learning history to make effective use of the metaphor.

As noted below, rote delivery of a therapeutic activity or technique, even one that is presented in an ACT manual, does not guarantee intended effects in targeted behavioral processes (Masuda, 2016; Pasillas & Masuda, 2014). What the functional and contextual framework allows clinicians to attain, if it is applied effectively, is a sensitivity to clients' socioculturally shaped unique learning histories, workability of treatment techniques used in sessions (i.e., whether a given technique used in session yields the intended effect), and adjustment of therapeutic strategies and steps accordingly. Therefore, from a functional and contextual perspective, the cultural adaptation of ACT is a continuous and ongoing process that unfolds in a given therapeutic relationship.

## ACT as Contextually and Pragmatically Situated Acts of Clinicians

From the standpoint of the therapist, ACT can be viewed as a *contextually situated, purposeful act of a clinician* in a therapeutic context that is principle-informed and experientially guided (Masuda, 2014a, 2016). More specifically, ACT is said to be *purposeful* in that the clinician's actions are intentionally directed toward a client's greater behavioral adaptation (i.e., psychological flexibility) regardless of how psychological flexibility is manifested topographically in that client. ACT is also said to be principle-informed, as the clinician's behavior is always guided by the psychological flexibility model of prosperity and behavior change. From its inception (see Hayes, Barnes-Holmes, et al., 2012; Hayes, Long, et al., 2013), the ACT community has made great efforts to improve and refine the psychological flexibility model as a case formulation and treatment planning tool to be pragmatic across diverse clinical cases. The following clinical implications are derived from the psychological flexibility model (Hayes, Strosahl, et al., 2012; Masuda, 2016, 2014b):

a.   Many of clients' presenting concerns (e.g., problematic behaviors, negative affect, loss of purpose, apathy, negative self-appraisal, relationship conflicts) are cognitively enmeshed and regulated, and their efforts to solve these concerns are also cognitively regulated.

b.   These cognitively regulated phenomena are learned and socioculturally shaped and maintained.

c.   An ACT case conceptualization is formulated in terms of the extent to which clients engage in unworkable and automatic behavioral and cognitive efforts to downregulate unwanted private events (e.g., experiential avoidance), the deficits in activities that are meaningful or fulfilling (e.g., lack of committed action) for clients, and factors that maintain these behavioral patterns.

d.   It is important to identify contextual factors that can be systematically manipulated by client, clinician, or both.

e.   Clients' sociocultural factors (e.g., upbringing, learning history, verbal antecedent and consequence, verbal community) are functionally understood and are translated into the target behavioral processes identified in (c).

f.   The promotion of greater behavioral adaptation does not necessarily require the elimination of presenting concerns in form or frequency.

g.   Change in how one relates or responds to problematic internal events (e.g., psychological openness) along with the promotion of intrinsically reinforcing and adaptive behaviors (e.g., committed action) is sufficient to promote greater behavioral adaptation (psychological flexibility).

While the psychological flexibility model is theorized to be relatively universal, the practice of ACT is extremely idiographic. That is, the behavior of an ACT clinician is shaped and adjusted functionally and contextually through the *ongoing* interaction with a client. This is the experiential part of therapeutic work that shapes the clinician's therapeutic behavior.

# Cultural Adaptation of ACT

Given its functional and contextual nature, the course of ACT typically follows that of clinical behavior analysis (Hayes, Barnes-Holmes, et al., 2012; Hayes, Long, et al., 2013). More specifically, unlike a content-focused approach, a therapist does not want to start any intervention work until the client's presenting concerns, general functioning, and treatment goals are understood and formulated both functionally and contextually. Cultural adaptations of ACT are not exempt from this guiding heuristic.

## Psychological Flexibility as Socioculturally Situated Behavioral Repertoires

The promotion of psychological flexibility is the overarching treatment goal and direction of ACT. From an ACT perspective, the functional quality of psychological flexibility (e.g., open, centered, and engaged living) is universally applicable, although its topographical manifestations can vary significantly across individuals (Masuda, 2014a, 2016). This is because of different sociocultural contingencies that operate within these individuals. For example, for some, an individualistic worldview (e.g., individuality, personal achievement, and autonomy) continues to be the driving force that shapes psychologically flexible behavioral patterns (Markus & Kitayama, 1991; Weisz, Rothbaum, & Blackburn, 1984). For others, such as those in non-Western cultures, a collective and interdependent worldview (e.g., harmony and conformity to the collective whole) may serve as an underlying principle of valued living (Markus & Kitayama, 2010).

As discussed extensively elsewhere (Markus & Kitayama, 1991, 2010; Weisz et al., 1984), these differential social contingencies may shape behaviors of individuals differently across key life domains, including family relations, parenting, peer socialization, and intimacy. For example, the direct expression of intimacy (e.g., saying "I love you" to one's partner) tends to be valued in a Western culture, and is often viewed as part of a psychologically flexible behavioral pattern. However, expressing intimacy in this behavioral form may not be a culturally supported practice for individuals from other cultures (for example, I never see my Japanese parents, who have been married fifty years, saying "I love you" to each other). Once again, what is crucial for ACT clinicians is to judge whether a given behavior of a client is linked to psychological flexibility for that client in a given sociocultural context by looking at its functional and adaptive quality (e.g., open, centered, and engaged living). In practice, culturally and individually sensitive understanding of psychological flexibility can start with asking the client questions, such as "If this (i.e., presenting concern) is no longer an issue, what do you hope to see more of in your life?"

## ACT Case Conceptualization

Generally, an ACT clinician examines (a) whether the psychological flexibility model can be applied to the case formulation of a client's presenting concerns and overall functioning, (b) if so, which behavior patterns of the client fit which key behavioral processes (e.g., psychological acceptance, committed action) in the model, and (c) whether a tentative treatment goal informed by the model is *socioculturally* sound for both the client and therapist.

While there is a generic functional contextual case conceptualization framework presented in an ACT approach, understanding a given client must be extremely idiographic (Hayes & Toarmino, 1995; Masuda, Cohen, Wicksell, Kemani, & Johnson, 2011). More specifically, whether a given behavioral pattern fits a given ACT process is determined not by its form, but rather, by its function in a given context. Take a case of a sixteen-year-old Black adolescent male with sickle cell disease (SCD) as an example (see Masuda et al., 2011 for a detailed case conceptualization of this case). In the United States, SCD is most common among people whose ancestors come from Africa. To prevent a sickle cell pain crisis, which can begin suddenly and last several hours to several days, individuals with SCD are often encouraged to drink at least eight twelve-ounce glasses of water daily, especially during warm weather. Depending on the individual patient, if the behavior (i.e., water intake) is limited and is conceptualized to yield greater functional disability due to regular sickle cell crises and prevent values-reflected activities, it should be conceptualized as a target behavior to be increased. On the other hand, if the behavior is excessive and serves as an extreme safety behavior that is regulated by negative affect and interferes with daily functioning (e.g., socialization with peers), it may be viewed as a behavior to be decreased to a certain extent. For this adolescent male patient with SCD, the water intake was conceptualized to be the former (Masuda et al.,

2011), and the ACT intervention focused on increasing his water intake and other crisis management behaviors (e.g., moderate levels of exercises, such as walking).

Furthermore, this sixteen-year-old adolescent male's perceived gender role/expectation, peer socialization, family system, practice of religion and spirituality, social norms, and perceived social discrimination were explored to determine how extant contingencies approximated by these social factors influenced the promotion of water intake and other crisis management behaviors (Masuda et al., 2011). Of these factors, his endorsement of masculinity role/expectation and peer relations were conceptualized to be particularly relevant to the behavioral deficits of symptom management, including regular water intake. More specifically, they seemed to maintain his attachment to the notion of "a strong Black man" and not wanting to appear "weak," which in turn strengthened the view that pain management behaviors are a sign of weakness or unimportance (Rose, Kim, Dennison, & Hill, 2000; Wade, 2008). At the same time, the reframing of a Black masculinity role was conceptualized to be therapeutic for promoting crisis management behaviors and personal autonomy (e.g., "to be a strong Black man and become independent, you may want to take care of yourself really well first"). To summarize, in an ACT case conceptualization, the client's presenting concerns are translated into key behavioral processes in the psychological flexibility model, and relevant sociocultural factors are translated into the contingencies of these behavioral processes.

## Therapeutic Relationship and Stance of the Therapist

In ACT, a therapeutic relationship is viewed as the *contextually situated*, ongoing and dynamic interplay between the client and the therapist as *historical and situational beings* (Hayes, Strosahl, et al., 2012, see pp. 141–149). For clients, the therapeutic relationship is a context where they can learn a new set of behaviors or insights through interacting with a clinician (Robins, Schmidt III, & Linehan, 2004), and where the therapist serves as a crucial contextual factor for the client's behavior change. For clinicians, the therapeutic relationship is also an interpersonal context that requires them to be flexible in response to ongoing changes in each therapeutic moment with the client (Kohlenberg & Tsai, 2007).

As seen in the work of Kelly Wilson (Wilson & Dufrene, 2008) and other celebrated ACT clinicians and trainers, extant ACT manuals (e.g., Hayes, Strosahl, et al., 2012, pp. 141–142) often encourage the therapeutic relationship to be intense and experiential with a strong interpersonal and emotional connection between client and therapist. However, from a functional and contextual perspective, one cannot assume that this *form* of interpersonal style (e.g., the therapist's being warm, empathic, and validating) is universally effective for all clients. In fact, a therapeutic interaction that is vertical, prescriptive, and directive may be more effective for some clients in particular therapeutic contexts (e.g., primary care setting). For example, when I work with Asian American and Native Hawaiian clients in Hawaii who are younger than I am, I tend to present myself as an authority figure—at least initially in order to build their perceived confidence in me as their clinician—and I tend to be more directive than I am usually in session. This is in part because Hawaiian cultures often value the wisdom of age and respect for elders, and behaving in this way tends to be congruent with their cultural expectations. Similarly, when I work with Asian American and Native Hawaiian clients, and even some White Americans, in Hawaii who are older than I am, I tend to present myself as polite and humble to them in order to directly express my respect for them.

As such, my therapeutic relationship with clients in Hawaii is not necessarily horizontal, as is often suggested by extant ACT manuals. However, I would argue that this *form* of therapeutic relationship is still ACT-consistent if it *functions to* promote greater psychological flexibility. The take-home message here is that effective styles of therapeutic relationships can vary greatly across different client-therapist dyads, and it is crucial for the therapist to have the ability to fine-tune their relationship in each moment accordingly in service of the promotion of psychological flexibility (Koerner, 2012; Sue et al., 2009).

Relatedly, a therapist's self-disclosure in session is often discussed in cultural adaptation literature, and is often a central topic in ACT therapist training (Hayes, Strosahl, et al., 2012). Once again, it is important to note that the therapist's self-disclosure may not always be therapeutic, at least initially. This is because, for some clients, self-disclosure is not part of their sociocultural norm, at least not during the initial phase of an interpersonal relationship. Given the potential pitfalls of therapist self-disclosure, it is important for clinicians to be mindful of the timing and content of their own self-disclosure. For some clients, I will not self-disclose any of my own previous struggles unless the client and I have created a safe therapeutic context where experiential learning is validated and encouraged. Similar to that of the therapeutic relationship, the general consensus about self-disclosure is to self-disclose only if it is therapeutic for the client.

## Awareness of One's Own Assumptions

Clinicians are also historical beings who are influenced by their previous and current learning history. This means that a therapist's standards of adaptive and maladaptive behavior are also functionally and contextually shaped within a given sociocultural context (e.g., verbal community). For this reason, it is crucial for the clinician to be careful not to make assumptions regarding which client behaviors are adaptive or not adaptive without carefully assessing their functions in the context in which they occur. As I have already discussed potentially biased assumptions in terms of case conceptualization, the therapeutic relationship, and self-disclosure, here I will focus on potential biases in the domain of actual practice, using values and commitment work as an example.

Striving for personal growth in the domains of occupation and school is often valued in Western cultural contexts. This is also the case for many clients in non-Western cultural contexts. However, while the pursuit of personal growth tends to be individualistic in mainstream Western cultures, pursuits in non-Western cultures are often collectivistic and interpersonal (e.g., "I will pursue education for my family and its prosperity"). For Westernized therapists, this collectivistic quality may come across as too pliant or disingenuous. However, within collectivistic cultural views, incorporating such interpersonal and relational qualities into values work can be quite adaptive personally and socially.

Assertiveness is another example that has been discussed in the domains of values and committed actions. Speaking up for one's own thoughts, beliefs, and "wants" is often valued in many Western cultural contexts, including those in the US. For example, ACT therapists often encourage clients to be assertive to their partners in their intimate relationships. As the proverb "The squeaky wheel gets the grease" goes, the act of assertiveness is often followed by favorable outcomes, and this is in part because Western sociocultural contexts tend to encourage such interpersonal communication styles. However, in other cultural contexts, such as some racial and ethnic minority cultures in the US, assertiveness is viewed as a sign of hostility, aggression, selfishness, and disruption of interpersonal harmony. It is important to clarify that I do not contend that assertiveness should be discouraged for non-Western clients in non-Western cultures. However, what I attempt to clarify here is that the kind of assertiveness that is encouraged in Western cultural contexts ("I want…") may not be an effective *form* of behavior to effectively navigate in social contexts in other cultures. As the Japanese proverb "A nail that stands will be hammered down" goes, it may actually result in unintended negative outcomes. In these contexts, it is important for the therapist and client to identify alternative ways to navigate through their interpersonal, cultural contexts for the intended outcomes.

As described by Hayes and Toarmino (1995), a given behavior of a client in a given moment is the function of multiple contingencies of reinforcement that augment and conflict with one another. In other words, a given behavior (e.g., self-disclosure) is perhaps adaptive in one domain (e.g., personal growth and prosocial action), but not quite so adaptive in another (e.g., family relationship, community relationship). As such, it is important for the therapist to demonstrate cultural sensitivity and humility in regard to the client's sociocultural context (e.g., social and verbal contingencies) to navigate with a client throughout the course of therapy.

## Modification of Therapeutic Techniques

From the perspective of a functionally and contextually informed approach (Hayes et al., 2011; Masuda, 2016), structural modifications of treatment are always expected. As implied above, clinicians may not serve as effective therapists initially, but being cognizant of the actual function of the ongoing therapeutic interaction allows them to fine-tune their therapeutic techniques. In ACT, some modifications may include modifying the content or length of mindfulness exercises, metaphors, and session activities or even modifying the session format.

Take ACT values and commitment work with Japanese clients as an example. Unlike a content-focused adaptation, a functional and contextual adaptation of ACT for a given client starts with identifying behavioral processes to increase or undermine. For example, primary behavioral processes to be strengthened in terms of values and committed actions are (a) the construction and experience of values as the freely chosen sense of life's meaning and direction, (b) identification of committed actions that reflect those values, and (c) continuous engagement in committed action (i.e., process) regardless of its initial failures or successes (outcomes).

The next step for this cultural adaption of ACT is to identify potential strategies to move these behavioral processes and judge whether strategies recommended by ACT manuals would be likely to promote these behavioral processes. For the promotion of the third behavioral process above, ACT manuals often suggest the use of the Skiing metaphor (Hayes, Strosahl, & Wilson, 1999, pp. 220–221) and the Path Up the Mountain metaphor (Hayes et al., 1999, p. 221-222), as well as the Passengers on the Bus metaphor (Hayes et al., 1999, pp. 157–158). If these recommended strategies are judged to be effective, there is no reason not to try it and see if it in fact yields intended change in the client. If not, it is important to identify other potential metaphors that can be substituted for that client.

When I work with Japanese clients on increasing continuous engagement in committed action, I often use proverbs and common personal mottos familiar to many Japanese people, instead of metaphors listed in ACT manuals. These include "継続は力なり(putting continuous efforts is wisdom)," "思い立ったが吉日 (Never put off until tomorrow what you can do today)," "七転び八起き(Fall seven times, stand up eight)," and similar others. It is also important to note that these proverbs and mottos are not therapeutically useful for all Japanese clients. For this reason, when I use them in therapy, I pay close attention to their workability in terms of intended effects. If the intended process (e.g., constant, continuous engagement in value-reflection and perceived importance of doing so) is not moved, I will revisit it again later, perhaps with another proverb or so. In sum, the modification of ACT must be done functionally in the service of promoting greater behavioral adaptation and psychological flexibility, and it should be idiographically tailored to a given client. To do so, metaphors and experiential exercises presented in ACT manuals should be viewed merely as exemplars that *can be* adapted to a given client.

## Research Support

The synthesis of knowledge and evidence regarding the cultural adaption of ACT is still in its infancy. To date, the importance of effective cultural adaptation of ACT has been discussed in the context of multicultural competencies and mindfulness- and acceptance-based cognitive behavioral therapies (Masuda, 2014b), treatment development (Hayes, Long, et al., 2013), and the inclusion of understudied racial and ethnic groups in ACT studies (Woidneck, Pratt, Gundy, Nelson, & Twohig, 2012). Similarly, some scholars have examined cross-cultural utility and validity of ACT and the psychological flexibility model to various cultural and anthropological contexts (Fung, 2015; Pasillas & Masuda, 2014; Sabucedo, 2017; Stewart et al., 2016; White, Gregg, Batten, Hayes, & Kasujja, 2017).

## Future Directions

What may be a beneficial future direction for the adaptation of ACT to diverse cultures is the synthesis of relevant ACT studies and reports in order to examine and develop a model and effective strategies of cultural adaptation with precision and scope. In other words, as discussed by Hayes and his colleagues in the context of treatment development (Hayes, Long, et al., 2013), we can conduct the same level of careful investigation regarding the cultural adaptability of the ACT model as we have done for a wide variety of behavioral health issues (e.g., depression, anxiety, chronic pain).

ACT is now recognized as an evidence-based procedure for a range of behavioral health concerns. The present chapter argues that while the dissemination and cultural adaptation of ACT is encouraging, such an effort is likely to fall short if it is merely a content-focused transportation without sensitivity to the client's context (e.g., learning history and current sociocultural environment). In response to the pitfalls of this content-focused cultural adaptation, the present chapter argues for the importance of principle-informed, bottom-up ACT practice that allows a clinician to be functionally and contextually oriented to a given clinical case. Framing ACT as the purposeful behavior of a clinician in therapeutic contexts that are both principle-informed and experientially guided allows a clinician to fine-tune their therapeutic interaction with a given client.

## References

A-tjak, J. G., Davis, M. L., Morina, N., Powers, M. B., Smits, J. A., & Emmelkamp, P. M. (2015). A meta-analysis of the efficacy of acceptance and commitment therapy for clinically relevant mental and physical health problems. *Psychotherapy and Psychosomatics, 84*(1), 30–36.

Atkins, P. W., Ciarrochi, J., Gaudiano, B. A., Bricker, J. B., Donald, J., Rovner, G., . . . Hayes, S. C. (2017). Departing from the essential features of a high quality systematic review of psychotherapy: A response to Öst (2014) and recommendations for improvement. *Behaviour Research and Therapy, 97,* 259–272.

Bernal, G., Jiménez-Chafey, M. I., & Domenech Rodríguez, M. M. (2009). Cultural adaptation of treatments: A resource for considering culture in evidence-based practice. *Professional Psychology: Research and Practice, 40*(4), 361–368. doi: 10.1037/a0016401

Cardemil, E. V. (2010). Cultural adaptations to empirically supported treatments: A research agenda. *The Scientific Review of Mental Health Practice. 7*(2), 8–21.

Cheng, J. K. Y., & Sue, S. (2014). Addressing cultural and ethnic minority issues in the acceptance and mindfulness movement. In A. Masuda (Ed.), *Mindfulness and acceptance in multicultural competency: A contextual approach to sociocultural diversity in theory and practice* (pp. 21–37). Oakland, CA: Context Press/New Harbinger Publications.

Fung, K. (2015). Acceptance and commitment therapy: Western adoption of Buddhist tenets? *Transcultural Psychiatry, 52*(4), 561–576.

Hall, G. C. N. (2001). Psychotherapy research with ethnic minorities: Empirical, ethical, and conceptual issues. *Journal of Consulting and Clinical Psychology, 69*(3), 502–510. doi: 10.1037/0022-006X.69.3.502

Hall, G. C. N., Hong, J. J., Zane, N. W. S., & Meyer, O. L. (2011). Culturally competent treatments for Asian Americans: The relevance of mindfulness and acceptance-based psychotherapies. *Clinical Psychology: Science and Practice, 18*(3), 215–231. doi: 10.1111/j.1468-2850.2011.01253.x

Hall, G. C. N., Yip, T., & Zárate, M. A. (2016). On becoming multicultural in a monocultural research world: A conceptual approach to studying ethnocultural diversity. *American Psychologist, 71*(1), 40–51. doi: 10.1037/a0039734

Hayes, S. C. (1984). Making sense of spirituality. *Behaviorism, 12,* 99–110.

Hayes, S. C. (2015). Making sense of spirituality. In S. C. Hayes (Ed.), *The Act in Context: The canonical papers of Steven C. Hayes* (pp. 68–82). New York, NY: Routledge.

Hayes, S. C., Barnes-Holmes, D., & Wilson, K. G. (2012). Contextual Behavioral Science: Creating a science more adequate to the challenge of the human condition. *Journal of Contextual Behavioral Science, 1*(1–2), 1–16. doi: 10.1016/j.jcbs.2012.09.004

Hayes, S. C., Levin, M. E., Plumb-Vilardaga, J., Villatte, J. L., & Pistorello, J. (2013). Acceptance and commitment therapy and contextual behavioral science: Examining the progress of a distinctive model of behavioral and cognitive therapy. *Behavior Therapy, 44*(2), 180–198. doi: 10.1016/j.beth.2009.08.002

Hayes, S. C., Long, D. M., Levin, M. E., & Follette, W. C. (2013). Treatment development: Can we find a better way? *Clinical Psychology Review, 33*(7), 870–882. doi: 10.1016/j.cpr.2012.09.009

Hayes, S. C., Muto, T., & Masuda, A. (2011). Seeking cultural competence from the ground up. *Clinical Psychology: Science & Practice, 18*(3), 232–237. doi: 10.1111/j.1468-2850.2011.01254.x

Hayes, S. C., Strosahl, K. D., & Wilson, K. G. (1999). *Acceptance and commitment therapy: An experiential approach to behavior change.* New York, NY: Guilford Press.

Hayes, S. C., Strosahl, K. D., & Wilson, K. G. (2012). *Acceptance and commitment therapy: The process and practice of mindful change* (2nd ed.). New York, NY: Guilford Press.

Hayes, S. C., & Toarmino, D. (1995). If behavioral principles are generally applicable, why is it necessary to understand cultural diversity? *The Behavior Therapist, 18,* 21–23.

Hwang, W.-C. (2006). The psychotherapy adaptation and modification framework: Application to Asian Americans. *American Psychologist, 61*(7), 702–715. doi: 10.1037/0003-066x.61.7.702

Koerner, K. (2012). *Doing dialectical behavior therapy: A practical guide.* New York, NY: Guilford Press.

Kohlenberg, R. J., & Tsai, M. (2007). Functional analytic psychotherapy. In *Functional Analytic Psychotherapy* (pp. 169–188). Boston, MA: Springer.

Markus, H. R., & Kitayama, S. (1991). Culture and the self: Implications for cognition, emotion, and motivation. *Psychological Review, 98*(2), 224–253.

Markus, H. R., & Kitayama, S. (2010). Cultures and selves: A cycle of mutual constitution. *Perspectives on Psychological Science, 5*(4), 420–430. doi: 10.1177/1745691610375557

Masuda, A. (2014a). Psychotherapy in cultural context. In A. Masuda (Ed.), *Mindfulness and acceptance in multicultural competency: A contextual approach to sociocultural diversity in theory and practice.* (pp. 39–55). Oakland, CA: New Harbinger Publication.

Masuda, A. (Ed.) (2014b). *Mindfulness and acceptance in multicultural competency: A contextual approach to sociocultural diversity in theory and practice.* Oakland, CA: Context Press/New Harbinger Publications.

Masuda, A. (2016). Principle-based cultural adaptation of cognitive behavior therapies: A functional and contextual perspective as an example. *Japanese Journal of Behavior Therapy, 42*(1), 11–19.

Masuda, A., Cohen, L. L., Wicksell, R. K., Kemani, M. K., & Johnson, A. (2011). A case study: Acceptance and commitment therapy for pediatric sickle cell disease. *Journal of Pediatric Psychology, 36*(4), 398–408. doi: 10.1093/jpepsy/jsq118

Masuda, A., Muto, T., Hayes, S. C., & Lillis, J. (2008). Acceptance and commitment therapy: Application to a Japanese client. *Japanese Journal of Behavior Therapy, 34,* 137–148.

Messer, S. B., & Gurman, A. S. (2011). *Essential psychotherapies: Theory and practice* (3rd ed.). New York, NY: Guilford Press.

Pasillas, R. M., & Masuda, A. (2014). Cultural competency and acceptance and commitment therapy. In A. Masuda (Ed.), *Mindfulness and acceptance in multicultural competency: A contextual approach to sociocultural diversity in theory and practice* (pp. 109–125). Oakland, CA: Context Press/New Harbinger Publications.

Robins, C. J., Schmidt III, H., & Linehan, M. M. (2004). Dialectical behavior therapy: Synthesizing radical acceptance with skillful means. In S. C. Hayes, V. M. Follette, & M. M. Linehan (Eds.), *Mindfulness and acceptance: Expanding the cognitive-behavioral tradition* (pp. 30–44). New York, NY: Guilford Press.

Rose, L. E., Kim, M. T., Dennison, C. R., & Hill, M. N. (2000). The contexts of adherence for African Americans with high blood pressure. *Journal of Advanced Nursing, 32*(3), 587–594. doi: 10.1046/j.1365-2648.2000.01538.x

Sabucedo, P. (2017). The Psychological Flexibility Model from a cultural perspective: An interpretative analysis of two Native American healing rituals. *International Journal of Culture and Mental Health, 10*(4), 367–375.

Stewart, C., G. White, R., Ebert, B., Mays, I., Nardozzi, J., & Bockarie, H. (2016). A preliminary evaluation of acceptance and commitment therapy (ACT) training in Sierra Leone. *Journal of Contextual Behavioral Science, 5*(1), 16–22. doi: 10.1016/j.jcbs.2016.01.001

Sue, S. (1998). In search of cultural competence in psychotherapy and counseling. *American Psychologist, 53*(4), 440–448. doi: 10.1037/0003-066x.53.4.440

Sue, S. (1999). Science, ethnicity, and bias: Where have we gone wrong? *American Psychologist, 54*(12), 1070–1077. doi: 10.1037/0003-066x.54.12.1070

Sue, S., Zane, N., Hall, G. C. N., & Berger, L. K. (2009). The case for cultural competency in psychotherapeutic interventions. *Annual Review of Psychology, 60,* 525–548. doi: 10.1146/annurev.psych.60.110707.163651

Wade, J. C. (2008). Masculinity ideology, male reference group identity dependence, and African American men's health-related attitudes and behaviors. *Psychology of Men & Masculinity, 9*(1), 5–16.

Weisz, J. R., Rothbaum, F. M., & Blackburn, T. C. (1984). Standing out and standing in: The psychology of control in America and Japan. *American Psychologist, 39*(9), 955–969.

Whaley, A. L., & Davis, K. E. (2007). Cultural competence and evidence-based practice in mental health services: A complementary perspective. *American Psychologist, 62*(6), 563–574. doi: 10.1037/0003-066x.62.6.563

White, R. G., Gregg, J., Batten, S., Hayes, L. L., & Kasujja, R. (2017). Contextual behavioral science and global mental health: Synergies and opportunities. *Journal of Contextual Behavioral Science, 6*(3), 245–251. doi: 10.1016/j.jcbs.2017.07.001

Wilson, K. G., & Dufrene, T. (2008). *Mindfulness for two: An acceptance and commitment therapy approach to mindfulness in psychotherapy.* Oakland, CA: New Harbinger.

Woidneck, M. R., Pratt, K. M., Gundy, J. M., Nelson, C. R., & Twohig, M. P. (2012). Exploring cultural competence in acceptance and commitment therapy outcomes. *Professional Psychology: Research and Practice, 43*(3), 227–233.

# CHAPTER 18

# Implementing ACT in Sierra Leone

Beate Ebert

*Private Practice Aschaffenburg*
*Commit and Act*

Hannah Bockarie

*Commit and Act,*

Corinna Stewart

*Institute of Health & Wellbeing*

Thomas Szabo

*Florida Institute of Technology*

Ross G. White

*University of Liverpool*

## Overview

This chapter describes a nongovernmental organization (NGO) called Commit and Act (CAA) and its use of acceptance and commitment therapy (ACT; Hayes, Strosahl, & Wilson, 1999) to support the mental health needs of people in the West African country of Sierra Leone. A key concept is *task sharing,* the process of delegating tasks ordinarily performed by highly qualified individuals to other, less educated workers (Sashidharan, White, Mezzina, Jansen, & Gishoma, 2016) in order to reach otherwise inaccessible populations and regions. In this chapter, we outline a reticulated task-sharing model of psychosocial service delivery in lower income countries (LICs) where deep poverty is compounded by a marked lack of mental health professionals (World Health Organization [WHO], 2014). Additionally, we elucidate challenges of working with ACT in diverse cultures and identify factors that are crucial for success in disseminating a Western therapeutic approach in LICs and, more generally, in crisis-afflicted regions.

# Global Context of ACT in Low-Income Countries

Mental health difficulties are associated with high levels of disability worldwide, accounting for 22.7% of documented lifespan disabilities (Vos et al., 2013), and are a significant barrier to economic development (All-Party Parliamentary Group on Global Health, 2014). Unaddressed mental health needs have global impacts that are disproportionately experienced in LICs, given their comparative lack of economic, human policy, and legislative supports. LICs such as Sierra Leone have virtually no economic and human resources to meet the mental health needs of the population (Collins et al., 2011). Whereas the global average of mental health expenditure is $2.50 per capita per year, in the African region this figure is $0.10 (WHO, 2018). Resource limitations in LICs such as Sierra Leone also include the lack of mental health governance instruments that outline minimum standards for the care, treatment, and human rights of people experiencing mental health difficulties. Of all WHO regions, Africa has the lowest percentage (58%) of countries with updated mental health policies. In Sierra Leone, the Ministry of Health and Sanitation coordinated a new mental health policy that was ratified in 2014, but this has only been partially implemented (WHO, 2014).

# History of Commit and Act

CAA was founded in Germany in 2010 with the aim of supporting vulnerable populations in LICs with evidence-based psychotherapeutic care. CAA's premise is that *functional contextual* approaches to understanding difficult behaviors (i.e., identifying relevant context factors that maintain the behavior and finding response options more aligned with the individual's values) should be helpful in tackling the broad range of problems that can occur in settings plagued by posttraumatic stress after armed conflict, gender-based violence, Ebola, and other calamities. The core strategy is the provision of coaching workshops by experienced ACT trainers to local health workers and other professionals (e.g., teachers, religious leaders, community leaders, police). The goal is to help these workers develop applications suitable to their unique cultural and professional contexts and train others to apply the method. The ultimate task-sharing aim is that those trained by ACT experts will teach others to train the next generation after them in a self-replicating, reticulated fashion. To this end, a regional, independent branch of CAA, Commit and Act Foundation in Sierra Leone (CAF-SL), was registered in 2014. This marked an important step forward in ensuring local ownership and autonomy of CAA activities in the region. Since then, in addition to annual training and supervision provided by international trainers, CAF-SL has provided a permanent local hub for the implementation of ACT and PROSOCIAL (described later in this chapter). Furthermore, the majority of ACT training is now delivered by local trainers.

CAA developed its approach incrementally, starting with our visit to Sierra Leone in 2010 and a desire to provide psychotherapy support to address the prolonged suffering of people in Sierra Leone after its eleven-year civil war. The intention was not to "bring

Western expertise" but to connect cultures and codesign interventions suitable to the local contexts. Conversations with amputees, priests, teachers, social workers, and politicians uncovered the many physical and mental health difficulties that resulted from the civil war. These issues, compounded by a lack of resources and infrastructure, led many to hopelessness, drug abuse, and violence. In this context, CAA partnered with local institutions who invited local health workers to the first ACT training workshops.

## Description of ACT Training Workshops

In the initial workshops delivered in Sierra Leone in 2011, Western trainers labored to examine their assumptions about the kinds of metaphors and exercises that would be relevant and acceptable, given that those attending the workshops had recently experienced violence, loss, and extreme poverty. We invited input from Sierra Leonean attendees—about thirty participants, women and men equally, from different tribes and religions. We asked about the populations that they worked with (e.g., survivors of the civil war, street kids, HIV-positive clients, perpetrators of violence), their experiences and challenges, the problems their clients faced (e.g., emotional pain, anxiety, physical violence, stigma), and the supports they offered. Participants reported therapeutic interventions ranging from reassuring ("It will all be well again") and giving advice ("Best you obey your husband so he will not beat you again") to cognitive behavioral interventions ("Is this thought true?").

The inner struggles that participants described were similar to what is reported in Western contexts, such as *Maybe my suffering in the civil war was God's punishment for something I committed.* In an acceptance intervention used in such situations, one attendee would perform the role of a difficult emotion, and another would play with wrestling with the emotion and then trying something new, like physically taking their hands off the emotion, as though to release the struggle against it.

Early CAA workshop leaders often used "classic" ACT exercises and evaluated the outcomes, for example the Passengers on the Bus exercise or a present moment exercise involving chewing gum mindfully. A participant who was doing important work as a counselor for the blind shared feelings of regret, as he had always dreamed of becoming a priest. When soldiers had violently assaulted him during the civil war, he lost one eye and lost his ability to study. The opportunity to pursue that goal had passed. We encouraged him to allow the grief about the loss and to express what was valuable for him in the aspiration he had to be a priest. In the end, this participant recognized with relief that his current work was aligned with his deepest value, helping others; and importantly, this new perspective put him into the driver's seat of a newly fueled bus on the way to self-efficacy.

Another activity introduced early on was the Life Line exercise (Dahl, Plumb-Vilardaga, Stewart, & Lundgren, 2009). In this exercise, we laid a rope on the ground as a metaphor for the path you travel in life. We asked participants to write their values on a sheet of paper and place them on the floor at one end of the line. We invited partici-pants to write short notes about moments of loss and to put them on the life line in chronological order. We then asked them to place notes along the line chronologically where they went "off track." We asked participants to walk toward their values, stopping to experience the moments where they had fallen away, becoming deeply aware of the pain and difficulty, and also of the gain, in stepping off their line. The last step was recommitting to pulling forward in the direction they were choosing for their lives and embracing the hurt that this involved, if they were willing to do so.

We encouraged participants to adapt ACT techniques for use in their unique health care environments. For example, a social worker adapted the Life Line exercise to support a young boy who lived on the streets, robbed people, and abused drugs. The social worker asked the child what mattered most to him and what the barriers were to getting there. The child reported that he wanted an education but was afraid of his father, who physi-cally abused him, so he had run away. He then wrote two notes—the first about wanting an education, which he placed at the end of the life line, and the second about being afraid of his father, who had physically abused him, which he placed on the life line where he had left home. The social worker asked the child to step on the place where he had left his home, compromising his life values. Exploring this place meant facing the fear of his father's abusive temper and the losses he was incurring. In contrast, the social worker then asked the boy to imagine life in an expanded context in which he could receive education and exchange the rewards immediately available on the streets (e.g., not being abused by his father, feeling powerful through robbing people) for larger, more important rewards that were available only upon facing his fears. Practicing the Life Line exercise helped this child to select a new course of action and to ask for support. He went home accompanied by a social worker and talked to his father. The social worker then brokered an agreement with the father to accept parenting supervision in exchange for having his son back. The child in turn agreed to go home and back to school, as long as his father abstained from corporal punishment. From an ACT perspective, this child learned that avoidance of difficult emotions came at the price of giving up a life that mattered; and in contrast, approaching situations in which these emotions surfaced led to valued outcomes and a life worth living.

In the next few years, CAA trained Sierra Leoneans to lead ACT workshops and to develop novel metaphors that grew directly out of their own cultural context. For example, the mango tree is ubiquitous across the region and is notable for its long, flowing limbs with clusters of fruit that sway in the wind. To illustrate the advantages of behaving flexibly in light of life's difficulties, we asked the workshop participants to stand and imagine that they are Sierra Leonean mango trees, tall and proud. We then asked whether life for mango trees was always easy, and what they do when the weather gets rough, particularly during the rainy season. Respondents said that mango trees swayed in the wind, and we then asked them to move like mango trees in the wind. After a minute of this, we invited them to share or imagine challenges they faced and to generate ideas for how they might face these trials with greater resilience, the way a mango tree might do. In this way we did not instruct, but rather evoked discrimination of flexible movement with life's difficulties in contrast to potentially counterproductive rigidity and resistance.

Encouraging workshop participants to examine their geography for familiar features that related to their lives facilitated individuals' developing their own unique metaphors and exercises. For example, one group of participants developed the following metaphor describing behavioral change in the face of life barriers. On hot days people cool off in Sierra Leone's majestic rivers. Rivers flow with life toward the ocean, and on their way, they face barriers such as fallen trees and giant boulders that impede their flow. In the midst of these great barriers, the river may slow and collect itself in brackish eddies or ponds that do not support life. But as water continues to press forward, new pathways emerge, and the river once again makes its way toward the living sea.

Attendees, who were health workers and not trained psychologists, reported that they were able to help their clients more efficiently after ACT trainings, particularly after they tried using ACT with their own struggles. This example of task sharing led to the establishment of regular supervision sessions from which workers refined and augmented their emerging ACT skills. Free supervision was provided online by ACT trainers and by local supervisors who traveled to different parts of the country to teach others. Funding from the Association for Contextual Behavioral Science (ACBS) and other sources allowed a few Sierra Leonean counselors to go to ACBS World Conferences to deepen their learning and bring home new skills to share with others.

## Workshop Approaches: Working in Partnership

As the form and function of CAA's ACT workshops evolved, a few crucial strategies have remained constant. First, CAA trainers respect the local customs, such as starting every workshop with prayers (Christian and Muslim, the most prevalent religions in Sierra Leone). We also ask locals for guidance before presenting material. Our emphasis is on drawing out the local expertise rather than dominating with Western knowledge and assumptions. Second, we look closely at the impact of interventions, examine and rework exercises, and identify missing pieces in collaboration with our Sierra Leonean colleagues. Third, we practice sharing when there are misunderstandings or upsets, which is especially relevant due to our cultural differences. It takes courage, but the gain is an open and responsible team spirit.

## Addressing Community Concerns with PROSOCIAL

Coming back to Sierra Leone as trainers every year created trust with our local colleagues and allowed us a deeper insight into the daily challenges and emergencies—like diseases, domestic violence, severe weather, and loss of family members—and the traditional ways to resolve these problems. The Sierra Leonean culture is strongly community based. Families and villages generate support for those in need, in the face of limited resources. In order to expand the functional contextual tools to enhance these traditional support systems, CAA and CAF-SL decided to adopt an approach to increase flexibility in groups, called PROSOCIAL. PROSOCIAL is based on the Nobel-prize winning work of economist Elinor Ostrom in conjunction with biologist David Sloan Wilson and psychologist Steven C. Hayes (Wilson, Ostrom, & Cox, 2013). The PROSOCIAL approach involves teaching groups to identify their shared values and to manage behavioral and cultural change to achieve goals in the service of these values (see https://evolution-institute.org/projects/prosocial/). PROSOCIAL workshops teach groups to assess their strengths in eight core areas:

1.   Group vision and purpose

2.   Fair distribution of costs and benefits

3.   Fair and inclusive decision making

4.   Monitoring agreed-upon behaviors

5.   Graduated consequences for misbehaviors

6.   Fair and fast conflict resolution

7.   Authority to self-govern

8.   Appropriate relations with other groups

Keeping important group cultural practices in place while simultaneously undertaking change in any of these eight domains is difficult. While this may be perceived as an exciting opportunity for the group, it can also be challenging, perhaps eliciting fear, apprehension, and even resistance in some group members. An application of ACT known as the matrix (Polk & Schoendorff, 2014; see chapter 6 for a more detailed description) is a tool used to help bring openness and curiosity to the prospect of cultural and individual change. Using the ACT matrix, participants learn to sort experiences into four categories in a way that promotes psychological distancing and the deriving of new responses to difficult situations. Taking into consideration their purpose as a group and each of the remaining seven domains listed previously, we invite participants to state (1) their values; (2) memories, thoughts, emotions, and bodily sensations that get in the way; (3) the way others see them behave when they are obstructed by these private events; and finally, (4) the way others see them act when they are freely engaging in synchrony with their values. The process is light, engaging, and in many cases, filled with humor and excitement with the possibility of change. The level of engagement with the approach can be enhanced through small adaptions like drawing the four quadrants of the matrix on the floor and walking participants through each.

## ADDRESSING GENDER-BASED VIOLENCE

We have used PROSOCIAL to address various issues in Sierra Leone. One of the most effective applications of this approach has been in our efforts to tackle gender-based and domestic violence. After learning about PROSOCIAL, we (led by the CAF-SL workshop facilitators) started to use it with women experiencing poverty, spousal abandonment, and gender-based violence. We have encouraged women to meet in groups and to share their difficult experiences. We ask them what they most deeply care about in their family relationships. Invariably, women say that they love to see their families united, healthy, and mutually supportive, and their children receiving a good education. We then ask them about what keeps them from living these values. Mostly, women report memories of being berated and physically abused. Many report being abandoned by their husbands, being left without money, feeling helpless, and being unable to provide food and education for their children. When asked what others see them doing when these memories and emotions are present, women characteristically reply that they weep, plead, hang their heads low, and try to make themselves invisible. Some admit that they provoke their husbands, belittling them when they do not earn enough money to provide for their family. When asked, "What will others observe when you no longer act this way and instead stand for the family values you have articulated?" women seem to come alive with hope; they share images of personal strength and gaining support from other women or family members; those who have husbands begin to create partnerships and mutual respect with them. Women start to discuss how to establish structures at the level of community to protect themselves and their children, for example, by reporting cases of domestic and gender-based violence to elders in their communities or to institutions like police and CAF-SL, instead of compromising with the perpetrators.

CAF-SL workers also meet with villagers and community leaders to discuss the principles of resource distribution, shared decision making, conflict management, and strategies for dealing with misbehavior. Groups form, develop leadership, and plan grassroots actions in various regions. While these groups act independently, they also come together periodically to plan collective actions, learn from each other, and share their accomplishments. For instance, women's groups have generated a vision of economic well-being and initiated the practice of giving each other microloans. As a result, many have been able to start business ventures like buying and selling spices or firewood. This has moved a number of women from positions of dependency to powerful engagement in the construction of their lives.

## ACT IN RESPONSE TO THE EBOLA CRISIS

In 2014, the Ebola outbreak brought all CAA planned activities to a halt. In an atmosphere of increasing uncertainty and fear, the local CAF-SL staff discussed with the international CAA team and experts in PROSOCIAL (David Sloan Wilson and Steven C. Hayes) how to best complement the efforts of the Sierra Leonean Government Ebola Task Force, Ministry of Health and Sanitation, and other local and international organizations in the fight against the disease. A rapid behavior change of hundreds of thousands of people was necessary, and PROSOCIAL seemed to provide a powerful framework for achieving this.

Preliminary workshops were facilitated in gatherings of several hundred villagers. They involved two parts: (1) providing information about the Ebola virus and how it is spread, and (2) using the matrix to help participants speak about the pain that their communities were facing, clarify their values, and identify and implement new behaviors to break the chain of transmission and save lives in their communities. The pivotal challenge was the cultural practice of laying the deceased family members out, washed and dressed in white linen, so that the community and relatives from farther away could visit and honor them, hug them, and wish them well before their burial. Health workers identified this as the leading cause of human-to-human transmission of the Ebola virus across districts. For Sierra Leoneans, the inability to practice burial rites had a profound impact on their emotional well-being. For example, one woman indicated that the pain of losing her brother to Ebola was exceeded by the pain of not being able to honor him according to the cultural practices, as she had to deliver the dead body to the government burial team. This conflict between ingrained traditions and life-saving health practices for their families lead to additional suffering and sometimes to disregard of the health rules (e.g., hiding the dead bodies to perform the traditional ceremonies). During one workshop, participants faced with this conflict suggested a "symbolic reparation ceremony" whereby a small banana tree trunk, symbolizing the deceased, would be dressed in white cotton and laid to rest in a loving ceremony. The actual bodies, delivered to official burial teams, would no longer pose a safety risk, and bereaved families could gain access to psychosocial support at the symbolic reparation ceremonies. Twenty-five Sierra Leonean psychosocial assistants and fifty teachers were trained by CAF-SL to lead these PROSOCIAL workshops, and the new ceremony spread across the entire district of Bo with funding from NGOs and individuals. Infection rates in Bo district dropped rapidly compared with other hot spots. After the crisis ended, psychosocial assistants continued to apply the PROSOCIAL approach combined with theater plays to help Ebola survivors who experienced stigma so they could be reintegrated in their communities, for example by showing how Ebola survivors could safely be hugged without risk of infection.

# Research Support

There is preliminary evidence for the efficacy of ACT in middle-income nations such as Uganda (Tol et al., 2018), Iran (e.g., Hoseini, Rezaei, & Azadi, 2014), and South Africa (Lundgren, Dahl, Melin, & Kies, 2006). In West Africa, our research team conducted a preliminary evaluation of ACT for local NGO workers in Sierra Leone. We investigated the acceptability of ACT methods and their usefulness in increasing psychological flexibility and well-being. Participants rated the workshops positively and reported applying some of the techniques that they had learned during training to their clinical work. In addition, participants demonstrated improvements in psychological flexibility and life satisfaction following training (Stewart et al., 2016).

## Effectiveness of Treatment of Gender-Based Violence

With respect to treating gender-based violence, ACT researchers have demonstrated some effectiveness in treating unwanted sexual behavior (e.g., Paul, Marx, & Orsillo, 1999). Zarling, Lawrence, and Marchman (2015) evaluated ACT with a clinical sample of adult male perpetrators of gender-based violence and reported that participants receiving ACT had significantly greater reductions in psychological and physical aggression from pre- to posttreatment and from pretreatment to follow-up compared to controls; they also reported that six-month treatment outcomes were partially mediated by levels of experiential avoidance and emotion dysregulation at posttreatment. Peterson, Eifert, Feingold, and Davidson (2009) reported results of two uncontrolled case studies in which they used ACT to treat couples experiencing distress. Both couples reported gains in global marital adjustment and marital satisfaction that were maintained at six-month follow-up, and corresponding reductions in interpersonal distress. Taken together, these studies suggest that ACT can be applied in low-income countries to address complex issues such as gender-based violence.

## DARE to Connect to Reduce Family Violence

In 2016, CAA research team members secured funds to conduct ACT training for couples with histories of partner violence. Nine couples from three villages received a one-month long, four-session intervention called DARE to Connect (Szabo et al., 2019). DARE stands for Defuse, Accept, Re-center, and Engage—in contrast to FEAR, which stands for Fusion, Experiential Avoidance, and Reason-giving (Hayes et al., 1999).

The DARE approach includes experiential exercises that do not involve revealing intimate personal details. Rather than employing talk therapy, we invite partners to engage in games, problem-solving initiatives, and trust exercises housed in metaphorical situations that capture the gestalt of their experiences helping and hurting one another. Activities move from low to high threat over a period of time so that couples develop sufficient trust to sustain the forward movement of the experience during emotionally charged experiences. The intervention is thus consistent with experiential education (e.g., Smart & Csapo, 2007) as opposed to psychotherapy. It can therefore be implemented by behavior analysts, school teachers, community leaders, coaches, and importantly, by the initial recipients of the intervention themselves when they in turn train other couples. The ultimate aim of DARE to Connect is to train couples to become trainers of other couples.

A preliminary, low-threat exercise may involve a partner who complains he is worried that he will be a bad father when his wife gives birth and senses the expectations are mounting. The facilitator can take the word "mounting" and, together with the partners, build a metaphor about climbing a "mountain" with each other's support. To physicalize the metaphor, the facilitator can invite the partners to stand up, and then invite the partner with this thought to climb over a chair or a table, with manual assistance from his partner or the facilitator. A high-threat activity could be helpful later with the same couple when they begin working through self-as-context issues that emerge around decision making and taking the other's perspective. Another physicalized exercise might be to ask the less dominant of the partners to blindfold the more dominant of the two and lead their partner through a series of obstacles. If the couple has a history of making demands rather than requests of each other, a facilitator could ask the leader to refrain from using words and to instead guide with touch, using one hand on her partner's elbow and the other holding the palm of his hand.

In our research, we measured observable microaggressions, which can be understood as an escalating pattern of interaction occurring when one partner behaves in an uncharacteristic way and the other presses unsuccessfully for a return to the status quo. The pattern may escalate until one concedes or there is physical violence. For example, a partner comes home, where he is usually greeted with a kiss and a meal. But on a given occasion, he returns late and instead of a kiss and a meal, his partner asks why he did not come home on time. Instead of supplying an answer, he avoids the question by loudly complaining that the house is a mess. His partner asks again, he makes a sudden jerking physical motion that subtly warns her to back off, she raises her voice, and after a few more volleys, this escalating pattern of microaggression ends in physical confrontation.

We measured within-session microaggression and asked couples to record home episodes of microaggression, aggression, and functionally equivalent replacement behaviors (e.g., making requests instead of demands, holding hands when bringing up difficult topics) that we taught in session. We later followed up on couple reports by asking individuals to endorse or refute their partner's responses. Results from this study showed that couples were able to learn ACT skills with each other, become reinforcers for each other, and use replacement behaviors instead of aggressive or avoidant behavior (Szabo et al., 2019). The effects were observed by others, and subsequently the couples were asked by tribal leaders in two chiefdoms to teach other couples. In one village, several couples trained in the DARE approach formed a collective and proposed the purchase of a cassava grater that will be used to raise money for traveling to teach and support other couples.

## Challenges

Professionals from the West conducting ACT training in low- and middle-income countries (LMICs) of sub-Saharan Africa face three notable challenges: (1) language, (2) cultural rules, and (3) unequal power, privilege, and bias. In Sierra Leone, indigenous languages such as Mende have comparatively fewer words for emotions. Men especially are taught to conceal emotions. Only by creating a safe place in our workshops and by inviting the healthy expression of emotions do men and women share them. Attendees often report a remarkable relief after sharing their emotions in a safe environment and indicate that they no longer feel compelled to react to them.

Metaphoric phrases and idiomatic expressions common in English or German are likewise foreign to Sierra Leoneans (e.g., "autopilot"), so Western trainers learn to speak with careful attention to the catchphrases that they might otherwise use offhandedly. An important practice is to learn local idioms that can be interpreted from an ACT perspective. For example, a saying in Krio (the Sierra Leonean colloquial English-based creole language) that CAA trainers have found particularly useful is "If yu tek tem kil anch, yu go si in gut." The literal translation is "If you kill an ant slowly, you see his guts." From an ACT perspective, this means "Go slowly, lighten up, and your biggest problems will break down into smaller, more manageable ones." It is a local saying that invariably brings laughter to Krio speakers in Sierra Leone, which fosters the defusion context in which it is used in ACT training and therapy.

Western CAA trainers have found that Sierra Leonean customs pertaining to gender in particular are vastly different from Western practices. For example, it is not uncommon to hear statements like "It is my right to beat my wife when she disobeys me," a sentiment that may be difficult and yet important for us to hear without reacting personally. Even if violence is unacceptable for us, we can allow this point of view as one contextual factor and work with it, for example, by asking if this stance helps the participant to gain the relationship he desires.

In some cases, cultural rules and expectations can produce barriers to effective ACT work. For example, Western ACT practitioners often use variants of the Eyes-On exercise to promote perspective taking. In Sierra Leone, eye contact between genders or from younger people to elders is considered disrespectful. Therefore, CAA trainers discuss the challenges of eye contact in the local context and the healing that comes from seeing and being seen. They then ask for consent among members of the group to try to make eye contact given this challenge in the current situation.

In general, Western trainers are afforded tremendous unconditional respect that can blind them to their privilege and expectations, so a general strategy that CAA trainers adopt is to seek multicultural training, anticipate being biased, and respond with openness and vulnerability.

Another important challenge to consider is that the level of hardship that CAA trainers encounter in sub-Saharan Africa is difficult to prepare for. It can be overwhelming to connect to people and their distress. Some stories are too cruel to tell; and bearing witness can become a burden to even the most prepared therapist, sometimes continuing to affect them after returning to the West. It is often a journey to the edges of willingness and compassion, to the limits of time and finances. It is important to acknowledge the contribution one is making to alleviation of suffering—despite the fact that the problems Sierra Leoneans face will still be present when one is back home in a safe and comfortable environment.

A final note on challenges is to be mindful of the impact that Western trainers can have on the local context and the potential for causing unintentional harm. It is important to consider how the sharing of new approaches can be integrated into the local context in both a culturally sensitive and sustainable way after Western trainers have left. CAA has worked in partnership with local people to develop a shared vision and create structures for supporting and empowering local people to adapt and apply ACT skills to their own contexts.

## Future Directions

At this time, it seems safe to say that ACT combined with PROSOCIAL in Sierra Leone has led to helpful behavior change in various areas including gender-based violence, health behaviors, and economic practices. The approach has spread widely, and CAF-SL has become one of the leading organizations in the country offering training and development programs, supported with funding and expertise by CAA in Germany and the US. Key lessons have emerged from CAA's decade of work in Sierra Leone regarding effective practices. These include engaging local trainers; networking with local political, medical, and spiritual leaders; adapting ACT to the cultural context; establishing structures to support and sustain this work (e.g., supervision); and evaluating the acceptability and effectiveness of these approaches in this context.

The next step will be to expand services to other districts in Sierra Leone, which means working with representatives from other tribes and seeing if changes can occur there too. The DARE for couples approach will be expanded by local trainers who train individual couples to train others in new partner behaviors and to build their economic futures, as described above. It will also be important to obtain research grants to evaluate the impact of our interventions on violence rates and broader health outcomes.

Sierra Leoneans offer tremendous care to visiting professionals. They show remarkable openness to new psychosocial interventions. Most notably, they decelerated Ebola with the use of an intervention generated during a PROSOCIAL workshop. Long-term gender-based violence has also receded following partner training with ACT methods, and a new social context is evolving in which violence against women is no longer tolerated. We end this chapter with these final questions: How could we bring this care and openness to our Western countries? How might we move our individualistic societies forward in a healthier, communitarian direction? And, perhaps more importantly, what novel insights might we gain, what new contexts might we create, what achievements might we collectively achieve by sharing our experiences, understanding, and wisdom to collaborate and form partnerships between nations?

# References

All-Party Parliamentary Group on Global Health (2014). *Mental health for sustainable development.* UK: Mental Health Innovation Network.

Collins, P. Y., Patel, V., Joestl, S. S., March, D., Insel, T. R., & Daar, A. S. (2011). Grand challenges in global mental health. *Nature, 475,* 27–30.

Dahl, J., Plumb-Vilardaga, J., Stewart, I., & Lundgren, T. (2009). *The art and science of valuing in psychotherapy.* Oakland, CA: New Harbinger.

Hayes, S. C., Strosahl, K. D., & Wilson, K. G. (1999). *Acceptance and commitment therapy: The process and practice of mindful change.* New York, NY: Guilford.

Hoseini, S. M., Rezaei, A. M., & Azadi, M. M. (2014). Effectiveness of acceptance and commitment group therapy on the self-management of Type 2 diabetes patients. *Journal of Clinical Psychology, 5,* 55–64.

Lundgren, T., Dahl, J., Melin, L., & Kies, B. (2006). Evaluation of acceptance and commitment therapy for drug refractory epilepsy: A randomized controlled trial in South Africa. *Epilepsia, 47,* 2173–2179.

Paul, R. H., Marx, B. P., & Orsillo, S. M. (1999). Acceptance-based psychotherapy in the treatment of an adjudicated exhibitionist: A case example. *Behavior Therapy, 30,* 149–162.

Peterson, B. D., Eifert, G. H., Feingold, T., & Davidson, S. (2009). Using acceptance and commitment therapy to treat distressed couples: A case study with two couples. *Cognitive and Behavioral Practice, 16,* 430–442.

Polk, K. L., & Schoendorff, B. (2014). *The ACT matrix: A new approach to building psychological flexibility across settings and populations.* Oakland, CA: New Harbinger.

Sashidharan, S. P., White, R. G., Mezzina, R., Jansen, S., & Gishoma, D. (2016). Global mental health in high income countries. *British Journal of Psychiatry, 209,* 3–5.

Smart, K. L., & Csapo, N. (2007). Learning by doing: Engaging students through learner-centered activities. *Business Communication Quarterly, 70,* 451–457.

Stewart, C., White, R. G., Ebert, B., Mays, I., Nardozzi, J., & Bockarie, H. (2016). A preliminary evaluation of acceptance and commitment therapy training in Sierra Leone. *Journal of Contextual Behavioral Science, 5,* 16–22.

Szabo, T. G., Bockarie, H., White, R. G., Tarbox, J. Stewart, C., & Ebert, E. (2019). Microaggression, intimate partner gender-based violence, and behavioral flexibility in Sierra Leonean couples. *Journal of Applied Behavior Analysis.* Manuscript submitted for publication.

Tol, W. A., Augustinavicius, J., Carswell, K., Leku, M. R., Adaku, A., Brown, F. L., . . . van Ommeren, M. (2018). Feasibility of a guided self-help intervention to reduce psychological distress in South Sudanese refugee women in Uganda. *World Psychiatry, 17,* 234–235.

Vos, T., Flaxman, A. D., Naghavi, M., Lozano, R., Michaud, C., Ezzati, M., . . . Abraham, J. (2013). Years lived with disability (YLDs) for 1160 sequelae of 289 diseases and injuries 1990–2010: A systematic analysis for the Global Burden of Disease Study 2010. *The Lancet, 380,* 2163–2196.

Wilson, D. S., Ostrom, E., & Cox, M. E. (2013). Generalizing the core design principles for the efficacy of groups. *Journal of Economic Behavior and Organization, 90,* S21–S32.

World Health Organization (2018). *Mental health atlas 2017.* Geneva, Switzerland: WHO.

Zarling, A., Lawrence, E., & Marchman, J. (2015). A randomized controlled trial of acceptance and commitment therapy for aggressive behavior. *Journal of Consulting and Clinical Psychology, 83,* 199–212.

**Michael E. Levin, PhD**, is associate professor at Utah State University. Levin's research focuses on web/mobile interventions and mechanisms of change in acceptance and commitment therapy (ACT). He has published more than one hundred peer-reviewed articles and book chapters, primarily related to ACT and contextual behavioral science (CBS).

**Michael P. Twohig, PhD**, is professor at Utah State University, former president of the Association of Contextual Behavioral Science, and peer-reviewed ACT trainer. He has published over one hundred peer-reviewed papers on the application of ACT to obsessive-compulsive and related disorders.

**Jennifer Krafft, MS**, is a doctoral student in clinical and counseling psychology at Utah State University. Krafft has published more than twenty articles and book chapters related to ACT, and has collaborated with Levin and Twohig on numerous studies investigating applications of ACT delivered through innovative platforms and for novel problem areas.

Foreword writer **Kelly G. Wilson, PhD**, is professor of psychology at the University of Mississippi, and founder of Onelife, LLC. He has authored or coauthored eleven books, including *Acceptance and Commitment Therapy* and *Mindfulness for Two*.

# Index

# MORE BOOKS *from*
# NEW HARBINGER PUBLICATIONS

**EVOLUTION & CONTEXTUAL BEHAVIORAL SCIENCE**

An Integrated Framework for Understanding, Predicting & Influencing Human Behavior

9781626259133 / US $39.95

**CONTEXT PRESS**
An Imprint of New Harbinger Publications

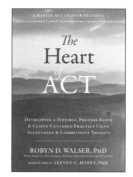

**THE HEART OF ACT**

Developing a Flexible, Process-Based & Client-Centered Practice Using Acceptance & Commitment Therapy

9781684030392 / US $49.95

**CONTEXT PRESS**
An Imprint of New Harbinger Publications

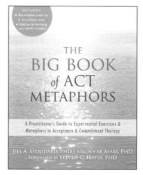

**THE BIG BOOK OF ACT METAPHORS**

A Practitioner's Guide to Experiential Exercises & Metaphors in Acceptance & Commitment Therapy

9781608825295 / US $59.95

**LEARNING ACT FOR GROUP TREATMENT**

An Acceptance & Commitment Therapy Skills Training Manual for Therapists

9781608823994 / US $59.95

**CONTEXT PRESS**
An Imprint of New Harbinger Publications

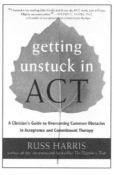

**GETTING UNSTUCK IN ACT**

A Clinician's Guide to Overcoming Common Obstacles in Acceptance & Commitment Therapy

9781608828050 / US $29.95

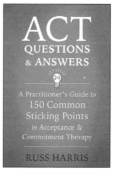

**ACT QUESTIONS & ANSWERS**

A Practitioner's Guide to 150 Common Sticking Points in Acceptance & Commitment Therapy

9781684030361 / US $29.95

**CONTEXT PRESS**
An Imprint of New Harbinger Publications

**newharbingerpublications**
1-800-748-6273 / newharbinger.com

(VISA, MC, AMEX / prices subject to change without notice)

Follow Us 📷 📘 🐦 ▶️ 📌 in

## QUICK TIPS *for* THERAPISTS
Fast and free solutions to common client situations mental health professionals encounter every day

Written by leading clinicians, Quick Tips for Therapists are short e-mails, sent twice a month, to help enhance your client sessions. **Visit newharbinger.com/quicktips to sign up today!**

Sign up for our Book Alerts at **newharbinger.com/bookalerts** ⇲

# PRAXIS

MANY VOICES | ONE WORK

A subsidiary of New Harbinger Publications, Inc.

## Enhance your practice with live ACT workshops

Praxis Continuing Education and Training—a subsidiary of
New Harbinger Publications—is the premier provider of evidence-based
continuing education for mental health professionals. Praxis specializes
in ongoing **acceptance and commitment therapy (ACT)** training—
taught by leading ACT experts. Praxis workshops are designed to help
professionals learn and effectively implement ACT in session with clients.

- **ACT BootCamp®: Introduction to Implementation**
  For professionals with no prior experience with ACT, as well as
  those who want to refresh their knowledge

- **ACT 1: Introduction to ACT**
  For professionals with no prior experience with ACT

- **ACT 2: Clinical Skills-Building Intensive**
  For professionals who practice ACT, but want more
  hands-on experience

- **ACT 3: Mastering ACT**
  For professionals actively using ACT who want to
  apply it to their most complex cases

## Receive 10% off Any Training!

Visit praxiscet.com and use code **EDU10** at checkout to receive 10% off.

### Check out our workshops and register now at
### praxiscet.com

***Can't make a workshop?*** Check out our online and
on-demand courses at **praxiscet.com**

CONCEPTUAL | EXPERIENTIAL | PRACTICAL

Register your **new harbinger** titles for additional benefits!

When you register your **new harbinger** title—purchased in any format, from any source—you get access to benefits like the following:

- Downloadable accessories like printable worksheets and extra content

- Instructional videos and audio files

- Information about updates, corrections, and new editions

Not every title has accessories, but we're adding new material all the time.

Access free accessories in 3 easy steps:

**1.** Sign in at NewHarbinger.com (or **register** to create an account).

**2.** Click on **register a book**. Search for your title and click the **register** button when it appears.

**3.** Click on the **book cover or title** to go to its details page. Click on **accessories** to view and access files.

That's all there is to it!

If you need help, visit:

NewHarbinger.com/accessories

**new harbinger**
CELEBRATING
**40** YEARS